Empire's daughters

Manchester University Press

## STUDIES IN IMPERIALISM

When the 'Studies in Imperialism' series was founded by Professor John M. MacKenzie more than thirty years ago, emphasis was laid upon the conviction that 'imperialism as a cultural phenomenon had as significant an effect on the dominant as on the subordinate societies'. With well over a hundred titles now published, this remains the prime concern of the series. Cross-disciplinary work has indeed appeared covering the full spectrum of cultural phenomena, as well as examining aspects of gender and sex, frontiers and law, science and the environment, language and literature, migration and patriotic societies, and much else. Moreover, the series has always wished to present comparative work on European and American imperialism, and particularly welcomes the submission of books in these areas. The fascination with imperialism, in all its aspects, shows no sign of abating, and this series will continue to lead the way in encouraging the widest possible range of studies in the field. 'Studies in Imperialism' is fully organic in its development, always seeking to be at the cutting edge, responding to the latest interests of scholars and the needs of this ever-expanding area of scholarship.

General editors:
Andrew Thompson, Professor of Global and Imperial History at Nuffield College, Oxford
Alan Lester, Professor of Historical Geography at University of Sussex and LaTrobe University

Founding editor:
Emeritus Professor John MacKenzie

Robert Bickers, University of Bristol
Christopher L. Brown, Columbia University
Pratik Chakrabarti, University of Houston
Elizabeth Elbourne, McGill University
Bronwen Everill, University of Cambridge
Kate Fullagar, Australian Catholic University
Chandrika Kaul, University of St Andrews
Dane Kennedy, George Washington University
Shino Konishi, Australian Catholic University
Philippa Levine, University of Texas at Austin
Kirsten McKenzie, University of Sydney
Tinashe Nyamunda, University of Pretoria
Dexnell Peters, University of the West Indies
Sujit Sivasundaram, University of Cambridge
Angela Wanhalla, University of Otago
Stuart Ward, University of Copenhagen

To buy or to find out more about the books currently available in this series, please go to: https://manchesteruniversitypress.co.uk/series/studies-in-imperialism/

# Empire's daughters

## Girlhood, whiteness, and the colonial project

Elizabeth Dillenburg

MANCHESTER UNIVERSITY PRESS

Copyright © Elizabeth Dillenburg 2024

The right of Elizabeth Dillenburg to be identified as the author of this work has been asserted in accordance with the Copyright, Designs and Patents Act 1988.

An electronic version of this book has been made freely available under a Creative Commons (CC BY-NC-ND) licence, thanks to the generous support of The Ohio State University Libraries, which permits non-commercial use, distribution and reproduction provided the author(s) and Manchester University Press are fully cited and no modifications or adaptations are made. Details of the licence can be viewed at https://creativecommons.org/licenses/by-nc-nd/4.0/

Published by Manchester University Press
Oxford Road, Manchester, M13 9PL

www.manchesteruniversitypress.co.uk

British Library Cataloguing-in-Publication Data
A catalogue record for this book is available from the British Library

ISBN 978 1 5261 6351 6 hardback

First published 2024

The publisher has no responsibility for the persistence or accuracy of URLs for any external or third-party internet websites referred to in this book, and does not guarantee that any content on such websites is, or will remain, accurate or appropriate.

Typeset
by Cheshire Typesetting Ltd, Cuddington, Cheshire

For my family
Mom, Dad, Jessica, Ben, and Emma

# Contents

| | |
|---|---:|
| List of figures | *page* viii |
| Acknowledgements | x |
| List of abbreviations | xiii |
| Introduction: Constructing and contesting girlhood and whiteness in the British empire | 1 |
| 1   Purity and the origins of the Girls' Friendly Society | 24 |
| 2   Imperial education programmes and the construction of colonial knowledge and racial difference | 55 |
| 3   Class, race, and competing objectives within girls' emigration programmes | 101 |
| 4   Contested ideas of whiteness and race in the Girls' Friendly Society | 131 |
| 5   Shifting colonial relations and ideas of girlhood and the decline of the Girls' Friendly Society | 167 |
| Conclusion | 198 |
| Appendix: List of key figures in the Girls' Friendly Society | 220 |
| Bibliography | 223 |
| Index | 241 |

# Figures

Every effort has been made to obtain permission to reproduce copyright material, and the publisher will be pleased to be informed of any errors and omissions for correction in future editions.

1.1 Girls from a Newcastle branch with a white flower banner, 1927 (Women's Library, London, 5GFS/04/127, 'Newcastle Branch, Bridgend, Glamorganshire', *G.F.S. Magazine*, April 1927, photo from Block Book VII, 1926–31) 30

2.1 Avonside branch in Christchurch, New Zealand, 1904 (From 'Candidates in New Zealand', *Our Letter: For G.F.S. Candidates all over the World*, September 1904, p. 3) 64

2.2 'The Quest', 1931 (Women's Library, London, 5GFS/04/127, '"The Quest." St. David's Diocese', *G.F.S. Magazine*, January 1931, photo from Block Book VII, 1926–31) 69

2.3 Candidates as 'caravaners' in the Isle of Wight pageant, 1927 (Women's Library, London, 5/GFS/04/127, 'Wingham Candidates as "Caravaners" in the Isle of Wight Pageant', *Our Letter: For G.F.S. Candidates all over the World*, September 1927, photo from Block Book VII, 1926–31) 70

2.4 Skipping display, 1933, photograph copyright by The Daily Sketch & Sunday Graphic Ltd. London (Women's Library, London, 5/GFS/11/003, Skipping display, 1933) 71

2.5 'Indian Tableaux at Endon', 1923 (Women's Library, London, 5GFS/04/086, 'Indian Tableaux at Endon', *G.F.S. Magazine*, September 1923, photo from Block Book, 1922–23) 73

2.6 'North Indian Tableaux', c. 1929 (Women's Library, London, 5GFS/04/127, 'North Indian Tableaux by Rhayader Branch', c. 1929, photo from Block Book VII, 1926–31) 73

2.7 Cwdandur Branch in 'The Lady with the Lamp', 1930 (Women's Library, London, 5GFS/04/127, 'Cwdandur Branch

Figures ix

|  |  |  |
|---|---|---|
|  | in "The Lady with the Lamp"', *G.F.S. Magazine*, February 1930, photo from Block Book VII, 1926–31) | 74 |
| 2.8 | GFS picnic in South Africa (Women's Library, London, 5GFS/02/260, 'These Speak for Themselves. Girls generally *can*!', in South Africa scrapbook, c. 1930) | 77 |
| 2.9 | Girls at church in Port Elizabeth (Women's Library, London, 5GFS/02/260, 'After service on Ascension Day. 1931', in South Africa scrapbook, c. 1930) | 78 |
| 2.10 | 'Candidates' Sewing' in West Australia (Women's Library, London, 5GFS/02/357, photo of the 'Candidates' Sewing' from 'G.F.S. Bassadean Candidate Class. 1930' page in West Australia scrapbook, c. 1930) | 79 |
| 2.11 | Candidates' picnic in Australia (Women's Library, London, 5GFS/02/357, photo of 'Miss Whatley and Junior St. Andrews at picnic' from 'St Andrews Junior Branch, Subiaco' page in West Australia scrapbook, c. 1930) | 80 |
| 2.12 | An African man and woman (Women's Library, London, 5GFS/02/260, photo from South African countryside page in South Africa scrapbook, c. 1930) | 82 |
| 3.1 | Durban GFS lodge, 1935, photograph by A. Cecil Covne (Women's Library, London, 5GFS/02/358, Durban GFS Lodge, 1935) | 113 |
| 4.1 | Candidates in Colombo (Women's Library, London, 5GFS/04/127, 'Candidates of Colombo, Ceylon', November 1931, photo from Block Book VII, 1926–31) | 138 |
| 5.1 | GFS Girl Guides (Women's Library, London, 5GFS/04/113, 6th Poplar G.F.S. Girl Guides at Fryerning', in *The Book of the G.F.S.: What It Is and What It Does*, June 1920) | 177 |
| 6.1 | Festival service marking the GFS's centenary at Chester Cathedral, 1975, photograph by Clifford Shirley (Women's Library, London, 5GFS/06/178, Girls' Friendly Society Centenary Scrapbook, 1975) | 206 |

# Acknowledgements

To call this *my* book seems like a misnomer, because in reality it is the product of so many people's time, energy, ideas, and sacrifices. The journey of writing this book has been a long, often challenging one, and I could not have done it without the support of the people around me.

Research for this book has been supported by the Ohio State University, University of Minnesota History Department, Hella Mears Graduate Fellowship in European Studies, the University of Minnesota Graduate School Thesis Research Travel Grant, and the University of Minnesota Graduate Research Partnership Program Fellowship. This book is available as open access through the Ohio State Open Access Monograph Initiative. I would like to thank the Ohio State University Libraries for their generous support and Maureen Walsh for her guidance through the process. Many archivists assisted me in my research, including those at the Derbyshire Record Office, the Keep in Brighton, the Modern Records Centre at the University of Warwick, the John Rylands University Library, Manchester, Lambeth Palace Library, Church of England Record Centre, London Metropolitan Archives, University of Liverpool Department of Special Collections and Archives, the British Library, and the National Archives. Martine King at Barnardo's was welcoming and accommodating and took time out of her busy schedule to talk with me. I am especially grateful to the workers and archivists at the Women's Library at the London School of Economics for their assistance and patience with my countless questions and requests and for scanning images for the book.

Portions of this book have been presented at various conferences and workshops, where I received feedback that refined my argument and writing. The participants of the Youth as Subjects, Objects, Agents research collaborative and Workshop on the Comparative History of Women, Gender, and Sexuality at the University of Minnesota encouraged me to think about my project in new ways. Attendees at the Social Science History Association, Society for the History of Childhood and Youth, and Children's History Society conferences raised thoughtful questions that enriched my writing.

*Acknowledgements*  xi

At these conferences, I met brilliant colleagues whose work and ideas inform this project, including Kristine Alexander, Katherine Cartwright, Catherine Ellis, Miriam Forman-Brunell, Jóhanna Jochumsdóttir, Susan Miller, Rachel Neiwert, Ashley Remer, and Mateusz Świetlicki. Parts of chapters appear in *The Journal of the History of Childhood and Youth* and the edited collections *New Perspectives on Gender* and *Empire* and *International Migrations in the Victorian Era*, and I am grateful to the reviewers and editors of those publications for their feedback. My thanks also go to the anonymous readers of the book manuscript and proposal, whose comments pushed my work in new directions and resulted in a stronger book. It has been a pleasure to work with Meredith Carroll, Humairaa Dudhwala, and Emma Brennan at Manchester University Press and the editors of the Studies in Imperialism series, who have supported this project and guided this book through the publication process with great skill, kindness, and understanding.

I am fortunate to have had the opportunity to work with scholars whose work I greatly admire. Since my first days as a graduate student at the University of Minnesota, Anna Clark and Mary Jo Maynes have been invaluable sources of advice and spent innumerable hours reading my work. MJ's enthusiasm for this project energised my work. I especially appreciate her support at conferences and her assistance as I thought through different ways to reconceptualise this project. Anna's constructive feedback made my writing stronger. Both MJ and Anna challenged me and saw potential in my work that I could not see. Their ideas infuse this book. I am also grateful to Howard Louthan, Andrea Sterk, and Ann Waltner for their continued guidance throughout the various stages of writing this book.

During my time at the University of Minnesota, I met students and colleagues who have remained close friends and provided valuable support while I wrote this book, including Emily Bruce, Ruchen Gao, Elisabeth Lefebvre, Kan Li, Sharon Park, Jürgen Pirker, Laura Weber, and Marie Wu. I could not have asked for a better friend and guide to the Buckeye state than Ellen Manovich Janzen, who always provides new perspectives and ideas that I greatly value. Kelly Condit-Shrestha's encouragement motivated me to keep working on the book. Leslie Nightingale offered support through the ups and downs of writing this book.

When I came to Ohio State, Jennifer Kowalsky and Sonia Gollance were among the first people I met. I appreciate Jen's friendship and insights over the past years and Sonia's assistance, especially in the early stages of this book project. Wonderful colleagues at the Newark campus and in the history department at Ohio State have supported me and this book project over the years, including Lucy Murphy, Mitch Lerner, Alcira Dueñas, Birgitte Søland, Scott Levi, Clay Howard, Víctor Espinosa, Greg Anderson,

Nicholas Breyfogle, Elizabeth Bond, Melissa Buelow, Sara Butler, Alice Conklin, Theodora Dragostinova, Bart Elmore, María Esther Hammack, Dodie McDow, Margaret Newell, Chris Otter, Amanda Respess, Mytheli Sreenivas, David Steigerwald, and Joan Flores-Villalobos. Harvey Graff has been an inestimable mentor. He and Vicki Graff have given me valuable advice throughout the process of writing this book and provided me a sense of community in Columbus.

My greatest thanks go to my family. Ben and Emma have brought endless love, laughter, and happiness into my life. Jessica has been my friend and role model throughout my life. Her love of British literature and culture started me on the path to being a British historian. Mom and Dad nurtured my interest in history and, through their example, instilled in me the importance of hard work and perseverance. Mom, Dad, and Jessica were my cheerleaders and my partners on every step of this journey, believing in me and giving me strength, courage, and confidence throughout the long process of working on this project. This book would not exist without their unwavering love and support.

# Abbreviations

| | |
|---|---|
| BWEA | British Women's Emigration Association |
| CFS | Children's Friend Society |
| CMS | Church Missionary Society |
| GFS | Girls' Friendly Society |
| SACS | South African Colonisation Society |
| YWCA | Young Women's Christian Association |

# Introduction
# Constructing and contesting girlhood and whiteness in the British empire

In 1907, *Our Letter: For G.F.S. Candidates all over the World* published a series entitled 'Stories of Brave Girls'. The first instalment recounts the life of Joan of Arc. It begins by describing Joan's childhood and how she was '[s]trong, brave, and merry above all her playmates' and 'a very good little girl, very careful about saying her prayers and going to church'. The story discusses how Joan exhibited both conventional feminine characteristics, like piety and duty, and traditionally masculine qualities of bravery and strength, and praises her military feats and skills, providing an unconventional model for the article's girl readers. Even though Joan was a French heroine, the article emphasises how her example could serve as model for all girls, including girls of the British empire, telling its readers: 'we can carry into our lives her spirit, the spirit of patriotism, of love and pride for England, and an earnest desire to serve her'. The last lines of the story encourage readers to remember the 'duty of every English girl' to the empire and to transform their knowledge about the empire into meaningful action: 'Perhaps, too, when you are older, you will be the more ready to go and build new homes in the "British Dominions beyond the seas," and make some real sacrifice, do some real service, for the Empire which at present is to you but patches of red in the map on the schoolroom wall'. The article concludes by encouraging its readers to observe the upcoming Empire Day holiday so they 'will then learn a little of the duties and privileges of a citizen of the British Empire'.[1]

Girls are often consigned to the shadows in studies of colonialism, but this story reveals that girls had an integral role in the British empire. Girls, specifically white girls, were encouraged to think of themselves as patriotic citizens who could contribute to the empire through building up settler societies abroad. In performing these roles, white girls were seen as vital to the futurity of settler colonial societies and the British empire more broadly. While girls did perform these prescribed roles, they also challenged these scripts. Girls did travel to 'British dominions beyond the seas', but their motives were not necessarily rooted in 'the spirit of patriotism' and 'love and pride for England', as the story of Joan of Arc would have one believe. Moreover, the charge to 'build new homes' was complicated by a myriad of factors.

In addition to challenging traditional conceptions of girls' roles in the empire, the story provides insights into the organisation that produced *Our Letter:* the Girls' Friendly Society (GFS). Founded in 1875, the GFS originally focused on providing shelter and protection to girls travelling in England, but, as reflected in the story of Joan of Arc, imperial matters fundamentally shaped the organisation. Within its first decade, the GFS had established branches for girls throughout the empire and orchestrated migration programmes to ensure the safe passage of girls and young women moving between various parts of the empire.[2] It also developed initiatives to educate girls about the empire and their role in it. Stories in newsletters, like the one of Joan of Arc, formed just one facet of these extensive programmes. The GFS's concerted efforts to educate and emigrate girls demonstrate how empire building depended on the mobility and labour of girls and young women.

*Empire's daughters* studies the GFS to uncover the ways in which girls and ideas of girlhood were central to the British empire and the construction of social, gendered, and racial structures of power. Although the GFS forms the framework for this book, *Empire's daughters* is not a traditional institutional history; it instead uses the organisation as a lens to explore the micropolitics of colonialism and whiteness. The GFS emerged at a key moment in the evolution of childhood and girlhood, the history of the British empire, and the promulgation of whiteness – phenomena that may seem disparate at first glance but were deeply intertwined. The GFS acted as a laboratory of empire. Its employment of girls and the concept of girlhood mirrored strategies used by other organisations and the broader colonial state to promote and reinforce colonial rule and white hegemony. Especially during times of imperial uncertainty, girls became an important means to reassert class, gender, and racial hierarchies. Yet girls' involvement in the empire was anything but straightforward. Girls not only supported – directly and indirectly – racialised systems of colonial power but also resisted them. These complexities of girls' participation in the British empire form the focus of *Empire's daughters*.

## Centring girls and girlhood in studies of colonialism

Despite the proliferation of scholarship about childhood history since the publication of Philippe Ariès's *Centuries of Childhood: A Social History of Family Life* in 1960, childhood is still often viewed as a 'gender-neutral' term.[3] The history of childhood consequently becomes *de facto* the history of boyhood, with boys' lives taken as the normative experience of childhood and girls relegated to a footnote, paragraph, or chapter in broader studies of childhood, especially in studies of colonial childhoods. In her book on girls in colonial Nigeria, Abosede George challenges the focus on boys and men in studies of African youth, asking: 'Where are the girls?'[4] George's question is applicable not only to the study of African childhoods but to the broader field of childhood history. Seeking to answer George's call, *Empire's daughters* uncovers the myriad experiences and roles of girls in the British empire and reorientates analyses of colonial childhood around the intersections of age *and* gender. In doing so, it builds on the long tradition of feminist scholarship about the British empire that has recovered women, their voices, and their experiences from the margins of colonial histories and demonstrated how gender is necessary for understanding colonialism.[5]

*Empire's daughters* also expands on innovative work by scholars in fields like literary and cultural studies who have examined representations of girls in British and colonial texts and how the figure of the girl played a significant symbolic role in colonial discourses.[6] In the introduction to their edited collection, *Colonial Girlhood in Literature, Culture and History, 1840–1950*, Michelle Smith and Kristine Moruzi articulate why the study of colonial girlhood is important, stating that '[t]elling the stories of colonial girls can help us to see aspects of colonialism that might not otherwise be visible'.[7] Centring girls in studies of colonialism can thus expand and challenge traditional narratives of empire. Drawing on the work of cultural and literary scholars, *Empire's daughters* analyses discursive constructions of girlhood and also foregrounds how girls acted as agents with their own views and voices who actively shaped their environment.[8] In colonial scripts, such as those in the story about Joan of Arc, girls, particularly white girls, were cast as imperial citizens, good servants, model mothers, and valued migrants. They were encouraged to exhibit the 'right spirit' by enduring the hardships of colonial life without complaint, but some girls contradicted these emotional norms and wrote honestly about the difficulties they faced and how they found themselves 'plunged into an utterly different life'.[9] Chapter 3 discusses Eliza Hobbs and Eliza Cook, two emigrant servants in Bulawayo (in present-day Zimbabwe) who, disillusioned with their working conditions and colonial life, absconded from their situations. Their testimonies in court and letters to emigration organisers paint a very different picture of life in southern Africa than the one that appears in propaganda and expose the paradoxes inherent in emigration programmes. Studying the relationship between ideas of girlhood and girls' lived experiences can thus provide insights into the diversity of girls' engagement with the empire.

## Demarcating childhood and girlhood in Victorian and Edwardian Britain

Like other categories of age, girlhood is shaped not only by gender but also by race and class. The constructed nature of girlhood makes it ambiguous, contested, and difficult to define. Even the GFS, an organisation that proclaimed its dedication 'to the service of girlhood' and cast itself as 'a guardian of girlhood', debated the ages and meaning of the term 'girl', a point further explored in the next chapter.[10] As Corinne T. Field and LaKisha Michelle Simmons note in their introduction to *The Global History of Black Girlhood*, 'The idea that girlhood ends at a specified age simply does not hold up in the archives'.[11] The plasticity of girlhood serves as a valuable starting point for this study, rather than a hindrance. As Field and Simmons observe, 'Chronological age offers a paradigmatic example of how people impose abstract categories upon the variable experience of individual lives and how those categories always remain incomplete and ripe for transformation'.[12] The development of girlhood did not occur in a vacuum, and a central theme of this book is how class, gender, racial, and imperial anxieties shaped conceptualisations of girlhood in the late nineteenth and early twentieth centuries and how these definitions were never fixed and often contested.

Legislation in Britain during the Victorian era attempted to define and standardise amorphous and variable concepts of children and childhood. While childhood could extend into the late teens and mid-twenties for upper-class and middle-class girls in Britain, childhood ended earlier for working-class girls, typically around the age of thirteen, when they assumed more adult responsibilities.[13] Laws, like the Factory Act of 1833 and the Education Act of 1870, established age parameters for child labour and education. In doing so, they constructed more rigid boundaries between childhood and adulthood and imposed middle-class notions of the 'cult of the child' on the working classes, even though the realities of poverty meant that childhood for the working classes diverged from this ideal, and it remained impractical for poorer families who relied upon children as an important source of labour and income.[14] Changing social, political, and economic landscapes drove these laws. The rise of juvenile delinquency, poverty, and working-class unrest combined with the growth of Social Darwinism and the emergence of new imperial competitors, namely Germany, in the late nineteenth century fomented anxieties about social order and national and racial decline.[15] The South African War at the turn of the century called into question beliefs about imperial security and Britain's supposed racial supremacy not just in southern Africa but throughout the empire. The prolonged nature of the war led to disillusionment and shone light on the unfitness of soldiers, with over a third of recruits being rejected on physical grounds.[16] This problem was not confined to the military; emigration organisations also found that many prospective migrants were unfit. For instance, a 1901 report by the South African Colonisation Society, an emigration society for women, found '[t]he sudden rise in the percentage of rejections ... has been partly due to the lower average in physique of the candidates offering'.[17] The declining fertility rate among white women in Britain and the settler colonies appeared to substantiate concerns about racial decline and degeneration.

These concerns over national and imperial prestige led to greater attempts to control children and extend the influence of the state over their lives. Children's education and health were no longer a personal or familial matter but one that had national and imperial ramifications. As future citizens and Britain's 'greatest asset', children became central to national prosperity, stability, prestige, and imperial power.[18] The supposed need both to 'civilise' children, particularly poor children, and teach them the necessary skills to keep Britain competitive internationally served as the impetus behind the Education Act of 1870 and the institution of compulsory schooling in England and Wales. Schools spread patriotic and pro-imperial values and socialised children to fulfil certain roles according to their social and racial status.[19] Like schools in England and Wales, schools in the colonies taught white children how to be future citizens and empire builders and reaffirmed racial hierarchies and privilege.[20] Schools also acted as key institutions of colonial governance that sought to educate and control children of colour.[21]

## Placing the Girls' Friendly Society in histories of youth organisations and colonial migration

While schools acted as the primary vehicle to inculcate imperial and racial ideologies, such efforts were not confined to the classroom.[22] Youth organisations, like schools, were crucial sites of girls' 'informal education' and 'the learning of place and race'.[23] The closing decades of the nineteenth century witnessed the proliferation of youth organisations that cultivated imperial ideals and values in children. While rich scholarship exists about contemporary organisations, most notably the Girl Guides, comparatively little research has been done on the GFS.[24] The scholarship that exists on the GFS primarily focuses on its operations in Britain and examines it within the context of women's growing social and political involvement in the Victorian and Edwardian eras.[25] Brian Harrison wrote one of the first scholarly studies about the GFS, 'For Church, Queen, and Family: The

Girls' Friendly Society 1874–1920', which examines the organisation in relation to the revival of conservativism in late nineteenth-century Britain.[26] Vivienne Richmond has written more extensively about the organisation, examining programmes like the Needlework Depot and its decline in the interwar years.[27] Julia Bush has analysed the GFS in its imperial context and specifically written about the organisation in relation to the growth of women's philanthropic and entrepreneurial participation in the empire.[28] *Empire's daughters* builds upon the work of Harrison, Richmond, and Bush, but its focus is more centrally on two important linchpins of the organisation: its imperial impetus and reach and its girl members.

To classify the GFS as simply a youth organisation does not do justice to the range of its programmes. As part of its increasing investment in the empire, the GFS also operated as an emigration society, instituting the 'very important' Department for Members Emigrating within a decade of its foundation.[29] This expansive purpose makes the GFS an especially valuable subject for understanding the construction and experiences of girlhood in the British empire. Scholarship on child migration largely focuses on programmes for both boys and girls and on major organisations, like Barnardo's.[30] Drawing greater attention to the distinctly gendered experiences of child migration and the operations of a lesser-known organisation like the GFS can expand and complicate our understandings of children's migration in the British empire. The GFS functioned differently from mainstream child emigration organisations in that its programmes did not institutionalise and force girls to migrate, but it nevertheless employed a variety of means – and many of them not dissimilar to methods used by these other organisations – to persuade girls to travel and settle in disparate parts of the empire.

White girls' value as migrants not only rested on their capacity as labourers but also depended on their perceived malleability and futurity. They were still in the process of 'becoming', which is reflected in the story of Joan of Arc and its emphasis on what girls can do 'when you are older'. Children were viewed as *tabulae rasae* who could be moulded into empire builders.[31] Emigration organisations like the GFS touted white girls as the ideal emigrants, because they could assimilate more quickly and were more adaptable, easier to train, and a better investment than adults, since they would likely stay in a position for a longer period of time. As future wives and mothers, they also represented an imagined future of white settler colonies.[32] As Laura Ishiguro details in her study of colonial families in British Columbia, 'the idea of children was fundamentally important to a collective politics of aspiration – what I call "settler futurity" – that lay at the very foundations of settler colonialism'.[33] This futurity and malleability gave children a heightened importance in the colonial project, but it had a flip side in that it also made them the source of anxieties, which led to beliefs that girls needed special protection and greater control.

## Interrogating whiteness and its relationship to girlhood

When the GFS emerged in the late Victorian and Edwardian eras, British imperial fervour appeared to be at its zenith, but this age of high imperialism was simultaneously a moment of imperial crisis when ideas of empire, nation, and national identities were being sharply contested throughout the empire, with the first decades of the twentieth century witnessing rising anticolonialism and nationalism and shifting colonial relations. During this period of imperial unease and transformation, a 'new religion of whiteness' emerged on the international stage.[34] Writing in 1910, W. E. B. Du Bois described how this 'new religion' held that 'whiteness alone is inherently and obviously better than brownness and tan'.[35] In 'The Souls of White Folks', Du Bois argued that '[t]he discovery of personal whiteness among the world's peoples is a very modern thing – a nineteenth and twentieth century matter, indeed'.[36] For Du Bois, part of what made whiteness 'modern' was 'the imperial width of the thing'.[37] Du Bois described whiteness as an international phenomenon that justified the 'domination of white Europe over black Africa and yellow Asia'.[38] Europeans used whiteness as a tool to create artificial distinctions – between the 'civilised' and 'uncivilised', the ruler and the ruled – to bolster beliefs in white supremacy and the necessity of colonial intervention.

Writing nearly half a century after Du Bois amid the fracturing of European empires, Frantz Fanon described whiteness as something to which all 'otherness' is compared.[39] This 'othering' is a cornerstone of whiteness. As Cheryl I. Harris observes in her influential 'Whiteness as Property', 'The fundamental precept of whiteness – the core of its value – is its exclusivity. But exclusivity is predicated not on any intrinsic characteristic, but on the existence of the symbolic "other," which functions to "create an illusion of unity" among whites.'[40] *Empire's daughters* examines how whiteness is forged relative to not only racial 'others' but also gendered, class, and sexual 'others'.[41] The first chapter in particular explores how anxieties about these various 'others' converged in the founding of the GFS. The inherently relational and constructed nature of whiteness means that it is never secure nor stable, and a recurring theme throughout this book is how definitions of 'whiteness' and who is 'white' shift across time and place and in reaction to changing social, imperial, and racial exigencies. This instability of racial categories is evident in debates surrounding the white identity of working-class English girls. As explored most extensively in the third and fourth chapters, the questioning of girls' whiteness was especially pronounced during times of imperial uncertainty and upheaval, when the '"illusion of unity" among whites' described by Harris appeared to fracture.

Numerous scholars – including Harris, Robin Bernstein, Richard Dyer, Ruth Frankenberg, George Lipsitz, and Aileen Moreton-Robinson – have observed that part of the insidious power of whiteness lies in its seeming invisibility and its operation as an unarticulated norm.[42] In his article 'The Possessive Investment in Whiteness', Lipsitz notes, 'As the unmarked category against which difference is constructed, whiteness never has to speak its name, never has to acknowledge its role as an organizing principle in social and cultural relations'.[43] Whiteness is, in many respects, at the heart of the GFS and simultaneously hyper-visible and ubiquitous but also unspoken. As analysed in the first chapter, white imagery and symbols permeated the GFS, and whiteness functioned within the organisation in different ways, yet GFS organisers referred to whiteness in coded language, in terms of 'purity'. At the most superficial level, 'purity' implied moral and sexual virtue or virginity, but the GFS's fervent commitment to 'purity' had racial implications and was intertwined with whiteness. In *The White Possessive*, Moreton-Robinson describes how whiteness 'is tied to power and dominance despite being fluid, vacuous, and invisible to white people'.[44] A recurring theme throughout this book is how the GFS used associations of whiteness, purity, superiority, and civilisation to bolster its own power and extend its reach in Britain and the empire. Through its education and emigration programmes for girls, the GFS constructed notions of whiteness that then circulated globally.

By identifying whiteness and making it a central analytical category, this book aims to interrogate its formation and influence and further explore its relationship with constructions of girlhood. This relationship has been studied by scholars like Corinne T. Field and Lakisha Michelle Simmons, who have highlighted the ways that whiteness was the defining feature of girlhood and womanhood, and Robin Bernstein, who has examined how childhood provided a cover for whiteness.[45] In *Racial Innocence: Performing American Childhood from Slavery to Civil Rights*, Bernstein argues: 'Childhood innocence – itself raced white, itself characterized by the ability to retain racial meanings but hide them under claims of holy obliviousness – secured the unmarked status of whiteness, and the power derived from that status in the nineteenth and into the early twentieth centuries'.[46] Building upon the insights of Bernstein, Field, Simmons, and other scholars, I further explore how childhood – and specifically girlhood – was central to the propagation of whiteness and argue that the construction and operation of whiteness in this era cannot be understood without greater attention to girlhood.

## Confronting the silences and challenges of the archive

Sources present one of the greatest challenges in the study of childhood and colonialism due to the nature of the archive, which continues to reflect colonial power relations and privilege European, male, and adult voices over Indigenous, female, and youth voices. The nature of the archive means that the motives and operations of the colonial state overshadow the experiences of children themselves and render children – and girls in particular – silent. As Kristine Alexander has observed in her work on colonial girlhood, the history of girlhood consequently reflects a tradition of girls being 'spoken for and about' by adults.[47] However, girls were not passive in the process of colonialism, and, while *Empire's daughters* does examine discourses about girlhood, it also uncovers how girls understood, experienced, and engaged with the empire.

While the colonial archive poses challenges in studying girlhood, this book employs the theories and methodologies of postcolonial and feminist scholars who have valuably demonstrated the need to rethink traditional analytical categories and utilise new sources.[48] Although girls leave comparatively few records, their voices do emerge in correspondence they penned to friends and family, in articles they authored for children's periodicals, and in scrapbooks they crafted. While all these sources must be approached with caution, since they are mediated by adults as well as genre conventions and archival practices, they nonetheless show how girls participated in wider discourses about the empire and acted as creators and transmitters of colonial knowledge. For instance, Chapter 2 analyses scrapbooks created by members of the GFS, and, even though adults were involved in the creation of the scrapbooks, girls wrote essays and made drawings for them. As a result, these scrapbooks served as a unique forum where girls acted as experts about colonial life and instructed others about colonial history and geography and everyday experiences.

Although girls' experiences rarely appear in the traditional sources of the British empire, postcolonial and gender scholars have demonstrated the need to appreciate and investigate the moments when girls do appear in the colonial archive as holding important clues about their lives and importance in the empire. The third and fourth chapters highlight examples of girls whose stories are preserved in the archives because they did not conform to the organisers' wishes and instead protested against the difficult and abusive situations they faced. Their resistance to the imperial objectives of the organisation complicate simplistic narratives about girls' roles in the empire. Researching colonial girlhoods requires reading both along and against the archival grain, exploring the gaps and contradictions within the archive and considering what erasures or misrepresentations might reveal about the aspirations, anxieties, and epistemologies of GFS organisers and colonial officials.[49] One of the greatest difficulties I encountered in my research about the GFS was finding information about girls of colour. Except for cursory references, the GFS's official records contain little information about girls of colour and their involvement, and even fewer records include their voices and perspectives. Yet this marginalisation is in itself revealing and significant; it exposes that *white* girls were the primary focus of GFS organisers. The GFS centred its identity on purity and whiteness, and the presence of girls of colour disrupted this identity. The erasure of girls of colour from the GFS records thus exposes deeply rooted anxieties about the fragility of whiteness and suggest the racial and imperial hierarchies that seemingly underpinned the British empire were more precarious than GFS organisers wanted to admit. Due to the nature of the sources and the focus of the GFS itself, white girls are discussed more extensively in the following chapters, but this book is not exclusively about white girls and girlhood. The latter chapters of the book in particular focus on girls of colour in the organisation and their experiences, and one of key arguments of the book is how imperial and racial objectives shaped the lives of all girls but in different ways. A variety of factors – including race, class, and geography – mediated girls' roles in the empire and their experiences of colonialism.

In addition to analysing erasures within the historical record, *Empire's daughters* compares the different – and often contradictory – narratives that emerge in sources and interrogates these moments of disconnect and misrepresentation. For instance, emigration societies were keen to emphasise the value of their programmes and therefore inflated their success rate at times. For example, Ellen Joyce – who founded and led the GFS's emigration department – painted a picture of girls' migration as an unqualified success. In an article in *The Times*, she described travelling to Canada in 1884 and 1890 and how 'I visited many of the children who had been sent out, and found them, without exception, healthy, contented, and beloved. I have no reason to think my experience exceptional.'[50] Yet, as the third chapter explores, other evidence, including girls' correspondence and testimonies in court cases, tells a different story and details the hostility that greeted emigrant children, the abuses they suffered, and their difficulties adapting to life in the colonies. Such exaggeration may cause one to overlook assessments like Joyce's statements entirely, but they should not simply be disregarded and instead interrogated more fully.[51] Looking beyond the surface of such claims in reports suggests that confidence in emigration programmes was not as absolute as it appeared at first glance. Reading along the archival grain, these inconsistencies should not be dismissed simply as misrepresentations but viewed as symptomatic of class, racial, and gender anxieties within the organisation.

## Employing a multi-sited framework in studying colonial girlhoods

As scholars – like Tony Ballantyne, Antoinette Burton, Frederick Cooper, Catherine Hall, Alan Lester, Satadru Sen, and Ann Laura Stoler – have demonstrated, the relationship between Europe and its empires were mutually constitutive.[52] The British metropole and the colonies cannot be studied as discrete entities and instead must be considered more holistically as parts of integrated processes. Scholars of colonial childhoods – including Kristine Alexander, David Pomfret, and Rebecca Swartz – have demonstrated how a multi-sited approach enables broader comparative analyses about the changes and continuities of childhood and draws attention to the various effects of politics, race, gender, economics, and education on ideas and experiences of childhood.[53] By employing this approach and studying girlhood in different areas of the British empire, *Empire's daughters* reveals how the diverse histories, societies, and strategic interests of these regions shaped girls' perceived roles in the empire and their experiences of colonialism. Despite organisers' attempt to create uniformity among its global branches, the GFS developed differently in these regions, with colonial branches facing unique challenges, a theme explored throughout *Empire's daughters* and especially in Chapters 4 and 5. Furthermore, a multi-sited approach foregrounds how events and debates in one part of the empire shaped ideas and discourses about girlhood in other areas. For instance, the effects of the South African War reverberated beyond the region and generated concerns about the strength and stability of the empire, leading Britons and British settlers in regions throughout the empire to take a renewed interest in the education and welfare of children.

A single study cannot capture the diversity and complexity of the GFS's history and girls' experiences in different parts of the empire. This book is not a comprehensive global history of the organisation. Instead the following chapters use specific regions as focal case studies to elucidate the themes of the chapters. For instance, Chapter 3 about the GFS's emigration programmes describes the GFS's efforts to send girls to the settler colonies of New Zealand, Australia, and Canada but concentrates on southern Africa, since the concerted efforts to emigrate girls following the end of the South African War in 1902 crystallise how white girls were important in constructing social and racial hierarchies and fortifying notions of whiteness in settler colonial societies. Similarly, Chapter 4 examines girls of colour within the GFS, and, while it does discuss southern Africa and other regions of the empire, the chapter centres on India and specifically how the GFS's programmes to train girls in India reveal anxieties surrounding whiteness and its instability.

## A note on terminology

Racial designations are complex and contested due to the diversity of racial, ethnic, linguistic, and cultural identities and the problematic construction and employment of racial terms during the colonial period and beyond. Racial classifications served as a key part of colonial governance and technology of colonial rule.[54] Sources often use derogatory terms to refer to the inhabitants of a region. In the case of southern Africa, I use 'African' to encompass people categorised as Black and Coloured, as a means to distinguish them from European settlers, both British and Afrikaner, in the late nineteenth and early twentieth centuries, although I recognise that such a broad category does not adequately capture the diversity and complexity of these groups.

Geographic designations are similarly fluid and debated, in large part because of their connection to colonialism. The GFS records often used the term 'South Africa' broadly, at times to refer to areas in Rhodesia (present-day Zimbabwe). Since South Africa as a political entity did not exist until 1910, I use 'southern Africa' to refer to the region before 1910. I use India to refer to areas on the subcontinent that today are in Pakistan and Bangladesh. This usage reflects the terms used for the region prior to independence and also the structure of the GFS, which included areas like Burma (present-day Myanmar) and Ceylon (present-day Sri Lanka) under the umbrella of 'India'.

For similar reasons, while I use the term 'British' to refer to the empire, I more often use the term 'England' when referring to the GFS and its work. England, rather than Britain as a whole, occupied a privileged place within the organisation. The GFS established a branch in Scotland shortly after the GFS was founded in 1875, but, according to Mary Heath-Stubbs in her history of the organisation, the GFS's early leaders saw the Scottish GFS as a distinct entity from 'the Parent Society' in England due to 'the essential differences between England and Scotland'.[55] These 'essential differences' were partly connected to the structure of the GFS. Reflecting its close connection with the Anglican Church, the GFS imitated the church's structure by organising the society along diocesan lines, but Scotland, Ireland, and other parts of the empire had distinct ecclesiastical structures that complicated the GFS's growth and development in different regions. The 'Parent Society' technically included both England and Wales, but the Welsh society was subsumed under the banner of England. Leaders identified the GFS as an 'English Society' that was devoted to 'English girlhood'.[56] As explored throughout the book, whiteness and the Anglocentrism of the organisation were intricately connected; for GFS leaders, whiteness was an integral part of English identity.[57]

## Chapter overview

To understand how and why the GFS evolved into an imperial organisation, its development must be situated within the broader context of the late Victorian era. The following chapter focuses on how anxieties around gender, class, empire, and race shaped the formation of the GFS and its overarching principle: purity. As part of its commitment to protecting the 'purity of the girlhood of the empire', the GFS required its members have 'a virtuous character' and be virgins.[58] These strict rules were not just a way to govern girls' sexual and moral behaviour; they were rooted in concerns about social and racial purity. As the first chapter explores, the GFS used purity as an instrument not only of reform in England but also to extend its reach in the empire through the establishment of colonial branches and the organisation of missionary programmes.

As the GFS grew, it served as a conduit by which ideas about girlhood – and specifically racialised girlhood – spread. The second chapter analyses how the GFS used various cultural forms – including newsletters, scrapbook exchanges and competitions, 'penfriend' schemes, and pageants and plays – to construct ideas of race, otherness, and whiteness and support the 'civilising mission' of imperialism. This chapter also examines how girls actively participated in the production of colonial knowledge and appropriated and reproduced broader discourses about empire and race through these cultural productions. The GFS used these different cultural forms to transform white girls into empire builders who would migrate to the colonies and build up settler societies. The third chapter further investigates how emigration programmes heralded white girls as cultural and racial bulwarks who would assist in the reformation of colonial home life, strengthen the bonds of empire, and fulfil labour needs, but this role – and girls' place in the broader colonial project – was called into question. Conflicts between organisers in England and the colonies, debates over the selection of servants, disputes between organisers and employers, and strained relationships between mistresses and their servants were rooted in doubts over the durability and authenticity of working-class emigrants' whiteness.

Anxieties over girls' whiteness also shaped the GFS's work in non-settler colonies. As in settler colonial societies, poor white and multiracial girls in places like India provoked considerable unease among GFS organisers, since they threatened notions of whiteness and purity. The fourth chapter examines how the GFS endeavoured to bolster ideas of whiteness and extend its imperial reach through the establishment of overseas branches, referred to as 'Colonial Daughters', and in particular explores how the GFS's educational and training programmes for poor white and multiracial girls in India were rooted in a desire to maintain social and racial hierarchies. Yet these efforts had limited success and reveal the GFS's broader failure to deal effectively with questions of race. The GFS encouraged its members to think of themselves as belonging to 'a very large family' and an 'Imperial sisterhood', but the treatment of girls of colour within the organisation reveal that not all girls were equal members in this sisterhood.[59] Instead this familial imagery reinforced hierarchies of power within the empire.

The last chapter turns to the decline of the organisation in the interwar years and connects it to shifting ideas of girlhood and broader changes in the British empire. Although the GFS had succeeded in making early inroads in Britain and the empire, other organisations supplanted it by the interwar years. Debates over the possible amendment of the organisation's central rule on purity created ruinous fractures within the GFS community that highlighted how out of touch the organisation had become to girls and their concerns. The decline of the organisation also coincided with the growth of national sentiment and unrest in many regions of the empire, especially India. Disputes within the organisation mirrored growing divisions within the empire, as members in the colonies and dominions increasingly challenged the hierarchical structure of the organisation.

The GFS continued to face endemic problems in the latter half of the twentieth century, and the conclusion provides a brief overview of the challenges faced by the organisation since the Second World War. The GFS, like Britain more broadly, struggled to find its place and redefine its identity in a post-imperial world. The organisation continues to exist today with around twenty thousand members in branches throughout the world, but, within recent decades, the locus of GFS activity and power has moved from England to South Africa. Furthermore, the Black Lives Matter Movement has opened new discussions about race and racism within the organisation. The conclusion also offers some reflections on how the legacies of colonialism continue to shape girls' lives and frame the contemporary politics of girlhood.

Studying the GFS illustrates how the construction of girlhood was intricately tied to ideas of whiteness and empire. Debates around girlhood and girls' education, employment, and emigration were not isolated discussions but intersected with broader political, economic, and social discourses in the British empire. As the following chapters explore, girls and ideas of girlhood were central to the production of colonial and racial structures of power, but they could also destabilise these structures. By drawing attention to girls' myriad roles in the colonial project, *Empire's daughters* challenges assumptions that girls were peripheral figures in the empire and argues that understandings of colonialism and whiteness remain incomplete without a consideration of girls and girlhood.

## Notes

1 Edith Brunette, 'Stories of Brave Girls I. Maids of War', *Our Letter: For G.F.S. Candidates all over the World* (Easter 1907), pp. 3–4.
2 Agnes L. Money, *History of the Girls' Friendly Society*, 2nd ed. (London: Wells, Garner, Darton & Co., Ltd., 1911), p. 44.
3 Giorgia Dona and Andrea Veale, 'Mobility-in-Migration in an Era of Globalization: Key Themes and Future Directions', in Giorgia Dona and Andrea Veale (eds), *Child and Youth Migration: Mobility-in-Migration in an Era of Globalization* (Basingstoke: Palgrave Macmillan, 2014), p. 239. Philippe Ariès, *Centuries of Childhood: A Social History of Family Life*, trans. Robert Baldick (New York: Vintage Books, 1962). For informative assessments of Ariès, see Colin Heywood, '*Centuries of Childhood*: An Anniversary – and an Epitaph?', *The Journal of Childhood and Youth*, 3:3 (Fall 2010), 341–65; Adrian Wilson, 'The Infancy of the History of Childhood: An Appraisal of Philippe Ariès', *History and Theory*, 19:2 (1980), 132–53; and Stephen Mintz, 'Reflections on Age as a Category of Analysis', *The Journal of the History of Childhood and Youth*, 1:1 (Winter 2008), 91–2. See also the exchange on 'Rethinking the History of Childhood', by Sarah Maza, Steven Mintz, Nina Milanich, Robin P. Chapdelaine, Ishita Pande, and Bengt Sandin in the *American Historical Review*, 125:2 (April 2020), 1260–322; and the 'Forum on Double Age in the History of American Childhood and Youth' in *The Journal of the History of Childhood and Youth*, 15:3 (Fall 2002), 355–439, especially the introduction by Holly N. S. White and Julia M. Gossard, pp. 355–61. On age as an important category of analysis, see Mary Jo Maynes, 'Age as a Category of Historical Analysis: History, Agency, and Narratives of Childhood', *The Journal of the History of Childhood and Youth*, 1:1 (2008), 114–24; and the roundtable on 'Chronological Age: A Useful Category of Analysis' by Corinne T. Field, Nicholas L. Syrett, Pat Thane, Bianca Premo, Ishita Pande, Corrie Decker, Sayaka Chantani, and Ashwini Tambe, in *American Historical Review*, 125:4 (October 2020), 371–459.
4 Abosede George, *Making Modern Girls: A History of Girlhood, Labor, and Social Development in Colonial Lagos* (Athens: Ohio University Press, 2014), p. 14.
5 This scholarship includes Antoinette Burton, *Burdens of History: British Feminists, Indian Women, and Imperial Culture, 1865–1915* (Durham, NC:

University of North Carolina Press, 2000); Julia Bush, *Edwardian Ladies and Imperial Power* (London: Continuum, 1999); Catherine Hall, *Civilising Subjects: Colony and Metropole in the English Imagination, 1830–1867* (Chicago: University of Chicago Press, 2002); Ruby Lal, *Coming of Age in Nineteenth-Century India: The Girl-Child and the Art of Playfulness* (New York: Cambridge University Press, 2013); Philippa Levine, *Prostitution, Race and Politics: Policing Venereal Disease in the British Empire* (New York: Routledge, 2003); Philippa Levine (ed.), *Gender and Empire*, Oxford History of the British Empire Companion Series (Oxford: Oxford University Press, 2004); Anne McClintock, *Imperial Leather: Race, Gender, and Sexuality in the Colonial Contest* (New York: Routledge, 1995); Clare Midgley, *Gender and Imperialism* (Manchester: Manchester University Press, 1998); Clare Midgley, *Feminism and Empire: Women Activists in Imperial Britain, 1790–1865* (London: Routledge, 2007); Mrinalini Sinha, *Colonial Masculinity: The Effeminate Bengali and the Manly Englishman* (Manchester: Manchester University Press, 1995); Gayatri Chakravorty Spivak, 'Can the Subaltern Speak?', in Cary Nelson and Lawrence Grossberg (eds), *Marxism and the Interpretation of Culture* (Basingstoke: Macmillan Education, 1988), pp. 271–313; Gayatri Chakravorty Spivak, 'The Rani of Sirmur: An Essay in Reading the Archives', *History and Theory*, 24:3 (1985), 247–72; and Kathleen Wilson, *The Island Race: Englishness, Empire, and Gender in the Eighteenth Century* (New York: Routledge, 2003).

6 See, for instance, Kristine Moruzi and Michelle Smith, 'Colonial Girlhood / Colonial Girls', in Kristine Moruzi and Michelle J. Smith (eds), *Colonial Girlhood in Literature, Culture and History, 1840–1950*, Palgrave Studies in Nineteenth-Century Writing and Culture (Basingstoke: Palgrave Macmillan, 2016), pp. 1–11; Kristine Moruzi, 'Feminine Bravery: *The Girls Realm* (1898–1915) and the Second Boer War', *Literature Association Quarterly*, 34 (2009), 241–54; Kristine Moruzi, '"The Freedom Suits Me": Encouraging Girls to Settle in the Colonies', in Tamara S. Wagner (ed.), *Victorian Settler Narratives: Emigrants, Cosmopolitans and Returnees in Nineteenth Century Literature* (London: Pickering & Chatto, 2011), pp. 177–91; Kristine Moruzi, '"I am content with Canada": Canadian Girls at the Turn of the Twentieth Century', *Jeunesse: Young People, Texts, Cultures*, 4 (2012), 119–31; Michelle Smith, *Empire in British Girls' Literature and Culture: Imperial Girls 1880–1915* (New York: Palgrave Macmillan, 2010); Michelle Smith, 'Wild Australian Girls?: The Mythology of Colonial Femininity in British Print Culture, 1885–1916', in Clare Bradford and Mavis Reimer (eds), *Girls, Texts, Cultures*, Studies in Childhood and Family in Canada (Waterloo: Wilfrid Laurier University Press, 2015), pp. 237–60; and Michelle Smith, Kristine Moruzi, and Clare Bradford, *From Colonial to Modern: Transnational Girlhood in Canadian, Australian, and New Zealand Children's Literature* (Toronto: University of Toronto Press, 2018).

7 Moruzi and Smith, 'Colonial Girlhood/Colonial Girls', p. 4.

8 For greater examinations of children's agency, see Maynes, 'Age as a Category of Historical Analysis'; Susan Miller, 'Assent as Agency in the Early Years of the

Children of the American Revolution', *The Journal of the History of Childhood and Youth*, 9:1 (2016), 48–65; Mona Gleason, 'Avoiding the Agency Trap: Caveats for Historians of Children, Youth, and Education', *History of Education*, 45:4 (2016), 446–59; Deborah Levison, Mary Jo Maynes, and Frances Vavrus, 'Children and Youth as Subjects, Objects, Agents: An Introduction', in Deborah Levison, Mary Jo Maynes, and Frances Vavrus (eds), *Children and Youth as Subjects, Objects, Agents: Innovative Approaches to Research across Space and Time* (New York: Palgrave Macmillan, 2021), pp. 1–9; and Karen Vallgårda, Kristine Alexander, and Stephanie Olsen, 'Against Agency', Society for the History of Childhood and Youth Featured Commentaries, 23 October 2018, www.shcy.org/features/commentaries/against-agency/, accessed 27 November 2022.
9 The Women's Library, London (hereafter WL), 5GFS/02/235, 'The India "At Home"', n.d., p. 1.
10 *The Book of the G.F.S.: What It Is and What It Does* (June 1920), p. 11. Mary Heath-Stubbs, *Friendship's Highway: Being the History of the Girls' Friendly Society, 1875–1935* (London: G.F.S. Central Office, 1935), p. 19.
11 Corinne T. Field and LaKisha Michelle Simmons, 'Looking for Black Girls in History', in Corinne T. Field and LaKisha Michelle Simmons (eds), *The Global History of Black Girlhood* (Chicago: University of Illinois Press, 2022), p. 14. See also the roundtable on 'Chronological Age: A Useful Category of Analysis' in the *American Historical Review*.
12 Field and Simmons, 'Looking for Black Girls in History', p. 15.
13 Mary Jo Maynes, Birgitte Søland and Christina Benninghaus, 'Introduction', in Mary Jo Maynes, Birgitte Søland and Christina Benninghaus (eds), *Secret Gardens, Satanic Mills: Placing Girls in European History, 1750–1960* (Bloomington: Indiana University Press, 2005), pp. 4–5, 7, 43; Anna Davin, 'Imperialism and Motherhood', *History Workshop Journal*, 5:1 (1978), 36; and Sally Mitchell, *The New Girl: Girls' Culture in England 1880–1915* (New York: Columbia University Press, 1995), p. 7.
14 Anna Davin, 'What Is a Child?', in Stephen Hussey and Anthony Fletcher (eds), *Childhood in Question: Children, Parents and the State* (Manchester: Manchester University Press, 1999), p. 16; Peter Stearns, *Childhood in World History*, 2nd ed. (New York: Routledge, 2006), p. 74.
15 Caroline Rowan, 'Child Welfare and the Working-Class Family', in Mary Langan and Bill Schwarz (eds), *Crises in the British State, 1880–1930* (London: Hutchinson, 1985), pp. 226–39; Seth Koven, 'Borderlands: Women, Voluntary Action, and Child Welfare in Britain, 1840 to 1914', in Seth Koven and Sonya Michael (eds), *Mothers of a New World: Maternalist Politics and the Origins of Welfare State* (New York: Routledge, 1993), pp. 94–135; and Hugh Cunningham, 'Saving the Children, c. 1830–1920', in *Children and Childhood in Western Society since 1500* (New York: Longman, 1995), pp. 134–62.
16 Davin, 'Imperialism and Motherhood', 15.
17 WL, 1/SAX/1/1, *South African Colonisation Society Report. Report for 1903–4*, p. 50.

18 Shurlee Swain and Margot Hillel, *Child, Nation, Race and Empire: Child Rescue Discourse, England Canada, and Australia, 1850–1915* (Manchester: Manchester University Press, 2010), pp. 3, 35, 72; Office of Special Enquiries and Reports of the Board of Education, *Report of the Imperial Education Conference, 1911* (London: Eyre and Spottiswoode, Ltd, 1911), p. 199.
19 Stephen Heathorn, *For Home, Country, and Race: Gender, Class, and Englishness in the Elementary School, 1880–1914* (Toronto: University of Toronto Press, 2000), especially p. 26.
20 Ann Laura Stoler, *Carnal Knowledge and Imperial Power: Race and the Intimate in Colonial Rule* (Berkeley: University of California Press, 2002). For more on the construction of racial hierarchies in British schools, see Heathorn, *For Home, Country, and Race*.
21 See, for instance, David Pomfret, *Youth and Empire: Trans-Colonial Childhoods in British and French Asia* (Redwood City: Stanford University Press, 2015), especially 'Introduction: Childhood and the Reordering of Empire'.
22 John MacKenzie and J. A. Mangan were among the first scholars to draw attention to the pervasive influence of colonial ideas on British childhood. See, for example, John M. MacKenzie (ed.), *Imperialism and Popular Culture* (Manchester: Manchester University Press, 1986), especially chapter 9, 'Imperial Propaganda and Extra-curricular Activities', pp. 228–52; John M. MacKenzie, *Propaganda and Empire: The Manipulation of British Public Opinion, 1880–1960* (Manchester: Manchester University Press, 1984); J. A. Mangan (ed.), *Making Imperial Mentalities: Socialisation and British Imperialism* (New York: St Martin's Press, 1990); and J. A. Mangan, *The Games Ethic and Imperialism: Aspects of the Diffusion of an Ideal* (New York: Viking, 1986).
23 Stoler, *Carnal Knowledge and Imperial Power*, p. 112. On informal education, see Sarah Mills and Peter Kraftl (eds), *Informal Education, Childhood and Youth: Geographies, Histories, Practices* (London: Palgrave Macmillan, 2014); and Stephanie Olsen, *Juvenile Nation: Youth, Emotions and the Making of the Modern British Citizen, 1880–1914* (New York: Bloomsbury, 2014), pp. 2, 7–11.
24 For more on the Girl Guides and the British Empire, see Kristine Alexander, *Guiding Modern Girls: Girlhood, Empire, and Internationalism in the 1920s and 1930s* (Vancouver: UBC Press, 2017); Tammy M. Proctor, '(Uni)Forming Youth: Girl Guides and Boy Scouts in Britain, 1908–1939', *History Workshop Journal*, 45 (Spring 1998), 103–34; Michelle Smith, 'Be(ing) Prepared: Girl Guides, Colonial Life, and National Strength', *Limina*, 12 (2006), 52–63; Mary Clare Martin, 'Race, Indigeneity and the Baden-Powell Girl Guides: Age, Gender and the British World', in Shirleene Robinson and Simon Sleight (eds), *Children, Childhood and Youth in the British World*, Palgrave Studies in the History of Childhood (Basingstoke: Palgrave Macmillan, 2016), pp. 161–79; and Allen Warren, '"Mothers for the Empire"? The Girl Guides Association in Britain, 1909–1939', in J. A. Mangan (ed.), *Making Imperial Mentalities: Socialisation and British Imperialism* (Manchester: Manchester University Press, 1990), pp. 96–109. For more on Boy Scouts and the British Empire, see John

O. Springhall, 'The Boy Scouts, Class and Militarism in Relation to British Youth Movements, 1908–1930', *International Review of Social History*, 16 (1971), 125–58; and Allen Warren, 'Citizens of the Empire: Baden-Powell, Scouts and Guides, and an Imperial Ideal', in John M. MacKenzie (ed.), *Imperialism and Popular Culture* (Manchester: Manchester University Press, 1986), pp. 232–56. On other youth organisations in Britain, see Sian Edwards, *Youth Movements, Citizenship and the English Countryside: Creating Good Citizens, 1930–1960* (Basingstoke: Palgrave Macmillan, 2018); and Mills and Kraftl (eds), *Informal Education, Childhood and Youth*. For youth organisations in the United States, see Jennifer Helgren, *The Camp Fire Girls: Gender, Race, and American Girlhood, 1910–1980* (Lincoln: University of Nebraska Press, 2022); Jennifer Helgren, *American Girls and Global Responsibility: A New Relation to the World during the Early Cold War* (New Brunswick: Rutgers University Press, 2017); Mischa Honeck, *Our Frontier Is the World: The Boy Scouts in the Age of America Ascendancy*, The United States in the World Series (Ithaca: Cornell University Press, 2018); Benjamin René Jordan, *Modern Manhood and the Boy Scouts of America: Citizenship, Race, and the Environment, 1910–1930* (Chapel Hill: University of North Carolina Press, 2016); Susan Miller, *Growing Girls: The Natural Origins of Girls' Organizations in America*, Rutgers Series in Childhood Studies (New Brunswick: Rutgers University Press, 2007); and Gabriel Rosenberg, *The 4-H Harvest: Sexuality and the State in Rural America* (Philadelphia: University of Pennsylvania Press, 2015).

25 For work on the GFS in Britain, see Susan Anderson-Faithful, 'A "Mission to Civilize": The Popular Educational Vision of the Anglican Mothers' Union and Girls' Friendly Society (1886–1926)', *Revista Brasileira de História da Educação*, 12:1 (2012), 15–44; Sue Anderson-Faithful, *Mary Sumner: Mission, Education and Motherhood: Thinking a Life with Bourdieu* (Cambridge: Lutterworth Press, 2018); Sue Anderson-Faithful and Catherine Holloway, '"We do not wish to be sofa cushions, or even props to men, but we wish to work by their side": Celebrating Women as Popular Educators at the Anglican Church Congresses 1881–1913', *History of Education*, 48:2 (2019), 180–96; Ray Fabes and Alison Skinner, 'The Girls' Friendly Society and the Development of Rural Youth Work 1850–1900', in Ruth Gilchrist, Tony Jeffs, and Jean Spence (eds), *Essays in the History of Community and Youth Work* (Leicester: Youth Work Press, 2001), pp. 64–7; and Kristine Moruzi, 'Encouraging Charitable Work and Membership in the Girls' Friendly Society through British Girls' Periodicals', in Alexis Easley, Beth Rodgers, and Clare Gill (eds), *Women, Periodicals and Print Culture in Britain, 1830s–1900s: The Victorian Period* (Edinburgh: Edinburgh University Press, 2019), pp. 140–52.

26 Brian Harrison, 'For Church, Queen, and Family: The Girls' Friendly Society 1874–1920', *Past and Present*, 61 (November 1972), 107–38.

27 Vivienne Richmond, 'Crafting Inclusion for "Invalid" Women: The Girls' Friendly Society Central Needlework Depôt, 1899–1947', in Janice Helland, Beverly Lemire, and Alena Buis (eds), *Craft, Community and the Material Culture of Place and Politics, 19th–20th Century* (Burlington: Ashgate, 2014),

pp. 161–76; and Vivienne Richmond, '"It Is Not a Society for Human Beings but for Virgins": The Girls' Friendly Society Membership Eligibility Dispute 1875–1936', *Journal of Historical Sociology*, 20:3 (September 2007), 304–27.
28 Julia Bush, 'Edwardian Ladies and the "Race" Dimensions of British Imperialism', *Women's Studies International Forum*, 21:3 (1998), 277–89. She also discusses the GFS in *Edwardian Ladies and Imperial Power*.
29 Money, *History of the Girls' Friendly Society*, p. 44.
30 See, for instance, Ellen Boucher, *Empire's Children: Child Emigration, Welfare, and the Decline of the British World* (Cambridge: Cambridge University Press, 2014); Tim Calabria, 'Agents of Settler Colonialism?: Childhood, Time and Exclusion in the Fairbridge Scheme, 1913–1924', *Settler Colonial Studies*, 13:1 (2023), 133–55; Chris Jeffery and Geoffrey Sherington, *Fairbridge: Empire and Child Migration* (London: Woburn Press, 1998); Morgan Brie Johnson, 'Settler Colonial Structures of Domestication: British Home Children in Canada', *Genealogy*, 5:3 (2021), 78; Scott Johnston, '"Only Send Boys of the Good Type": Child Migration and the Boy Scout Movement, 1921–1959', *The Journal of the History of Childhood and Youth*, 7:3 (2014), 377–97; Gillian Wagner, *Barnardo* (London: Weidenfeld and Nicolson, 1979); and Gillian Wagner, *Children of the Empire* (London: Weidenfeld and Nicolson, 1982).
31 Calabria, 'Agents of Settler Colonialism?', 140.
32 Calabria, 'Agents of Settler Colonialism?'. Sana Nakata, *Childhood Citizenship, Governance and Policy: The Politics of Becoming Adult* (New York: Routledge, 2015). Laura Ishiguro, '"Growing up and Grown up [...] in Our Future City": Children and the Aspirational Politics of Settler Futurity in Colonial British Columbia', *BC Studies: The British Columbian Quarterly*, 190 (2016), 15.
33 Ishiguro, 'Growing up and Grown up [...] in Our Future City', 15.
34 W. E. B. Du Bois, 'The Souls of White Folk', in *W. E. B. Du Bois: Writings* (New York: Library of America, 1987), p. 924. For more on this point, see Marilyn Lake and Henry Reynolds, *Drawing the Global Colour Line: White Men's Countries and the International Challenge of Racial Equality*, Critical Perspectives on Empire (Cambridge: Cambridge University Press, 2008), p. 2; and George Robb, *British Culture and the First World War* (Basingstoke: Palgrave Macmillan, 2002), p. 31. For more on whiteness, see, for instance, Richard Dyer, *White: Essays on Race and Culture* (New York: Routledge, 1997); Ruth Frankenberg, *White Women, Race Matters: The Social Construction of Whiteness* (Minneapolis: University of Minnesota Press, 1993); Ruth Frankenberg (ed.), *Displacing Whiteness: Essays in Social and Cultural Criticism* (Durham, NC: Duke University Press, 1997); Toni Morrison, *Playing in the Dark: Whiteness and the Literary Imagination* (Cambridge, MA: Harvard University Press, 1992); and Nell Irvin Painter, *The History of White People* (New York: W. W. Norton & Company, 2010). For a discussion of whiteness scholarship, see also Aileen Moreton-Robinson, 'Writing Off Treaties: Possession in the U.S. Critical Whiteness Literature', chapter 4 in *The White Possessive: Property, Power, and Indigenous Sovereignty* (Minneapolis: University of Minnesota Press, 2015), pp. 47–61; and Angela Woollacott's review article on recent scholarship on

whiteness, 'New Angles on Whiteness and the Making of the Modern World', *Itinerario*, 47 (2023), 138–45.
35 Du Bois, 'The Souls of White Folk', p. 923.
36 Du Bois, 'The Souls of White Folk', p. 923.
37 Du Bois, 'The Souls of White Folk', p. 932.
38 Du Bois, 'The Souls of White Folk', p. 930. For more on the emergence of whiteness as a transnational phenomenon, see Lake and Reynolds, *Drawing the Global Colour Line* and especially the introduction.
39 Frantz Fanon, *Black Skin, White Masks*, trans. Charles Lam Markmann (London: Pluto Press, 2008), especially the chapters on 'The Negro and Language' and 'The Lived-Experience of the Black Man'.
40 Cheryl I. Harris, 'Whiteness as Property', *Harvard Law Review*, 106:8 (June 1993), 1790.
41 Bill Schwarz, *The White Man's World (Memories of Empire)* (Oxford: Oxford University Press, 2012), pp. 20–1.
42 Harris, 'Whiteness as Property'; Robin Bernstein, *Racial Innocence: Performing American Childhood from Slavery to Civil Rights* (New York: New York University Press, 2011); Dyer, *White*; Ruth Frankenberg, 'Introduction: Local Whiteness, Localizing Whiteness', in Ruth Frankenberg (ed.), *Displacing Whiteness: Essays in Social and Cultural Criticism* (Durham, NC: Duke University Press, 1997), p. 6; George Lipsitz, 'The Possessive Investment in Whiteness: Racialized Social Democracy and the "White" Problem in American Studies', *American Quarterly*, 47:5 (1995), 369–87; and Moreton-Robinson, *The White Possessive*. I am grateful to the anonymous reviewer of the manuscript for encouraging me to articulate this point more clearly.
43 Lipsitz, 'The Possessive Investment in Whiteness', 369.
44 Moreton-Robinson, *The White Possessive*, p. 52.
45 Corinne T. Field and LaKisha Michelle Simmons, 'Girlhood', in Corinne T. Field and LaKisha Michelle Simmons (eds), *The Global History of Black Girlhood* (Chicago: University of Illinois Press, 2022), pp. 40–1.
46 Bernstein, *Racial Innocence*, p. 17.
47 Kristine Alexander, 'Can the Girl Guide Speak?: The Perils and Pleasures of Looking for Children's Voices in Archival Research', *Jeunesse: Young People, Texts, Cultures*, 4:1 (2012), 134.
48 For more on the difficulty of finding girls' voices in the colonial archive, see Corinne T. Field, Tammy-Charelle Owens, Marcia Chatelain, Lakisha Simmons, Abosede George, and Rhian Keyse, 'The History of Black Girlhood: Recent Innovations and Future Directions', *The Journal of the History of Childhood and Youth*, 9:3 (2016), 383–401; and Field and Simmons, 'Looking for Black Girls in History', pp. 1–27. On the colonial archive, see, for example, Anjali Arondekar, *For the Record: On Sexuality and the Colonial Archive in India* (Durham, NC: Duke University Press, 2009); Tony Ballantyne, 'Rereading the Archive and Opening up the Nation-State: Colonial Knowledge in South Asia (and Beyond)', in Antoinette Burton (ed.), *After the Imperial Turn: Thinking with and through the Nation* (Durham, NC: Duke University Press, 2003),

pp. 102–21; Antoinette Burton, *Dwelling in the Archive: Women, Writing, House, Home and History in Late Colonial India* (New York: Oxford University Press, 2003); Antoinette Burton (ed.), *Archive Stories: Facts, Fictions, and the Writing of History* (Durham, NC: Duke University Press, 2006); Liz Conor and Jane Lydon, 'Double Take: Reappraising the Colonial Archive', *Journal of Australian Studies*, 35:2 (June 2011), 137–43; Lachy Paterson and Angela Wanhalla, 'Introduction: Voice, Text and the Colonial Archive', in *He Reo Wāhine: Māori Women's Voices from the Nineteenth Century* (Auckland: Auckland University Press, 2017), pp. 11–35; Thomas Richards, *Imperial Archive: Knowledge and the Fantasy of Empire* (London: Verso, 1996); Spivak, 'Can the Subaltern Speak?'; Spivak, 'The Rani of Sirmur'; Ann Laura Stoler, 'Colonial Archives and Arts of Governance', *Archival Science*, 2 (2002), 87–109; and Ann Laura Stoler, *Along the Archival Grain: Epistemic Anxieties and Colonial Common Sense* (Princeton: Princeton University Press, 2008).
49 Stoler, *Along the Archival Grain*, pp. 86–9. See also Saidiya Hartman, *Wayward Lives, Beautiful Experiments: Intimate Histories of Riotous Black Girls, Troublesome Women, and Queer Radicals* (New York: W. W. Norton & Company, 2019), especially 'A Note on Method', pp. xiii–xv.
50 Hon Mrs Joyce, 'Children under the Poor Law', *The Times* (9 January 1897), p. 2.
51 Stoler, *Along the Archival Grain*, p. 53.
52 Tony Ballantyne, *Orientalism and Race: Aryanism in the British Empire*, Cambridge Imperial and Post-Colonial Studies (Basingstoke: Palgrave Macmillan, 2001); Burton, *Burdens of History*; Antoinette Burton, 'Introduction: On the Inadequacy and Indispensability of the Nation', in *After the Imperial Turn: Thinking with and through the Nation* (Durham, NC: Duke University Press, 2003), pp. 1–26; Frederick Cooper and Ann Laura Stoler, 'Between Metropole and Colony: Rethinking a Research Agenda', in Frederick Cooper and Ann Laura Stoler (eds), *Tensions of Empire: Colonial Cultures in a Bourgeois World* (Berkeley: University of California Press, 1997), pp. 1–56; Hall, *Civilising Subjects*; Alan Lester, 'Colonial Settlers and the Metropole: Racial Discourse in the Early 19th-Century Cape Colony, Australia and New Zealand', *Landscape Research*, 27.1 (2002), 39–49; and Satadru Sen, *Colonial Childhoods: The Juvenile Periphery of India, 1850–1945* (New York: Anthem, 2005).
53 Alexander, *Guiding Modern Girls*; Pomfret, *Youth and Empire*; and Rebecca Swartz, *Education and Empire: Children, Race and Humanitarianism in the British Settler Colonies, 1833–1880* (Basingstoke: Palgrave Macmillan, 2019). There are also edited collections that provide transnational studies of girlhood, like Moruzi and Smith (eds), *Colonial Girlhood in Literature, Culture and History*; Jennifer Helgren (ed.), *Girlhood: A Global History* (Piscataway: Rutgers University Press, 2012); and Helen May, Baljit Kaur, and Larry Prochner, *Empire, Education, and Indigenous Childhoods* (London: Routledge, 2016). For more on multi-sited methodologies, see George E. Marcus, 'Ethnography in/of the World System: The Emergence of Multi-Sited Ethnography', *Annual Review of Anthropology*, 24 (1995), 95–117.

54 Benedict Anderson analyses the census and its relation to colonial ordering and imagining in the South Asian context in 'Census, Map, Museum', in *Imagined Communities: Reflections on the Origin and Spread of Nationalism*, revised ed. (New York: Verso, 2006), pp. 164–70. For a discussion of the colonial census in the African context, see Karl Ittmann, Dennis D. Cordell, and Gregory H. Maddox (eds), *The Demographics of Empire: The Colonial Order and the Creation of Knowledge* (Athens: Ohio University Press, 2010).

55 Heath-Stubbs, *Friendship's Highway*, p. 166.

56 Heath-Stubbs, *Friendship's Highway*, p. 166. Edith Marion Welch, 'Anniversary, 1917. An Impression', *The Empire and Beyond*, Occasional Leaflet XVI (All Saints 1917), p. 3. On this point, see also Willoughby Jones, 'A Dialogue for G.F.S. Candidates', *Our Letter: For G.F.S. Candidates all over the World* (September 1910), p. 98. For a greater discussion on the distinction between British and English, see Wendy Webster, *Englishness and Empire 1939–1965* (New York: Oxford University Press, 2005), p. 17. My thanks to Geoffrey Parker for his clarification about this point.

57 For a greater discussion of the meanings of Englishness, Britishness, and their connection to race and ideas of racial purity, see, for instance, Ian Baucom, *Out of Place: Englishness, Empire, and the Locations of Identity* (Princeton: Princeton University Press, 2001), especially the introduction.

58 Lambeth Palace Library, London, Davidson 143, ff.215, Appeal for £20,000 for the Lodges and Homes of Rest of the Girls' Friendly Society, 1907. British Library, London, General Reference Collection 8275.b.23.(6.), Mary Elizabeth Townsend, *A Friendly Letter to Fathers and Mothers about the Girls' Friendly Society* (London: Hatchards, 1883), p. 1.

59 On the GFS as a 'very large family', see An Associate, 'A Friendly Letter to all Candidates Everywhere', *Our Letter: For G.F.S. Candidates all over the World* (June 1906), p. 1. On the GFS as an 'Imperial sisterhood', see WL, 5GFS/01/097, 'Colonial Committee Minutes of a Meeting held on Nov. 20th 1905', p. 10. This tension was also apparent in the Camp Fire Girls. See Jennifer Helgren, *The Camp Fire Girls*, p. 95.

# 1

# Purity and the origins of the Girls' Friendly Society

When Queen Victoria died in 1901, the newsletter *The Girls' Quarterly: A Paper for Workers in the Girls' Friendly Society* published an obituary honouring the late monarch and patron of the GFS.[1] The obituary pronounced how the Queen was mourned by her worldwide empire. The Queen's sixty-three-year reign witnessed tremendous social, economic, and technological changes, but the obituary contains little mention of them. Instead it focuses on Victoria's role as a mother and a model of virtue. In particular, it emphasises Victoria's 'purity of family life' and the 'purity of her court' and notes that her 'innocency' provides a 'message to all the girls of her land'.[2] The obituary also highlights Victoria's 'whiteness', both morally and racially, describing 'the white stainlessness of her life' and referring to her as 'their Great White Mother'.[3] Another commemorative essay, this one composed by the GFS's founder, Mary Elizabeth Townsend, echoed the obituary in *The Girls' Quarterly*, writing about 'the dark millions of India lamenting for their "great white mother"'.[4] As these tributes reveal, purity and whiteness were integral to the GFS and inextricably connected to colonialism and ideas of Victorian femininity.

Why did ideas of purity and whiteness become cornerstones of the GFS? How did the GFS, which initially appeared parochial in its remit, develop into an imperial organisation? The answers to these two seemingly disparate but interrelated questions lie in the broader contexts in which the GFS emerged. This chapter explores how concerns about gender, race, class, sex, and empire in the late Victorian era intersected with anxieties surrounding girls and girlhood and shaped the formation, development, and structure of the GFS. Contrary to what its name suggests, purity – not friendship – was the central ideal of the Girls' Friendly Society. Through its ardent commitment to purity, the GFS positioned itself as a key agent of not only social reform in England but also the 'civilising mission' of imperialism and the propagation of whiteness.

## 'The capture of the girlhood of the empire': social and racial anxieties and the emergence of the GFS

The Girls' Friendly Society was officially founded on 1 January 1875. However, the seeds of the organisation had been planted years earlier. The previous May, the GFS's founder, Mary Elizabeth Townsend, met with religious figures and philanthropists, including Catherine Tait, the wife of the archbishop of Canterbury; Elizabeth Browne, the wife of the bishop of Winchester; and the Reverend Thomas Vincent Fosbery, the chaplain to the bishop of Winchester. At this meeting at Lambeth Palace, Townsend put forward her vision for an organisation to 'help young girls to meet the trials, difficulties, and dangers which so often attend their first start in life for themselves, especially such as have to leave home to live, or work, amongst strangers'.[5] Following in the footsteps of other organisations, like the Travellers' Aid Society and the Salvation Army, Townsend wanted to ensure the safety of girls travelling in England and that they came under the right influences.[6]

Townsend and her fellow founding members envisioned the GFS as fulfilling the supportive, educative, and protective roles of families for girls, particularly orphaned and working girls in England who were separated from their homes and communities.[7] The informational booklet, *The Book of the G.F.S.: What It Is and What It Does*, described how the society acted as an supplementary family and that the friendship it provided 'will help to take away the desolate feeling which must come at times to every child with no home of her own. They will find that they are in a family – the family of the G.F.S.'.[8] Family and familial imagery were replete within the GFS. In another pamphlet about the GFS, Townsend encouraged girls to think of each other as sisters: 'when you go about the world, you may meet with other girls belonging to the same Society, and that will often give you a happy feeling, as if you had met a sister, or some one of the same family'.[9] Extending this familial metaphor, Townsend was referred to as the 'Mother of the G.F.S.', and the GFS was called 'a "mothering" Society'.[10] While cultivating a sense of inclusivity, this familial terminology also propagated racial and imperial hierarchies, a theme explored in greater length in the following chapters, and social prejudices. This positioning of the GFS as a pseudo-family was rooted in critiques about working-class domestic life. The upper-class and middle-class leaders of the GFS saw the society as creating a better family that compensated for the poor conditions of working-class families and homes.[11] The GFS did require parents' consent for girls to join the society and emphasised that girls should be dutiful to their families, but they believed working-class parents were not imparting the necessary moral habits and domestic skills in their daughters, leaving them 'untrained and ignorant'.[12] This lack of proper upbringing meant that, especially when they left home to work, girls would not be able to withstand the 'sin and misery' of city life and the dangers posed by working conditions.[13] Organisers thus framed the GFS's role as 'shield[ing] the Members from the dangers and temptations to which they may be specially exposed by poverty, by their youth, their ignorance, or by the lack of good influences'.[14] To counteract the perceived deficiencies of English working-class families, the GFS provided religious instruction, including Bible study classes. It also had classes to teach them domestic and homecraft skills, like needlework, basket-making, and cookery, and instil in them middle-class values, namely self-control, piety, domesticity, and, above all, purity.[15]

The emergence of the GFS coincided with a heightened awareness of children's developmental stages. In his landmark 1904 book, *Adolescence: Its Psychology and Its Relations to Physiology, Anthropology, Sociology, Sex, Crime, Religion and Education*, G. Stanley Hall identified adolescence as a distinct time characterised by 'storm and stress' that required carefully controlled, adult-monitored environments and activities to ensure healthy adjustment to adulthood.[16] In line with Hall's advice, the GFS hosted a wide range of classes – including lantern lectures, essay and scrapbook competitions, debates, and teas and picnics – to structure girls' free time with the 'right kind' of activities.[17] These supervised activities eased concerns that girls wasted their free time and limited earnings on frivolous things, such as visits to fortune-tellers, dresses, and novels, and instead ensured that 'the G.F.S. can fill the leisure hours of her life with wholesome and innocent interests'.[18] Alarmed by 'the poisonous literature daily circulating amongst our boys and girls', the GFS established a range of periodicals, the earliest being *Friendly Leaves*, which was first published in 1876, as well as reading circles and circulating libraries for members.[19] These efforts sought to 'spread as widely as possible the purifying influence of a holy, healthy, fresh, and attractive literature amongst our young people to counteract and supplant, if it may be, the evil leaven'.[20] The GFS also encouraged girls' physical activity through drill and sports, including hockey, as part of the effort to keep girls' bodies healthy and pure.[21]

The GFS was part of the social purity movement that arose in the late nineteenth century.[22] Orchestrated by upper-class and middle-class women, it aimed to impose their ideas of morality on working-class girls. In line with the broader social purity movement, GFS leaders stated that one of its long-term goals was 'to revolutionise the opinions and to reform the habits of our working classes upon the moral question'.[23] For GFS leaders, girls were the key to this 'revolution'. A speech on 'Some Ideals and Difficulties of Girl Life' by Miss Rich, the head of the GFS members' department, expressed the notion that the reformation of womanhood – and society more broadly – originated with the improvement of girlhood: 'Girlhood is an *important* time, for in it lies the preparation for the future ... Womanhood, wifehood, motherhood, are all much what girlhood has made them.'[24] The GFS's efforts to shape girls' actions and attitudes took on a renewed urgency amid transformations in women's position in society in the late nineteenth century.[25] Emerging in the 1890s, the 'New Woman', independent and self-assured, challenged conventional gender and class norms and enjoyed the greater freedoms and mobility provided by new educational and employment opportunities. As discussed more in the fifth chapter, these fears around changing gender norms would continue to trouble the GFS in the wake of the emergence of the modern girl in the first decades of the twentieth century. In this 'time when girlhood was changing', the GFS reaffirmed its commitment to uphold traditional, middle-class, Victorian ideals and 'to direct and consecrate the energies of girlhood'.[26] While framed altruistically, its training and educational initiatives helped strengthen upper-class and middle-class women's own position, elevating their sense of power and influence over other members of society.

The social purity movement encompassed a wide range of reforms aimed at controlling sexual behaviour, from the abolition of prostitution to the censorship of pornography to ending 'white slavery'. A decade after the GFS's foundation, the journalist W. T. Stead published his sensational exposé 'The Maiden Tribute of Modern Babylon' about the 'white slave trade' that detailed how English girls were lured into prostitution abroad.[27] The series of articles generated a proliferation of writings – everything from tracts to novels – about white slavery and the related evils of prostitution and venereal disease and led to the implementation of the Criminal Law Amendment Act of 1885, which raised the age of consent for girls from thirteen to sixteen in Britain and Ireland. These fears over white slavery reaffirmed the GFS's charge. In this atmosphere of moral panic, Townsend asserted the necessity of the GFS: 'There surely never was a time when more efforts were needed to preserve in purity the girlhood of England, to strengthen and protect character in virtue, and in chastity'.[28] At this time when girlhood was seemingly under threat, the GFS presented itself as 'the godparent of English girlhood ... whose scope is not one whit less narrow than the capture of the girlhood of the empire – nay, of the world – for Christ'.[29] The GFS 'captured' girlhood through its provision of activities, which were put in place ostensibly to protect girls but controlled their behaviour. The protection of girlhood – and specifically white girlhood – was increasingly cast as not just a familial or domestic matter but one of imperial and racial importance. The very designation of *white* slavery signals the fundamental role of racism and xenophobia in the construction of this phenomenon. Stories around white slavery often involved sinister non-English elements, with girls abducted by foreigners or lured to brothels abroad, and fomented fears about the corruption of white racial purity.[30]

Anxieties about girlhood were not just about girls themselves but instead symptomatic of broader social and imperial unease. The social purity movement was not simply about reforming English society; its goal was the preservation of white supremacy through the creation of more white families and, importantly, respectable white families.[31] However, this objective was imperilled by the apparent lack of moral training among the working classes. The South African War at the turn of the twentieth century made apparent low birth rates and the unfitness of soldiers and future solders in Britain and its consequences for the empire. These circumstances, which took place alongside the proliferation of Social Darwinist ideology, gave credence to fears that the British race was degenerating while 'inferior' or 'unfit' races were growing in strength and number.[32] As Anna Davin argues in her article 'Imperialism and Motherhood', women – and specifically their maternal ignorance and neglect – were blamed for low birth rates and children's poor health.[33] As 'mothers of the race', women had the responsibility of ensuring the success of the British empire by producing healthy children and training them as future citizens, soldiers, and colonists of the British empire.[34] This context gave a greater urgency to the GFS's efforts to teach girls maternal and domestic skills. Through training girls and improving their physical fitness, the GFS viewed itself as stemming the tide of white racial decline and helping ensure the futurity of the British empire.

### 'That most critical period of their lives': debates about age and purity within the GFS

Anxieties about white slavery, working-class morality, and social and racial purity infused the structure of the GFS, shaping its central principles and membership groups. The GFS had three main categories for participants in the organisation: associates, members, and candidates. The GFS initially focused its efforts on recruiting girls between the ages of twelve and fourteen as members. This time was – in the words of one early GFS leader – 'that most critical period of their lives, when after leaving school, they either remain idle at home or drift from one small situation to another'.[35] The GFS feared that girls would stop having any kind of formal religious education or allegiance after leaving school and were the most impressionable and susceptible to negative influences at this age.[36] They occupied a liminal position, what the scholar Sally Mitchell describes as the 'provisional free space' between childhood and adulthood.[37] Members who were older than twenty were considered 'Elder Members' and envisioned as 'guardian angels' who could serve as companions and models and assist the spiritual life of younger girls of the organisation.[38] Girls and women could remain members of the GFS until they married or reached the age of thirty-five.[39] Once girls married, they were no longer allowed to be members but could continue to participate in the GFS as 'married helpers' or associates.[40] Associates, typically upper-class and middle-class 'ladies', 'vowed themselves to the service of girlhood' and led branches for candidates and members.[41] According to the society's history, *Friendship's Highway*, 'Associates were to be the governing and the working force in the Society'.[42]

Considerable debate existed within the GFS about the ideal age of members. In the late 1890s, associates contemplated changing the name of the organisation to the Young Women's Friendly Society in an effort to recruit older girls. However, the proposal experienced resistance from some of the most influential associates, including Agnes Money, a long-time friend of Townsend who was a leading figure in the GFS during its early years and wrote a history of the organisation in 1911. She argued that the GFS 'was formed for the sake of the girlhood of England'.[43] GFS associates like Money opposed admitting older girls, fearing they would have a detrimental effect on younger members.[44]

Underlying these debates about the age of members and the admittance of older girls was the GFS's singular commitment to purity, the keystone of its social and imperial policies. The GFS stated that it was founded 'to preserve and protect the girls of England in purity and goodness' and that its 'central object' was to 'uphold Purity in Thought, Word, and Deed'.[45] To safeguard its reputation, the organisation required its members to be 'pure', with one of its central rules stating: 'No girl who has not borne a virtuous character to be admitted as a Member; such character being lost, the Member to forfeit her card'.[46] The implied meaning of 'virtuous' was virginity, so girls had to be virgins to be members of the society and leave the organisation if they were not. However, the vagueness of the term led to misunderstandings, with some members believing that being virtuous meant they could not even go dancing.[47]

Other contemporary youth organisations, like the Girl Guides, Boy Scouts, and Camp Fire Girls, also emphasised purity. For instance, Camp Fire Girls were encouraged to take the 'maiden's vow' that included 'the vow of purity'.[48] For Boy Scouts, 'purity' was often coded as 'cleanliness'. The Scout's Eleventh Law stipulated that a good Scout 'keeps clean in body and thought, stands for clean speech, clean sport, clean habits, and travels with a clean crowd'.[49] Yet they did not make virginity an explicit condition of membership, as the GFS did. As a result, the reputation of the

GFS became closely entwined with the ideal of purity. Randall Davidson, the archbishop of Canterbury from 1903 to 1928, heralded the work of the GFS as 'this great effort to preserve and protect the purity of the Girlhood of our Empire'.[50] GFS iconography reinforced this commitment to purity through white symbols. As seen in the photo of a branch from Newcastle (Figure 1.1), girls often wore white dresses, and white flowers featured prominently on GFS banners and in GFS publications.

The latter half of the nineteenth century witnessed the proliferation of social rescue organisations in England focused on helping 'fallen' girls and women, but the GFS distinguished itself from these organisations by concentrating its efforts on preventing girls from 'falling' and recruiting only girls who were honourable, respectable, and sexually pure.[51] A pamphlet produced by the GFS acknowledged, 'The Society does not attempt the sad work of reclaiming the fallen, nor even of holding such as are already drifting away'.[52] As Deborah Gorham has shown in her study of child prostitution in Victorian England, this anxiety about the corrupting influence of 'fallen' girls and the need to separate 'fallen' from 'unfallen' girls and

Figure 1.1 Girls from a Newcastle branch with a white flower banner, 1927 (Women's Library, London, 5GFS/04/127, 'Newcastle Branch, Bridgend, Glamorganshire', *G.F.S. Magazine*, April 1927, photo from Block Book VII, 1926–31)

women was a common concern within not just the GFS but also the wider social purity movement.[53] What especially troubled GFS leaders was that the virginity of girls could not be definitively proved, meaning that the GFS would have to take 'their characters and history, as must necessarily be the case, more or less, on trust'.[54] Yet relying on girls' own testimony did not provide an authoritative safeguard and consequently 'admits an element of uncertainty into the character of its Society, which must derogate from its value, and in the long run mar its work'.[55] GFS organisers feared that the possible admittance of an 'impure' girl could contaminate other members and would be potentially ruinous to the organisation.

The GFS's 'great effort to preserve and protect the purity of the Girlhood of our Empire' led the organisation to amend its structure in 1879.[56] Organisers created a new category of membership for girls between the ages of eight and twelve, who were referred to as candidates. The decision to introduce this category stemmed from a growing realisation that girls needed help earlier in life and from fears that a girl might already have 'fallen' by the time she could become a member of the GFS, or, in the view of Townsend, 'that the mischief was often done, and the first train of evil laid, before a child of twelve years of age, the earliest age at which she could be admitted as a Member of the Girls' Friendly Society'.[57] If the GFS recruited younger girls before they reached sexual maturity and became sexually active, it was more likely that their purity – and by extension the purity of the organisation – could be assured. As one early associate observed: 'a girl's connexion with the GFS thus early formed would underlie all her after life, and unbroken membership would be the most conclusive guarantee of character possible'.[58] GFS organisers viewed the development of the candidates as a way of 'drafting our young maidens from their very childhood into the ranks of an army of virtue'.[59] To ensure girls were prepared for membership in the GFS, candidates' classes focused on teaching girls the basic principles of the GFS and especially the importance of purity.[60]

To encourage children to join the GFS, branches appointed candidates' correspondents, and the GFS created a department for candidates, designated 'The Nursery of the Society', that specifically targeted children in workhouses and orphanages.[61] The organisation's leaders believed that children from workhouses and orphanages were especially susceptible to 'falling' and 'needed very special care before they could be admitted as Members'.[62] An account about the organisation's founding in the memoir *Some Memories of Mrs. Townsend* commented that 'these waifs and strays should not be regarded as a race apart'.[63] Nevertheless, prejudices against workhouse and orphan girls remained prevalent. A pamphlet produced by the GFS gave advice on how to recruit working-class girls and described them as an 'impulsive race' who 'had been very rough until the G.F.S.

tamed them'.⁶⁴ The belief that working-class girls were inferior did not go unnoticed by the girls themselves. A report by the GFS's 'Department for Members in Professions and Business' bemoaned 'the lack of sympathy amongst Associates' for factory and workhouse girls in particular. It also noted that members 'sometimes complain that the ladies do not understand them; they seem to look upon them as a kind of class apart, rather than as human beings with human interests and sympathies'.⁶⁵ As described more in the fifth chapter, this sense of disconnection between the leaders and the girls the GFS claimed to help persisted through the interwar years and led many girls to leave the organisation. While the GFS presented itself as a cross-class organisation and pledged to 'befriend girls, to whatever class of society they may belong', its attitudes towards girls working in factories and in workhouses called into question the validity of such statements. Associates' classist and paternalistic assumptions ultimately limited the GFS's influence among girls in factories and workhouses and, as discussed in the fourth and fifth chapters, remained a persistent problem for the society, limiting its reach among girls in England and the empire.⁶⁶

## 'Duty came first': the servant crisis and domestic servants within the GFS

Even though 'the G.F.S. [was] open to working girls of *all* classes and of every occupation', domestic service remained the principal occupation of members, composing 57 per cent of the total members of the GFS who were employed in 1891.⁶⁷ The dominance of this occupation was partly driven by the conditions of service, which often required girls to live apart from their families and home communities and work long hours for relatively low pay. GFS associates believed that these aspects of servant life easily led to sex work. This perceived connection between sex work and domestic service led to the creation of various reform groups to assist domestic servants, including the Metropolitan Association for Befriending Young Servants (MABYS), which taught servants or girls from the workhouses or industrial schools qualities like self-control and self-discipline.⁶⁸ The GFS's work aligned with these other societies, as it aimed to provide a sense of community to protect 'lonely' girls from 'perils' and 'falling'.⁶⁹

The GFS also provided practical resources for servants. It formed servants' homes that offered accommodations and information about training opportunities and open positions.⁷⁰ It also established registry offices and acted as a type of employment agency, vetting and connecting prospective employers and employees.⁷¹ These lodging homes and registry offices operated both independently and in conjunction with other organisations, like MABYS.[72] Since registry offices could sometimes be used 'as a cloak for the most infamous of practices' like the white slave trade, the GFS kept a 'white list' of respectable registry offices to prevent the 'moral ruin' of girls.[73] It also designed training programmes for servants, which included an examination process and certificate following completion.[74]

While the GFS's efforts to assist servants may appear altruistic, the organisation had the interests of its associates, who often employed servants, at heart. The GFS's training programmes were rooted in its prejudices towards the working classes. Miss Lyon, an associate from the Guildford branch, wrote about how servants went to their situations 'with scarcely any sense of what is true and straight' and that their time in service 'tends to weaken the sense of moral responsibility'.[75] She proceeded to observe that '[t]he majority of girls who pass through our Rescue Homes come from the class of domestic servants'.[76] Associates feared that servants – because of their working-class background – could corrupt rather than enhance the domestic life of their employers. The GFS's work with servants also contributed to its broader mission of reforming working-class domesticity. As *The Book of the G.F.S.* noted, 'our girls are the homemakers of the future, and our biggest work is to help them to prepare for the time when they will have husbands, children, and homes of their own'.[77] This idea was echoed in the GFS newsletter, *The Girls' Quarterly*, which expressed the hope that girls would apply these domestic skills not only in their roles as domestic servants but also in their future roles as wives and mothers and in their own 'bright and wholesome' homes that would serve as 'beautiful centre[s] of usefulness'.[78]

The GFS emerged in the context of the 'servant problem' or 'servant crisis' in the late nineteenth and early twentieth centuries. The attraction of better-paying, less labour-intensive, and more respectable jobs for girls and women made a good servant hard to find and even harder to keep. Girls eschewed the menial status and long hours of service for employment opportunities in hotels, shops, and factories. Increasing education and literacy rates led more girls and women to leave domestic service more quickly than the number entering service. The shortage of servants presented not only practical difficulties, leaving households without servants to perform domestic labour, but also threatened to undermine the key qualities of Victorian domesticity – purity, cleanliness, and order.[79] As explored more in the following chapters, particularly Chapter 3, the 'servant crisis' was not simply a domestic issue but had national and imperial implications.[80]

GFS associates, many of whom employed servants and thus had a personal interest in increasing the number of servants, attempted to solve this 'crisis' by improving the quantity and quality of domestic servants.[81] Part of the GFS's commitment to friendship was to make servants more content, since

Townsend and the other associates believed that '[n]o one can work well who is lonely'.[82] The GFS focused on training girls and facilitating relations between servants and mistresses. A leaflet about the organisation outlined how 'one of the great objects of the Society is to promote a better feeling between "mistress and maid," to encourage good and faithful service by inducing girls to remain in their situations; and many mistresses have joined it, that it may form another link between themselves and their servants'.[83] The organisers hoped that the GFS 'may help to bridge over the apparently ever-widening gulf between employers and servants, of which we now hear so much'.[84] It offered incentives to servants who stayed in their positions for a certain length of time. When the incentives became too expensive, the GFS instead awarded servants with certificates. It additionally sought 'to raise that status of Domestic Service to that of a skilled employment, and to make domestic servants, skilled workers', even developing the League of Skilled Housecraft in 1922, so that more girls would take a greater interest in service, although these programmes had limited success.[85]

The GFS also attempted to raise the standing and prestige of domestic service through stories in its newsletters. For instance, when the GFS periodical *Our Letter: For G.F.S. Candidates all over the World* printed a recurring series on 'Stories of Brave Girls' in 1907, it featured not only the story of Joan of Arc, discussed in the Introduction, but also an instalment, entitled 'Heroines of Storm and Fire', which recounted the life of Alice Ayers. During the night of 24 April 1885, the young servant Alice woke to find that her employers' house was on fire.[86] Alice alerted the family, and even though '[s]afety was then within Alice's reach', 'duty came first'. Instead of escaping the fire, she remained in the house where 'the flames were leaping' and rescued three girls under her care. When it came 'to save herself', the 'strain and exhaustion had done their work', and she fell while trying to leap out of the window and later died.

Instead of commenting on the horrific aspects of Alice's death, the article in *Our Letter* praises her 'unselfish courage' and 'calm dutifulness' and encourages girls to follow the 'wonderful' example of Alice, advising its readers: 'For girls are not only meant to be pure, gentle, obedient, and orderly. They are to be brave and honourable as well, content to prove their courage with the little things in life.'[87] The article presents Alice as an ideal model for the girl readers of *Our Letter*. In contrast to typical images of servants as passive and silent figures, the article shows how Alice had the ability to effect great change in the world around her and – in her commitment to quintessential Victorian values of duty, courage, and self-sacrifice – became a 'heroine'. Even though the article heralded the example of Alice, she was a dangerous, impractical model for girls, and her story implicitly conveyed the notion that servants' lives were less valuable than their employers' lives. The story of Alice was not an isolated example. A 1891 speech by the GFS associate Ellen Joyce, who is discussed at length in the third chapter, featured a similar story of Margaret, a 'nurse girl, who was burnt to death, though she saved her two infant charges'.[88] As in the article about Alice, Joyce praised Margaret's 'bravery' and example. Stories like those of Alice and Margaret provide insights into the principles that shaped the GFS, specifically its idealised notions of femininity and girlhood, as well as the class hierarchies and prejudices that underlay its structure.

## A 'seed now planted in different soils': the growing involvement of the GFS in the empire

The 'servant crisis' was not confined to Britain but endemic throughout the British empire. As the third chapter explores, the demand for servants in the settler colonies provided a powerful rationale for the expansion of the GFS. Greater interest and investment in the empire propelled the society's rapid growth in the closing decades of the nineteenth century. At the end of its first year in 1875, the GFS had 24 branches and about one thousand associates and three thousand girl members.[89] By 1881, the GFS had 553 branches with 16,850 associates and 58,077 members.[90] It grew not only in the number of members but also in its geographic reach, with a branch in Scotland inaugurated in October 1875. In 1877, it formed its first branches in Ireland and the United States. The establishment of colonial branches within a few years after the organisation's foundation solidified its involvement in the empire. The GFS established its first branches in the settler colonies of Canada, New Zealand, Australia, and South Africa and later founded branches in other parts of the empire, including India, Ceylon (present-day Sri Lanka), Burma (present-day Myanmar), the West Indies, and Malta.[91] By the commencement of the twentieth century, the GFS had transformed into a worldwide organisation with 1,359 branches throughout the British empire and included over 240,000 girls and women.[92] In 1910, it proclaimed itself 'the largest English-speaking Society of women in this Empire' and that it could be found '[w]here'er the English language has a place'.[93]

As the GFS expanded its imperial work, the GFS Central Council, which was the Society's main governing body based in London, struggled to define the place of the colonial branches in its structure and administration. In 1882, the GFS Central Council formalised the relationship between the GFS in England and other parts of the empire. The treaties that united overseas branches with the Central Council underscored the GFS's desire to control overseas branches. As Mary Heath-Stubbs states in her history of the organisation, the Central Council wanted to ensure that 'as year by year the Society has become organised in the Empire and beyond, each new centre has still remained in loyal union with the Mother Society'.[94] While the Central Council allowed the colonial branches to manage their own finances and draw up their own constitutions, it stipulated that colonial branches adhere to the same three central rules as branches in England, namely that associates should be members of the Church of England (or any church in communion with the Church of England), that associates and members should contribute annually to the funds of the organisation, and that girls must have 'a virtuous character'.[95] In 1896, the GFS formed the Colonial Committee, later known as the Imperial Committee and then the Imperial and Overseas Committee, that included the presidents of overseas branches and representatives in England as well as the heads of various departments, including the migration department, and editors of GFS newsletters.[96] The goal of the committee was to aid 'pioneer work for the Society in the far distant parts of the Empire' and 'to bring the leaders of the Society in the mother country and those in distant lands more into touch with one another'.[97] GFS organisers professed a desire for colonial branches to be 'indigenous' and adapted to local conditions.[98] For instance, in *Some Memories of Mrs. Townsend*, Kathleen Townsend described how the GFS had grown into an international organisation 'from one seed', but that 'we must avoid any conventional *stiffening* which would prevent that seed now planted in different soils taking its colour from local surroundings, and that each new organisation must *evolve* not *copy*, though each can strengthen and uphold the other'.[99] However, the actions of the organisation did not align with this professed desire, and the relinquishing of control was not always something that the Central Council was willing to do, a topic explored in the fourth and fifth chapters.

The GFS used familial imagery to cultivate a sense that girls belonged to a global community and make them feel more connected to each other and the empire and also to explicate the structure of the organisation and specifically the relationship among its disparate branches. The GFS Central Council in London viewed itself as 'the Parent Society' to the overseas branches, which it referred to as 'Colonial Daughters'.[100] While this imagery could create a feeling of inclusivity, it also replicated imperial and familial hierarchies and power relations. The Central Council expected its 'Colonial Daughters' to adhere to its rules and guidelines, even when the variances and realties of colonial life made such observances impossible. As later chapters explore, the inequity and inflexibility of these hierarchical power dynamics generated highly contentious – and in some cases ruinous – debates between the Central Council and colonial branches.

This use of familial terms was not unique to the organisation but reproduced in the wider empire. In broader imperial discourses and propaganda,

England as the 'Mother Country' or 'Motherland' and personified in the figure of 'their Great White Mother', Queen Victoria, acted as the supreme and authoritative head of the empire family, with the colonies assuming the role of subservient children.[101] This parent–child metaphor provided a persuasive justification for colonialism, since England and other European countries could claim that their 'civilising' guidance was needed until countries 'developed' and reached a state of maturity. The GFS built upon such ideas – implicitly and explicitly – in validating its own colonial projects. For instance, Sister Madeline Thomas, who established the Deaconess Home School and led the GFS in Jamaica, wrote to the Central Council in 1919 and referred to the Jamaican population as 'the child races of the empire who have not reached that point [of civilisation], who are the white man's burden'.[102] Evoking Rudyard Kipling's poem, Sister Madeline could portray her – and the GFS's – imperial work as necessary and benevolent.

The GFS's involvement in the empire coincided with growth of the popular imperialism, and the activities of GFS mirrored those of other contemporary organisations, including the Primrose League and the Victoria League. The GFS differed from these organisations, in that it was not primarily an imperial organisation. Nevertheless, imperial matters fundamentally shaped the organisation and its development. As Brian Harrison notes in his study of the GFS, 'the Empire was the Society's first love'.[103] Even before the GFS was officially founded, Mary Elizabeth Townsend imagined it as a 'vast organisation' spread 'throughout the world'.[104] Over the next decades, she worked to make this vision a reality, and in a speech in 1916, she proclaimed: 'The G.F.S. army has already its contingents throughout the Empire'.[105] Following Townsend's death in 1918, an obituary printed in the GFS periodical *The Empire and Beyond* extolls her contributions to the empire, including her encouragement of others to 'think imperially' and her concern for 'the wellbeing of the girlhood of the Empire'.[106] It also praised her worldwide influence: 'There is not a Branch of the G.F.S. in any part of the Empire that does not owe much to her far-sighted policy, her wonderful grip of its surroundings, her knowledge of the conditions of Church and State which prevailed in each particular Dominion, her deep abiding belief in the Mission which God had entrusted to the Society'.[107] Like other imperialists of this era, Townsend envisioned a united Christian British empire and employed the GFS as a means to promote this vision and strengthen the connections between different parts of the empire.[108]

As reflected in the obituary, Townsend and other organisers viewed the GFS as having an integral role in the building up of Britain's empire and a unifying force by providing 'a link of Empire' that could 'band together women and girls of all classes, not only in the home country, but all over the world'.[109] Associates regarded the GFS's connection with the empire as mutually beneficial. This view is expressed in a 1913 article in *The Empire and Beyond*, which noted: 'Surely we can use the Empire for the girls as well as the girls for the Empire'.[110] The GFS's identity was increasingly tied to the empire, and over time its motto became 'For Church and Empire'.[111] The empire initially served as a way for the GFS to grow and extend its 'spheres of influence'.[112] Later, especially as the GFS struggled to recruit and maintain members, associates turned to the empire to reinvigorate the organisation.[113]

In her *History of The Girls' Friendly Society*, Agnes Money stated that one of the key goals of the GFS was 'not only to be pure, but to purify'.[114] This charge of 'to be pure' and especially 'to purify' served as a persuasive justification for the GFS to extend its reach beyond England.[115] The connection between purity and the GFS's imperial work, and especially its emigration work, emerges in *The G.F.S. Who Knows: A Game for Candidates* designed to prepare girls for membership in the GFS, with one question asking: 'What do you mean by Purity?' The prescribed answer was 'Trying to be like Christ, white and clean and straight. It means fighting against all that is bad, and helping to make our Empire full of good homes.'[116] This answer reflects how the GFS saw its charge 'to purify' as including the extension of British home life and associated standards of domesticity, respectability, and morality to the colonies. As Antoinette Burton has argued, the imperial ethic of moral improvement and the ideal of imperial purification were incredibly powerful and helped to emphasise women's place in the British empire.[117] While notions of purification validated white women's expanding participation in the empire, they also served as a way to control girls and women of colour along with working-class women and girls, a theme examined in the following chapters.[118]

While GFS associates saw an acute need for its work in the empire, establishing and maintaining colonial branches were not without their challenges. The more diffuse nature of the population, the distance between branches, and the relative lack of transportation and communication infrastructure in many colonies and dominions hindered girls' ability to attend GFS meetings and events.[119] When a GFS associate from England, Miss V. Grenfell, visited New South Wales, she expressed astonishment that 'G.F.S. Branches were enormous distances apart' and reported that she 'had never before realised the tremendous isolation of people in the Dominions'.[120] The mobility of the British population provided a further complication, since it left the organisation without consistent leadership and a stable membership base.[121] A report by the GFS branches in India highlighted this hurdle in particular: 'One of the great difficulties with regard to the European Community is that they are such a migratory lot of people. We lose about one-third of the women in our populations during the hot weather, and it is desperately difficult to get any continuity in our work.'[122] The GFS in South Africa similarly struggled to retain members given the 'floating G.F.S. population' with girls who frequently travelled.[123] Members and associates rarely stayed in one place for a long time, often returning to the metropole, travelling as part of their work as missionaries or teachers, or, in India, escaping to the hill stations during the hot summer months.[124] Once workers left, they were difficult to replace, leading to constant calls for permanent workers who could help organise the GFS's work and ensure 'lasting results'.[125] Reports from the colonial branches informed the Central Council that workers who did go out to the colonies and dominions were 'greatly overworked' and needed 'grit' due to the 'overwhelmingly difficult circumstances'.[126] In many cases, the work proved too challenging for the resources and workers that the GFS had.[127] While all these practical problems posed difficulties to the GFS's operations, the varied social structures of different parts of the empire led to the greatest challenges. The GFS intended for its 'Colonial Daughters' to replicate the organisation in Britain, but, as explored with the case of India in Chapter 4, the unique circumstances of the colonies created unanticipated challenges to this vision.[128]

## 'A moral equivalent for war': the development of the GFS's missionary programmes

As with its broader imperial efforts, missionary activities became an increasingly key facet of the GFS's work. Associates celebrated 'the power of the G.F.S. as a Missionary force' and encouraged its girl members to think of missionary work as 'a moral equivalent for war' and their way to support national and imperial imperatives.[129] The society formally adopted missions as part of its organised work in 1897, although branches had been taking part in missionary activities before this time.[130] The GFS cultivated connections with missionary organisations, including the Society for the Propagation of the Gospel, the Church Missionary Society, the Zenana Missionary Society, Women's Missionary Association, and the Universities' Mission.[131] It also sponsored its own missionaries in Zanzibar, Cawnpore (present-day Kanpur), and Tokyo and supported Bible women, or local women who supported missionary efforts, in China.[132]

The society also encouraged girls to aid missionary efforts through raising money and taking part in missions in areas where there was the greatest need, specifically China, India, Japan, Uganda, and Canada.[133] Girls' support for missionaries took a variety of forms, including paying for the education of children in a mission school, purchasing materials and making garments for children, and collecting and sending books, cards, pictures, money, and supplies to missions.[134] Branches also 'adopted' children.[135] For instance, candidates from York reported that they adopted 'a little African girl connected with the Universities' Mission to Central Africa'.[136] These programmes also supported disadvantaged children in England, with the same branch in York assisting a poor candidate in London.[137] The GFS helped finance the education of girls who wished to be missionaries and arranged missionary pilgrimages, in which members and associates went to schools and distributed missionary literature.[138]

While the donation of goods and money was a key component of girls' support of missionaries, they participated in the movement in other ways. In *Protestant Children, Missions and Education in the British World*, Hugh Morrison challenges the traditional perception that children's involvement in the missionary movement was limited to their financial contributions; he instead draws attention to how the missionary movement was an educational endeavour. Morrison highlights the importance of juvenile missionary periodicals and how they created an 'empire-wide shared classroom' that facilitated children's participation in imperial networks of information exchange.[139] These publications went beyond informing readers and also encouraged a participatory relationship. Stories about missionaries appear frequently in GFS literature, and, like missionary periodicals, these publications interwove knowledge about the empire with encouragement to support the missions. This dual impulse is reflected in a report on 'Missionary Work' in the GFS's *A Jubilee Chronicle for Overseas*, which instructed branches to choose a missionary and 'make a study of the land of her work, pray for her, and provide money and also clothes, teaching outfits, sewing materials, and hospital supplies'.[140] Another article in the GFS periodical *Our Letter* urges girls to emulate women 'who left their homes to go to India for the love of Jesus'.[141] GFS newsletters thus acted as important forms of propaganda for missionaries that sought to actively engage children in the missionary cause in myriad ways.

The GFS's missionary endeavours, like its broader imperial work, were rooted in the organisation's dedication to purity and its efforts to reform domestic life.[142] Its charge to create 'pure' 'Christian' homes was seen as especially important because of the supposed lack of domesticity in colonial societies and the contaminating and degenerative effects of colonial environments. For instance, one instalment of 'News from the Mission Field' in *The Girls' Quarterly* quotes a missionary in the Cape Colony who reflected: 'I think the greatest difficulty we have is the absence of home-life among these people. They don't understand it, even the Christians find it hard to realise that they ought to make a Christian home.'[143] Since the home acted as microcosm of society, missionaries viewed the exportation of Victorian middle-class notions of family and domestic life as a means to elevate the morality of colonial societies. The key qualities of Victorian domesticity acted as markers of civilisation, with the adoption of European domestic practices portending the Europeanisation and 'civilisation' of groups within colonial societies.

As with social purity discourses in England, missionary efforts were framed in humanitarian terms but were rooted in more self-interested motives. Missionary work sought to reform girls, specifically girls of colour, in a way that would make them useful to the colonial enterprise and acted as a means for the colonial state to extend their policing into the 'uncolonised' sphere of the home, which largely remained outside the purview of colonial governance. In India, the exclusively female domain of the zenana in the home provided English women with their own version of imperial duty, what Burton has termed the 'white woman's burden'.[144] The prohibition of men in these female spaces underscored the utility and indispensability of white women's involvement in the mission field. An article in the *Girls' Quarterly* describes the importance of missionary work in India, noting that a missionary 'seems almost the only way to bring Christian teaching into Indian homes'.[145] Indian girls' and women's perceived malleability and their roles as wives and mothers made this work especially vital, since they could act as conduits through which Christian and English middle-class values, habits, and mores could enter Indian communities.[146] Girls and women thus had an important role in the empire but one that fell within the framework of dominant gender norms and Victorian mores. The GFS, like other organisations, took up the mantle of a 'white woman's burden' to justify its purpose and the expansion of its imperial work.

## 'Our absolute powerlessness': early fault lines within the GFS

Despite the importance and apparent enthusiasm for its imperial work, the GFS's involvement in the empire was not universally embraced within the society. One key issue of contention among organisers was that the GFS's imperial initiatives took valuable resources away from local problems within England. An article published in *The Empire and Beyond* in 1913 hints at this dissention within the organisation. The article opens with the observation that some '[a]ssociates [were] ostensibly adverse to "Empire Work"'. It continues: 'Perhaps some of us do find the Empire more romantic than our own High Street, and put our energy into Empire work to the neglect of our own branches. But surely if the Empire is romantic, so is the High Street, which is part of the Empire. What we need is a larger outlook over all our work, for we cannot help seeing how the Empire touches the lives of our own girls ... Perhaps we need to realise that the home and Empire are one.'[147] As evident in this article, the GFS faced criticism for investing money and time into 'rescuing' people abroad while ignoring similar problems in the metropole. This criticism of 'telescopic philanthropy' was not confined to the GFS but also levelled against other charitable and reform groups.[148] The GFS did establish 'Home Missions' designed to care for children in England, specifically those in orphanages and other institutions, including the Waifs and Strays' Society and Dr Barnardo's Homes, but its imperial work overshadowed these initiatives.[149]

Disagreements about where the GFS should focus its energy was just one of innumerable problems facing the organisation from its early days. While it grew rapidly in the initial years, this period was one of 'immense pressure and strain', according to Agnes Money. There were confusion and debates over the organisation's rules and constitution, which was ultimately finalised in 1880.[150] As early GFS leaders worked to build the organisation, they felt overwhelmed by the task before them. These pressures and 'the strain of work and anxiety' contributed to Townsend having a breakdown in 1880.[151] As the organisation grew, it struggled to find enough workers and money to finance its projects.[152] Eleanor Chute, who served as president of the GFS Central Council from 1901 to 1916, reflected on the limitations the GFS faced, particularly in its imperial work: 'The idea which is most deeply impressed on my mind as regards the whole work of the G.F.S. in the Colonies, is the greatness of the opportunity, and our absolute powerlessness to take advantage of it *with sufficient speed*'.[153] The GFS's lack of resources prohibited it from carrying out the work it envisioned and contributed to the organisation's decline during the interwar period, a topic analysed in the fifth chapter.

The GFS also continually struggled with disagreements over the central rule and its commitment to purity. From the outset, the rule provoked extensive debates. Critics of the rule highlighted the complications posed by the rule and its enforcement. Since girls could simply lie to gain admittance, some within and outside of the society wondered whether the GFS would resort to such extreme measures as medical inspections to ensure girls' virginity.[154] While organisers framed this unwavering allegiance to purity as a singular strength of the society, especially in the face of changing social and cultural mores, this strict adherence led to the perception of the organisation as out of touch and 'a sort of local police force', contributing to its decline.[155] Objections to this rule led to the resignation of some associates in 1879 and the formation of the Young Women's Help Society, later Women's Help, for girls and women who could not join the GFS because of the rule.[156]

The debates over the central rule were indicative of another long-standing problem for the GFS: its organisers' intransigence in the face of change and inability to reconcile different viewpoints. A statement in *The Girls' Friendly Society Reporter,* written shortly after the organisation's foundation in July 1875, expressed discomfort at the 'diversity of opinion' among its leaders.[157] As discussed earlier in the chapter, the GFS was built along hierarchical – not democratic – lines. Girl members were supposed to obey their 'mother' unquestioningly, specifically the upper-class and middle-class associates. However, as Heath-Stubbs conceded in *Friendship's Highway*, this structure led to criticisms that 'the government of our Society is too much of a despotism' and that it ignored 'the might majority' of its girl members.[158] Girls felt marginalised within the GFS, further contributing to the GFS's reputation as out of touch.

Despite mounting internal and external criticisms, GFS organisers failed to solve endemic issues within the organisation and instead turned to more superficial explanations for its problems. Associates claimed that criticisms were founded on misunderstandings and not any actual shortcomings of its policies. Louisa Knightley, an associate and pro-imperial activist who would later serve as president of the South African Colonisation Society, wrote in 1883 about how 'the poor G.F.S. gets into trouble' because the broader public failed to understand the organisation. She believed the solution was simply to clear up these misconceptions: 'I feel sure, however, that in many instances the prejudice arises in great measure from want of properly understanding the aims and objects of the Society'.[159] Even though associates like Knightley claimed that better publicity could improve the reputation of the organisation, the GFS struggled to change broader perceptions of the organisation, which is clearly evident in relation to its work with domestic servants.

While the GFS presented itself as a bridge between mistresses and servants, reports by associates also indicate that mistresses objected to their servants being a part of the GFS. Mistresses worried that GFS classes and activities took girls away from their work.[160] The GFS attempted to ease these concerns by requiring employers' consent for girls to join the GFS and claiming that mistresses had the right to prevent girls from going to classes and that girls did not need to attend all meetings, but resistance from mistresses continued.[161] Moreover, although associates were deeply invested in increasing both the quality and the quantity of domestic servants, they also struggled with the GFS's identity being closely associated with domestic service. People outside of the organisation often perceived the organisation as exclusively for domestic servants. Writing in 1883, Townsend sought to dispel notions that 'the G.F.S. is only for girls in service' and to attract girls in other occupations, stating: 'It is a Society in which every Member, of every age, and rank, and occupation, has her place and her work'.[162] Her efforts met with limited success. While the GFS did include girls from other occupations, including shop assistants, clerks, factory workers, and mill girls, as well as daughters of tradespeople and farmers, domestic service remained the dominant occupation of girls in the GFS. Especially in the interwar years when the organisation's numbers declined, associates blamed this misapprehension for limiting girls' interest in joining the organisation, although, as analysed in the fifth chapter, the reasons for its decline were more complicated and reflected systemic problems inherent in the structure and ideology of the GFS.[163]

## Conclusion

In the late nineteenth century, the purity of the white race was seemingly imperilled from many angles. For Townsend and other GFS organisers, the apparent lack of moral training among the working classes posed a dangerous threat to not only England but also the empire. Maintenance of white racial purity – and by extension white superiority – required the reformation of working-class habits and lifestyles, which the GFS sought to do through its provision of activities and classes and effectively replacing the role of working-class families in the upbringing and education of girls. The GFS's zealous commitment to purity not only served as the impetus behind its social reforms within England but also justified its greater involvement in the empire. The GFS was deeply invested in imperial matters from the beginning, evidenced by the formation of branches in different parts of the empire and its sponsorship and promotion of missionaries. The next two chapters further examine how the GFS's commitment to upholding white racial purity and 'helping to make the Empire full of good homes' informed its imperial work by examining the GFS's educational and emigration programmes.

## Notes

1 On Queen Victoria as patron of the GFS, see Kathleen M. Townsend, *Some Memories of Mrs. Townsend: Foundress of the Girls' Friendly Society* (London: G.F.S. Central Office, 1923), pp. 25–9.
2 L. M., 'Queen Victoria', *The Girls' Quarterly: A Paper for Workers in the Girls' Friendly Society*, 26 (April 1901), pp. 122–3.
3 L. M., 'Queen Victoria', p. 122.

4 Women's Library, London (hereafter WL), 5GFS/04/003, M. E. Townsend, 'Victoria: Queen and Empress. The Mother of Her People. A Memorial', in Sketches and Impressions, February 1901, p. 1.
 5 WL, 5GFS/04/021, [Objects and rules for candidates], n.d., p. 1. On the founding meeting, see British Library, London (hereafter BL), General Reference Collection 8275.aaa.18.(11.), *An Appeal to the Mistresses of Elementary Schools from the Girls' Friendly Society* (London: Hatchards, 1882), p. 7.
 6 For more on the Travellers' Aid Society, see Derbyshire Record Office, Matlock, D3287/88/2/37, Lady Frances Balfour, *Travellers' Aid Society* (London: Women's Printing Society, n.d.).
 7 Kathleen M. Townsend, *Some Memories of Mrs. Townsend*, p. 10.
 8 *The Book of the G.F.S.: What It Is and What It Does* (June 1920), p. 52.
 9 BL, General Reference Collection DRT Digital Store 8282.aaa.1.(21.), M. E. T. [Mary Elizabeth Townsend], *A Word to the Girls about the Girls' Friendly Society* (London: Hatchards, 1875), p. 2.
10 M. E. Townsend, 'For Home and Country', *Our Letter: For G.F.S. Candidates all over the World* (March 1915), p. 1. BL, General Reference Collection 1890.e.2.(70.), *The Girls' Friendly Society* (London: Hatchards, 1877), p. 3.
11 BL, General Reference Collection 8275.b.23.(6.), M. E. Townsend, *A Friendly Letter to Fathers and Mothers about The Girls' Friendly Society* (London: Hatchards, 1883), pp. 1–2.
12 'Overseas Reports. Canada', *The Empire and Beyond*, Occasional Leaflet VIII (1915), p. 10.
13 BL, General Reference Collection 8275.b.23.(4.), *The Need for the Girls' Friendly Society* (London: Hatchards, 1883), p. 2.
14 BL, General Reference Collection 8282.de.27.(4.), *Suggestions for G.F.S. Branch Organisation* (London: Hatchards, 1887), pp. 4–5.
15 *The Book of the G.F.S.*, p. 65.
16 G. Stanley Hall, *Adolescence: Its Psychology and Its Relations to Physiology, Anthropology, Sociology, Sex, Crime, Religion and Education* (New York: D. Appleton and Company, 1904), p. 306.
17 'Weybridge Branch Association', *The Girls' Friendly Society Reporter*, 1 (July 1875), p. 3. *The Book of the G.F.S.*, p. 65.
18 'Girls', *The Girls' Quarterly: A Paper for Workers in the Girls' Friendly Society*, 14 (April 1898), p. 36.
19 'The Girls' Friendly Society', *The Girls' Friendly Society Reporter*, 2 (January 1876), p. 6.
20 'The Girls' Friendly Society', p. 5.
21 *The Book of the G.F.S.*, pp. 18–21. On the connection between exercise and purity, see *The Book of the G.F.S.*, p. 58.
22 For more on the relationship between the GFS and social purity movements, see Vivienne Richmond, '"It Is Not a Society for Human Beings but for Virgins": The Girls' Friendly Society Membership Eligibility Dispute 1875–1936', *Journal of Historical Sociology*, 20:3 (September 2007), 304–27. Social movements in Victorian and Edwardian England

and the idea of purity as a means of uplifting and reforming society have been examined by numerous scholars. See, for instance, Judith R. Walkowitz, *City of Dreadful Delight: Narratives of Sexual Danger in Late-Victorian London* (Chicago: University of Chicago Press, 2013); Judith R. Walkowitz, *Prostitution and Victorian Society: Women, Class, and the State* (Cambridge: Cambridge University Press, 1980); Alison Bashford, *Purity and Pollution: Gender, Embodiment, and Victorian Medicine*, Studies in Gender History (New York: St Martin's Press, 1998); Deborah Gorham, 'The "Maiden Tribute of Modern Babylon" Re-Examined: Child Prostitution and Childhood in Late-Victorian England', *Victorian Studies*, 21:3 (Spring 1978), 353–79, especially p. 375; Edward Bristow, *Vice and Vigilance: Purity Movements in Britain since 1700* (Dublin: Gill and Macmillan, 1977); and Frank Mort, *Dangerous Sexualities: Medico-Moral Politics in England since 1830* (New York: Routledge, 2002).
23 Lambeth Palace Library, London (hereafter LPL), Tait 268 ff. 234, 'Some Remarks on the Present Crisis in the Girls' Friendly Society, By One of its Earliest Associates and Member of a Diocesan Council', 1880.
24 WL, 5GFS/04/024, Miss Rich, *The Path with the Blue Marks: An Address on Some Ideals and Difficulties of Girl Life* (London: George Allen & Co., Ltd, 1911), p. 2. Emphasis in the original.
25 For more on this point, see Carol Dyhouse, *Girl Trouble: Panic and Progress in the History of Young Women* (London: Zed Books, 2013), chapter 1.
26 'The Wandering Thoughts of an Empire Correspondent', *The Empire and Beyond*, Occasional Leaflet II (1913), p. 12.
27 For more on Stead, see Walkowitz, *City of Dreadful Delight*; Gorham, 'The "Maiden Tribute of Modern Babylon" Re-Examined'; Dyhouse, *Girl Trouble*, pp. 17–20; and Cecily Devereux, '"The Maiden Tribute" and the Rise of the White Slave in the Nineteenth Century: The Making of an Imperial Construct', *Victorian Review*, 26:2 (2000), 1–23.
28 Kathleen M. Townsend, *Some Memories of Mrs. Townsend*, p. 20.
29 Edith Marion Welch, 'Anniversary, 1917. An Impression', *The Empire and Beyond*, Occasional Leaflet XVI (All Saints 1917), p. 3.
30 For more on white slavery and race, see, for instance, Devereux, '"The Maiden Tribute" and the Rise of the White Slave'.
31 For more on this point, see, for instance, Antoinette Burton, *Burdens of History: British Feminists, Indian Women, and Imperial Culture, 1865–1915* (Durham, NC: University of North Carolina Press, 2000); and Margaret Tennant, '"Magdalens and Moral Imbeciles": Women's Homes in Nineteenth-Century New Zealand', *Women's Studies International Forum*, 9:5 (1986), 492. For more on social purity and the class dimensions, see, for instance, Lucy Bland, *Banishing the Beast: English Feminism & Sexual Morality, 1885–1914* (London: Tauris Parke, 1995).
32 Anna Davin, 'Imperialism and Motherhood', *History Workshop Journal*, 5:1 (1978), 9–66.

33 Davin, 'Imperialism and Motherhood', 26.
34 Ellen Joyce, *30 Years Imperial Work with the Girls Friendly Society* (London: G.F.S., 1912), p. 1.
35 'Some Remarks on the Present Crisis in the Girls' Friendly Society'. M. E. T., *A Word to the Girls about the Girls' Friendly Society*, p. 9. BL, General Reference Collection 8275.b.23.(11.), Mrs Egerton Hubbard, *A Few Words to School and Schoolroom Girls* (London: Hatchards, 1887), p. 6.
36 BL, General Reference Collection 8282.de.24.(17.), *Report of Conference of the Department for Members in Professions and Business* (London: Hatchards, 1887), pp. 7, 9. M. Howard Bell, 'Ministering School-Girls', *The Girls' Quarterly: A Paper for Workers in the Girls' Friendly Society*, 20 (October 1899), p. 182.
37 Sally Mitchell, *The New Girl: Girls' Culture in England 1880–1915* (New York: Columbia University Press, 1995), p. 3. See also Hall, *Adolescence*.
38 On the role of older members, see 'How Can Elder Members Help the Spiritual Life of Younger Girls?', *The Girls' Quarterly: A Paper for Workers in the Girls' Friendly Society*, 13 (October 1897), p. 7; Jane F. Scott, 'The Elder Member in New Zealand: Her Significance', *The Empire and Beyond*, Occasional Leaflet XXIII (Winter 1919), p. 3; *The Handbook of Elder Members' Work* (London: Wells Gardner, Darton & Co., 1892).
39 WL, 5GFS/02/302, *The Girls' Friendly Society: Constitution of the Society By-Laws of Central Committees, and Minutes of Council Binding on the Whole Society* (London: G.F.S. Central Office, 1927), p. 44.
40 For more on the membership categories and structure of the GFS, see *The Book of the G.F.S.*, pp. 47–52.
41 *The Book of the G.F.S.*, p. 11. On associates being 'ladies', see Mary Heath-Stubbs, *Friendship's Highway: Being the History of the Girls' Friendly Society, 1875–1935* (London: G.F.S. Central Office, 1935), p. 19.
42 Heath-Stubbs, *Friendship's Highway*, p. 19.
43 Agnes L. Money, 'Elder Members' Page', *The Girls' Quarterly: A Paper for Workers in the Girls' Friendly Society*, 13 (October 1897), p. 177.
44 'Some Remarks on the Present Crisis in the Girls' Friendly Society, By One of its Earliest Associates and Member of a Diocesan Council'.
45 *The Handbook of Elder Members' Work*, p. 7; WL, 5GFS/05/011, 'Object of the Society', *Girls' Friendly Society Leaflet for India and the Far East*, 2:3 (January 1930), p. i.
46 For more on this rule and its controversy, see Richmond, 'It Is Not a Society for Human Beings but for Virgins'.
47 WL, 5GFS/02/306, 'Report of the Special Meeting of the Incorporated Central Council of the Girls' Friendly Society, Held at Townsend House, Greycoat Place, Westminster on Wednesday, April 27th, 1932 at 11 a.m.', p. 19.
48 For more on purity in the Camp Fire Girls, see Jennifer Helgren, *The Camp Fire Girls: Gender, Race, and American Girlhood, 1910–1980* (Lincoln: University of Nebraska Press, 2022), pp. 56, 59, 87.

49 For more on this point, see Benjamin René Jordan, *Modern Manhood and the Boy Scouts of America: Citizenship, Race, and the Environment* (Chapel Hill: University of North Carolina Press, 2016), p. 60; and Mischa Honeck, *Our Frontier Is the World: The Boy Scouts in the Age of American Ascendency* (Ithaca: Cornell University Press, 2018).
50 LPL, Davidson 143, ff. 215, 'Appeal for £20,000 for the Lodges and Homes of Rest of the Girls' Friendly Society', 1907.
51 Agnes L. Money, *History of the Girls' Friendly Society*, 2nd ed. (London: Wells, Garner, Darton & Co., Ltd, 1911), p. 4.
52 *The Need for the Girls' Friendly Society*, p. 3.
53 Gorham, 'The "Maiden Tribute of Modern Babylon" Re-Examined', 371.
54 'Some Remarks on the Present Crisis in the Girls' Friendly Society'.
55 'Some Remarks on the Present Crisis in the Girls' Friendly Society'.
56 'Appeal for £20,000 for the Lodges and Homes of Rest of the Girls' Friendly Society'.
57 Kathleen M. Townsend, *Some Memories of Mrs. Townsend*, p. 54. Similar ideas are also expressed in M. E. T., *A Word to the Girls about the Girls' Friendly Society*, p. 9; and *The Handbook of Elder Members' Work*.
58 'Some Remarks on the Present Crisis in the Girls' Friendly Society'.
59 *The Need for the Girls' Friendly Society*, p. 3.
60 *The Book of the G.F.S.*, pp. 48–51. WL, 5GFS/05/016, Question 23 in *Games for Candidates*, 1st series, 1930s.
61 WL, 5GFS/05/009, 'Report of the Candidates' Department for 1930', *G.F.S. Colombo Quarterly Diocesan Leaflet and Report Jan 1931*, p. 15.
62 Kathleen M. Townsend, *Some Memories of Mrs. Townsend*, p. 53.
63 Kathleen M. Townsend, *Some Memories of Mrs. Townsend*, p. 54.
64 BL, General Reference Collection 8275.b.23.(12.), N. Parker, *A Year's Work Amongst Factory Girls* (London: Hatchards, 1884), p. 8.
65 *Report of Conference of the Department for Members in Professions and Business*, p. 5.
66 Rev. Harry Jones, 'G.F.S.', *The Girls' Quarterly: A Paper for Workers in the Girls' Friendly Society*, 2 (March 1895), p. 28.
67 'Some Remarks on the Present Crisis in the Girls' Friendly Society'. Emphasis in the original. Brian Harrison discusses the class dynamics and servant composition of the GFS in 'For Church, Queen, and Family: The Girls' Friendly Society 1874–1920', *Past and Present*, 61 (November 1972), 117.
68 Heath-Stubbs, *Friendship's Highway*, p. 67. Gorham, 'The "Maiden Tribute of Modern Babylon" Re-Examined', 375.
69 M. E. T., *A Word to the Girls about the Girls' Friendly Society*, pp. 3, 5.
70 'The Central Fund', *The Girls' Friendly Society Reporter*, 1 (July 1875), p. 2. 'The Girls' Friendly Society', *The Girls' Friendly Society Reporter*, 2 (January 1876), p. 7.
71 *Report of Conference of the Department for Members in Professions and Business*, pp. 15–18. *The Book of the G.F.S.*, pp. 27–8. 'Weybridge Branch Association', *The Girls' Friendly Society Reporter*, 1 (July 1875), p. 3.

72 'The Girls' Friendly Society Reporter', *The Girls' Friendly Society Reporter*, 1 (July 1875), p. 1.
73 WL, 5GFS/03/022, M. E. Townsend (ed.), *Report of the Work and Progress of the Girls' Friendly Society in 1897* (London: Hatchards, 1897), pp. 16–17; WL, 5GFS/03/024, M. E. Townsend (ed.), *Report of the Work and Progress of the Girls' Friendly Society in 1898* (London: Hatchards, 1898), pp. 62–3; WL, 5GFS/03/022, M. E. Townsend (ed.), *Report of the Work and Progress of the Girls' Friendly Society in 1900* (London: Hatchards, 1900), p. 60.
74 *The Book of the G.F.S.*, p. 26.
75 WL, 5GFS/04/024, H. Lovett Cameron, 'The G.F.S. in Relation to Domestic Servants', [1906?], in Members' Department Scrapbook, p. 8.
76 Lovett Cameron, 'The G.F.S. in Relation to Domestic Servants', p. 8.
77 *The Book of the G.F.S.*, p. 71.
78 'From Seventeen to Twenty-Seven', *The Girls' Quarterly: A Paper for Workers in the Girls' Friendly Society*, 22 (April 1900), p. 29.
79 For more on domestic service in the British colonial context, see, for instance, Victoria K. Haskins and Claire Lowrie (eds), *Colonization and Domestic Service: Historical and Contemporary Perspectives* (New York: Routledge, 2014); Swapna M. Banerjee, *Men, Women and Domestics: Articulating Middle-Class Identity in Colonial Bengal* (New York: Oxford University Press, 2003); and Fae Dussart, *In the Service of Empire: Domestic Service and Mastery in Metropole and Colony* (New York: Bloomsbury Academic, 2022).
80 Anne McClintock, *Imperial Leather: Race, Gender, and Sexuality in the Colonial Contest* (New York: Routledge, 1995), especially p. 5.
81 WL, 5GFS/01/039, 'Minutes of a Meeting of the Aid and Reference Department for Registry Work, Held at the G.F.S. Central Employment Office, 14 Victoria Street, S.W. on Tuesday, November 3rd, 1914 at 2:30 P.M.', p. 102.
82 'The Objects', *Our Letter: For G.F.S. Candidates all over the World* (September 1915), p. 4.
83 *The Girls' Friendly Society*, p. 2.
84 'The Girls' Friendly Society Reporter', p. 2. See also 'The G.F.S. in Relation to Domestic Servants', p. 8.
85 *The Book of the G.F.S.*, p. 30. For more on this point, see Richmond, 'It Is Not a Society for Human Beings but for Virgins', 319.
86 For more on stories about Alice Ayers, see John Price, 'Heroism in Everyday Life: The Watts Memorial for Heroic Self Sacrifice', *History Workshop Journal*, 63 (2007), 254–78; and John Price, *Everyday Heroism: Victorian Constructions of the Heroic Civilian* (London: Bloomsbury, 2014).
87 Edith Brunette, 'Stories of Brave Girls III. Heroines of Storm and Fire', *Our Letter: For G.F.S. Candidates all over the World* (September 1907), p. 4.
88 WL, 5GFS/05/013, Hon. Mrs Joyce, 'Footsteps: An Address delivered at the Rhyl Church Congress, October 1891', p. 5.
89 M. E. Townsend (ed.), *Report of the Work and Progress of the Girls' Friendly Society in 1878*, p. 6.
90 *An Appeal to the Mistresses of Elementary Schools*, p. 1.

91 Money, *History of the Girls' Friendly Society*, p. 97. WL, 5GFS/02/285, M. E. Townsend, 'G.F.S. in the Colonies', 1882.
92 These numbers include all categories of membership – members, candidates, associates, married helpers, and branch workers – for 1901. They are taken from Money, *History of the Girls' Friendly Society*, p. 128.
93 Willoughby Jones, 'A Dialogue for G.F.S. Candidates', *Our Letter: For G.F.S. Candidates all over the World* (September 1910), p. 98.
94 Heath-Stubbs, *Friendship's Highway*, p. 154. See also Money, *History of the Girls' Friendly Society*, p. 149.
95 M. E. Townsend, 'G.F.S. in the Colonies'.
96 *The Girls' Friendly Society: Constitution of the Society By-Laws of Central Committees, and Minutes of Council Binding on the Whole Society*, p. 34. Heath-Stubbs, *Friendship's Highway*, p. 154.
97 WL, 5GFS/01/105, 'Minutes of the Sub-Committee appointed by the Colonial Committee in March 1911 to consider further developments of the Committee held at the G.F.S. Central Office, 39 Victoria Street, London, S.W. on Tuesday 13th June 1911 at 2:30 p.m.', p. 17. Money, *History of the Girls' Friendly Society*, p. 99.
98 WL, 5GFS/01/009, 'Canadian Sectional Meeting of the Colonial Committee Minutes of a Meeting Held at the GFS Central Office, June 4th, 1901', p. 39.
99 Kathleen M. Townsend, *Some Memories of Mrs. Townsend*, p. 46. Emphasis in the original.
100 M. E. T., *A Word to the Girls about the Girls' Friendly Society*, p. 11. Money, *History of the Girls' Friendly Society*, p. 97.
101 For more on how the language of childhood and family reinforced colonial hierarchies and paternalism, see Ashis Nandy, 'Reconstructing Childhood: A Critique of the Ideology of Adulthood', in *Traditions, Tyranny, and Utopias: Essays in the Politics of Awareness* (London: Oxford University Press, 1987), pp. 56–76. For other examinations on the operation of familial metaphors in colonialism, see Elsbeth Locher-Scholten, 'Orientalism and the Rhetoric of the Family: Javanese Servants in European Household Manuals and Children's Fiction', *Indonesia*, 58 (October 1994), 19–39; and Alison Brysk, Craig Parsons, and Wayne Sandholtz, 'After Empire: National Identity and Post-Colonial Families of Nations', *European Journal of International Relations*, 8:2 (2002), 267–305, especially pp. 273–4.
102 WL, 5GFS/02/299, *Girls' Friendly Society. Report of a Conference for the Consideration of the Central Rules, held at the G.F.S. Central Office, 39 Victoria Street, S.W. 1, on Friday and Saturday, June 13th and 14th, 1919*, p. 61.
103 Harrison, 'For Church, Queen, and Family', 126.
104 Kathleen M. Townsend, *Some Memories of Mrs. Townsend*, p. 10.
105 Edith Marion Welch, 'Fellowship', *The Empire and Beyond*, Occasional Leaflet XII (Anniversary Week 1916), p. 4.
106 K. M. T. [Kathleen M. Townsend], 'A Great Leader', *The Empire and Beyond*, Occasional Leaflet XX (All Saints 1918), p. 3.

107 K. M. T., 'A Great Leader', p. 3.
108 See Julia Bush, *Edwardian Ladies and Imperial Power* (London: Continuum, 1999).
109 Money, *History of the Girls' Friendly Society*, pp. 95, 139. For similar themes of unity, see Welch, 'Fellowship', p. 4.
110 Editor [Constance M. Thompson], *The Empire and Beyond*, Occasional Leaflet III (1913), p. 14.
111 Title page of *The Book of the G.F.S.*
112 WL, 5GFS/02/246, Overseas – New Zealand 'Annual Rally' article clipping, c. 1933–39.
113 See, for instance, Editor [Constance M. Thompson], 'The Empire Aspect of G.F.S', *The Empire and Beyond*, Occasional Leaflet V (1914), pp. 11–12.
114 Money, *History of the Girls' Friendly Society*, p. 95.
115 On this point, see, for instance, WL, 5GFS/02/299, *Girls' Friendly Society. Report of a Conference for the Consideration of the Central Rules, held at the G.F.S. Central Office 29 Victoria Street, S.W. 1, on Friday and Saturday, June 13th and 14th, 1919*, p. 21. There is a rich scholarship on the ideology of purity in the imperial context and its connection to the civilising mission of imperialism. See, for instance, Philippa Levine, *Prostitution, Race, and Politics: Policing Venereal Disease in the British Empire* (New York: Routledge, 2013); Burton, *Burdens of History*; Anne McClintock, *Imperial Leather: Race, Gender, and Sexuality in the Colonial Contest* (New York: Routledge, 1995); Ann Laura Stoler, *Race and Education of Desire: Foucault's History of Sexuality and the Colonial Order of Things* (Durham, NC: Duke University Press, 1995); Ann L. Stoler, 'Making Empire Respectable: The Politics of Race and Sexual Morality in 20th-Century Colonial Cultures', *American Ethnologist*, 16 (November 1989), 634–52; Vron Ware, *Beyond the Pale: White Women, Racism, and History* (New York: Verso, 1992); Marjory Harper and Stephen Constantine, 'A Civilizing Influence? The Female Migrant', in *Empire and Migration*, Oxford History of the British Empire Companion Series (New York: Oxford University Press, 2010), pp. 212–46; Margaret Tennant, '"Magdalens and Moral Imbeciles": Women's Homes in Nineteenth-Century New Zealand', *Women's Studies International Forum*, 9:5 (1986), 491–502, especially pp. 491–2; and Margaret Jacobs, *White Mother to a Dark Race: Settler Colonialism, Maternalism, and the Removal of Indigenous Children in the American West and Australia 1880–1940* (Lincoln: University of Nebraska Press, 2009).
116 WL, 5GFS/05/017, Question 50 of *The G.F.S. Who Knows: A Game for Candidates*, 2nd series, 1940s.
117 Burton, *Burdens of History*, p. 152.
118 For more on this point, see McClintock, *Imperial Leather*, especially p. 47. See also Michelle Smith, Kristine Moruzi, and Clare Bradford, 'Introduction', in *From Colonial to Modern: Transnational Girlhood in Canadian, Australian, and New Zealand Children's Literature* (Toronto: University of Toronto Press, 2018), pp. 3–19.

119 WL, 5GFS/01/091, 'Sectional Committee for South Africa Minutes of a Meeting Held on Friday Nov. 17th 1905', p. 143; WL, GB/106/BWE/B/4/4, letter to Ellen Joyce, 17 January 1900; WL, 5GFS/02/263, letter from Fanchette G. Parrish to Mrs. Calvert, 11 October 1943; WL, 5GFS/02/248, letter from Winifred Preston to Miss Angus, 1 May 1939, pp. 2 and 4; WL, 5GFS/01/098, 'Minutes of a Meeting of the Overseas Council held at Townsend House, Greycoat Place, London, S.W. 1, on Tuesday, November 28th, 1950', p. 276; WL, 5GFS/02/263, letter from Sarah Angus to Miss Rudd, 10 November 1938; and 'Overseas Reports', *The Empire and Beyond*, Occasional Leaflet IX (1915), pp. 6–8.

120 'Minutes of a Meeting of the Overseas Council held at Townsend House, Greycoat Place, London, S.W. 1, on Tuesday, November 28th, 1950', p. 276. On this point, see also WL, 5GFS/02/270, letter from Overseas Secretary to Miss Chaderton, 26 February 1938; and 'Sectional Committee for South Africa Minutes of a Meeting Held on Friday Nov. 17th 1905', p. 143.

121 See, for instance, WL, 5GFS/02/230, letter from Winifred Paine to Miss Mytton, 29 January 1931; and 'Industrial Training Scheme for the Punjab', *The Empire and Beyond*, Occasional Leaflet II (1913), p. 5.

122 WL, 5GFS/02/235, 'The India "At Home"', n.d., p. 3. On this point, see also Money, *History of the Girls' Friendly Society*, p. 26; and WL, 5GFS/02/237, N. E. Grenside, 'G.F.S. in India', n.d., p. 1.

123 WL, 5GFS/02/263, letter from Sarah Angus to Mrs Craster, 18 February 1938.

124 'Overseas Reports. Ceylon', *The Empire and Beyond*, Occasional Leaflet IX (1915), p. 11.

125 Money, *History of the Girls' Friendly Society*, p. 69.

126 'Overseas Reports. Ceylon', *The Empire and Beyond*, Occasional Leaflet IX (1915), pp. 9 and 11.

127 Letter from Fanchette G. Parrish to Mrs Calvert, 11 October 1943.

128 On how colonies were not direct copies of European countries, see Ann Laura Stoler, 'Rethinking Colonial Categories: European Communities and the Boundaries of Rule', *Comparative Studies in Society and History*, 31:1 (January 1989), 136.

129 Money, *History of the Girls' Friendly Society*, p. 135. K. M. T. [Kathleen M. Townsend], 'The G.F.S. Imperial Conference', *The Empire and Beyond*, Occasional Leaflet IX (1915), p. 6.

130 WL, 5GFS/05/015, *The Story of the G.F.S.* (London: The G.F.S. Central Office, 1946), p. 5.

131 A. E. M. Anderson-Morshead, 'The Land of the Rising Sun', *The Girls' Quarterly: A Paper for Workers in the Girls' Friendly Society*, 11 (July 1897), pp. 156–8. See also 'News from the Mission Field', *The Girls' Quarterly: A Paper for Workers in the Girls' Friendly Society*, 23 (July 1900), p. 23. On the Women's Missionary Association, see WL, 5GFS/01/107, Agnes L. Money, 'Committee of Council for the G.F.S. in India Minutes of a Meeting Held at the GFS Central Office on January 20th 1903', p. 6.

132 'Our G.F.S Missionaries', *Our Letter: For G.F.S. Candidates all over the World* (August 1920), p. 3.

133 WL, 5GFS/02/229, letter from Secretary to Mrs Sandys, 19 January 1931. 'Needs Still Unfilled', *The Empire and Beyond*, Occasional Leaflet IX (1915), p. 8. Kathleen M. Townsend, 'Dear Children', *Our Letter: For G.F.S. Candidates all over the World* (September 1913), pp 1–2.

134 'Home Reports', *The Empire and Beyond*, Occasional Leaflet XVIII (Easter 1918), pp. 10–12. 'What Candidates Are Doing', *The Girls' Quarterly: A Paper for Workers in the Girls' Friendly Society*, 23 (December 1920), p. 3. '"G.F.S. Missionary" in India', *The Girls' Quarterly: A Paper for Workers in the Girls' Friendly Society* (July 1900), p. 53.

135 'Something about Melanesia', *Our Letter: For G.F.S. Candidates all over the World* (Michaelmas 1903), p. 53.

136 'What Candidates Are Doing', *Our Letter: For G.F.S. Candidates all over the World* (June 1911), p. 4.

137 'What Candidates Are Doing', *Our Letter: For G.F.S. Candidates all over the World* (June 1911), p. 4.

138 WL, 5GFS/04/128, 'Missionary Work', *A Jubilee Chronicle for Overseas* (1935), p. 26. Edith Marion Welch, 'Home Reports', *The Empire and Beyond*, Occasional Leaflet XVI (All Saints 1917), pp. 10–14.

139 Hugh Morrison, *Protestant Children, Missions and Education in the British World*, Brill Research Perspectives in Religion and Education Series (Boston: Brill, 2021), p. 49.

140 'Missionary Work', *A Jubilee Chronicle for Overseas* (1935), p. 26.

141 Kathleen A. Dawson, M.D., 'Our Picture', *Our Letter: For G.F.S. Candidates all over the World* (December 1917), pp. 1–2.

142 M. F., 'On, to the City of God', *The Empire and Beyond*, Occasional Leaflet XXIII (Winter 1919), p. 6.

143 'News from the Mission Field', *The Girls' Quarterly: A Paper for Workers in the Girls' Friendly Society*, 2 (March 1895), p. 48.

144 Burton, *Burdens of History*, particularly chapter 5.

145 'News from the Mission Field', *The Girls' Quarterly: A Paper for Workers in the Girls' Friendly Society*, 7 (July 1896), p. 72.

146 For more on the education and training of girls, see, for example, Nancy L. Stockdale, 'Palestinian Girls and the British Missionary Enterprise, 1847–1948', in Jennifer Helgren (ed.), *Girlhood: A Global History* (Piscataway: Rutgers University Press, 2012), pp. 217–33.

147 'The Wandering Thoughts of an Empire Correspondent', *The Empire and Beyond*, Occasional Leaflet II (1913), p. 11.

148 For a greater discussion of 'telescopic philanthropy', see Hugh Cunningham, '*The Times* and "telescopic philanthropy"', in *The Reputation of Philanthropy since 1750: Britain and Beyond* (Manchester: Manchester University Press, 2000), pp. 224–35.

149 'What Candidates Are Doing', *Our Letter: For G.F.S. Candidates all over the World* (June 1911), p. 4. Kathleen M. Townsend, 'Letter from the Editor', *Our Letter: For G.F.S. Candidates all over the World* (June 1909), p. 1.

150 Money, *History of the Girls' Friendly Society*, p. 13.

151 Money, *History of the Girls' Friendly Society*, p. 17.
152 Money, *History of the Girls' Friendly Society*, p. 15.
153 WL, 5GFS/01/091, Eleanor Chute, 'Colonial Committee Meeting Held on June 16th 1902', p. 68. Emphasis in the original.
154 WL, 5GFS/02/306, *Report of the G.F.S. Special Committee* (Oxford: C. A. Press, 1932). WL, 5GFS/02/306, *Report of the Special Meeting of the Incorporated Central Council of the Girls' Friendly Society, Held at Townsend House, Greycoat Place, Westminster on Wednesday, April 27th, 1932 at 11 a.m.*, pp. 20–1.
155 WL, 5GFS/04/024, 'As Others See Us', n.d., in Members' Department Scrapbook, p. 59.
156 *Report of the Special Meeting of the Incorporated Central Council of the Girls' Friendly Society*, p. 24. Richmond also talks about this split in 'It Is Not a Society for Human Beings but for Virgins', p. 309, as does Harrison in 'For Church, Queen, and Family', p. 318.
157 'The Girls' Friendly Society Reporter', p. 1.
158 Heath-Stubbs, *Friendship's Highway*, p. 22.
159 BL, General Reference Collection 8275.b.23.(4.), Louisa M. Knightley, 'Hints on the Work of the G.F.S. in County Parishes', 1883, p. 6. On this point, see also *The Need for the Girls' Friendly Society*, p. 3; and 'The Girls' Friendly Society Reporter', p. 1.
160 Knightley, 'Hints on the Work of the G.F.S. in County Parishes', p. 2.
161 On this point, see also *The Need for the Girls' Friendly Society*, pp. 2–3.
162 BL, General Reference Collection 8275.b.23.(4.), M. E. Townsend, *Friendly Letters to Young Women in Business* (London: Hatchards, 1883), p. 1.
163 WL, 5GFS/01/006, Margaret Antrim, 'Minutes of a Meeting of the Employment and Migration Committee Held at Townsend House, Greycoat Place, S.W. 1 on Thursday, October 4th 1935 at 11 A.M.', p. 2; 'Some Ideas and a Little News', *The Girls' Quarterly: A Paper for Workers in the Girls' Friendly Society*, 9 (January 1897), p. 119.

# 2

# Imperial education programmes and the construction of colonial knowledge and racial difference

In 1913, *Our Letter: For G.F.S. Candidates all over the World* published a story entitled 'The Banner over us is Love', which relates the story of Georgina and Patricia, two sisters who are proud members of the GFS. They love attending GFS meetings and are especially interested in the lectures given by its emigration department, which feature 'vivid description[s]' of the colonies and dominions, particularly Canada, Australia, and New Zealand. At the meetings, the girls learn 'that we in the Home Country must have a great self-sacrificing love for all the countries which form our great Empire' and that 'even little girls could help their Empire ... [b]y trying to advance the work of the GFS abroad' and 'do something for the great Empire of India or our Colonies – something that would cost some sacrifice'. Georgina and Patricia leave the meetings 'burning with zeal to do their share for the good of our great Empire'. Their opportunity comes after they learn that their father, a farm labourer, has been given notice to leave because 'farming had been bad for so many years'. Georgina and Patricia tell their father what they learned at the GFS meetings about emigration. Following the girls' recommendation, the family departs for Alberta, and, although Georgina and Patricia are sad about leaving their 'Home Country', they are excited about their new life and go to Canada 'with the same bright ideals of a beautiful home-life, a strong sense of duty, and a great love for our Empire'.[1] This story of Georgina and Patricia represents one of a multitude of strategies employed by the GFS to educate girls about the empire and make them good empire builders. GFS organisers hoped their efforts to inculcate imperial ideals in its members would have tangible results, with girls, specifically white girls, deciding to undertake missionary work or, like Georgina and Patricia, emigrate and 'build new homes' in different parts of the empire.[2]

This chapter explores the different methods utilised by the GFS to generate interest in the empire and how its educational programmes reinforced colonial structures and racial identities. The chapter begins by providing an overview of the GFS's imperial education programmes before proceeding to a more focused study of four aspects of these efforts: newsletters, pageants and plays, scrapbooks, and penfriend programmes. Analysing these educational initiatives illustrates how constructions of girlhood were intricately tied to the empire and race and how white girls actively engaged in the performance of imperial, racial, and gendered identities. Through these cultural forms, the GFS constructed and projected imaginings of whiteness and idealised visions of colonial societies that marginalised people of colour and obscured the violence inherent in colonisation.[3] The society also served as a mode for systems of knowledge about girlhood, race, and colonial life to circulate globally.

## 'Bringing home to them their responsibilities as citizens of the Empire': the development of the GFS's empire education programmes

The empire formed a central part of the GFS's educational work from its early years. The society's education programmes, which paralleled its growing interest and investment in the empire, became more pronounced and co-ordinated in the early decades of the twentieth century, culminating with the establishment of the Empire Education Committee in 1924.[4] Through 'the study of the history and economic development of the Empire', the committee aimed not only to 'teach young people everything we can about the Empire' but also to increase their sense of patriotism and duty by 'bringing home to them their responsibilities as citizens of the Empire'.[5] The story of Georgina and Patricia illustrates that fostering interest in migration and cultivating the 'right type' of emigrant were a pre-eminent concern of empire education.[6]

As examined in the first chapter, the GFS viewed its connection with the empire as mutually beneficial: the empire served as a way for the GFS to grow and extend its 'spheres of influence', and the organisation also saw its role as integral to the empire's continuation by providing 'a link of Empire' that could 'band together women and girls of all classes, not only in the home country, but all over the world'.[7] Since GFS organisers viewed the interests of the GFS and the empire as interdependent, lessons sought 'to interweave with an interest in the Empire a knowledge of GFS in the Empire'.[8] The importance of imperial knowledge to the GFS is evident in the candidates' central examination, a series of questions administered to girls around the ages of twelve to fourteen who wished to become members of the GFS. 'The G.F.S. in the Colonies' formed one of only three sections of the exam, indicating the centrality of the empire to the organisation. Questions in this section focused on girls' knowledge of imperial geography and the GFS's work in the colonies. For example, a question on the 1907 exam instructed girls to draw a map of one colony and 'mark on it any places where you know the G.F.S. is at work'.[9] Another question posed to candidates was 'How does the work in South Australia show the advantage of belonging to the G.F.S.?'[10] As these questions reveal, in addition to increasing girls' interest in the empire, educational initiatives also acted as propaganda for the GFS and its imperial work.

The GFS organised myriad activities – from imperial stamp clubs to Empire Day celebrations to lending libraries – with the goal of enhancing girls' knowledge and appreciation of the empire. These activities also reaffirmed the GFS's identity as a key partner in the imperial enterprise. Educational programmes included talks and lantern lectures on topics like 'The Vision and Mission of Girlhood in the Empire and Beyond', 'our Imperial Heritage', 'Empire Citizenship for Girls', and 'Round the World with the G.F.S.'.[11] These lantern lectures educated girls throughout the empire and cultivated a sense of an imperial community. For instance, in 1918 the GFS's Committee for India, Ceylon (present-day Sri Lanka), and the Far East sent the lantern lecture of 'The G.F.S. Jewel and Its Imperial Settings' to Colombo and 'felt that the slides would be of some immense value in bringing before members in Ceylon the world-wideness of the G.F.S. and it was hoped that not only would the slides be used in Ceylon but that they would be sent to India and if possible to the Chekiang Diocese'.[12] Even events like garden parties provided occasions to learn about the empire. For instance, candidates in Wakefield in West Yorkshire hosted a party that included a talk 'about the G.F.S. and where it is to be found'. Following the presentation, the girls 'all dressed in costumes to represent those different countries'.[13] These garden parties, which often featured plays and pageants, supported the GFS's missionaries.[14]

Garden parties were just one of a variety of activities used by the GFS to generate greater interest in missionary work. The society encouraged girls to make models of mission scenes and ones of Chinese streets, village schools, and Indian bazaars.[15] In a report to the GFS publication *The Empire and Beyond*, a branch in London described how it organised events, including 'a two days' School upon Mission work, Costume Scenes, a pageant for 100 performers, also lectures and a six weeks' Study Circle'. The report expressed the hope that '[t]his may well produce G.F.S. Missionary workers' and concluded with a success story of its efforts: 'Recently a little girl working at an elaborate alphabet scrap-book for the St. Agnes' School, Baraisal [*sic*; Barisal in present-day Bangladesh], where the Oxford Mission to Calcutta takes Hindoo village children, expressed an ardent wish to go out and work there some day'.[16] This special attention given to missionaries signifies their importance to the GFS. As discussed in the first chapter, missionary work was closely entwined with the GFS's identity as an organisation committed to purity and also acted as one of the rare spheres of activity that enabled women to display their dedication to the empire while simultaneously adhering to Victorian gender mores and ideas of respectability.[17]

Reading unions and circles similarly fostered girls' interest in imperial and particularly missionary work by teaching them about the places they might travel to one day, as either migrants or missionaries.[18] In addition to patriotic subjects, like the Spanish Armada and St George, imperialist works – such as 'The Pipes of Lucknow' about the Indian Rebellion of 1857 and 'The Beginning of the Colonial Enterprise', which detailed the origins and evolution of the British empire – formed the focus of the unions.[19] The GFS used the unions and circles to make girls feel more connected to the empire by having branches in disparate parts of the empire focus on a common subject.[20] An article in *The Empire and Beyond* touted the success of the programmes by relating how a member of a London branch started her training as a nurse after being 'urged to this step by the "Women of other Lands" course in the E.R.U. [Elementary Reading Union]'. The article proceeds to describe the impact of the 'Women of other Lands' course on other girls:

> It *is* possible to use the interest in other countries which is abroad in the girls' minds and forge it into the sort of link which will help draw the Empire together under the Cross. We cannot possibly know what the girls have it in them to do and be and what use they might be to the Empire later on. A Devonshire Associate remarked that 'emigration couldn't possibly touch' her girls, and the very next week had to arrange for one of her own Members to go off with a G.F.S. party.[21]

As evidenced by this article, GFS associates saw a clear correlation between greater imperial knowledge and increased interest in migration and missionary work.

Like reading circles, study circles educated girls about the empire and the GFS's imperial work. For example, study circles in Lancashire, the chief region for the cotton industry in England, taught students about cotton production in India.[22] Another study circle in Bradford, a town central to the woollen industry in England, discussed wool production in Australia. Study circles also involved reading letters from missionaries and missionary literature and talks by missionaries about their experiences.[23] For instance, a branch in Southwell hosted a talk by a missionary, Miss Whitaker, and report how 'G.F.S. and Mothers' Union Members together went partly round the world with Miss Whitaker when she described the work being done for and by both, in Australia, New Zealand, and India, and the deep interest taken in the Societies by our far-off Sisters and their children'.[24] These visits provided a personal point of connection to the empire for girls to augment their interest in missionary work.[25]

The GFS also orchestrated large-scale events promoting the empire, including pageants, which are discussed in detail later in the chapter, as well as a 'Festival of Empire', which the GFS held at the Crystal Palace in London on 20 July 1911. This event celebrated the imperial work of the society, and, in the words of an account in *Friendly Leaves*, 'one visited distant colonies and thought of our Members far away in foreign lands' through the festival.[26] The GFS also hosted an Imperial Conference in June 1919 that welcomed visitors from different parts of the empire.[27] One of the keynote speakers at the conference was Mary Sorabji, a teacher at the High School for Indian Girls in Poona (present-day Pune) and a sister of the reformers and activists Cornelia and Susie Sorabji.[28] An article about the conference in *The Empire and Beyond* described how 'Miss Mary Sorabji, in a very pathetic and touching appeal on behalf of the women of India, spoke of the extraordinary way in which they look with admiration to the women of England, trusting us to free them from the tyranny of the ancient customs of the East, which freedom can only be compassed by taking the knowledge and spirit of Christ to India'.[29] These contrasts between the cultures of the 'West' and 'East' and the supposedly degraded status of Indian women formed a recurring theme in GFS programmes and imperial propaganda more broadly and justified the need for white women's 'civilising' influence.[30]

## 'Little sisters across the seas': the creation of imagined imperial communities and colonial knowledge in GFS newsletters

Newsletters formed a cornerstone of the GFS's imperial educational work and were integral to the construction of white girlhood. Like the GFS's events and activities, its newsletters endeavoured both to 'teach [girls] what the G.F.S. means' and 'to foster in each Member an intelligent interest in G.F.S. Imperial and Missionary work'.[31] The GFS produced a variety of newsletters – including *G.F.S. Candidate*, *G.F.S. Associates Journal and Advertiser*, *G.F.S. Reading Union Leaflet*, and *G.F.S. Workers' Journal* – each aimed at a different category of participants in the GFS. As discussed later in the chapter, white girls and girls of colour living throughout the empire read the newsletters, but the target audience was white girls in England, which shaped the newsletters' content and message. Despite the broad audience and different purposes of the newsletters, almost all the newsletters contained regular features about the empire, and in 1913, the GFS's Imperial Committee began a periodical, *The Empire and Beyond*, specifically designed 'to supply more knowledge' about the 'special needs' of the empire.[32] Articles in the various periodicals instructed girls about geography and history. For instance, *Our Letter* directed its readers to 'get some one to show them a map of India, and then they must find Burma [present-day Myanmar], and then Rangoon [present-day Yangon]'.[33] Contemporary events, like the plague and famine in India, form a common theme in the newsletters.[34] The frequency of such topics challenges perceptions that girls' periodicals were apolitical and concerned only with trivial matters and instead exemplifies the strong emphasis placed on girls' knowledge of imperial affairs and girls' engagement with imperial matters.[35]

*Friendly Leaves* was the first newsletter published by the GFS, with its inaugural issue appearing in 1876, just a year after the organisation's foundation. In 1911, it published a series of articles on 'Our Colonies'. The newsletter provides the rationale behind the series:

> The papers on Colonies will deal with their origin and their developments. We read and hear a great deal about Canada and Australia, for instance; our friends go there. We hear in these days much about the far ends of the world, but how each of these young nations began to be, how they started in life, and why they are part of our Empire many of us don't know, and these papers will try to tell.[36]

The introduction underscores the didactic rationale behind the series. Yet its purpose was not only to teach girls about the empire but also to cultivate a sense of imperial unity and loyalty. Accompanied by photographs and drawings, the articles of 'Our Colonies' detail what life was like for girls in these regions and attempted to promote a sense of familiarity by drawing parallels with life in England.

While the professed aims of 'Our Colonies' were to increase girls' knowledge about the empire, the subject matter of the articles reveals that the series also had another implicit goal: to facilitate emigration. The series had six instalments, with the settler colonies of Canada, New Zealand, Australia, and South Africa each given its own article, while Ceylon, Aden, Malta, the West Indies, and Hong Kong received briefer treatment in two articles on the 'Crown Colonies'. The decision to focus attention on the settler colonies indicates how these articles aimed to foster interest in areas of the empire that needed emigrants. The tone and themes of the articles also underscore this objective. Most instalments of 'Our Colonies' read like advertisements for emigration, with the articles providing advice for readers who wished to travel and settle there. For instance, the article about New Zealand draws attention to the freedoms and advantages girls enjoy there, describing how 'girls live in the open air, and are very carefully educated.

They generally learn to swim and can ride and take part in all outdoor games ... New Zealand girls and women are very much like English girls and women of their class, but they may be said to possess more force and more decision.'[37] The article concludes by encouraging girls to settle there, noting that New Zealand is 'waiting for the pioneer'.[38] Similarly, the article on Canada includes the plea: 'Come over and help us'.[39] The instalment about Australia also ends with an entreaty to prospective migrants: 'There is room enough and to spare in Australia'.[40] The Australia article provides advice to prospective emigrants with descriptions of the different regions where girls can settle: 'If one of you wanted to emigrate to Australia, it would be wise to consider what part, and to give each of the large five great colonies and states which comprise the whole country due consideration'.[41] These calls to emigrate in 'Our Colonies' are reinforced by another regular section of *Friendly Leaves*, 'Emigration News', which provides updates about parties of girls and young women who emigrated to the colonies and dominions and advertises free passages to different parts of the empire and job openings.[42]

Given the purpose of the 'Our Colonies' series, it is not surprising that these articles emphasise the best features of the regions. Canada is described as 'one of the most important parts of the British Empire' with 'her immense natural resources' and 'prosperity'.[43] The New Zealand essay capitalises on the country's reputation as 'not only British, but the best British'.[44] The article draws parallels between New Zealand and England and how settlers in New Zealand 'call England home, and never forget her. In fact, New Zealand is the most English place imaginable ... New Zealand is really the Britain of the South.'[45] The articles also foreground the egalitarian nature of these regions. For instance, the New Zealand essay comments: 'For the most part there are neither rich nor poor' and '[t]here is no aristocracy, and nobody worries about position'.[46] These articles exaggerate the opportunities and benefits that awaited girls in the colonies and dominions and minimise the difficulties of colonial life in their efforts to attract emigrants. This misrepresentation of colonial life was common in the propaganda of the GFS as well as other emigration organisations, but, as examined more in the next chapter, it could backfire and enhance discontentment among migrants.

Like the other instalments of 'Our Colonies', the South Africa essay reiterates myths to appeal to prospective migrants. Echoing broader emigration propaganda, the article extols the beauty of the region and its climate, which it describes as 'one of the finest in the world', while glossing over the racial realities of the region.[47] It presents a benign view of race relations and relegates racial problems to the past, stating: 'In the early days of colonisation, the few whites suffered much from the natives, and life in the colony was an incessant anxiety ... Life was a precarious and uncertain thing in those days, but now it is very different, and Europeans and Kafirs live peaceably together.'[48] It describes the Africans in paternalistic terms as 'genial and kindly, placid and good-natured, but capable of becoming excited'.[49] Even though the article acknowledges that South Africa is 'the land of the black man', it simultaneously accentuates the whiteness of the region, stating for instance: 'The air, we are told, seems to be washed clean and white'.[50] Such descriptions intended to dispel racial anxieties by indicating that, at its heart, South Africa was white and any hint of non-whiteness or uncleanliness could be easily remedied. Yet these images of settler societies presented in the newsletters were mirages that obscured the violence of settler colonialism, which depended upon the elimination and dispossession of Indigenous inhabitants of the regions.[51]

As illustrated by the South Africa feature, considerable space is devoted to the peoples living in the different regions, and the articles frequently employ stereotypes that reflected superficial understandings and racist views of Indigenous cultures and histories. For instance, the article on Australia presents Aboriginal people as 'ugly and unprepossessing' and observes that 'the women are generally treated as mere slaves'.[52] The comparison of women's status to slavery builds upon common tropes at the time that used women's status as a marker of civilisation.[53] The article on New Zealand presents a different picture of the Māori, referring them as 'an interesting race' who 'seem to be fairly contented and happy'. It further describes the Māori as 'very intelligent ... and is strong, courageous, a good shot, a good wrestler, and a keen observer'.[54] The article reiterates beliefs about racial hierarchies, including that the Māori were 'better blacks' and superior to other Indigenous peoples. This notion of the Māoris as 'better blacks' developed following the New Zealand Wars (1845–72) and the publication in 1885 of Edward Tragear's *The Aryan Maori*, which argues that the Māori shared an ancient origin with Britons and other northern Europeans.[55] While describing the Māoris as 'better blacks' might at first appear conciliatory, such views conceal more self-interested motives. This idea of Māoris as 'better blacks' elevated not only the Māori people but also the Pākehā (European settlers) in New Zealand, since they could claim that they interacted with a superior type of 'native' and thus reinforced New Zealand's professed superiority to other white settler societies, especially Australia. Pākehā New Zealanders could also use this notion to propagate the belief that they had the best race relations in the world and emphasise its relative racial harmony.[56]

Celebrating the benefits of European colonisation and the success of the 'civilising mission' forms another common theme in these articles, especially in the ones about the 'Crown Colonies'. One of the instalments on the

'Crown Colonies' notes: 'In the last hundred years much has been done by the English for Ceylon'.[57] It supports this contention by drawing attention to various developments in the region, including railways, commerce, roads, and schools.[58] The description of Malta in the same article proclaims how the Maltese 'believed that they were better off under our rule than under any other'.[59] Such descriptions frame British rule as desirable and benevolent. While praising the success of the European 'civilising mission', the articles make it clear that more work remains to be done. The description of the West Indies in the 'Crown Colonies' article expresses how '[t]he Barbadian Negroes are very fine specimens of humanity' and '[t]hey are healthy, cheerful, and sober, as a rule; but if left to themselves they are apt to degenerate'. It also provides a description of 'a very interesting and remarkable people, called the "poor whites"' who 'are now utterly degenerate'.[60] As the next chapters analyse in greater depth, poor whites posed a danger to colonial societies by destabilising racial hierarchies and undermining notions of white prestige and, like West Indians, were the targets of reform by the colonial state. The descriptions of these groups in the article therefore underline the need for white emigrants and missionaries, who could reaffirm white respectability and continue the work of Britain's 'civilising mission'.

Like *Friendly Leaves*, another GFS periodical – *Our Letter: For G.F.S. Candidates all over the World* – regularly contains articles about the lives of women and girls around the world and the GFS's work in different areas of the empire. Circulated throughout the empire and designed for candidates under the age of twelve, *Our Letter* features articles and often pictures submitted by girls that share the activities of their branches and give the girl readers a sense of their 'home-life' and 'help one another to understand something of each other's lives'.[61] Like the articles in *Friendly Leaves*, the essays in *Our Letter* fostered girls' interest in the empire, hoping it would encourage girls to emigrate to the colonies.[62] One article from 1904 about 'Candidates in New Zealand' reflects common motifs that appear throughout the newsletters. It draws parallels between candidates in New Zealand and in England, observing how in New Zealand '[t]hese children love *Our Letter*, which goes to them by post across the sea; they have Candidates' Classes just as you have in England'.[63] A photograph that accompanies the article (Figure 2.1) features a group of girls from Christchurch, New Zealand, affirming how the GFS acted as a family for girls. Familial imagery forms a common theme in the articles. For instance, an article published in 1906 describes the organisation as 'a very large family' composed of 'thousands of G.F.S. Candidates at home and abroad', and one of the newsletter's regular columns – 'What Candidates are Doing' – informed girls 'about life and surroundings of these little sisters across the seas'.[64]

Figure 2.1 Avonside branch in Christchurch, New Zealand, 1904 (From 'Candidates in New Zealand', *Our Letter: For G.F.S. Candidates all over the World*, September 1904, p. 3)

The recurring use of familial motifs highlights how GFS newsletters fostered an 'imagined community' for girls.[65] In her study of colonial literature, Kristine Moruzi explains how fiction and periodicals encouraged girls to emigrate and that one of the key ways they accomplished this purpose was 'to situate colonial girlhood within an international sisterhood that promoted the ties of imperialism in an effort to reassure girls that life in the colonies and dominions would allow them to maintain their purity and virtue'.[66] The GFS newsletters connected girls in disparate parts of the empire and encouraged girl readers to think of their 'sisters' across the world. For girls in England contemplating emigration, familial motifs could ease trepidations about colonial life and its dangers. For girls, especially white girls, living in the colonies and dominions, this imagery made them feel more connected to the empire and their 'home'. As Moruzi observes, 'Often colonial girls had little direct experience with England or other colonies. Through their magazines, however, they could see themselves as part of the community but also as uniquely situated within the empire, thereby creating a model of girlhood that is simultaneously transnational, imperial, and colonial.'[67] Like other girls' periodicals, GFS newsletters allowed girls to visualise their place within both the GFS and the empire. For instance, an article in *Our Letter* notes the importance of the community provided by the GFS: 'Pray sometimes for these G.F.S. friends of yours so far away.

You and they belong to one great Society, and though you may never see each other's faces, you can help each other by your prayers, your letters, and your love.'[68] Through its emphasis on commonalities and sisterhood across the disparate parts of the empire, these newsletters made esoteric ideas about empire and their 'home' more tangible.

Like the activities and events described in the previous section, newsletters endeavoured to raise money for missionaries and stimulate girls' interest in missionary work by drawing attention to the vital role of 'brave' and 'indispensable' missionaries.[69] The GFS's efforts to inspire interest in missionaries is reflected in a 1917 story in *Our Letter*, entitled 'Our Hope for the World'. It depicts the lives of children in Africa, India, China, and Samoa and their conversion to Christianity and concludes by encouraging girls to pursue missionary work. The story is followed by questions, including: 'How can we best help Missions?' and 'Why is it so important to teach the Chinese Christianity?'[70] These questions illustrate how the GFS hoped girls would read the stories and then put the missionary ideas into practice. Other articles similarly testify to the necessity of missionary work and connect it to the 'civilising mission' of imperialism. For instance, an article in *The Girls' Quarterly* about Japan argues for the need for missionaries and ends with the pronouncement, 'Now is key time for civilization'.[71]

While articles about the white settler colonies emphasise the commonalities with England, articles about other regions – particularly China, India, and Japan, which were the focus of the GFS's missionary activities – highlight their differences from England to accentuate the necessity of English intervention.[72] For instance, one article in *Our Letter* from 1906, with the title of 'Topsy Turvy Land', describes China as 'a land where manners and customs are in many ways the opposite to what they are in England'.[73] Another essay in a 1904 issue of *Our Letter* expresses similar views about India. The editor, Kathleen Townsend, details her experiences travelling in India, referring to it as 'a far country, a country strange and wonderful in many ways, and very different from the dear old England from whence I have come'. Despite the emphasis on India's 'otherness' and a recognition of the difficulties of journeying there, Townsend reassures her young readers that the GFS has eased many of the challenges of travelling and highlights the success of the GFS's work: 'And yet here, in this great empire of India, I rejoice to know that our dear G.F.S. is taking root, and will, I trust, help many girls, whose homes are out here, to live lives of purity, and love, and service to others'.[74] Townsend's comments demonstrate how the GFS saw its role as integral in constructing 'pure' homes, which was foundational to the reformation of colonial societies.

Comments on the religion of other cultures foregrounded the need for the 'civilising' work of the GFS and its missionaries. For instance, one article in *Our Letter* from 1906 accentuates the seeming backwardness of China: 'Isn't it strange to think of some of our Candidates living in a land where the native people worship such a god? We hope that all our G.F.S. Members and Candidates will be real missionaries in these distant countries by showing in their lives what the religion of Jesus Christ really is.'[75] Another article, this one in *The Girls' Quarterly* from 1901, details the experience of a girl in the zenana and cites the lack of Christian beliefs as a cause for the poor treatment of women: 'But at the cost of what terrible suffering to the girls and women are such scenes enacted! They make one realise the essential difference between East and West, the Christian and non-Christian civilisation.'[76] As this article reflects, the GFS justified the importance of its missionary work by privileging and elevating the position of British girls and contrasting their lives with the apparent backwardness of girls' lives in other regions. Articles frame missionary work as rescuing girls and women from their supposedly degraded condition and providing girls with a happy childhood. For instance, an article from *The Empire and Beyond* features a letter from a Dr Laura C., who was in charge of a dispensary for Indian women and wrote: 'All the children ... look so happy, being free from much Hindu caste and religion'.[77] Such observations indicate that missionaries fulfilled roles not only as educators but also as maternal figures who could atone for the shortcomings of the home through their moral guidance.[78] This emphasis on otherness and the poor status of women in China, Japan, and India provided a persuasive rationale for the GFS's missionary work and, on a broader level, supported white women's engagement in the empire and the British right to colonise these regions.[79]

As this section has examined, the empire features prominently in GFS newsletters in a variety of ways, indicating not only its centrality to the GFS but also girls' importance to the empire. The newsletters thus provide singular insights into the role that the GFS envisioned girls, specifically white girls, playing in the empire. GFS organisers wanted white girls to be knowledgeable and loyal members of the imperial family who contributed to the project of empire building by undertaking missionary work and migrating and building homes and 'lives of purity' in the colonies. These roles as empire builders were shaped not only by gender ideals but also by racial prescriptions, as demonstrated by the description of different groups in 'Our Colonies' and the frequent contrasts between the lives of English girls and girls in Japan, China, and India. Through the juxtaposition of girls' lives in England and other parts of the world, the newsletters reinforced what Partha Chatterjee has termed the 'rule of difference' between the coloniser and the colonised and reaffirmed notions of white girlhood as more 'civilised' and fundamentally distinct from – and superior to – other girlhoods.[80] In addition to reinforcing these colonial myths, newsletters projected conceptions of settler colonial societies as white and 'neo-Europes' that concealed the violent realities of colonialism. The representations of these regions in the newsletters illustrate how, as Lorenzo Veracini has observed, 'settler migration operates within a register of sameness' and settler colonialism depends on its 'regenerative capacity' with settlers attempting to reproduce whiteness by claiming sovereignty and permanency over 'virgin' land while aggressively eliminating Indigenous peoples and dispossessing them of their land.[81] As explored in the next section, pageants and plays produced by the GFS complemented the themes in the newsletters. Like newsletters, pageants and plays served not only as powerful publicity tools for the GFS but were also integral in constructing ideas of white girlhood and racial difference, evidenced by the staging of imperial scenes and the use of blackface and brownface.

### 'Instructing and inspiring enthusiasm and loyalty': enacting whiteness and racial difference in pageants and plays

In the early twentieth century, 'pageant fever' struck England. While pageants have a long history extending back to the Middle Ages, their popularity in England spread following the success of Louis Napoleon Parker's pageant in Sherborne, Dorset, in 1905.[82] In subsequent decades, pageants became a staple in schools, youth organisations, and community life, with hundreds of thousands of people taking part in these displays as performers, musicians, organisers, and spectators. The GFS was not immune to 'pageantitis' and, like other organisations, including the Girl Guides, recognised the value of such spectacles and mass public performances.[83] Pageants often involved not only short plays and tableaux vivants but also other events, including lectures and exhibits. This 'pageant fever' also extended beyond England, with reports in GFS newsletters recounting how members in different parts of the empire engaged in these performances.[84]

Pageants and plays fulfilled a variety of purposes. On a practical level, they were key sources of revenue for the organisation. Money raised through the production of GFS pageants and plays assisted branches and the imperial work of the GFS, with funds being used to support GFS workers and missionaries in different parts of the empire.[85] For instance, when the St Albans and Chelmsford branch hosted the 'Pageant of GFS in the Empire' in 1914, the proceeds were sent to support a worker in Lahore.[86] Similarly, the money raised from a Southwark branch's 'Pageant of Greenwich History' in 1915 aided a missionary in Burma.[87] In addition to this financial incentive, pageants had an educational purpose. Pageants and plays increased the visibility of the organisation, promoted its programmes, and resolved misconceptions about the GFS. This purpose was especially important as the GFS struggled with declining membership in the interwar years, a topic discussed more in Chapter 5.[88] When branches in New Zealand organised a pageant, they had high hopes about its effects: 'Apart from the financial success, the Pageant will have been invaluable in bringing G.F.S. before the general public, showing that it is a live, efficient, and progressive Society'.[89] Their importance as a propaganda tool is also reflected in an article in *Our Letter* that describes pageants as 'a means of instructing and inspiring enthusiasm and loyalty'.[90] The inclusion of descriptions and images of pageants and plays in GFS newsletters indicates that they were a source of pride for the organisation and ensured that their message extended beyond immediate audience of these productions. Girl readers of the newsletters who viewed images of the pageants and plays or read details about them were encouraged not only to learn from them but also to emulate them through putting on their own pageants and plays. Pageants and plays, like newsletters, also fostered a sense of belonging and community in the GFS.[91] The GFS used these events to fashion – or refashion – a narrative about the organisation and its identity. They allowed the GFS to convey a specific version of the past and the organisation and by extension shape its present and future.

Women's involvement in historical pageantry has largely been overlooked, yet pageants were a significant part of women's and girls' culture. In her study of women's involvement in pageants, the historian Zoë Thomas observes: 'Historical pageants provided a particularly compelling way to construct popular "usable" pasts which cemented group cohesion, and enabled these groups visually to depict the history and interests peculiar to each organisation – from institutional histories and women's historic religious, political and professional roles to the importance of international "sisterhood"'.[92] This effort to create a 'usable past' and sense of international sisterhood is evident in the GFS pageants and especially its 'Pageant of the Girls' Friendly Society'.[93] Devised and primarily written by the 'Great Master of Pageantry' Louis Napoleon Parker, the pageant was first performed on 20 July 1920, to an audience of over 1,700. Featuring three hundred performers, it opened with girls assuming roles of famous women leaders in history, including Hatshepsut, Boadicea, St Helena, Joan of Arc, and Queen Elizabeth I.[94] The pageant then celebrated the growth of the GFS and its ideals of friendship and purity before concluding with a parade of girls of different occupations: nurse, business girl, student, domestic servant, teacher, factory girl, doctor, policewoman, and land girl. The pageant also highlighted the different departments of the GFS, 'the variety of privileges and advantages enjoyed by its Members', and representatives of 'the vast field in which it operates'.[95] Other GFS pageants followed a similar pattern. For instance, 'The Quest', which was authored by Parker and first performed in Albert Hall to mark the society's Golden Jubilee in 1925, featured six hundred members and was similarly divided between a historical tableau – featuring St Elizabeth of Hungary, St Hilda, Joan of Arc, Queen Elizabeth I, Elizabeth Fry, and Florence Nightingale – and then 'Girls of Today' (see Figure 2.2).[96] Pageants presented a female-oriented view of the past with the celebration of women, including ones who stepped outside traditional feminine roles. Their emphasis on having girls perform adult occupations reveals how ideas of girlhood were intricately tied to notions of futurity.[97] Pageants provided a space where womanhood, and more specifically the qualities of white womanhood promoted by the GFS, could be learned and practised by girl members.

While pageants reified traditional feminine roles, girl performers at times subverted social markers and traversed gender lines by donning masculine clothing.[98] Pageants provided girl performers with an opportunity to escape the confines of traditional gender norms.[99] Yet such transgressions were possible because they were transitory and contained within the controlled space of plays and pageants. When the plays and pageants ended, girls removed their masculine clothing and resumed traditional gender roles. Consequently, despite these disruptive moments, pageants ultimately preserved traditional gender – and, as discussed below, racial – roles and hierarchies.

**Figure 2.2** 'The Quest', 1931 (Women's Library, London, 5GFS/04/127, '"The Quest." St. David's Diocese', *G.F.S. Magazine*, January 1931, photo from Block Book VII, 1926–31)

The centrality of pageants and plays to the GFS's outreach and educational work is evident in *The G.F.S. in Picture and Pageant*, a booklet that provides instructions on how to stage pageants. This booklet includes information for producing scenes, including 'Caravan Scene', 'Members' Drilling Class', 'Camp Scene', 'Hampstead Heath Temperance Stall', and 'Missions: an Indian Scene'.[100] These scenes reveal how pageants aimed to teach girls how to be members and engage in the activities of girlhood, as defined by the GFS. In the 'Caravan Scene' (Figure 2.3), girls would act as adult GFS 'caravaners', who travelled to different towns as a means of fundraising, publicising the organisation, and recruiting and training new members.[101] Like the scenes of the 'Pageant of the Girls' Friendly Society', the 'Caravan Scene' accentuated the futurity of girls and provided an opportunity for white girls to rehearse roles that the GFS hoped they would undertake as adults.

Another common feature of pageants was exercise and drill displays (Figure 2.4).[102] *The G.F.S. in Picture and Pageant* provides a description of what such a display might include, instructing performers to 'march on to music, single file, take up positions, do exercises, etc., form in line again, do running exercise, form a maze, etc., etc., and march off in single file as

**Figure 2.3** Candidates as 'caravaners' in the Isle of Wight pageant, 1927 (Women's Library, London, 5/GFS/04/127, 'Wingham Candidates as "Caravaners" in the Isle of Wight Pageant', *Our Letter: For G.F.S. Candidates all over the World*, September 1927, photo from Block Book VII, 1926–31)

**Figure 2.4** Skipping display, 1933, photograph copyright by The Daily Sketch & Sunday Graphic Ltd. London (Women's Library, London, 5/GFS/11/003, Skipping display, 1933)

they came on'.[103] This display of drill reflects shifting notions of femininity. By the late Victorian era, Britons increasingly eschewed traditional ideals of female fragility and women's sedentary lifestyle and instead viewed women's health as indicative of the nation's – and empire's – strength. This recognition led to a greater incorporation of physical exercise in schools. For instance, Frances Dove, the founder and headmistress of the girls' school Wycombe Abbey, explicitly tied the individual benefits of exercise with the well-being of the whole nation by emphasising the importance of physical education for 'the future ... both of women in particular and of the nation as a whole'.[104] She elaborated on this significance, writing: 'I think I do not speak too strongly when I say that games, i.e. active games in the open air, are essential to a healthy existence, and that most of the qualities, if not all, that conduce to the supremacy of our country in so many quarters of the globe, are fostered, if not solely developed, by means of games'.[105] Through these drill displays, the girls manifested not only their strength and vigour but also the ideals of discipline, co-operation, self-control, and obedience, all of which were important to the continuation of the British empire. These presentations also demonstrated the sublimation of individual identity to broader group pride and loyalty.[106]

The empire and imperial work of the GFS formed a prominent theme of pageants. Imperial-themed pageants produced by the GFS include 'Britannia and her Colonies', 'Pageant of the Empire', 'GFS in the Empire',

'Out West', 'Sunrise Land', 'The Lady with the Lamp', 'The Sign Post', 'Round the Fair World', and 'Comrades of the World'.[107] Even pageants not explicitly about the empire often included segments devoted to the GFS's imperial work. For instance, *The G.F.S. in Picture and Pageant* contains instructions for creating a pageant section on 'Expansion'. It opens with a monologue about how England is the 'stem' and the colonies are the 'branches' of the 'Tree of Empire'. This section is followed by a procession of girls bearing the banners of countries of the empire and the singing of the national anthem.[108] As evident from these descriptions, pageants promoted ideas of imperial citizenship and made explicit the connection between the growth of the GFS and Britain's empire.

Missionaries also formed a principal theme in GFS pageants and plays. Like newsletters and other activities described in the previous sections, pageants and plays advertised and promoted the GFS's missionary programmes and sought to inspire girls' interest in being missionaries. It educated girls about missionary life and gave them the opportunity to rehearse the roles of missionaries that the GFS hoped they would fulfil in the future. An article on 'The Missionary Pageant' in *Our Letter* articulates the importance of these performances: 'It gives Candidates a wonderful opportunity of learning about the different nations, who are just now stretching out their hands to Christ'. It continues that the pageants may 'really help in making known the great needs of the heathen world, and how we can all help send out the good news to these nations'.[109] Within these pageants, missionaries – and by extension girls – occupied a central place in the imperial story. Significantly, girls played not only roles typical of white women but also the roles of women of colour. India was a common setting of missionary plays and pageants, and in these performances, girls both acted as nurses and doctors to Indian women and assumed the guise of Indian women (see Figures 2.5 and 2.6).[110] These pageants drew attention to the supposedly lowly status of girls and women of colour and underscored the responsibility of white girls to rectify this situation by 'saving' these women.[111]

Pageants and plays provided spaces where both gender roles were enacted and racial roles were constructed, performed, and rehearsed, evidenced most clearly by the use of blackface and brownface. Blackface and brownface had been part of entertainment in Britain since the early 1800s, when minstrel shows were brought to Britain by American performers.[112] Thomas D. Rice first acquired fame with his performance of 'Ethiopian operas' in the 1820s and thereby initiated a cultural form that would enjoy enduring popularity into the twentieth century.[113] While minstrel shows were perhaps the most visible and well-known enactment of racial stereotypes, the appropriation of other cultures and the performance of racial roles were not isolated to these shows and infiltrated British culture. Photographs of GFS pageants and plays reveal

*Imperial education programmes* 73

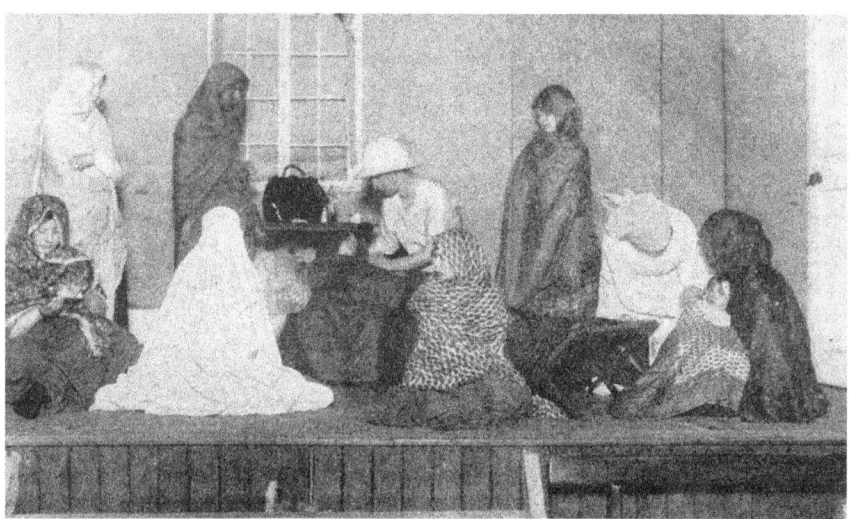

Figure 2.5 'Indian Tableaux at Endon', 1923 (Women's Library, London, 5GFS/04/086, 'Indian Tableaux at Endon', *G.F.S. Magazine*, September 1923, photo from Block Book, 1922–23)

Figure 2.6 'North Indian Tableaux', c. 1929 (Women's Library, London, 5GFS/04/127, 'North Indian Tableaux by Rhayader Branch', c. 1929, photo from Block Book VII, 1926–31)

CWMDANDUR BRANCH IN 'THE LADY WITH THE LAMP.'

**Figure 2.7** Cwdandur branch in 'The Lady with the Lamp', 1930 (Women's Library, London, 5GFS/04/127, 'Cwdandur Branch in "The Lady with the Lamp"', *G.F.S. Magazine*, February 1930, photo from Block Book VII, 1926–31)

how girls imitated minstrels and similar cultural scripts. A photograph of a branch in Wales performing the play 'The Lady with the Lamp' features girls and young women in brownface and dressed in Indian clothing (Figure 2.7).[114]

These representations in the plays and pageants impose flawed identities on colonised peoples.[115] Through the use of blackface and brownface, these performances reaffirmed not only the 'otherness' of girls from India and Africa but also the whiteness of the English performers.[116] As Bill Schwarz argues in *A White Man's World*, the imperial experience allowed the British 'to imagine oneself as white – or to recognise that others were imagining one to be white'.[117] By enacting ideas of racial difference and the supposed superiority of white girls and women, pageants and plays were instrumental to this imagining of whiteness and the construction of white identities. The performances also underscored girls' importance in the imperial project as civilising agents.

Pageants demonstrate that children did not passively receive cultural scripts but actively engaged in the performance of imperial, racial, and gendered identities.[118] In her incisive study *Racial Innocence: Performing American Childhood from Slavery to Civil Rights*, Robin Bernstein notes that scholars have often understood minstrelsy as a realm of adult, working-class men and thus overlooked the connection between blackface minstrelsy and children's representational play. GFS plays and pageants reveal how minstrelsy became an inextricable part of children's culture not only in America but also in Britain during the nineteenth and early twentieth centuries and, as a result, informed girls' understanding of the world and their role in it. In *Racial Innocence*, Bernstein investigates how white children – particularly middle-class children – adopted racialised practices through playing with Black dolls.[119] The GFS also used dolls – often in conjunction with pageants – to construct and maintain racial hierarchies. For instance, candidates in Ardingly produced a missionary exhibition that featured a doll pageant with a 'Native American Indian Wigwam' in the hope that it would interest people in missionary work.[120] The GFS also held pageants accompanied by an exhibition in which '[t]iny dolls, beautifully dressed in native African costumes, were placed in groups showing the practical work done by the Missionaries in Zanzibar'.[121] These events support Bernstein's contention that 'the idea of childhood innocence and the bodies of living children have historically mystified racial ideology by hiding it in plain sight'.[122] Their seeming innocuousness helped to make plays and pageants powerful vehicles of imperial ideology and masked the racial violence being enacted in these events.

## 'Our friends at home': narratives of colonial life and the marginalisation of racial 'others' in GFS scrapbooks

In addition to pageants, the GFS capitalised on another effective medium in girls' culture to support its imperial efforts: scrapbooks. Like pageants, plays, and newsletters, scrapbooks fostered colonial connections and aimed to strengthen girls' sense of patriotism towards the empire.[123] Scrapbooks created and reproduced narratives about colonial life and, in doing so, also constructed ideas of white girlhood and racial difference. This section begins by outlining the ways that the GFS used scrapbooks. It then proceeds to a detailed analysis of two scrapbooks produced around 1930 – one by a GFS branch in Port Elizabeth (present-day Gqeberha), South Africa, and the other by various branches in West Australia – to examine the motifs and imagery employed by the GFS to garner support for its emigration and imperial work and to affirm racial hierarchies.

Initially popular among middle-class girls in the mid-nineteenth century, scrapbooks developed into a more mass cultural form by the early twentieth century. Scrapbooks originally served personal purposes, such as preserving one's own or familial memories or exhibiting accomplishments, like drawing or writing. By the late nineteenth century, they acquired an educative dimension with parents and teachers viewing scrapbooks as a productive activity that could cultivate children's interest in culture or the natural sciences and teach them artistic and practical skills, like how to collect and categorise.[124] Scrapbooks' growing popularity was the result of the greater affordability of materials – namely paper, scissors, and glue – as well as developments in printing and photograph technology and the consequent plethora of printed materials emerging in this period, including greeting and calling cards, postcards, and periodicals. The introduction of Eastman Kodak's folding cameras in the 1890s and the Brownie camera in 1900 moved photography beyond the world of studios and allowed amateurs to take part in it. Highlighting their affordability, portability, and ease of use, Kodak specifically marketed his cameras to women and children.[125] As part of his efforts to reach girls, Kodak advertised his cameras in Girl Guide publications and even introduced the Girl Guide Kodak camera in the 1930s.[126] Like the Girl Guides and other organisations, the GFS recognised the power of visual media and their utility in publicising its work, evidenced by the prominence of photographs in newsletters and scrapbooks.

The GFS utilised scrapbooks in two ways: by organising scrapbook competitions and by facilitating the exchange of scrapbooks between 'linked' branches in different parts of the empire. For scrapbook competitions, GFS associates chose a region of the empire and gave participants specific guidelines about the format and content of the books, demonstrating the didactic impulse behind these competitions. The guidelines directed girls to include maps, not only of the region of focus and its provinces and cities but also of the empire, and to designate which places were self-governing dominions, Crown Colonies, and mandated territories. The directions also stipulated that scrapbooks should include cuttings from newspapers, magazines, and leaflets as well as postcards and letters girls received from that region of the empire.[127] Winning the competition was a source of pride for the branches, especially when branches from the colonies or dominions prevailed over English branches.[128]

Like scrapbook competitions, scrapbook exchanges educated girls about the empire and promoted the work of the GFS. With scrapbook exchanges, girls compiled a book about their own branch and region and then sent this book to other branches. Explaining the value of scrapbook exchanges, the GFS's Imperial and Overseas Committee expressed the belief that 'it could help – and in the past had helped enormously – the growth of G.F.S. work overseas'.[129] The exchanges also fostered a sense of camaraderie by providing insights into girls' lives in disparate parts of the empire.[130] The instructions for scrapbook exchanges were more flexible than for competitions. Girls were informed that '[t]he ideal one was to contain about two to three pages of snapshots and writing from each of our Links [branches]'.[131] The volumes feature drawings, photographs, and essays, but the topics covered in the books vary. Pages from some branches focus solely on the activities of GFS members, like field trips, charitable work, and picnics. Others present postcards and descriptive essays of the region's landmarks and geographic and social landscapes and include observations about colonial life and pictures of buildings, beaches, and wildlife. The photographs of GFS members, along with the essays, reflect a self-fashioning and performativity, shaped by their purpose and the perceived expectations of their intended audience. The essays reveal girls' consciousness about their audience and a desire to please and entertain them, with lines such as 'I hope that you will like the pages that St. Albans are putting in the Album' and 'I hope this will be of interest to some of friends at home'.[132] The photographs and essays indicate that girls in Port Elizabeth and West Australia were influenced by girls in England – or at least by their perceptions of what girls in England did and liked.

As in newsletters, familial imagery forms a recurring motif in the scrapbooks. One of the essays in the scrapbook created by the Port Elizabeth branch describes the purpose of the book as a way of 'giving our friends at home' a sense of what life was like in South Africa. In the scrapbook created by various branches in West Australia, essays contain salutations like 'To a Dear G.F.S. Friend' and 'Dear Sister Candidates Overseas'.[133] Photographs reaffirm this sense of community by showing girls together, appearing almost as a family (Figure 2.8).[134] The idea of the GFS as a family, coupled

Figure 2.8 GFS picnic in South Africa (Women's Library, London, 5GFS/02/260, 'These Speak for Themselves. Girls generally *can*!', in South Africa scrapbook, c. 1930)

with the ubiquitous emphasis on knowing and understanding the lives of girls in other parts of the empire, produced a consciousness of girls' roles in and connection to the GFS and the empire. Scrapbooks, like newsletters, showed audiences 'at home' in England that their lives were not dissimilar to girls' lives in the colonies and dominions. Both the Port Elizabeth and West Australia scrapbooks contain images of churches and girls attending church, showing their religious commitment and the maintenance of their virtue in these distant places (Figure 2.9).[135] The West Australia scrapbook features a carefully posed photograph of girls sewing outside (Figure 2.10).[136] Such photos demonstrated girls' continued commitment to traditional ideas of femininity and domesticity and, by extension, the preservation of their English identity and the successful reproduction of Englishness abroad.[137]

The scrapbooks tried to convey that West Australia and South Africa were inviting places to settle and live, but such descriptions rested on the perpetuation of settler colonial myths. GFS scrapbooks reaffirmed emigration discourses and propaganda by portraying Australia and South Africa as places that offered girls opportunities not possible in England. Like newsletters, the images in the scrapbooks celebrate the freedom and benefits

Figure 2.9 Girls at church in Port Elizabeth (Women's Library, London, 5GFS/02/260, 'After service on Ascension Day. 1931', in South Africa scrapbook, c. 1930)

Figure 2.10 'Candidates' Sewing' in West Australia (Women's Library, London, 5GFS/02/357, photo of the 'Candidates' Sewing' from 'G.F.S. Bassadean Candidate Class. 1930' page in West Australia scrapbook, c. 1930)

of colonial life. Girls in the scrapbooks are pictured enjoying the outdoors (Figures 2.8 and 2.11).[138] Such pictures built upon common tropes in emigration propaganda that drew contrasts to the cramped and overcrowded conditions of London and other British cities.[139] These images of open, empty landscapes also perpetuated settler colonial beliefs in these regions as *terra nullius* that in turn was used to justify white sovereignty over these lands.[140]

The scrapbooks further reinforced the imperatives of settler colonialism by accentuating the modernity of these regions. Descriptions and images wanted to show that Port Elizabeth and West Australia should not be written off as unrefined backwaters. For instance, an essay in the Port Elizabeth scrapbook, 'Walking to Work in South Africa', begins by dismissing any idea that it is a wild and untamed place: 'there will be no thrilling accounts of encounters with lions and tigers!'. The essay instead highlights the town's features, like the 'up-to-date Hotel' and 'a fine Public Library' and 'the Shops', which 'contain everything, almost, that mankind, or womankind, could want'.[141] Photographs of buildings and monuments – including one described in a caption as 'One of the finest Memorials in the world' – reaffirm these descriptions.[142] The West Australia scrapbook contains pictures of the region's buildings and infrastructure,

Figure 2.11 Candidates' picnic in Australia (Women's Library, London, 5GFS/02/357, photo of 'Miss Whatley and Junior St. Andrews at picnic' from 'St Andrews Junior Branch, Subiaco' page in West Australia scrapbook, c. 1930)

including Mundaring Weir, which it proclaims to be 'the greatest scheme in the world'.[143] Such descriptions were not simply propagandistic but also reflected settlers' desire to control and master the land. In the introduction to their edited collection *Making Settler Colonial Space: Perspectives on Race, Place and Identity*, Tracey Banivanua Mar and Penelope Edmonds draw attention to how settler colonialism redefined the landscapes of these regions and describe how the process of settler colonialism 'has involved a much more thoroughgoing rewriting of land and production of social space'.[144] Banivanua Mar in particular explores how 'settler cities were discursively narrated as spaces of progress, commerce and modernity – spaces of the highest stage of development in the Western historicising narrative aggressively exclusive of Indigenous peoples. The bustling settler city, imagined as a rational, ordered and triumphal place of settler commerce and progress, became a symbol of empire which served to further justify the expropriation of Indigenous land.'[145] Building upon Banivanua Mar and Edmonds's insights, one can see that these descriptions served to reaffirm and celebrate common myths that settler colonialism brought prosperity and civilisation.

The portrayal and marginalisation of African and Aboriginal peoples in the scrapbooks complemented settler colonial objectives by projecting an idealised version of colonial society centred on whiteness. Although branches for Black and Coloured (mixed-race) girls existed in South Africa and for Aboriginal girls in Australia, the scrapbooks contain no photographs of these girls or essays about their activities. This erasure is rooted in the settler colonial project, which operated by what Patrick Wolfe has termed a 'logic of elimination' that sought to dispossess and destroy Indigenous peoples.[146] The GFS sought to construct an image of the organisation – and these societies more broadly – as white, homogeneous, and racially pure spaces in which Indigenous peoples and peoples of colour did not exist.[147] Although photographs of Aboriginal and African people are present in the scrapbooks, they are not shown interacting with white people, appearing to affirm the settler colonial myth that Indigenous people and people of colour were confined, controlled, and separate and could be removed and relocated and did not threaten the homogeneity of white society.[148]

When African and Aboriginal people appear in the scrapbooks, they are used for specific purposes, namely to reassert racial hierarchies and reinforce the 'civilising mission' of imperialism.[149] Images within the West Australian scrapbook reaffirm the transition of Aboriginals from a 'primitive' to a 'civilised' people. One photograph of an Aboriginal man features a caption that describes him as a drunken 'heathen' previously but who 'is a good Christian now'.[150] Aboriginal children are pictured playing cricket and boxing, Aboriginal men attending church, and Aboriginal women waiting for their tea.[151] For the British, such images served as undeniable markers of the success of the 'civilising mission'.[152]

The Port Elizabeth book similarly contains images and stereotypes about African peoples and myths about the positive effects of colonialism. One of the essays in the Port Elizabeth scrapbook describes the transition of Africans to a 'civilised' society: 'The Basutos have their own religious and witch doctors, but, as they are becoming more civilised, they are generally giving up their superstitions'.[153] Photos perpetuate narratives about Africans' supposed backwardness. For instance, one photo shows an African man and woman outside their home with the caption: 'The Native Boy would not allow his wife to be snapped without him'.[154] The caption brands the African woman as submissive and an object of sympathy, underscoring the supposed repressiveness of African societies and the necessity of Britain's 'civilising mission'. In another photograph (Figure 2.12), a woman stands behind her husband, with the caption: 'A Fine Native. His Wife peeps from behind.'[155] The African women's passiveness and powerlessness stand in contrast to the GFS girls, who are pictured moving freely in South Africa (see, for instance, Figure 2.8). Throughout the scrapbook, African women are barely visible, and when they are, they appear in the shadows or as stock figures. Besides these brief descriptions, the scrapbooks contain no information about who took the photographs and the people featured in the photographs.

**Figure 2.12** An African man and woman (Women's Library, London, 5GFS/02/260, photo from South African countryside page in South Africa scrapbook, c. 1930)

A sense of unease about people of mixed-race descent suffuses the Port Elizabeth scrapbook and is perhaps most evident in an essay, 'Walking to Work in South Africa'. The author of the essay, likely a GFS member or associate, begins by describing the topography of Port Elizabeth before providing an ethnography of the city, devoting over a page of the three-page essay to the 'wide diversity' of races: the English, 'South African Dutch', 'Natives', Chinese, Malays, Indians, and Coloured people. The author provides the following description of this last category: 'the Coloured People – whom one could almost call tragic. They are of course, descendants of children born to parents one of whom has been White and one Native. Through the years by intermarriage, they have built up practically a separate race of people.'[156] The description of Coloured people as 'tragic' suggests a perception not only that they are a source of shame but that their existence is regrettable and even disastrous to South African society. This disquiet reflects deeper anxieties about the liminal position of mixed-race children and their inclusion within the GFS, a topic discussed at greater length in the fourth chapter.

In creating and circulating these scrapbooks, girls appropriated and reproduced discourses about race and consequently contributed to the construction and maintenance of a racialised empire. These scrapbooks cannot be taken as neutral or authentic representations of colonial life and instead functioned as an apparatus of the settler colonial state.[157] As Homi Bhabha cautions, 'the image is only ever an *appurtenance* to authority and identity; it must never be read mimetically as the appearance of reality'.[158] Understanding the scrapbooks and specifically the photographs within them requires looking beyond the surface and disentangling the layers of meaning embedded within them. The scrapbooks presented how the GFS wished for it – and colonial societies more broadly – to be seen: as civilised, modern, and white where African and Aboriginal peoples were separate, carefully controlled, and dispensable.[159] Through these books, the GFS could reaffirm its identity as a beacon of whiteness and purity and the success of the settler colonial project.

## 'Not very suitable': assessing questions of production and reception

One key challenge in researching the history of childhood is judging the extent to which child-produced sources are mediated by adults. Given the limited information in the archives about the process of making these scrapbooks, it is difficult to assess the degree to which adults intervened in scrapbooks' production, but it is clear that they were a collaborative project, involving both adult associates and girl members and candidates, who wrote essays and made drawings for the books. The scrapbooks show how the GFS, like other youth organisations, including the Camp Fire Girls, acted as 'hybrid cultures' created and fashioned by both adults and girls and the struggle between them.[160] Even though adults were involved in their creation, scrapbooks nevertheless acted as a rare forum where girls could share their perspectives and experiences, act as experts about colonial life, and instruct others about colonial history and geography. They also provide insights into how girls viewed the empire and their place in it. What is particularly significant about the scrapbooks is that they are sources produced not only by girls but for an audience of girls, something made clear by salutations in the essays, like 'Dear Sister Candidates Overseas'. Following their completion, scrapbooks were sent to other parts of the empire and circulated among various GFS branches. The scrapbook from Port Elizabeth circulated among fourteen branches mainly located around the Cheshire area of England, while the one from West Australia was sent to London.[161] The circulation of the scrapbooks to England demonstrates how the GFS served as a mode for systems of knowledge about race to circulate in the wider empire.

Like scrapbooks, newsletters were circulated and read by girls throughout the empire. Subscription numbers show that newsletters were sent to every region where the GFS had branches. In addition to subscription numbers, sections in the newsletters like 'Our Imperial Mail-bag' and 'Correspondence', which feature letters by girls, also reflect a geographically broad readership. Reports from branches in different parts of the empire about girls requesting more copies of newsletters also attest to the popularity of the newsletters among members.[162] Yet there are indications that girls were not entirely happy with the content of the newsletters. Associates from colonial branches wrote to the GFS Central Council in London requesting that more news from overseas be included in the newsletters.[163] For example, a representative from West Australia informed the GFS Imperial and Overseas Committee in 1925 that 'what was suitable for girls at home had very little interest for girls in the Dominions. In West Australia, the complaint often heard was that the Magazine was "too English"'.[164] Similar criticisms came from India. In 1931, Vera Westmacott, the president of the GFS Diocesan Council in Calcutta, described how '[t]he literature does not appeal out here'.[165] Instead of making readers feel as if they were a part of an 'international sisterhood', the Anglocentrism of the newsletters exacerbated feelings that the GFS was out of touch with girls' lives in regions like India and Australia. Yet the Imperial and Overseas Committee rejected requests for the inclusion of more information about overseas branches, arguing that there was not enough general interest in the events of these branches.[166] Similar critiques about the suitability – or the lack thereof – also emerged of GFS pageants and plays. For instance, the GFS in South Africa criticised plays sent to it to promote the organisation, finding them 'not very suitable for S. Africa'.[167] As examined more in Chapter 5, this inability to understand and adapt to girls' lives in different parts of the empire would contribute to the organisation's decline in the interwar years.

The question of how girls interpreted and understood the pageants and plays, scrapbooks, and stories in the newsletters is difficult to ascertain. Did they shape girls' views of the empire and perhaps even encourage them to emigrate, as GFS organisers had hoped? Or did girls view the photographs, watch the pageants and plays, and read the essays and articles and find the descriptions of colonial life unappealing? The archives provide only glimpses into girls' reactions. For instance, when members of the North Adelaide branch in Australia performed *The Wonderful Wood: A Short Play for G.F.S. Candidates* in 1916, they reported 'the play brought in all the different privileges and benefits of the G.F.S. It helped us, too, because in learning the parts we realised what it means to become a Member.'[168] This response indicates that the play served as an effective medium of propaganda, as the GFS intended, yet such reactions must be interpreted with circumspection, since the GFS sought to emphasise the success of these efforts. Other evidence suggests girls did not always interpret these cultural forms in the way that associates hoped. For instance, a 1935 booklet published by the GFS mentions how members in Bradford were fascinated by life in Australia after receiving a scrapbook from Queensland. They reported: 'The one we received had photos of G.F.S. Members in all sorts of unexpected happenings. Some were on horseback, some bathing in shark-infested seas; those from Thursday Island were very unusual and interesting. There were pictures, too, of weird birds and animals and beautifully pressed flowers.'[169] This reaction indicates that the scrapbooks succeeded in presenting an interesting view of colonial life but one that was exotic, unfamiliar, and not necessarily enticing to girls in England. Even if the archives contained more evidence of girls' reactions, each girl who viewed the scrapbooks, watched the plays and pageants, and read the newsletters understood them and was influenced by them in different ways. Girls also did not always partake in activities in the ways that the GFS intended, which is illustrated by the problems with the GFS's 'penfriend' programme.[170]

## 'Arresting the progress of G.F.S. work': the problems with 'penfriend' programmes

Like its other imperial activities, the GFS's 'penfriend' programmes sought to educate members about the empire and connect girls living in different parts of the empire.[171] According to a GFS pamphlet about the programme, it had 'not only a friendly, but an educational value in widening the interests of Members, and uniting them with other girls all the world over'.[172] The establishment of these personal connections was seen as the foundation of 'friendship and understanding between countries' and a way 'to bring our G.F.S. Empire still closer', reaffirming notions of the GFS as a 'very large family'.[173] Participants in the programme exchanged letters along with magazines, leaflets, and small gifts, like vases.[174] The GFS reported great enthusiasm for this programme among its members and candidates.[175] When candidates at the Mayo School in India wanted to exchange letters with English girls, they wrote: 'If there are any little girls whose lives we might help to brighten in *any* way, it would be a great pleasure to us'.[176] After providing a brief description of India, they continued: 'We wish very much it were in our power to share all these delights with others; but we can do something, we know, towards sending sunshine abroad'.[177] Similarly, when a branch in Port Elizabeth was linked with the English town of Henley-on-Thames, the members in Port Elizabeth wrote of their excitement in receiving 'many interesting letters from these friends overseas' and promised that they 'shall succeed in interesting them in our own doings in sunny South Africa'.[178] This enthusiasm suggests that – in line with organisers' wishes – girls had a strong interest in not only relating details of their own lives but also gaining a greater understanding of girls' lives in other parts of the empire.

The GFS viewed these programmes as important to its migration endeavours. For girls living in England, GFS organisers hoped that the penfriend programme would generate interest and knowledge in the empire that would then translate into them emigrating to the colonies. The GFS was not alone in its use of such programmes and its appreciation of the effects correspondence could have. For instance, in 1895 E. M. Hance, the clerk of the Liverpool School Board, addressed concerns about how to encourage reluctant children to emigrate: 'there was some difficulty in getting children to go but since then children have written back favourably to their old school fellows. A constant influx of such letters has caused emigration to be looked forward to by the children.'[179] Hance's response indicates how correspondence from peers acted as a powerful and effective mode of propaganda for emigration. Such programmes were mutually beneficial, also aiding recent migrants. GFS organisers hoped the exchange of letters and small gifts would ease both the transition and hardships of life in the colonies for members who had recently migrated. Harriet Wemyss, the head of the GFS branch in Gloucestershire, noted this benefit of the exchange: 'letters are so valuable when far away and any news from familiar places so precious, and these memories will help to keep them true to their Church and to the best traditions of the old country, and so help to elevate and make beautiful their lives that they will be good citizens of the new country which will be their home'.[180] Exchanges of letters were seen as having an elevating influence by reminding girls of their English identity and counteracting the potentially contaminating effects of the colonial environment.[181]

However, as the GFS discovered, the problem with penfriend programmes is that girls did not always adhere to prescribed scripts. For example, in 1911, Miss Whitley, who oversaw one of the GFS branches in South Africa, wrote to the GFS in London and 'spoke strongly on the inadvisability of correspondence between Members at home and in S. Africa'.[182] Whitley 'found that Correspondence with English Members ... was not always appreciated by Members in the Colonies and had often in fact been the cause of arresting the progress of G.F.S. work'.[183] She particularly highlighted how letters from England increased the frustration felt by emigrant domestic servants, since '[d]omestic service in S. Africa, being almost entirely performed by coloured people, is looked upon in a different light to what it is at home'.[184] Although the GFS envisioned penfriend programmes as supporting their emigration efforts, Whitley's comments demonstrate how the letters actually highlighted the differential notions of domestic service in England and regions like southern Africa and the difficulties of colonial life, a topic returned to in the next chapter. As the problems with the penfriend programme illustrate, GFS efforts could actually have the opposite effect that organisers intended.

## Conclusion

The pervasiveness of the empire across the different cultural forms described in this chapter indicates its centrality to the GFS and girls' lives in this period. Far from being innocuous and apolitical forms of entertainment, pageants and plays, scrapbooks, and newsletters served myriad purposes. Capitalising on their imaginative and emotive power, the GFS used these cultural productions and activities as vehicles of propaganda and educational tools for the organisation and empire, and they became instrumental in the creation and circulation of knowledge about the empire, girlhood, and whiteness. The presentation of the empire in newsletters, scrapbooks, and pageants and plays propagated myths central to British colonialism, including colonisation as a civilising and necessary process, white superiority, and the settler colonies as *terra nullius*.

These cultural forms also reveal paradoxes and contradictions within the GFS's imperial ideology, a theme that the following chapters continue to explore. The GFS encouraged girls, specifically white girls, to be empire builders who needed to create 'pure' white homes and settler societies abroad, but this propaganda backfired at times and the idealised view it presented came into conflict with the realities of colonial life, a theme returned to in the next chapter. Images within GFS newsletters and scrapbooks of a unified, harmonious 'very large family' masked widening divisions within the organisation. The GFS encouraged its members to think of themselves as belonging to an 'Imperial sisterhood', yet it is evident from the privileging of English girls in newsletters, plays and pageants, and scrapbooks and the erasure of girls and women of colour, specifically in scrapbooks, that not all were welcome or equal members in this sisterhood.[185] Pageants and plays, newsletters, scrapbooks, and other imperial education efforts reinforced the notion that England was the head of the imperial family and the colonies and dominions were subordinate. This bias did not go unnoticed by candidates and members, as evidenced by their frustration at the Anglocentric nature of the periodicals.[186] Such tension would portend larger fractures within the GFS 'family'. As the fourth and fifth chapters explore, although the GFS intended for branches in the colonies and dominions to replicate the organisation in England, the unique circumstances of different regions created unanticipated challenges, and issues over race created fractures within the GFS community and complicated the GFS's apparent commitment to 'the care of the girlhood of the empire'.[187]

## Notes

1. 'The Banner over Us Is Love', *Our Letter: For G.F.S. Candidates all over the World* (March 1913), pp. 2–3.
2. Edith Brunette, 'Stories of Brave Girls I. Maids of War', *Our Letter: For G.F.S. Candidates all over the World* (Easter 1907), p. 3.
3. For more on this point, see Bill Schwarz, *The White Man's World (Memories of Empire)* (Oxford: Oxford University Press, 2012), p. 16.
4. Agnes L. Money, *History of the Girls' Friendly Society*, 2nd ed. (London: Wells, Garner, Darton & Co., Ltd, 1911), p. 99.
5. Women's Library, London (hereafter WL), 5GFS/02/223, letter from the Diocesan Imperial Correspondent to Sir, 1924. WL, 5GFS/02/225, GFS Empire Education Committee, 'Conference at the Mansion House on Empire Citizenship for Girls', c. 1927–31, p. 1. WL, 5GFS/02/223, letter to Mrs Orde, June 1927, p. 1.
6. WL, 5GFS/01/098, 'Minutes of a Meeting of the Imperial and Overseas Committee held at Townsend House, on Monday, June 16th 1930 at 11.30 a.m.', pp. 72–3. See also letter from the Diocesan Imperial Correspondent to Sir; WL, 5GFS/01/006, Margaret Antrim, 'Minutes of a Meeting of the Employment and Migration Committee Held at Townsend House, Greycoat

Place, Westminster, S.W. 1 on Friday, November 7th 1930 at 11:30 a.m.', pp. 108–9; and Mary Heath-Stubbs, *Friendship's Highway: Being the History of the Girls' Friendly Society, 1875–1935* (London: G.F.S. Central Office, 1935), p. 74.

7 Money, *History of the Girls' Friendly Society*, pp. 95, 139. WL, 5GFS/02/246, Overseas – New Zealand 'Annual Rally' article clipping, c. 1933–39.

8 WL, 5GFS/01/098, W. Searth, 'Report on GFS Empire Education Committee', in 'Minutes of a Meeting of the Imperial & Overseas Committee held at Townsend House, Greycoat Place SW on Monday, March 19th 1928 at 2.30 p.m.', p. 45.

9 'Candidates' Central Examination', *Our Letter: For G.F.S. Candidates all over the World* (Easter 1907), p. 4.

10 'Candidates' Central Examination', p. 4.

11 'Home Reports', *The Empire and Beyond*, Occasional Leaflet IX (1915), p. 11. 'Some Ideas and a Little News', *The Girls' Quarterly: A Paper for Workers in the Girls' Friendly Society*, 9 (January 1897), p. 119. WL, 5GFS/01/098, 'Report on GFS Empire Education Committee', 'Minutes of a Meeting of the Imperial & Overseas Committee held on Monday October 22nd 1928 at Townsend House at 2.30 p.m.', p. 50. Edith Marion Welch, 'Vision and Mission Slides', *The Empire and Beyond*, Occasional Leaflet XII (Anniversary Week 1916), p. 14. 'What Candidates Are Doing', *Our Letter: For G.F.S. Candidates All over the World* (Christmas 1909), p. 8.

12 WL, 5GFS/01/107, 'Minutes of a Meeting of the Committee of Council for the G.F.S. in India, Ceylon, and the Far East held at the GFS Central Office, 39 Victoria Street, S.W., on Friday November 8th, 1918 at 2.30 p.m.', p. 185.

13 'What Candidates Are Doing', *Our Letter: For G.F.S. Candidates all over the World* (September 1917), p. 3.

14 'Home Reports', *The Empire and Beyond*, Occasional Leaflet VIII (1915), p. 13.

15 'Home Reports', *The Empire and Beyond*, Occasional Leaflet XVIII (Easter 1918), pp. 10–12. 'What Candidates Are Doing', *Our Letter: For G.F.S. Candidates all over the World* (Christmas 1909), p. 8.

16 'Home Reports. Province of Canterbury', *The Empire and Beyond*, Occasional Leaflet XXI (Spring 1919), p. 7.

17 M. F., 'On, to the City of God', *The Empire and Beyond*, Occasional Leaflet XXIII (Winter 1919), p. 6.

18 Heath-Stubbs, *Friendship's Highway*, pp. 50, 56. Editor [Constance M. Thompson], 'As Others See Us', *The Empire and Beyond*, Occasional Leaflet VII (1914), pp. 11–16. The Editor [Constance M. Thompson], 'My Dear Candidates', *Our Letter: For G.F.S. Candidates all over the World* (June 1918), p. 2. For more on reading unions, see Susann Liebich, 'Connected Readers: Reading Practices and Communities across the British Empire, c. 1890–1930' (PhD thesis, Victoria University of Wellington, 2012), especially pp. 171 and 191.

19 On the British flag and St George, see '"Our Letter" Readers' Union', *Our Letter: For G.F.S. Candidates all over the World* (December 1919), p. 2. On the Siege of Lucknow and the Spanish Armada, see 'Test Scheme for Candidates', *Our Letter: For G.F.S. Candidates all over the World* (April 1920), p. 4.
20 'Overseas Reports', *The Empire and Beyond*, Occasional Leaflet XVII (Epiphany 1918), p. 9.
21 'The Experiences of an Empire Correspondent', *The Empire and Beyond*, Occasional Leaflet III (1913), p. 11. Emphasis in the original.
22 Letter to Mrs Orde, June 1927, pp. 1–2.
23 'Home Reports', *The Empire and Beyond*, Occasional Leaflet V (1914), p. 11. 'Home Reports', *The Empire and Beyond*, Occasional Leaflet IX (1915), p. 10. On lantern lectures, see 'Overseas Reports. Canada', *The Empire and Beyond*, Occasional Leaflet VIII (1915), p. 11. 'Overseas Reports. China', *The Empire and Beyond*, Occasional Leaflet VI (1914), p. 13.
24 'Home Reports', *The Empire and Beyond*, Occasional Leaflet IX (1915), p. 14. For a similar report by a Norwich branch, see 'Home Reports. Province of Canterbury', p. 8.
25 'The Experiences of an Empire Correspondent', pp. 10–11.
26 C. M. Spender, 'The G.F.S. Day: Festival of Empire', *Friendly Leaves*, 36:421 (September 1911), p. 307.
27 K. M. T. [Kathleen M. Townsend], 'The G.F.S. Imperial Conference', *The Empire and Beyond*, Occasional Leaflet IX (1915), p. 6.
28 Richard Sorabji, *Opening Doors: The Untold Story of Cornelia Sorabji, Reformer, Lawyer and Champion of Women's Rights in India* (Delhi: Penguin Books India, 2010), p. 14.
29 'One and All', *The Empire and Beyond*, Occasional Leaflet XXII (Summer 1919), p. 7. For more on the Sorabjis, see Tim Allender, *Learning Femininity in Colonial India, 1820–1932* (Manchester: Manchester University Press, 2016), pp. 494–6.
30 For more on this point, see Antoinette Burton, *Burdens of History: British Feminists, Indian Women, and Imperial Culture, 1865–1915* (Chapel Hill: University of North Caroline Press, 1994).
31 C. M. Thompson, 'Editor's Letters', *Our Letter: For G.F.S. Candidates all over the World* (March 1917), p. 2. 'Home Reports', *The Empire and Beyond*, Occasional Leaflet XXII (Summer 1919), p. 9.
32 'The Empire and Beyond', *The Empire and Beyond*, Occasional Leaflet II (1913), p. 1. WL, 5GFS/01/105, 'Report of a Conference between the Chairwoman of the Imperial Committee, the Central Representatives, the Chairwoman of the Publications Committee and the Head of the Literature Department, held at the G.F.S. Central Office on Monday, 1st May 1916 at 2.15 p.m.', p. 36.
33 'What Candidates Are Doing', *Our Letter: For G.F.S. Candidates all over the World* (September 1906), p. 3.
34 'Notes on Current Events', *The Girls' Quarterly: A Paper for Workers in the Girls' Friendly Society*, 9 (January 1897), p. 118. 'Notes on Current Events',

*The Girls' Quarterly: A Paper for Workers in the Girls' Friendly Society*, 14 (April 1898), p. 46.
35 For more on this point, see Helen Sunderland, '"Politics for Girls": Representations of Political Girlhood in the *Girls' Own Paper* and the *Girl's Realm*', *Victorian Periodicals Review*, 52:1 (Spring 2019), 1–26, especially p. 2; and Natalie Coulter and Kristine Moruzi, 'Woke Girls: From *The Girl's Realm* to *Teen Vogue*', *Feminist Media Studies*, 22:4 (2020), 765–79, especially p. 766.
36 'Friendly Notes', *Friendly Leaves*, 36:413 (January 1911), p. 33.
37 'Our Colonies. II. – New Zealand', *Friendly Leaves*, 36:415 (March 1911), p. 105.
38 'Our Colonies. II. – New Zealand', p. 107.
39 Constance Spender, 'Our Colonies. I. – Canada', *Friendly Leaves*, 36:413 (January 1911), p. 44.
40 Constance M. Spender, 'Our Colonies. III. – Australia', *Friendly Leaves*, 36:417 (May 1911), p. 175.
41 Spender, 'Our Colonies. III. – Australia', p. 173. The South Africa article also contained information about the different regions. See C. M. Spender, 'Our Colonies. IV. – South Africa', *Friendly Leaves*, 36:419 (July 1911), p. 239.
42 See, for instance, Hon. Mrs Joyce, 'Emigration News', *Friendly Leaves*, 36:423 (November 1911), p. 375.
43 Spender, 'Our Colonies. I. – Canada', p. 47.
44 Robert Francis Irvine, Oscar Thorwald, and Johan Alpers, *The Progress of New Zealand in the Century* (London: W. & R. Chambers, Limited, 1902), p. 421. On New Zealand's identity as the 'best British', see especially James Belich's *Paradise Reforged: A History of the New Zealanders from the 1880's to the Year 2000* (Honolulu: University of Hawaii Press, 2002). See also David Thomson, 'Marriage and Family on the Colonial Frontier', in Tony Ballantyne and Brian Moloughney (eds), *Disputed Histories: Imagining New Zealand's Past* (Dunedin: Otago University Press, 2006), p. 140; Barbara Brookes, Annabel Cooper, and Robin Law, 'Situating Gender', in Barbara Brookes, Annabel Cooper, and Robin Law (eds), *Sites of Gender: Women, Men and Modernity in Southern Dunedin, 1890–1939* (Auckland: Auckland University Press, 2003), p. 3; Barbara Brookes, 'Gender, Work and Fears of a "Hybrid Race" in 1920s New Zealand', *Gender & History*, 19:3 (November 2007), 514; and Jock Philips and Terry Hearn, *Settlers: New Zealand Immigrants from England Ireland and Scotland 1800–1945*, AUP Studies in Cultural and Social History Series (Auckland: Auckland University Press, 2008).
45 'Our Colonies. II. – New Zealand', p. 105.
46 'Our Colonies. II. – New Zealand', p. 105.
47 Spender, 'Our Colonies. IV. – South Africa', p. 237.
48 Spender, 'Our Colonies. IV. – South Africa', p. 238.
49 Spender, 'Our Colonies. IV. – South Africa', p. 238.
50 Spender, 'Our Colonies. IV. – South Africa', p. 236.

51 Lorenzo Veracini, *Settler Colonialism: A Theoretical Overview* (Basingstoke: Palgrave Macmillan, 2010), especially the introduction and chapter on 'Sovereignty'; and Lorenzo Veracini, *Colonialism: A Global History* (New York: Routledge, 2023), pp. 2–3.
52 Spender, 'Our Colonies. III. – Australia', p. 175.
53 For more on these points, see Leila Ahmed, *Women and Gender in Islam: Historical Roots of a Modern Debate* (New Haven: Yale University Press, 1992); and Burton, *Burdens of History*.
54 'Our Colonies. II. – New Zealand', p. 107.
55 Edward Tregear, *The Aryan Maori* (Wellington: G. Didsbury, 1885).
56 For more on this point, see Belich, *Paradise Reforged*, pp. 229 and 545; James Belich, *New Zealand Wars and the Victorian Interpretation of Racial Conflict* (Auckland: Penguin, 1986), especially 'The Wars and the Pattern of New Zealand Race Relations', pp. 298–310; Miles Fairburn, *The Ideal Society and Its Enemies: The Foundations of Modern New Zealand Society, 1850–1900* (Auckland: Auckland University Press, 1989); Tony Ballantyne, *Orientalism and Race: Aryanism and the British Empire* (London: Palgrave, 2001); and Colin McGeorge, 'Race, Empire, and the Maori in the New Zealand Primary School Curriculum 1880–1940', in J. A. Mangan (ed.), *The Imperial Curriculum* (London: Routledge, 2012), pp. 65–78.
57 C. M. Spender, 'Our Colonies. V. – Crown Colonies', *Friendly Leaves*, 36:421 (September 1911), p. 299.
58 Spender, 'Our Colonies. V. – Crown Colonies', p. 299.
59 Spender, 'Our Colonies. V. – Crown Colonies', p. 301.
60 'Our Colonies. VI. – Crown Colonies (Continued)', *Friendly Leaves*, 36:423 (November 1911), p. 363. For more about these concerns, see David Pomfret, 'Tropical Childhoods: Health, Hygiene and Nature', chapter 2 in *Youth and Empire: Trans-Colonial Childhoods in British and French Asia* (Redwood City: Stanford University Press, 2015), pp. 22–53.
61 'A Spring Greeting', *Our Letter: For G.F.S. Candidates all over the World* (March 1905), p. 1. See also Ethel S. Thompson, 'Correspondence: A Letter from A G.F.S. Candidate in Canada', *Our Letter: For G.F.S. Candidates all over the World* (Summer 1904), p. 4.
62 'G.F.S. Overseas.', *Our Letter: For G.F.S. Candidates all over the World* (June 1918), p. 2.
63 'Candidates in New Zealand', *Our Letter: For G.F.S. Candidates all over the World* (September 1904), p. 3.
64 An Associate, 'A Friendly Letter to all Candidates Everywhere', *Our Letter: For G.F.S. Candidates all over the World* (June 1906), p. 1. 'What Candidates are Doing', *Our Letter: For G.F.S. Candidates all over the World* (September 1906), p. 3.
65 Benedict Anderson, *Imagined Communities: Reflections on the Origin and Spread of Nationalism*, revised ed. (New York: Verso, 2006).
66 Kristine Moruzi, '"I am content with Canada": Canadian Girls at the Turn of the Twentieth Century', *Jeunesse: Young People, Texts, Cultures*, 4 (2012), 119.

67 Moruzi, 'I am content with Canada', 123.
68 Kathleen M. Townsend, 'Dear Children', *Our Letter: For G.F.S. Candidates all over the World* (June 1914), p. 1.
69 'News from the Mission Field', *The Girls' Quarterly: A Paper for Workers in the Girls' Friendly Society*, 23 (July 1900), p. 70. 'Our Own G.F.S. Missionary in India', *Our Letter: For G.F.S. Candidates all over the World* (Christmas 1909), p. 3.
70 M. E. R., 'Our Picture. "The Hope of the World"', *Our Letter: For G.F.S. Candidates all over the World* (September 1917), p. 2.
71 A. E. M. Anderson-Morshead, 'The Land of the Rising Sun', *The Girls' Quarterly: A Paper for Workers in the Girls' Friendly Society*, 11 (July 1897), p. 158.
72 This observation follows what Partha Chatterjee describes as the colonial 'rule of difference' in 'The Colonial State', in *The Nation and Its Fragments: Colonial and Postcolonial Histories* (Princeton: Princeton University Press, 1993), especially pp. 14–34. On this point, see also Veracini, *Colonialism*, pp. 2–3.
73 'Topsy Turvy Land', *Our Letter: For G.F.S. Candidates all over the World* (March 1906), p. 4.
74 Kathleen M. Townsend, 'A Letter from India', *Our Letter: For G.F.S. Candidates all over the World* (Summer 1904), p. 2.
75 'What Candidates Are Doing', *Our Letter: For G.F.S. Candidates all over the World* (September 1906), p. 3.
76 'News from the Mission Field', *The Girls' Quarterly: A Paper for Workers in the Girls' Friendly Society*, 27 (July 1901), p. 166.
77 'From A G.F.S. Letter-Bag', *The Empire and Beyond*, Occasional Leaflet XVIII (Easter 1918), p. 14.
78 For more on how the concept of childhood served as a metaphor for progress and modernity, see Ashis Nandy, 'Reconstructing Childhood: A Critique of the Ideology of Adulthood', in *Traditions, Tyranny, and Utopias: Essays in the Politics of Awareness* (London: Oxford University Press, 1987), pp. 56–76.
79 Ahmed, *Women and Gender in Islam*, p. 161. See also Burton, *Burdens of History*.
80 Chatterjee, *The Nation and Its Fragments*, p. 10.
81 Veracini, *Settler Colonialism*, pp. 4, 3. See also Morgan Brie Johnson, 'Settler Colonial Structures of Domestication: British Home Children in Canada', *Genealogy*, 5:3 (2021), 78; and Adele Perry, *On the Edge of Empire: Gender, Race, and the Making of British Columbia, 1849–1871* (Toronto: University of Toronto Press, 2001).
82 For more on pageants, see Angela Bartie, Linda Fleming, Mark Freeman, Alexander Hutton, and Paul Readman, 'Introduction', in Angela Bartie, Linda Fleming, Mark Freeman, Alexander Hutton, and Paul Readman (eds), *Restaging the Past: Historical Pageants, Culture and Society in Modern Britain* (London: UCL Press, 2020), p. 1; and Angela Bartie, Linda Fleming, Mark Freeman, Tom Hulme, Paul Readman, and Charlotte Tupman, 'The Redress

of the Past: Historical Pageants in Twentieth-Century England', *International Journal of Research on History Didactics, History Education, and History Culture*, 37 (2016), 19–35.
83 See Kristine Alexander's discussion of historical pageantry in chapter 5 of *Guiding Modern Girls: Girlhood, Empire, and Internationalism in the 1920s and 1930s* (Vancouver: UBC Press, 2017).
84 WL, 5GFS/01/107, Kathleen M. Townsend, 'Minutes of a Meeting of the Committee of Council for the G.F.S. in India, Ceylon, and the Far East Held at the GFS Central Office, 39 Victoria Street, S.W., on Friday June 7th, 1918 at 2.45 p.m.', p. 181. 'G.F.S. Overseas', *Our Letter: For G.F.S. Candidates all over the World* (June 1918), p. 3. See also the discussion of pageants in India in WL, 5GFS/01/107, 'Minutes of a Meeting of the Committee of Council for the G.F.S. in India, Ceylon, and the Far East Held at the GFS Central Office, 39, Victoria St. S.W. 1 on June 4, 1920 at 2.45 p.m.', p. 208.
85 'Home Reports', *The Empire and Beyond*, Occasional Leaflet VI (1914), pp. 7–9.
86 'Home Reports', *The Empire and Beyond*, Occasional Leaflet VII (1914), p. 13.
87 'Home Reports', *The Empire and Beyond*, Occasional Leaflet IX (1915), p. 12.
88 WL, 5GFS/05/018, Edith Murray, *The G.F.S. in Picture and Pageant* (London, G.F.S. Central Office, [c. 1910]), p. 16.
89 WL, 5GFS/04/128, 'Missionary Work', *A Jubilee Chronicle for Overseas* (1935), p. 20.
90 'What Candidates Are Doing', *Our Letter: For G.F.S. Candidates all over the World* (Christmas 1909), p. 8.
91 Bartie, Fleming, Freeman, Hutton, and Readman, 'Introduction', p. 4.
92 Zoë Thomas, 'Historical Pageants, Citizenship and the Performance of Women's History before Second-Wave Feminism', in Angela Bartie, Linda Fleming, Mark Freeman, Alexander Hutton, and Paul Readman (eds), *Restaging the Past: Historical Pageants, Culture and Society in Modern Britain* (London: UCL Press, 2020), p. 110.
93 For more on the concept of a 'usable past', see Van Wyck Brooks, 'On Creating a Usable Past', *The Dial* (11 April 1918), 337–41.
94 Heath-Stubbs, *Friendship's Highway*, p. 110.
95 Heath-Stubbs, *Friendship's Highway*, p. 111.
96 Heath-Stubbs, *Friendship's Highway*, p. 134. For more details on this pageant, see Angela Bartie, Linda Fleming, Mark Freeman, Tom Hulme, Alex Hutton, and Paul Readman, 'The Quest', *The Redress of the Past: Historical Pageants in Britain*, https://historicalpageants.ac.uk/pageants/1072/, accessed 1 December 2022. WL, 5GFS/04/127, '"The Quest." St. David's Diocese', *G.F.S. Magazine*, January 1931, photo from Block Book VII, 1926–31.
97 On childhood and futurity, see Laura Ishiguro, '"Growing up and Grown up […] in Our Future City": Children and the Aspirational Politics of Settler Futurity in Colonial British Columbia', *BC Studies: The British Columbian Quarterly*, 190 (2016), 15–37.

98 WL, 5GFS/04/127, 'Stoney Stanton Members in a Missionary Pageant', November 1928, photo from Block Book VII, 1926–31.
 99 Marjorie Garber, *Vested Interests: Cross-dressing and Cultural Anxiety* (New York: Penguin Books, 1993), p. 16. See also Anne McClintock, *Imperial Leather: Race, Gender, and Sexuality in the Colonial Contest* (New York: Routledge, 1995), especially chapter 3 on 'Imperial Leather: Race, Cross-dressing and the Cult of Domesticity'.
100 Murray, *The G.F.S. in Picture and Pageant*, pp. 6–8.
101 WL, 5GFS/05/015, *The Story of the G.F.S.* (London: The G.F.S. Central Office, 1946), pp. 10–11. WL, 5GFS/04/127, 'Wingham Candidates as "Caravaners" in the Isle of Wight Pageant', *Our Letter* (September 1927), photo from Block Book VII, 1926–31.
102 WL, 5GFS/11/003, Skipping display, 1933. The photo was also printed in the *G.F.S. Magazine* in August 1933 with the caption 'The Skipping Display at the Revel. Our Central Presiding Associate is Watching from the Royal Box.' See WL, 5GFS/04/088, Block Book VIII, 1932–36.
103 Murray, *The G.F.S. in Picture and Pageant*, p. 6.
104 Elsie Edith Bowerman, *Stands There a School: Memories of Dame Frances Dove, D.B.E., Founder of Wycombe Abbey School* (High Wycombe: Wycombe Abbey School, 1966), p. 54.
105 Jane Frances Dove, 'Cultivation of the Body', in Dorothea Beale (ed.), *Work and Play in Girls' Schools* (London: Longmans, Greens, & Co., 1901), p. 416.
106 Alexander, *Guiding Modern Girls*, pp. 140, 154, and 159.
107 'What Candidates Are Doing', *Our Letter: For G.F.S. Candidates all over the World* (September 1918), p. 4. Townsend, 'Minutes of a Meeting of the Committee of Council for the G.F.S. in India, Ceylon, and the Far East Held at the GFS Central Office, 39 Victoria Street, S.W., on Friday June 7th, 1918 at 2.45 p.m.', p. 181. 'Home Reports', *The Empire and Beyond*, Occasional Leaflet VII (1914), p. 13.
108 Murray, *The G.F.S. in Picture and Pageant*, pp. 8–9.
109 'Candidates and Missions', *Our Letter: For G.F.S. Candidates all over the World* (Christmas 1910), p. 4. See also 'Our Missionary Corner', *Our Letter: For G.F.S. Candidates all over the World* (Christmas 1911), pp. 3–4.
110 WL, 5GFS/04/086, 'Indian Tableaux at Endon', *G.F.S. Magazine* (September 1923), photo from Block Book, 1922–23. WL, 5GFS/04/127, 'North Indian Tableaux by Rhayader Branch', c. 1929, photo from Block Book VII, 1926–31.
111 For more on this point, see Gayatri Chakravorty Spivak, 'The Rani of Sirmur: An Essay in Reading the Archives', *History and Theory*, 24:3 (1985), 247–72; and Burton, *Burdens of History*.
112 George F. Rehin, 'Blackface Street Minstrels in Victorian London and Its Resorts: Popular Culture and Its Racial Connotations as Revealed in Polite Opinion', *Journal of Popular Culture*, 15:1 (Summer 1981), 20.
113 For more on the history of blackface, see Michael Pickering, *Blackface Minstrelsy in Britain* (New York: Ashgate, 2008); David Taylor '"The

Minstrels Parade"': Blackface Minstrelsy and the Music Hall', chapter 12 in *From Mummers to Madness: A Social History of Popular Music in England, c. 1770s to c. 1970s* (Huddersfield: University of Huddersfield Press, 2021), pp. 197–214; and David Olusoga, *Black and British: A Forgotten History* (London: Macmillan, 2016), p. 271.

114 WL, 5GFS/04/127, 'Cwdandur Branch in "The Lady with the Lamp"', *G.F.S. Magazine* (February 1930), photo from Block Book VII, 1926–31, p. 118. See also WL, 5GFS/04/086, '"A Call from India" at Weybridge', *G.F.S. Magazine* (September 1922), photo from Block Book 1922–24; and WL, 5GFS/04/086, 'Prestatyn Candidates in the Missionary Play "Go Tell"', *Our Letter: For G.F.S. Candidates all over the World* (September 1922), photo from Block Book 1922–24.

115 Homi Bhabha, *The Location of Culture* (New York: Routledge, 1994), p. 86.

116 Other youth organisations, including the Camp Fire Girls, also used blackface. See Jennifer Helgren, '"Wohelo Maidens" and "Gypsy Trails": Racial Mimicry and Camp Fire's Picturesque Girl Citizen', chapter 2 in *The Camp Fire Girls: Gender, Race, and American Girlhood, 1910–1980* (Lincoln: University of Nebraska Press, 2022), especially p. 56.

117 Schwarz, *The White Man's World*, p. 16.

118 Robin Bernstein, *Racial Innocence: Performing American Childhood from Slavery to Civil Rights* (New York: NYU Press, 2011), p. 29.

119 Bernstein, *Racial Innocence*, p. 212

120 'What Candidates Are Doing', *Our Letter: For G.F.S. Candidates all over the World* (Christmas 1909), p. 8.

121 Edith Marion Welch, 'Home Reports', *The Empire and Beyond*, Occasional Leaflet XVI (All Saints 1917), p. 14.

122 Bernstein, *Racial Innocence*, p. 18.

123 WL, 5GFS/02/261, letter from Overseas Secretary to Miss Timewell, 22 November 1932. On encouraging girls to make scrapbooks, see 'What Candidates Can Do', *Our Letter: For G.F.S. Candidates all over the World* (Christmas-tide 1901).

124 See Susan Tucker, Katherine Ott, and Patricia Buckler, 'Introduction', in Susan Tucker, Katherine Ott, and Patricia Buckler (eds), *The Scrapbook in American Life* (Philadelphia: Temple University Press, 2006), pp. 10, 12. On scrapbooks, see also Ellen Gruber Garvey, *Writing with Scissors: American Scrapbooks from the Civil War to the Harlem Renaissance* (Oxford: Oxford University Press, 2012); Susan Tucker, 'Reading and Re-Reading: The Scrapbooks of Girls Growing into Women, 1900–1930', in Anne H. Lundin and Wayne A. Wiegand (eds), *Defining Print Culture for Youth: The Cultural Work of Children's Literature* (Westport: Libraries Unlimited, 2003), pp. 1–26; Clare Pettitt, 'Topos, Taxonomy and Travel in Nineteenth-Century Women's Scrapbooks', in Mary Henes and Brian H. Murray (eds), *Travel Writing, Visual Culture and Form, 1760–1900*, Palgrave Studies in Nineteenth-Century Writing and Culture (Basingstoke: Palgrave Macmillan, 2016), pp. 21–41; and Haley Aaron, 'Spaces of self: Girls' scrapbooks at the Alabama Department

of Archives and History', in Tiffany R. Isselhardt (ed.), *A Girl Can Do: Recognizing and Representing Girlhood* (Wilmington: Vernon Press, 2022), pp. 109–28.
125 Silvan Niedermier, 'Colonial Self-positioning. Approaching the Snapshots of an American Woman in the Philippines (1900–1902)', in Ulrike Lindner and Dörte Lerp (eds), *New Perspectives on the History of Gender and Empire* (New York: Bloomsbury Academic, 2018), pp. 121–2. Kristine Alexander, 'Picturing Girlhood and Empire: The Girl Guide Movement and Photography', in Kristine Moruzi and Michelle J. Smith (eds), *Colonial Girlhood in Literature, Culture and History, 1840–1950*, Palgrave Studies in Nineteenth-Century Writing and Culture (London: Palgrave Macmillan, 2014), p. 200.
126 Alexander, 'Picturing Girlhood and Empire', p. 201.
127 See, for instance, WL, 5GFS/02/222, 'Empire Education Scheme. 1937–8. Seventh Empire Scrap-book Competition'.
128 WL, 5GFS/02/263, letter from Sarah Angus to Miss Parrish, 28 June 1938.
129 WL, 5GFS/01/098, 'Meeting of the Imperial and Overseas Committee of the Girls' Friendly Society held at GFS Headquarters, Townsend House, Greycoat Place, London, S.W. 1, on Thursday, 18 July 1948, at 11.30. am.', p. 236.
130 Letter from Overseas Secretary to Miss Timewell, 22 November 1932.
131 WL, 5GFS/04/128, 'Links and Logbooks', in *A Jubilee Chronicle for Overseas* (1935), p. 14.
132 WL, 5GFS/02/357, letter from Mollie Thomas to 'Dear Sister Candidates Overseas', Perth, in West Australia scrapbook, c. 1930; WL, 5GFS/02/260, 'A Trip By Motor Car to Basutoland', in South Africa scrapbook, c. 1930.
133 WL, 5GFS/02/357, Blanche Neave, 'To a Dear G.F.S. Friend', 27 May 1929, in West Australia scrapbook.
134 WL, 5GFS/02/260, 'These Speak for Themselves. Girls generally *can*.!', in South Africa scrapbook, c. 1930.
135 WL, 5GFS/02/260, 'After service on Ascension Day. 1931', in South Africa scrapbook, c. 1930. For more on the Christian ideals of the GFS, see Vivienne Richmond, '"It Is Not a Society for Human Beings but for Virgins": The Girls' Friendly Society Membership Eligibility Dispute 1875–1936', *Journal of Historical Sociology*, 20:3 (September 2007), 304–27; Brian Harrison, 'For Church, Queen, and Family: The Girls' Friendly Society 1874–1920', *Past and Present*, 61 (November 1972), 107–38; and Julia Bush, 'Edwardian Ladies and the "Race" Dimensions of British Imperialism', *Women's Studies International Forum*, 21:3 (1998), 277–89.
136 WL, 5GFS/02/357, photo of the 'Candidates' Sewing' from 'G.F.S. Bassadean Candidate Class. 1930' page in West Australia scrapbook, c. 1930.
137 On the importance of 'the cult of domesticity' to the empire, see McClintock, *Imperial Leather*, p. 5. Omni Gust discusses how the preservation of ties to Britain provided reassurances for morality in *Unhomely Empire: Whiteness and Belonging, c. 1760–1830* (London: Bloomsbury Academic, 2020), see especially the introduction and chapter 2 on 'Dugald Stewart and the Colour

of Progress'. See also Ishiguro, 'Growing up and Grown up [...] in Our Future City', 26; and Perry, *On the Edge of Empire*.
138 'These Speak for Themselves. Girls generally *can*.!'. WL, 5GFS/02/357, photo of 'Miss Whatley and Junior St. Andrews at picnic' from 'St Andrews Junior Branch, Subiaco' page in West Australia scrapbook, c. 1930.
139 Emigration societies, like Barnardo's, regularly printed images in its annual reports that juxtaposed the squalor of the British cities and the openness and independence of the colonies. See, for instance, 'A Study in Contrast', *For God and Country: Dr. Barnardo's Homes 53rd Annual Report Year 1918* (n.p.).
140 Tracey Banivanua Mar and Penelope Edmonds, 'Introduction: Making Space in Settler Colonies', in Tracey Banivanua Mar and Penelope Edmonds (eds), *Making Settler Colonial Space: Perspectives on Race, Place and Identity* (New York: Palgrave Macmillan, 2010), p. 13.
141 WL, 5GFS/02/260, 'Walking to Work in South Africa', in South Africa scrapbook, c. 1930.
142 WL, 5GFS/02/260, monuments page in South Africa scrapbook, c. 1930.
143 WL, 5GFS/02/357, Mundaring Weir page in West Australia scrapbook, c. 1930.
144 Banivanua Mar and Edmonds, 'Introduction: Making Space in Settler Colonies', p. 6.
145 Banivanua Mar and Edmonds, 'Introduction: Making Space in Settler Colonies', p. 11.
146 Patrick Wolfe, 'Settler Colonialism and the Elimination of the Native', *Journal of Genocide Research*, 8:4 (December 2006), 387. See also Veracini, *Settler Colonialism*.
147 Bush, 'Edwardian Ladies and the "Race" Dimensions of British Imperialism', 285. Wolfe, 'Settler Colonialism and the Elimination of the Native', 396. See also Patrick Wolfe, *Settler Colonialism and the Transformation of Anthropology* (London: Cassell, 1999).
148 For more on this point, see Veracini, *Colonialism*, p. 76.
149 For more on the portrayals of Aboriginal women, see Liz Conor, *Skin Deep: Settler Impressions of Aboriginal Women* (Crawley: UWA Publishing, 2016).
150 WL, 5GFS/02/357, photograph of '"Armless" Ned', in West Australia scrapbook, c. 1930.
151 WL, 5GFS/02/357, 'A young cricketer', 'A boxing match', 'Camp men leaving the Church after Service', and 'Single girls waiting for their tea', in West Australia scrapbook, c. 1930.
152 Keith A. P. Sandiford, *Cricket and the Victorians* (Aldershot: Scolar Press, 1994), p. 145.
153 'A Trip By Motor Car to Basutoland'.
154 WL, 5GFS/02/260, photo from South African farm page in South Africa Scrapbook, c. 1930.
155 WL, 5GFS/02/260, photo from South African countryside page in South Africa scrapbook, c. 1930.

156 'Walking to Work in South Africa'.
157 Elizabeth Siegel, *Galleries of Friendship and Fame: A History of Nineteenth-Century American Photograph Albums* (London: Yale University Press, 2010), pp. 7, 10. See also Tucker, 'Reading and Re-Reading', pp. 2 and 5; and James Ryan, *Picturing Empire: Photography and the Visualization of the British Empire* (Chicago: University of Chicago Press, 1998), pp. 19–20.
158 Bhabha, *Location of Culture*, p. 81. Emphasis in the original.
159 On the dispensability of Indigenous people as an integral part of settler colonialism, see Wolfe, *Settler Colonialism and the Transformation of Anthropology*, p. 163; and Veracini, *Settler Colonialism*, p. 8.
160 Jennifer Helgren, *The Camp Fire Girls: Gender, Race, and American Girlhood, 1910–1980* (Lincoln: University of Nebraska Press, 2022), p. 6; and Mischa Honeck, *Our Frontier Is the World: The Boy Scouts in the Age of America Ascendancy*, The United States in the World Series (Ithaca: Cornell University Press, 2018), p. 14.
161 WL, 5GFS/02/260, log page, in South Africa scrapbook, c. 1930.
162 See, for instance, Mary D. Williams, 'Dear Editor', *Our Letter: For G.F.S. Candidates all over the World* (September 1918), p. 1.
163 WL, 5GFS/01/096, 'Colonial Committee Minutes of a Meeting held on June 15th, 1903', pp. 93–5.
164 WL, 5GFS/01/098, 'Minutes of a Meeting of the Imperial and Overseas Committee held in the National Society's Hall on Monday, November 16th 1925, at 2.30 p.m.', p. 13.
165 WL, 5GFS/02/229, letter from V. Westmacott to Miss Grenside, 26 November 1931. See also WL, 5GFS/02/229, letter from V. Westmacott to Miss Mytton, 3 March 1932.
166 'Minutes of a Meeting of the Imperial and Overseas Committee held in the National Society's Hall on Monday, November 16th 1925, at 2.30 p.m.', p. 13. WL, 5GFS/02/231, letter from Mabel R. Goodrich to Miss Mytton, 20 February 1931.
167 WL, 5GFS/02/262, letter from Fanchette G. Parrish to Madam, 25 May 1938.
168 'Letters from Candidates', *Our Letter: For G.F.S. Candidates all over the World* (June 1916), p. 2.
169 'Links and Logbooks', in *A Jubilee Chronicle for Overseas*, p. 15.
170 Sara L. Schwebel, 'The Limits of Agency for Children's Literature Scholars', *Jeunesse: Young People, Texts, Cultures*, 8:1 (August 2016), 280.
171 WL, 5GFS/02/257, *Linked Branches* (London: G.F.S. Central Office, n.d.).
172 *Linked Branches*, p. 1. On this point, see also WL, 5GFS/02/225, Mrs Orde, 'Speech at the Conference at the Mansion House on Empire Citizenship for Girls', 24 October 1918.
173 'Home Reports', *The Empire and Beyond*, Occasional Leaflet IX (1915), p. 14. WL, 5GFS/01/098, 'Minutes of a Meeting of the Imperial and Overseas Committee (now Council) of the Girls' Friendly Society, Townsend House, Greycoat Place, London, S.W. 1 on Monday 11th October 1945 at 3.0. p.m.', p. 250. On the use of familial terminology, see, for instance, 'G.F.S. Candidates

in India', *Our Letter: For G.F.S. Candidates all over the World* (March 1906), p. 3.
174 Edith Marion Welch, 'The Story of Some G.F.S. "Links"', *The Empire and Beyond*, Occasional Leaflet XV (Trinity 1917), pp. 9–10.
175 Townsend, 'A Letter from India', p. 2.
176 'G.F.S. Candidates in India', p. 3. Emphasis in the original.
177 'G.F.S. Candidates in India', p. 3.
178 WL, 5GFS/02/260, 'St. Paul's G.F.S. Port Elizabeth Junior Branch', in South Africa scrapbook, c. 1930.
179 The National Archives, London, HO 144/495/X42032, 'Emigration of Industrial School Children', 8 February 1895, p. 23.
180 Harriet Wemyss, 'Emigration', *Gloucester Diocesan Report for 1911* (Gloucester: H. Osborne, 1912), p. 23.
181 On the dangers of the climate in colonial regions, see, for instance, Barnardo's, London, A2/52/115, letter from Stuart Barnardo to Thomas Barnardo, 9 November 1902. See also Ann Laura Stoler, *Carnal Knowledge and Imperial Power: Race and the Intimate in Colonial Rule* (Berkeley: University of California Press, 2002); Elizabeth Buettner, *Empire Families: Britons and Late Imperial India* (New York: Oxford University Press, 2004), p. 157; and Pomfret, 'Tropical Childhoods: Health, Hygiene and Nature'.
182 WL, 5GFS/01/102, 'Minutes of a Meeting of the Sectional Committee for S. Africa held at the G.F.S. Central Office, 39 Victoria Street, London S.W. on Wednesday 4 October 1911', p. 58.
183 'Minutes of a Meeting of the Sectional Committee for S. Africa', p. 58.
184 'Minutes of a Meeting of the Sectional Committee for S. Africa', p. 59.
185 A similar tension with the outward message of inclusivity and universality also existed within the Camp Fire Girls. See Helgren, *The Camp Fire Girls*, p. 54 and chapter 3, '"All Prejudices Seem to Disappear": Race, Class, and Immigration in the Camp Fire Girls'.
186 'G.F.S. Overseas.', *Our Letter: For G.F.S. Candidates all over the World* (June 1918), p. 3. 'What Candidates Are Doing', *Our Letter: For G.F.S. Candidates all over the World* (July 1920), p. 4. On girl readers shaping the nature of conversations in periodicals, see Coulter and Moruzi, 'Woke Girls', p. 768.
187 Lambeth Palace Library, Davidson 143, ff. 215, 'Appeal for £20,000 for the Lodges and Homes of Rest of the Girls' Friendly Society', 1907.

# 3

# Class, race, and competing objectives within girls' emigration programmes

In February 1902, Eliza Hobbs and Eliza Cook appeared before a magistrate's court in Bulawayo, Rhodesia (present-day Zimbabwe), charged with infringement of the Masters' and Servants' Ordinance.[1] They had arrived in June 1901 and were contracted to work as servants for the Robinson household for a minimum of two years. However, upon their arrival, Hobbs and Cook found life in Rhodesia laborious, alien, and full of hardships, very different from the 'Great Garden' promised in emigration propaganda.[2] Hobbs wrote to Ellen Joyce and Edith Lyttelton Gell, who had helped arrange her passage, about the difficulties in adjusting to life in Bulawayo and her sense of loneliness and isolation, confiding: 'I cannot tell you how earnestly I have longed for one friend since I have been here'.[3] She described the challenges of 'be[ing] in a strange land penniless' and expressed resentment at the false promises of emigration propaganda.[4] In contrast to finding a land full of sunshine with greater freedom and opportunities, Hobbs related to Joyce: 'I must say I do dislike the little I have seen of S. Africa'. She reiterated this belief in a later letter, concluding: 'I cannot see that servants should come to a strange place to be treated just anyhow'.[5] These frustrations were compounded by Hobbs's difficult relationship with her mistress, Sidonia Robinson, whom Hobbs described as 'dreadful to live with'.[6] Hobbs and Cook ultimately decided to leave their situations eight months after their arrival. They were eventually arrested, and at the trial, Hobbs testified that she would rather 'go to prison' than return to work for Mrs. Robinson, stating that, if she was compelled to stay, it would mean that 'the law seems to uphold tyranny'.[7] She pleaded her case to Joyce, writing 'we have done no crime, only took ourselves out of an unhappy life'.[8] The magistrate ruled in favour of Robinson and fined Hobbs and Cook £2 and ordered them to fulfil their contracts and return to work for the Robinsons. Hobbs lamented the verdict and broader legal system, writing: 'it is not justice, the law seems made for monied people'.[9] Ultimately Robinson released Hobbs from her contract, but, unable to pay for her passage back to

England, Hobbs remained in Bulawayo and found a new position as a housekeeper.[10]

Proponents framed emigration in terms of imperial duty, but as the cases of Eliza Hobbs and Eliza Cook demonstrate, emigrants cared little for these broader imperial objectives and instead viewed emigration in terms of their own interests and as a means to achieving their personal goals. The trials of Eliza Hobbs and Eliza Cook underscore inherent contradictions within emigration ideology and the limitations of imperial ideals. Organisations like the GFS had a clear view of how colonial societies should be structured and the role of girls in them. They heralded girls as empire builders and cultural and racial bulwarks, but within shifting colonial contexts, this role was called into question, and, as the cases of Hobbs and Cook demonstrate, girls did not always adhere to prescribed roles.

The previous chapter examined how whiteness was central to imaginings of settler colonial societies, evidenced in plays, pageants, newsletters, and scrapbooks produced by the GFS; this chapter considers how the GFS tried to make these imaginings a reality through its emigration programmes, which sought to reproduce whiteness abroad through populating and building up settler societies. The chapter begins by outlining the wider contexts in which the GFS's emigration programmes emerged and situates their development in relation to similar emigration schemes for girls that evolved over the course of the nineteenth century. It then traces the different motives that informed the development of the GFS's programmes. Child rescue and emigration organisations argued for the necessity of removing girls from the perceived dangers of poverty and urban life in England to the more wholesome environment of the colonies. Girls also provided valuable labour to colonial societies and were integral in making the empire white by ensuring the construction of English households abroad. Despite these compelling motives and the high demand for emigrants in settler colonies, the GFS and other emigration organisations faced myriad difficulties, which were rooted in broader class and racial anxieties and specifically concerns about the whiteness of emigrants and white prestige in colonial societies. These challenges reveal the competing, rather than complimentary, objectives among emigration organisers, settlers, and girl migrants and fault lines within emigration programmes and the settler colonial project.

## 'To build up our Empire': the development of emigration programmes in the nineteenth century

The earliest child migration programmes in the British empire emerged shortly after the establishment of the first permanent British settlements in North America in the early 1600s. Over the course of the next two centuries, state institutions co-ordinated the forced emigration of children, the majority of whom had criminal convictions, initially to North America and then to the Australian colonies until the transportation of children ended in 1853. In the nineteenth century, emigration efforts received renewed attention and expanded beyond the purview of the state to religious groups and private enterprises, like the Children's Friend Society (CFS). When the CFS emerged in 1830, issues of child labour and child poverty had acquired a new visibility and children became the target of governmental intervention.[11] The Factory Act of 1833, which prohibited the employment of children younger than nine years of age and limited the hours that children between nine and eighteen might work, transformed labour relations in Britain. The Factory Act did not end child labour – and there was not the expectation that it would – but instead limited a specific type of child labour. The Factory Act in particular aimed to mitigate the presence of children on the streets and ensure that children's, and specifically girls', labour remained within the home.

Although programmes in the first half of the nineteenth century, like the CFS, were short-lived and comparatively small-scale endeavours, the 1860s and 1870s marked the proliferation of more centralised, systematic child migration programmes, first by the Ragged School Movement in 1849 and then by Annie Macpherson's Home Children, Dr Barnardo's Homes, William Booth's Salvation Army, and John Middlemore's Children's Emigration Homes and, in the early twentieth century, by the Catholic Emigration Association and Kingsley Fairbridge's Child Emigration Society (later the Fairbridge Society).[12] The quick rate of expansion of child migration during this era is apparent in the programmes of Maria Rye and Thomas Barnardo. Hailed as 'the most successful of the priestesses of emigration', Rye organised the emigration of her first party of 76 children to Canada in 1869, and by 1875, Rye's Home for the Emigration of Destitute Little Girls had arranged for the emigration of six hundred children – 98 per cent of whom were girls – to 'Our Western Home' in Niagara, Canada.[13] By 1895, when Rye effectively retired, her organisation had sent four thousand children to Canada.[14] Thomas Barnardo sent the first party of emigrants to Canada in 1882, and by 1900, approximately 11,100 of 'Barnardo's children' had emigrated to the region.[15] The GFS developed its own migration programmes within this broader context. The GFS established the 'very important' Department for Members Emigrating in 1883 to ensure the safe passage of girls and young women travelling in the empire.[16] The GFS's emigration department assisted in the migration of around 150 girls a year from Britain to different parts of the empire during its first decade.[17] The GFS's emigration programmes operated differently from other programmes, like those of Fairbridge, Barnardo, and Rye. The GFS did not institutionalise workhouse and orphan girls as these other organisations did. Emigration was also not the primary undertaking of the GFS, although it increasingly became a more central facet of the GFS's work.

Emigration societies were not without their critics. High-profile cases of abuse and neglect led the CFS to acquire the nickname the 'white-flesh exportation company', while Barnardo's was accused of 'philanthropic kidnapping'.[18] Perhaps because of these criticisms, the GFS attempted to distinguish itself from these programmes. The 1885 Report of the Department for Members Emigrating made this point clear, declaring: *'the G.F.S. is not an Emigration Society;* it merely provides advice and direction, and the greatest possible supervision and protection, with reception on landing by Associates of its own body'.[19] Another report by the GFS correspondingly reassured wary parents: 'The Society neither wishes nor intends to take the children out of their parents' hands', and their goal was 'only to help parents by giving the little ones another friend who cares for them and is interested in encouraging them to grow up the pure, noble, upright women God meant them to be'.[20] Despite these disavowals, other GFS literature celebrated the emigration work of the GFS. For instance, a memoir about the GFS founder, *Some Memories of Mrs. Townsend*, proclaimed: 'High Commissioners and Emigration Overseas Authorities have acknowledged how real is the debt owed to the Girls' Friendly Society for the type of girls sent over to build up our Empire in the distant spaces of the earth'.[21] Such pronouncements reveal that the GFS's contributions to emigration were widely recognised and a point of pride for the organisation. Moreover, even though the GFS attempted to distance itself from other emigration societies, it employed many of the same techniques and discourses used by child rescue and emigration organisations and collaborated with them. For instance, the GFS established candidate and member groups among children of the Church of England Waif and Stray Society who were going to emigrate to Canada.[22] Dr Barnardo's Homes featured updates about the work of the GFS in its annual reports, indicating the complementarity of their objectives.[23]

Key figures in the GFS also connected its programmes to other emigration societies. GFS associates served on the councils of emigration organisations, including the United British Women's Emigration Association (BWEA) and the South African Colonisation Society (SACS).[24] Most significantly, Ellen Joyce – one of Hobbs's correspondents – instituted and led the Department for Members Emigrating. In developing the GFS's department, Joyce worked with the BWEA and the Society for Promoting Christian Knowledge.[25] Under her leadership, emigration became a cornerstone of the GFS and its imperial work. For the next fifty years, the GFS supported emigration in manifold ways, facilitating the movement of girls through its own department and programmes and through its connection to other societies and, as discussed in the previous chapter, producing propaganda that extolled the necessity and benefits of migration. Joyce's involvement with the GFS's department acted as a springboard for more extensive colonial migration programmes. Joyce built upon her experience with the GFS in the formation of the SACS to encourage female emigration following the conclusion of the South African War.[26] She also applied the lessons from her work with the GFS when she served as the president of the BWEA from 1901 to 1919.[27] Joyce's emigration efforts led to her being honoured as a Commander of the British Empire, and a memorial in Winchester Cathedral paid tribute to her as 'a pioneer / Of protected emigration' and 'her devoted work / On behalf of the women and girls / Of the Empire'.[28]

## A 'splendid safety-valve': emigration as a mechanism of social reform

Why did the GFS become so invested in emigration? The GFS's emigration programmes were rooted in the same anxieties that underlay the foundation of the organisation and formed an extension of its social reform efforts and especially its social purity work, discussed in the first chapter. Like other emigration proponents, Joyce viewed emigration as the antidote to myriad problems at home and abroad, referring to it as a 'splendid safety-valve' and 'the wisest solution for our home troubles'.[29] In a speech at a GFS conference in Winchester in 1883, Joyce detailed how emigration could solve problems in England and specifically the difficulties posed by 'redundant' or 'surplus' women. She contended: 'we have too many women in England for them to get bread to eat honestly' which 'is the strongest, saddest reason for Emigration'.[30] In making this argument, Joyce built upon discourses that had been circulating for decades. In 1862, William Rathbone Greg provided perhaps the most famous formulation of this 'problem' in his pamphlet 'Why Are Women Redundant?' Citing the 1851 census, Greg observed that nearly '1,248,000 women in the prime of life, i.e. between the ages of twenty and forty years ... were unmarried, out of a total number of rather less than 3,000,000'.[31] To correct this demographic discrepancy, Greg recommended sending women to the colonies '[t]o transport the half million from where they are redundant to where they are wanted'.[32] Emigration of women to the colonies was presented as an expedient and mutually beneficial solution.

The problem of surplus women was not just about quantitative gender imbalances. It also reflected broader anxieties about national strength and social stability during a period of rapid industrialisation and sharpening class divisions.³³ For figures like Greg and Joyce, the problem of 'surplus women' was intricately connected to other social troubles, including poverty, criminality, and working-class unrest. Greg predicted that, without the security of marriage, women would be condemned to lives of 'celibacy, struggle and privation'.³⁴ Joyce likewise warned that the lack of a male breadwinner would leave girls and women facing 'endless drudgery and poverty' and force them to resort to crime and prostitution to survive.³⁵ In another speech, this one at the Conference of Women Workers in Birmingham, Joyce argued that the movement of girls and women to the colonies could serve as a remedy to these manifold problems:

> Emigration is an open door of Salvation to many of our girls, an important preventative work. I think so on these grounds: It seems to me that, if you remove temptation, you remove crime; and therefore, by removing the over-population of women from this country, and sending them to a country where the men are largely an excess of the women, you adopt one of the greatest means of checking crime.³⁶

Joyce's speech touches upon many of the key justifications for emigration, including that it rebalanced the population by transporting 'surplus' women from Britain to the colonies, which had a disproportionate number of European men. This transference of population would not only limit poverty and crime but also curb class conflict and the threat of revolution.³⁷ According to Joyce, 'If we would avoid and avert disaster in England, it can only be done by Emigration'.³⁸ The economic depression in the 1870s and rising unemployment and poverty gave a new impetus to these beliefs.³⁹

Emigration also supported the GFS's mission of keeping girls 'pure' and preventing them from 'falling'.⁴⁰ Joyce argued that stemming the tide of pauperism would ensure that girls remained 'unsullied'.⁴¹ As described in Chapter 1, racial purity and white prestige were at the heart of social purity campaigns and rhetoric. Given this broader context, it is not surprising that Joyce touted emigration as a solution to not only social but also imperial and racial problems, a theme that emerges clearly in her leaflet on *Responsibility to the Church with Regard to Emigration*: 'Out of the evils, then, of overpopulation, out of the miseries of over-crowding, out of the ashes of many sorrows, rises, Phoenix-like, a brighter life, out of present evil a far-spreading good … the vigour of our Anglo-Saxon race asserts itself'.⁴² By ensuring girls did not engage in criminal activity, including sex work, emigration could ensure the purity and respectability of the white race.

Like other emigration proponents, Joyce portrayed emigration as a redemptive enterprise. Emigration not only removed children from the negative influences associated with poverty and urban life where crime and vice supposedly ran rampant but also allowed them to grow up in the more wholesome environment of the colonies. In a speech about emigration to the Girls' Friendly Society Imperial Conference in 1912, Joyce elaborated on this point and described how the colonies provided a better place for girls to grow up:

> The GFS has done the very best Imperial work that has been done, in sending women who have been under the highest influences from cultural, refined, religious women; to become the mothers of a race, not dwarfed by poverty; or cramped by pressure as in the Nest and Nursery of the Mother-Land; but free, contented, God-fearing women in the Great Garden of the British Empire.[43]

As reflected in Joyce's speech, changing children's surroundings was seen as having the power to undo any deficiencies associated with poverty. Her emphasis on the importance of environmental change echoed broader discourses that had been employed throughout the nineteenth century by emigration proponents, such as William Booth, the founder of the Salvation Army, who also advocated removing the poor from 'darkest England' to the colonies.[44] Building upon these common tropes, Joyce's speech portrays the colonies as an environment free from the problems and potential contamination of urban life in England and one where girls could more fully realise their potential as wives and mothers.

## 'You cannot have a real home without a woman': the importance of girls' domestic roles in the settler colonies

For Joyce and other proponents, emigration was not just a national reform project but also an imperial one that would benefit all parts of the empire by providing colonies, and especially settler colonies, with needed labourers. As described in the first chapter, Britain faced a 'servant crisis' in the late nineteenth and early twentieth centuries. Despite the continued demand for domestic labour, the supply of servants was declining, as more girls eschewed the drudgery of service for new, better paying, less labour-intensive, and more respectable jobs. This crisis was not confined to Britain and reverberated to the wider empire, creating a constant need for servants and giving a new impetus to emigration programmes. In her speech on the necessity of emigration at the GFS Conference in Winchester, Joyce reported that '[t]he demand for servants is so great, that in one instance 104 ladies had four girls to choose from'.[45] The GFS's Department for Members Emigrating emerged within this context of growing demand for servants in the settler colonies of New Zealand, Australia, Canada, and South Africa.

The 'servant crisis' was not just an issue of economics or a domestic problem but had national and imperial implications and brought racial, class, sexual, and gender anxieties to the fore.[46] In addition to fulfilling important labour needs, the emigration of white servants reinforced racial hierarchies by making colonial societies more white. In their capacities as future wives, homemakers, and mothers, girls helped ensure the futurity of the British empire through the building up white colonial settlements.[47] In advocating for emigration, Joyce emphasised this importance of girl emigrants:

> If England believes herself and the English-speaking people to be the power entrusted with the evangelisation of that vast part of the globe which is entrusted to their jurisdiction, then the duty of fully populating the fringes of the huge Oversea Empire becomes paramount. If, again, it is the exponent of Purity, it must focus its efforts to distribute its daughters under protection where they can find their mates and help make homes pure, happy, and Christian.[48]

Colonial societies required increased settlement and the building up of the colonies physically through the movement of people – 'fully populating the fringes' and 'distribut[ing] its daughters' – as well as a broader social reformation that began with the domestic sphere. Creating 'homes pure, happy, and Christian' was the foundation of a stable white society in the colonies.

Like Joyce, George Parkin – a self-described 'evangelist of Empire' – drew attention to how the home served as a microcosm of the state and society in a speech on 'The Future and Unity of Empire' given at the GFS's Imperial Conference on 23 June 1916.[49] In the speech, he 'explain[ed] how women and girls can influence the history of our British Empire' and their 'great responsibilities'. He specifically heralded the importance of women's domestic and maternal roles in the empire:

> These vast spaces are to be filled up with homes. You cannot have a real home without a woman in it, and it is the quality of woman who goes into their homes which will settle the future of these countries ... The Christian character of women is the greatest security they can have, not only for themselves, but for our nation and race.[50]

As alluded to in Parkin's speech, the building up of white homes and communities through the migration of white women and children became a central facet of colonial policies. While men might have the immediate responsibility of creating the empire's greatness, its success – or failure – ultimately rested with women. As Adele Perry observes in her study of colonial British Columbia, white women were an 'imperial panacea' that could 'turn a small and disorderly white population into a large and prosperous colonial community'.[51] Girls and women, and specifically domestic servants, were cast as cultural bulwarks and guards of the 'interior frontiers' of the home.[52] By helping preserve notions of Englishness and thus fortifying white settlers' professed racial superiority, emigrant servants were fulfilling not just a domestic responsibility but an imperial one.

## 'A country full of poor whites': resistance to emigration programmes

While proponents like Joyce championed emigration as a mutually beneficial solution to problems in both England and the colonies, this view was not shared by all. Emigration programmes by the GFS and other organisations faced criticisms that they deprived English homes of a valuable labour source. In developing her emigration programmes, Maria Rye faced such resistance. In her 1876 pamphlet *The Emigration of Infant Life to Canada,* Rye lamented the common complaint against emigration societies was that the 'enriching of our colonies is the impoverishing of England'.[53] Fifteen year later, she similarly noted that a servant's 'departure was looked upon as tending to thin the ranks of efficient domestics – for whom there is always more than room in the Home Country'.[54] A report produced by the emigration department of the GFS in 1915 indicates the persistence of this criticism, commenting that '[e]migration is looked upon as an uncomfortable way of losing servants'.[55] Emigration organisations attempted to quell such opposition by emphasising the need to consider the good of the entire empire. For instance, Lady Cecilie Cunliffe, who served as president of the GFS Central Council from 1917 to 1931, gave an address at the Conference on Empire Citizenship for Girls and praised the GFS's efforts 'to help with the right distribution of women throughout the British Empire'. She reminded her fellow Britons that '[t]hey must work for the good of every part of the British Empire, not for the good of Britain alone'.[56] While emigration societies often invoked ideas of imperial duty and patriotism to gain support, Cunliffe's comment suggests that in reality personal or local interests still took precedence over broader imperial needs. Emigration was acceptable as long as it did not deprive England of 'good' children and servants.

Resistance to emigration schemes came not only from people in England. Settlers in the colonies aspired to create a community centred on whiteness, but there always lingered questions about whether working-class emigrants truly belonged to this white community.[57] The first chapter discussed doubts over the morality and purity, and by extension whiteness, of the working classes in England, and this questioning of the working classes' whiteness and its durability and authenticity persisted in the colonies. As in England, the working classes remained on the margins of colonial societies. Although emigration organisations heralded girls as empire builders and conduits of 'civilisation', settlers feared that, instead of bringing English values with them, emigrant girls and women would spread the supposed vice and immorality associated with poverty and urban life in England to the colonies and destabilise fragile class and racial hierarchies within colonial societies.[58] Adelaide Ross, one of the founders of the BWEA, succinctly and crudely captured the misgivings surrounding working-class emigrants, writing that 'our national emigration has often ... sent forth the ugliest hussies in creation, to be the mothers – the model mothers – of new empires'.[59] Her perceptions were echoed by the wife of the governor of the Cape Colony, Lady May Hely-Hutchinson, who thought 'it undesirable that the mothers of the next generation should be domestic servants'.[60] While there was a high demand for the labour of servants in the settler colonies, they were not the ideal candidates to populate settler societies.

Women like Ross and Hely-Hutchinson were concerned about the long-term implications of emigration programmes to the creation of ideal colonial societies, but settler women also cast doubt on whether emigration was the best way to solve the more immediate problem of the 'servant crisis'. Lady Mary Ann Broome – who wrote extensively about her experiences living in various parts of the empire in works like *Colonial Memories, A Year's Housekeeping in South Africa*, and *Station Life in New Zealand* – frequently opined on the difficulties created by the perceived incompetence and impertinence of servants. In *Colonial Memories*, Broome writes about how her servants 'were all immigrants, and seemed drawn almost entirely from the ranks of factory girls. They were respectable girls apparently, but with very free and easy manners.'[61] Broome portrays servants as lacking in morality and integrity, as evident in this description, and also unreliable, emotionally unstable, and immature. She moreover casts doubt on their domestic abilities, noting that they had 'never seen a broom'.[62] For her, no amount of training could remedy the perceived deficiencies of working-class girls. She further writes about how 'the absolute and profound ignorance of these damsels' posed a serious barrier to her efforts to create 'a very pretty and comfortable home', suggesting that servants did not bolster the domestic life of the colonies but actually threatened to undermine it.[63]

In southern Africa, fears that the working-class emigrants could thwart – rather than support – settler colonial goals were especially acute due to the demographic imbalances of the region. The Black and Coloured population outnumbered white settlers nearly four to one, and British settlers remained a minority among the white population, with Afrikaners (Dutch settlers) composing approximately three-fifths of the white population in South Africa.[64] To correct this demographic discrepancy, Alfred Milner, the High Commissioner in South Africa (1897–1905), advocated for the increased emigration of girls and young women to South Africa who could produce more white homes and white children but, at the same time, expressed concern about the potential detrimental effect that poor white emigrants could have. In a speech, he reflected:

> Our welfare depends upon increasing the quantity of our white population, but not at the expense of its quality. We do not want a white proletariat in this country. The position of the whites among the vastly more numerous black population requires that even their lowest ranks should be able to maintain a standard of living far above that of the poorest section of the population of a purely white population ... However you look at the matter, you always come back to the same root principle – the urgency of that development which alone can make this a white man's country in the only sense in which South Africa can become one, and that is, not a country full of poor whites, but one in which a largely increased white population can live in decency and comfort.[65]

In this speech, Milner draws attention to the relational nature of whiteness; settlers' whiteness depended upon their apparent superiority – specifically their economic superiority – over the Black population.[66] The existence of poor whites therefore threatened the status and power of white society. Milner's speech and references to the tension between quantity and quality of emigrants encapsulates the inherent contradictions of the racial and class objectives of emigration. In order to achieve the racial objective of emigration and make the settler colonies – in this case South Africa – 'a white man's country', the region needed a large quantity of emigrants. Yet, as Milner makes clear, this project also depended on emigrants of a certain quality or class. While emigration programmes might help solve the problem of quantity, critics saw it doing so at the expense of quality, making South Africa a 'country full of poor whites' and undermining notions of white prestige.[67]

## 'Maintaining and fostering the most valued traditions of home life': mediating the problems of emigration and colonial life

Faced with criticisms from various quarters, the GFS, like other emigration organisations, worked to assure sceptics that they sent out only 'the right sort' of emigrants and had safeguards in place to ensure that girls were 'of the highest character'.[68] Emigration societies instituted a vetting process for potential emigrants that assessed an 'applicant's moral and physical fitness' to guarantee they selected only girls and young women who 'were the very pick of their class'.[69] For the GFS, Joyce personally checked the references of prospective emigrants, corresponded with them, and made the final decision about whether they should emigrate.[70] Yet, as evidenced by the frequent complaints about servants, such safeguards did not prevent 'unqualified' servants from emigrating. One letter from Judith Wimbush at the Rhodes

Hostel in southern Africa expressed her irritation at an emigrant servant, noting 'she had good references and testimonials and we cannot understand how it is she came by them'.[71] Criticisms about the shortcomings of the selection process also circulated in broader public forums. For instance, a letter to the editor of the South African newspaper *The Natal Witness* questioned the rigour of the vetting process and argued for the inclusion of additional references and greater punishments for fraud if girls were 'not in fact *bona fide* domestic servants'.[72] Emigration societies responded by arguing that such problems were the exception rather than the rule.[73] They also attempted to mitigate growing consternation by arguing that problems would be remedied over time.[74] However, even with such vetting processes in place, emigration societies had no guaranteed formula to predict how girls would adjust once they reached the colonies.

To facilitate girls' adaptation to colonial life, the GFS focused on carefully controlling and monitoring girls and their environment. These efforts began before the girls left England. The journey to the colonies brought its own perils, with GFS associates expressing apprehension that girls would lose their virginity – and thus their purity – during the voyage or fall victim to the 'white slave trade'. As discussed in the first chapter, the trafficking of white girls for sex work was a key source of concern for emigration organisers.[75] Working-class girls – and particularly domestic servants – were seen as particularly vulnerable, since they apparently lacked the proper upbringing and values that would allow them to withstand potential threats to their morality and purity.[76] Reports about the changes in girls' behaviour upon their arrival in the colonies appeared to substantiate concerns about voyages.[77] The secretary of the GFS Diocesan Council in Christchurch, New Zealand, Mrs. Wood, wrote to the Department for Members Emigrating about how '[g]irls [*sic*] heads are turned on voyage out'.[78] Similarly, in *Colonial Memories*, Broome observed a change in her servants when travelling to southern Africa, writing that she had

> three English servants, whom I had to get rid of as soon as possible after my arrival. They had all been with me some time in England, and I thought I knew them perfectly; but the voyage evidently 'wrought a sea change' on them, for they were quite different people by the time Durban was reached.[79]

Organisers feared that undesirable effects of voyages could continue after the girls landed and that these negative influences would have a contagious effect, spreading among other girls.[80]

To mediate the risks of travelling, the GFS focused its efforts on ensuring that girls were surrounded by respectable influences and 'literally protected from door to door' by 'making their journeys across the seas safe as well as comfortable, and ensuring for them a friendly reception on the other side'.[81]

They secured 'responsible matrons' to accompany 'protected parties' of girls on the voyages. These matrons segregated girls from other passengers, specifically male passengers, and provided supervised recreation for girls on the long voyages, since, according to Joyce, '[o]ccupation is the great remedy against mischief'.[82] A 1901 GFS report emphasised that '[n]early all who have emigrated through the G.F.S. during the past year, write most gratefully of the help it has been to them, of the kindness of the Matron, during the voyage, and of their reception on arrival by those to whom they were commended or had letters of introduction'.[83] Upon arrival, the GFS's emigration department ensured that girls had a place to stay by making 'introductions from branch to branch, and from one country to another'.[84] The department connected girls with people, primarily clergymen or GFS associates, in the colonies. A letter from Alice Wyche, an associate in Grahamstown (present-day Makhanda), South Africa, praised the importance of the GFS networks and system of introductions, describing them as 'a sort of open sesame all the world over'.[85]

The GFS increasingly moved beyond simply making introductions for girls when they arrived in the colonies and focused its efforts on constructing lodges or hostels. By 1933 the GFS had built 67 hostels, including ones in Durban (Figure 3.1), Port Elizabeth (present-day Gqeberha), and Cape Town in South Africa; Melbourne, Sydney, and Brisbane in Australia; Hamilton, Toronto, and Montreal in Canada; Bathsheba in Barbados; Wellington, Wanganui, and Auckland in New Zealand; and

Figure 3.1 Durban GFS lodge, 1935, photograph by A. Cecil Covne (Women's Library, London, 5GFS/02/358, Durban GFS Lodge, 1935)

Delhi in India.[86] They acted as 'a happy haven for many girls far from their homes in a strange land' and engendered a sense of community for girls by offering accommodations, amusements, and 'companionship and support' for newly arrived emigrants.[87] A settler woman in Salisbury (present-day Harare), Rhodesia, wrote about the necessity of hostels in a letter: 'I think the life here for a servant is lonely, and one of great temptation, but I am trying to get to know all the servant girls here and let them feel they can come to me at any time. I think it helps them to know there is a house independent of their situations where they can come for help or advice.'[88] Hostels catered not only to domestic servants but to girls and young women in business, teachers, and nurses and those travelling for both work and holidays.[89] Besides seeking to 'provide friends for the friendless', hostels also provided resources for both girls and potential employers, effectively serving as an employment agency, where girls could find out about job openings and obtain advice about necessary training.[90]

While hostels fulfilled an important supportive role for girls, they also functioned as a way to control girls' behaviour and mobility. Paternalistic employers and GFS associates expressed unease about how girls spent their rare moments of leisure time and about how girls wasted their wages and free time on frivolous activities.[91] To mitigate these concerns, the GFS organised supervised entertainment and activities, like field trips, parties, plays, and Bible study groups. These activities attempted to alleviate girls' sense of loneliness and ease the difficulties of transitioning to life in the colonies. The GFS branch in Durban, for instance, sponsored lectures on 'Native life' for its members to help acquaint them with the country.[92] In addition to acclimating girls to the colonies, these activities were viewed as preserving girls' purity, since, as mentioned above, Joyce believed that '[o]ccupation is the great remedy against mischief'.[93]

By protecting girls' purity, hostels also safeguarded girls' whiteness. The hostels provided girls with a home away from home and, significantly, an English home away from home and a way to ensure that girls would not lose touch with their English roots. The GFS even named its lodge in Bombay (present-day Mumbai) the 'White House', leaving little ambiguity about its desire for hostels and lodges to serve as centres of whiteness and Englishness in India.[94] Expressing the importance of hostels, Joyce wrote that they 'carried the traditions of old England … to the Colonies'.[95] An article in the GFS's *A Jubilee Chronicle for Overseas* published in 1935 underscored the English character of hostels in South Africa: 'Perhaps it is necessary to travel 6,000 miles fully to realise the joy of finding our "three magic letters" on a gate, ensuring an English welcome within'.[96] Edith Gell – one of Hobbs's correspondents, the chair of the SACS, and a member of the BWEA – made a similar point in an article for the BWEA's publication *The*

*Imperial Colonist*, referring to hostels as 'potent factors in Colonial life'. She noted that 'it is a great relief to their relations in England to know that they will start their new life from an English home surrounded by friendly sympathy'.[97] Hostels not only provided shelter but also formed part of a broader support network for emigrants who lacked the familial and kinship ties they enjoyed in England.[98] Led by lady superintendents – who were required to be 'women of high character' – hostels ensured that emigrant girls fell under the right influences and, in the words of BWEA organisers, 'the presence and welfare of good women is of incalculable importance in maintaining and fostering the most valued traditions of home life'.[99] While the GFS and other organisations framed the purpose of hostels in terms of girls' interests and their protection, these institutions also reflected anxieties about the potential loss of girls' English identity and whiteness and their susceptibility to negative influences in the colonies.[100]

## 'The right spirit for an emigrant': the contradictions of emigration propaganda

For some girl migrants, the GFS's emigration programmes did ease the trepidations of travelling to and settling in a new place. For instance, in a letter to Joyce, Madeline Skeels spoke positively about her voyage to Cape Town, reporting that 'belonging to the GFS seems to make travelling so easy'.[101] She also wrote enthusiastically about life in the colony, which she found 'not at all unlike English life, in some ways perhaps a little freer'.[102] Another migrant, Ruth Rudd, wrote to the GFS and also drew similarities between life in England and in southern Africa, describing how she worked as a servant on a farm owned by 'a very charming *very* English family'. Rudd described her situation as 'most happy and comfortable' with the 'only regret being that I am not nearer to the town'. She also commented on the 'lovely' weather of Port Elizabeth.[103] Such correspondence seemed to validate the aims of the GFS's emigration programmes, confirming that girls found favourable positions and that life in the colonies was similar to life in England but 'freer'. However, other emigrants found life in the colonies very different from the one that had been promised in emigration propaganda. The previous chapter analysed the concerted efforts of the GFS to entice girls and women to emigrate, but, like other emigration societies, the GFS often exaggerated the opportunities and benefits that awaited girls in the colonies and minimised the difficulties of colonial life. As this section explores, such misrepresentations were not without consequences and brought into focus competing agendas among emigrants, settlers in the colonies, and emigration organisers in England.

One way that organisations tried to enhance the appeal of service was underscoring the higher standing of servants in the colonies. For instance, the GFS's *Report for Members Emigrating* for 1890 trumpeted the more equitable status of servants and how 'the household work [was] shared with the mistress of the house in the way a sister would undertake it'.[104] Correspondence from GFS members substantiated such claims. For instance, a member in Dunedin wrote in 1886 that 'her mistress treated her like a relation, and made her birthday quite a *fete* day, and that she cleans the boots herself, so that the girl may go out'.[105] This notion that servants would become extended family members also emerges in a speech on emigration delivered by Joyce in 1883. Joyce shared the experience of 'a little girl, who I fear never could have been a G.F.S. [member] if she had stayed inhabiting one room with father and brother, speaks in favour of sending out even G.F.S. candidates at an early age'. By suggesting that the girl would not have been able to join the GFS, she implies that the girl would not have remained a virgin if she stayed in her home and thus employs common justifications for removing working-class children from their home environment. According to Joyce, the girl spoke positively of the voyage and her new home, describing her employers as 'very kind' who acted as parents to her: 'They learn me to milk and to churn, and a great many other things besides ... I have grown so much, that they have bought me a new dress and new stockings. I have got a nice room to myself, and a nice bed.' The girl also wrote about being raised in a Christian household and attending church on Sunday. Joyce used the example of the girl to emphasise the 'special attractions' held by Canada, specifically that 'it is so nearer than any other colony' and 'religious and temperate' and 'the young servants are treated as "one of the family", and share with them the simple pleasures of farmhouse life'.[106]

While this example validated claims that the colonies provided girls with a better environment, other emigrants found their situations little changed in the colonies and even worse than in England. Instead of being treated as extended family members, Eliza Hobbs reported that she and Cook were 'unjustly treated' by Robinson, who referred to her and Cook as 'low-grade'.[107] She wrote: 'I can truthfully say I have never been so much insulted all my life put together, as I have been the short time I have been with Mrs. Robinson'.[108] An annual report by the National Council of Women of New Zealand indicated that Hobbs's and Cook's experiences were not anomalous or singular to southern Africa. Published in 1900, the report painted a less egalitarian picture of servant life than the one portrayed in emigration propaganda and detailed how a servant is 'looked down upon with gentle contempt by her employers, and frequently spoken of as "the slavey" and "our Biddy"; and even where the elders are more outwardly considerate, the children of the family – with the brutal candour of their age – soon make the girl understand that they consider her of an inferior and altogether lower order of flesh and blood than themselves'.[109] As reflected in this report and the experiences of Hobbs and Cook, servants found that they were still a class apart in the colonies, which enhanced their dissatisfaction and led to contentious relationships with their mistresses.[110]

In southern Africa, this discontentment was compounded by the employment of African servants. Like other emigration organisations, the GFS emphasised how the employment of African servants constituted a singular advantage of the region, since they could do the more difficult, labour-intensive work.[111] Yet emigrants, like Hobbs and Cook, found living and working alongside African servants one of the more difficult aspects of adapting to life in southern Africa. Hobbs found that she still had to perform demanding labour, writing to Joyce: 'Anywhere else here the washing is put out, or done by blacks, and the scrubbing and dirty work done by them also, but I have had all to do, and people tell me it is not the custom for white women and that I am silly to do it'.[112] She also observed that Robinson 'is much more considerate to Kaffirs than to us'.[113] Instead of elevating her position in the colonial household, Hobbs found that the presence of African servants and the seeming parity between African and white servants depreciated her already lowly position in the household.[114]

Like Eliza Hobbs and Eliza Cook, Sarah Elliot found life in southern Africa was not at all what she had envisioned. In 1903, the twenty-four-year-old Elliot applied to travel to Johannesburg with the assistance of the SACS.[115] The SACS approved Elliot's application, but, instead of arranging for her passage to Johannesburg as she specified in her application, they sent her to work as a servant for a family in Salisbury, a fact that she learned only upon landing in Rhodesia. Elliot wrote to the SACS, criticising their lack of transparency and deceiving her: 'I think it very unpleasant that any young girl should be brought out and misled in this way'.[116] Like Hobbs, Elliot found life in the region difficult, writing about disagreements with her mistress and that 'life is too quiet' in Salisbury.[117] Mother Annie, who ran the SACS hostel in Salisbury, found that Elliot's discontentment originated in part with the voyage, which made her aware of the disadvantages of working in more rural areas. She consequently advised organisers in London: 'I wonder if it would be possible to send our people in another boat – not with the Johannesburg emigrants. They get dissatisfied on the voyage out with the comparatively small wages, etc. and of course this is a quieter place than Johannesburg and all that they learn on the voyage out.'[118] Mother Annie's correspondence illustrates the ways in which emigration societies sought to exert power over girls by controlling their access to knowledge about emigration and colonial life.

Elliot's resentment at the false pretences that brought her to Salisbury created tension with her employers, who wrote back to the SACS describing how they had 'such trouble with the girl'.[119] The sister of Elliot's employers, Geraldine Glasgow, wrote to the SACS detailing these complaints and condemned Elliot's attitude, remarking: 'This does not seem quite the right spirit for an emigrant does it?'[120] Joyce had a similar response to Eliza Hobbs. When Hobbs wrote about the difficulties she faced in the employment of the Robinsons and her plans to leave, Joyce advised her to stay in her position, telling her to 'make the best of things' and invoking the principles of loyalty and duty:

> People never better themselves when they break their word and you must remember this when a lady is rude to you, it is because you are not used to the ways of the country. People in the colonies do not always speak quite in the same way as people in England, and believe me, it would be far better for you to stop where you are for the present, and keep your word, and have a good name in the Colony for doing so.[121]

Joyce's attribution of the problem to the servant rather than the mistress was common. When problems arose with emigrants, organisers expressed little sympathy towards the girls and women and the challenges they faced in acclimating to a new country and instead blamed them for any difficulties. The experiences of Elliot, Hobbs, and Cook reveal how organisers sought to cultivate and control emigrants' emotions and the emotional labour that emigrants were supposed to perform in addition to domestic work.[122]

As evidenced by the situations of Elliot, Hobbs, and Cook, misleading propaganda and the lack of transparency could backfire by increasing servants' dissatisfaction. It also became a growing source of consternation between settlers in the colonies and emigration organisers, with settlers criticising emigration organisations for perpetuating unreasonable expectations and not preparing emigrants adequately. Hely-Hutchinson blamed emigrants' 'most lamentable ignorance of conditions of life in a colony' to the inadequate training and information they received from organisations in England.[123] Lady Lucy Jervois – the president of the GFS's Diocesan Council in Christchurch and the wife of William Jervois, the governor of New Zealand from 1883 to 1889 – similarly complained that emigrants often had 'a very exaggerated view of the prosperity which they expected to await them'.[124] Settler women like Jervois and Hely-Hutchinson recognised that emigration societies should be more forthcoming about the realities of colonial life and that the misrepresentations and underhanded tactics did more harm than good to the overall cause of emigration. These disagreements over emigrants' lack of preparation reflected broader frustrations among settlers that emigration organisers in England did not fully grasp the reality of the situation in the colonies and thus could not train girls properly for the challenges they would encounter. The perception of England being out of touch with the difficulties of colonial life emerges in the correspondence of women in the colonies to emigration organisers in England. Organisers in England viewed emigration in abstract, idealistic terms – emphasising how the colonies were prosperous and paradisical gardens – while girls and women in the colonies were confronted with the practical challenges and realities – including the isolation and arduous labour.[125] These differing views were emblematic of the systemic tensions and competing agendas within emigration programmes.

### 'The ties between the Mother Country and the Colonies have been strengthened': assessing the scale and objectives of the GFS's emigration programmes

Studying emigration programmes for girls raises myriad questions: How many girls emigrated? Did emigration societies achieve their objectives? What was the experience of emigration like for girls? Qualitative and quantitative evidence from the GFS's archives provides some insights into questions about the scale of the programmes – but with important qualifications. GFS emigration reports typically use the vague phrasing of 'some hundreds' when referring to the number of girls who travelled to the colonies, but other reports use more precise figures.[126] For instance, in the 1897 *Report for Members Emigrating*, Joyce relates:

> One thousand nine hundred and thirty-five young women have all been safely met and welcomed, and experienced the advantages and support of finding their Girls' Friendly Society in their new homes. The ties between the Mother Country and the Colonies have been strengthened by the care taken of the daughters of the Home land.[127]

Given that the department was established in 1883, the number of emigrants quoted by Joyce – 1,935 – would mean that the GFS assisted in the emigration of around 150 girls a year. These numbers are comparable to the number of girls sent out by Barnardo's, which relayed in the *Annual Report* for 1898 that the organisation emigrated 910 girls between 1892 and 1898, an average of 130 girls a year.[128] However, there are caveats with these figures, since the GFS sometimes allied with other emigration societies, including the BWEA and the SACS, to send out girls and young women or assisted migrants more informally. Some girls did not travel in protected parties arranged by the GFS but benefited from introductions made by GFS associates. Therefore, it is possible that the GFS assisted in the emigration of more girls than reflected in the reported number. Moreover, as discussed in the Introduction, the self-reported numbers of emigration societies must be approached with caution, since they were eager to emphasise the value of their endeavours and therefore sometimes inflated their success rate.

In seeking to answer questions about girls' experiences, one is constantly confronted with the challenges posed by the colonial archive, specifically its gaps and misrepresentations and the power relations implicit in its construction. As described in this chapter, girls' experiences of migration varied widely and defy easy categorisation. Some emigrants like Eliza Cook, Eliza Hobbs, and Sarah Elliot experienced abuse, loneliness, and frustration, with life very different from the one promised by emigration propaganda, but others like Ruth Rudd and Madeline Skeels found new opportunities through migration to the colonies. Their stories – or at least parts of their stories – are preserved in the archives, but thousands of girls' stories are not, making it difficult to paint a more holistic picture of girls' experiences of migration. While the concerns of emigration organisers and settler women pervade the reports and correspondence of emigration societies, little space is given to the concerns and ambitions of the emigrant girls themselves. Even when considering the trials of Cook and Hobbs, Hobbs's voice comes through in her impassioned letters to Joyce, but Cook remains largely silent in the archival records. There are excerpts of her testimony in newspaper reports covering her trial, but no correspondence or writings from her are preserved in the archive, and the available evidence presents a contradictory picture of her experiences with Robinson. Robinson maintained that she had less trouble with Cook, stating that she was 'very well satisfied' with her, and portrayed Cook as negatively influenced by Hobbs. She even claimed that she wanted to take Cook's sister, who planned to emigrate to Rhodesia, as Hobbs's replacement.[129] However, in a rare moment when Cook's voice does emerge, she presents a different view. While Robinson's testimony portrays Cook as under the control of Hobbs, Cook testifies she made the deliberate decision to act to change her situation, declaring at her trial that 'she left because she was not happy. Mrs. Robinson had been at times very nice and at other times not so.' Cook also reveals how Robinson subjected the two to mistreatment, stating that '[s]he had overheard her [Mrs Robinson] say that Mrs. Hobbs and herself were two low common women'.[130] The nature of the archive reflects how settlers and organisers saw girls as passive figures in the process of emigration and ones who did not need to have a say in their own future, as reflected in the placement of Sarah Elliot. This blind spot meant that organisers failed to take into account the ways that girls would resist the poor conditions and hardships they faced in the colonies. The actions of Hobbs and Cook as well as Elliot undercut the façade of colonies as a 'Great Garden' and instead highlighted the dangers, challenges, and complexities of colonial life and societies. As Lorenzo Veracini has argued, settler colonialism depends on its 'regenerative capacity' and the reproduction of Englishness and English society abroad, but the strangeness and alienation that Hobbs, Cook, and Elliot experienced in Rhodesia reveal the limitations of the settler colonial project in achieving its aims.[131]

## Conclusion

As this chapter has investigated, a variety of factors propelled emigration programmes for girls, including economics, social problems, racial anxieties, and concerns about the futurity of white settler societies and the British empire. While these different motives and agendas may appear compatible at first glance, they became increasingly irreconcilable. Criticisms of working-class emigrants as 'the ugliest hussies in creation' who endangered – rather than upheld – notions of whiteness and white prestige in settler colonies indicate that the objectives of settler colonial societies did not always align with the goals of organisers in England. The challenges faced by emigration programmes was also emblematic of a growing divide between imperial and regional interests that became more marked in the first decades of the twentieth century and especially after the First World War, a topic returned to in the fifth chapter. Moreover, organisers failed to foresee how girls like Hobbs, Cook, and Elliot would use organisations to accomplish their own personal ends, which did not necessarily support the aims of emigration programmes, and prioritise their own well-being over national, imperial, or racial concerns. Abstract notions of imperial duty and the need to exhibit 'the right spirit', which the GFS had worked to cultivate through its empire education programmes discussed in the previous chapter and were promoted by figures like Joyce, meant little to Hobbs, Cook, and Elliot faced with innumerable hardships living in 'a strange land'. Far from being insignificant and compliant figures, girls had the potential to destabilise settler colonial societies.

## Notes

1 In some reports and correspondence, Eliza Cook's surname is spelled 'Cooke', but it is more frequently spelled 'Cook', so I have chosen to use that spelling. Similarly, Eliza Hobbs's given name is sometimes spelled 'Elisa', but I use 'Eliza', since this spelling is used more often. I am unable to determine the ages of Eliza Hobbs and Eliza Cook. The archival records and correspondence do

not refer to their ages, and a search through the census records provided too many results for each name to ascertain their identities definitively.
2 Ellen Joyce, *30 Years of Imperial Work with the Girls Friendly Society* (London: G.F.S., 1912), p. 1.
3 Derbyshire Record Office, Matlock (hereafter DRO), D3287/67/11/84, letter from Eliza Hobbs to 'Honoured Madam', 20 January 1902.
4 Letter from Eliza Hobbs to 'Honoured Madam', 20 January 1902.
5 DRO, D3287/67/11/79, letter from Eliza Hobbs to 'Honoured Madam', 23 May 1902.
6 Letter from Eliza Hobbs to 'Honoured Madam', 20 January 1902.
7 Letter from Eliza Hobbs to 'Honoured Madam', 20 January 1902.
8 DRO, D3287/67/11/79, letter from Eliza Hobbs to 'Honoured Madam [Ellen Joyce]', 11 February 1902.
9 Letter from Eliza Hobbs to 'Honoured Madam', 23 May 1902.
10 Letter from Eliza Hobbs to 'Honoured Madam', 23 May 1902.
11 For more on the Children's Friend Society, see Rebecca Bates, 'From Suppression to Sponsorship: Juvenile Emigration and the Preservation of Pre-Industrial Labor', in Maria Ruiz (ed.), *International Migrations in the Victorian Era* (Leiden: Brill, 2018), pp. 507–31; Geoff Blackburn, *The Children's Friend Society: Juvenile Emigrants to Western Australia, South Africa and Canada, 1834–1842* (Northbridge: Access Press, 1993); Edna Bradlow, 'The Children's Friend Society at the Cape of Good Hope', *Victorian Studies*, 27:2 (1984), 155–77; Elizabeth Dillenburg, '"The Foundation of British Home Life": Domestic and Imperial Crises and the Evolution of Emigration Programs for Girls to South Africa and New Zealand, c. 1830–1900', chapter one in 'Constructing and Contesting "the Girlhood of Our Empire": Girls' Culture, Labor, and Mobility in Britain, South Africa, and New Zealand, c. 1830–1930' (PhD dissertation, University of Minnesota, 2019), pp. 43–59; Elaine Hadley, 'Natives in a Strange Land: The Philanthropic Discourse of Juvenile Emigration in Mid-Nineteenth-Century England', *Victorian Studies*, 33:3 (1990), 411–39; and Rebecca Swartz, 'Child Apprenticeship in the Cape Colony: The Case of the Children's Friend Society Emigration Scheme, 1833–1841', *Slavery & Abolition*, 42:3 (2021), 567–88.
12 For more on these emigration societies, see Ellen Boucher, *Empire's Children: Child Emigration, Welfare, and the Decline of the British World* (Cambridge: Cambridge University Press, 2014); Kenneth Bagnell, *The Little Immigrants: The Orphans Who Came to Canada* (Toronto: Dundurn Press, 1980); Tim Calabria, 'Agents of Settler Colonialism?: Childhood, Time and Exclusion in the Fairbridge Scheme, 1913–1924', *Settler Colonial Studies*, 13:1 (2023), 133–55; Gail Corbett, *Nation Builders: Barnardo Children in Canada* (Toronto: Dundurn Press, 1997); Alan Gill, *Orphans of the Empire: The Shocking Story of Child Migration to Australia* (New York: Vintage, 1998); Phyllis Harrison, *The Home Children: Their Personal Stories* (Winnipeg: Watson and Dwyer, 1979); Chris Jeffery and Geoffrey Sherington, *Fairbridge: Empire and Child Migration* (London: Woburn Press, 1998);

Morgan Brie Johnson, 'Settler Colonial Structures of Domestication: British Home Children in Canada', *Genealogy*, 5:3 (2021), 78; Joy Parr, *Labouring Children: British Immigrant Apprentices to Canada, 1869–1924* (Toronto: University of Toronto Press, 1980); Janet Sacks and Roger Kershaw, *New Lives for Old: The Story of Britain's Home Children* (London: The National Archives, 2008); Shurlee Swain and Margot Hillel, *Child, Nation, Race and Empire: Child Rescue Discourse, England Canada, and Australia, 1850–1915* (Manchester: Manchester University Press, 2010); Gillian Wagner, *Barnardo* (London: Weidenfeld and Nicolson, 1979); and Gillian Wagner, *Children of the Empire* (London: Weidenfeld and Nicolson, 1982). For more on the Boy Scouts' involvement in emigration programmes, see Scott Johnston, '"Only Send Boys of the Good Type": Child Migration and the Boy Scout Movement, 1921–1959', *The Journal of the History of Childhood and Youth*, 7:3 (Fall 2014), 377–87.

13 'Little Emigrants', *The Times* (29 October 1869), p. 10. Women's Library, London (hereafter WL), 1FME/1/2, 'Report', in *Female Middle Class Emigration Society*, 1862–72. University of Liverpool Department of Special Collections and Archives, Liverpool (hereafter UL), D630/1/19, 'Miss Rye's Emigration Home for Destitute Girls', 1875. For more on Rye, see Nupur Chaudhuri, '"Who Will Help the Girls?": Maria Rye and Victorian Juvenile Emigration to Canada', in Rita S. Kranidis (ed.), *Imperial Objects: Victorian Women's Emigration and the Unauthorized Imperial Experience* (New York: Twayne Publishers, 1998), pp. 19–42; Marion Diamond, *Emigration and Empire: The Life of Maria S. Rye* (New York: Routledge, 1999); Marion Diamond, 'Maria Rye's Journey: Metropolitan and Colonial Perceptions of Female Emigration', in Rita S. Kranidis (ed.), *Imperial Objects: Victorian Women's Emigration and the Unauthorized Imperial Experience* (New York: Twayne Publishers, 1998), pp. 126–43; Charlotte Macdonald, *A Woman of Good Character: Single Women as Immigrant Settlers in Nineteenth-Century New Zealand* (Wellington: Allen & Unwin, 1990); Parr, *Labouring Children*; and Wagner, *Children of the Empire*.

14 UL, D630/1/19, *Report for 1895 of Miss Rye's Emigration Home for Destitute Little Girls*.

15 'Emigrants to Canada: 1867–1911', *For God and Country: Dr. Barnardo's Homes 46th Annual Report. Year 1911* (London: L. Upcott Gill & Son, Limited), p. 31.

16 Agnes L. Money, *History of the Girls' Friendly Society*, 2nd ed. (London: Wells, Garner, Darton & Co., Ltd, 1911), p. 44. *The Book of the G.F.S.: What It Is and What It Does* (June 1920), p. 38.

17 DRO, D3287/68/1/3, Ellen Joyce, 'Preface', in *Girls' Friendly Society. Reports of the Department for Members Emigrating. 1883 to 1897*, p. 1.

18 'Philanthropic Kidnapping', *The Journal* (15 February 1886), pp. 9–10. For information on some of the high profile court cases, see The National Archives, London (hereafter NA), HO 144/310/B6159, letter from Mrs Giles as to Departure of Her Daughter (Mary Ann Giles) to Canada, Dr Barnardo's,

30 October 1893; NA, HO 144/310/B6159, 'The Queen v. Barnardo Gossage's Case', 25 January 1890; 'Dr. Barnardo Again', *The Personal Rights Journal* (October 1889), p. 70; London Metropolitan Archives, London, A/FWA/C/DIO/7, '"Before My Judges:" Being a Verbatim Report of Dr. Barnardo's Speech on the Gossage Case, Delivered on Friday, 24th, and Monday, 27th January, 1890, Before Lord Esher, Master of the Rolls, and Lord Justice Fry, Judges of the Court of Appeal, with Summary of Their Lordships' Decision, as Given by the Timer'.
19 DRO, D3287/68/1/3, Ellen Joyce (ed.), 'Report for 1885', in *Girls' Friendly Society. Reports of the Department for Members Emigrating. 1883 to 1897,* p. 14. Emphasis in the original.
20 WL, 5GFS/04/021, [Objects and rules for candidates], n.d., p. 1.
21 Kathleen M. Townsend, *Some Memories of Mrs. Townsend: Foundress of the Girls' Friendly Society* (London: G.F.S. Central Office, 1923), p. 42.
22 WL, 5GFS/01/109, 'Standing Committee. Meeting of the Committee held at the G.F.S. Central Office, 39 Victoria Street, London, S.W. June 1912'.
23 See, for instance, 'The World of Childhood', *Night and Day: A Record of Christian Missions and Practical Philanthropy*, 16 (December 1892), p. 120.
24 Mary Heath-Stubbs, *Friendship's Highway: Being the History of the Girls' Friendly Society, 1875–1935* (London: G.F.S. Central Office, 1935), p. 75.
25 WL, 5GFS/05/013, Hon. Mrs. Joyce, *Emigration – A Paper Read at the Barnsley Conference on Women Work, March 1889*, p. 3. For more on Joyce, see Lisa Chilton, *Agents of Empire: British Female Migration to Canada and Australia, 1860s–1930* (Toronto: University of Toronto Press, 2007), pp. 29–30.
26 Lady Rockley, 'Women Settlers in South Africa', *Journal of the Royal African Society*, 33:131 (1934), 124.
27 For more on how the GFS served as a testing ground for the BWEA, see *The Book of the G.F.S.*, pp. 37–8.
28 'Mrs. Joyce', *The Times* (23 May 1924), p. 16. *The Book of the G.F.S.*, p. 37.
29 DRO, D3287/68/1/3, Ellen Joyce, *Department for G.F.S. Members Emigrating* (1898), p. 6.
30 British Library, London, General Reference Collection 8275.b.23.(9.), The Hon. Mrs Joyce, *Emigration. A Paper. Read at the G.F.S. Winchester Diocesan Conference, Southampton, October 25th, 1883; Revised, April, 1884.* (London: Hatchards, 1884), p. 2.
31 William Rathbone Greg, *Why Are Women Redundant?* (London: Trübner, 1869), p. 12.
32 Greg, *Why Are Women Redundant?*, p. 15.
33 Kathrin Levitan, 'Redundancy, the "Surplus Woman" Problem, and the British Census, 1851–1861', *Women's History Review*, 17:3 (2008), 359–76. For more on the problem of 'surplus women' and specifically how it was connected to broader social shifts and debates about women's place in society, see Judith Worsnop, 'A Reevaluation of "the Problem of Surplus Women" in 19th-century England: The Case of the 1851 Census', *Women's Studies International Forum*, 13:1 (1990), 21; and Julia Bush, '"The Right

Sort of Women": Female Emigrators and Emigration to the British Empire, 1890–1910', *Women's History Review*, 3 (1994), 388–9.
34 Greg, *Why Are Women Redundant?*, p. 12.
35 WL, 5GFS/05/013, Hon. Mrs Joyce, *Responsibility to the Church with Regard to Emigration: A Paper read at the Portsmouth Church Congress, October 1885*, p. 2.
36 WL, 5GFS/05/013, Hon. Mrs Joyce, *Emigration. Paper Read at a Conference of Women Workers at Birmingham*, p. 2.
37 Joyce, *Emigration. A Paper. Read at the G.F.S. Winchester Diocesan Conference*, p. 4. On this point, see also Julia Cartwright (ed.), *The Journals of Lady Knightley of Fawsley* (New York: E. P. Dutton & Company, 1917), p. 293.
38 Joyce, *Emigration. A Paper. Read at the G.F.S. Winchester Diocesan Conference*, p. 4.
39 Wagner, *Children of the Empire*, p. 47.
40 Joyce, *Emigration. A Paper. Read at the G.F.S. Winchester Diocesan Conference*, p. 2.
41 Joyce, *Emigration. A Paper. Read at the G.F.S. Winchester Diocesan Conference*, p. 2.
42 Joyce, *Responsibility to the Church with Regard to Emigration*.
43 Joyce, *30 Years of Imperial Work*, p. 1.
44 William Booth, *In Darkest England and the Way Out* (London: International Headquarters of the Salvation Army, 1890). See also Lydia Murdoch, *Imagined Orphans: Poor Families, Child Welfare, and Contested Citizenship in London*, Rutgers Series in Childhood Studies (New Brunswick: Rutgers University Press, 2006), especially chapter 1, '"A Little Waif of London, Rescued from the Streets": Melodrama and Popular Representations of Poor Children'.
45 Joyce, *Emigration. A Paper. Read at the G.F.S. Winchester Diocesan Conference*, p. 7. See a similar report in '"The Bane of My Life": The Servant Girl Problem', *Night and Day: A Record of Christian Missions and Practical Philanthropy*, 26 (April 1903), p. 34.
46 Anne McClintock, *Imperial Leather: Race, Gender, and Sexuality in the Colonial Contest* (New York: Routledge, 1995), especially p. 5. On the importance of domestic servants in the British colonial context, see, for instance, Victoria K. Haskins and Claire Lowrie (eds), *Colonization and Domestic Service: Historical and Contemporary Perspectives* (New York: Routledge, 2014); and Fae Dussart, *In the Service of Empire: Domestic Service and Mastery in Metropole and Colony* (New York: Bloomsbury Academic, 2022).
47 Joyce, *Emigration. Paper Read at a Conference of Women Workers at Birmingham*, p. 4. WL, 5GFS/02/225, GFS Empire Education Committee, 'Conference at the Mansion House on Empire Citizenship for Girls', 1928.
48 Heath-Stubbs, *Friendship's Highway*, p. 76.
49 On Parkin as an 'evangelist of empire', see G. R. Parkin, 'Empire Day', *Cheltenham Ladies' College Magazine*, 60 (Spring 1909), p. 173.

50 Edith Marion Welch, 'The Future and Unity of Empire', *The Empire and Beyond*, Occasional Leaflet XII (Anniversary Week 1916), p. 8.
51 Adele Perry, *On the Edge of Empire: Gender, Race, and the Making of British Columbia, 1849–1871* (Toronto: University of Toronto Press, 2001), p. 4. See also her discussion of emigration programmes in chapter 6, '"Fair Ones of a Purer Caste": Bringing White Women to British Columbia'.
52 Ann Laura Stoler, 'Sexual Affronts and Racial Frontiers: European Identities and the Cultural Politics of Exclusion in Colonial Southeast Asia', *Comparative Studies in Society and History*, 3:4 (1992), 514–51. See also Ann Laura Stoler, *Carnal Knowledge and Imperial Power: Race and the Intimate in Colonial Rule* (Berkeley: University of California Press, 2002).
53 UL, D630/2/8, Maria S. Rye, *The Emigration of Infant Children to Canada* (December 1876), p. viii.
54 UL, D630/1/76, *Report for 1892 of Miss Rye's Emigration Home for Destitute Little Girls*, p. 14.
55 WL, 5GFS/01/044, 'A Meeting of the Aid and Reference Committee for the Emigration Department Held at the GFS Central Office, 39 Victoria Street London SW on Thursday 6th May 1915 at 11.30 a.m.', p. 3.
56 'Conference at the Mansion House on Empire Citizenship for Girl: Mrs Amery and Mrs. Philip Snowden Present', *The G.F.S. Workers' Journal* (December 1928), p. 200.
57 Boucher, *Empire's Children*, p. 15. On the notion of whiteness and belonging, see Omni Gust, *Unhomely Empire: Whiteness and Belonging, c. 1760–1830* (London: Bloomsbury Academic, 2020). On the goal of settlers see Lorenzo Veracini, *Settler Colonialism: A Theoretical Overview* (Basingstoke: Palgrave Macmillan, 2010), p. 4.
58 For more on anxieties about poor whites in India, see Teresa Hubel, 'In Search of the British Indian in British India: White Orphans, Kipling's *Kim*, and Class in Colonial India', *Modern Asian Studies*, 38:1 (2004), 227–51.
59 Adelaide Ross, 'Emigration for Women', *Macmillan's Magazine*, 45 (February 1882), p. 312.
60 Barnardo's, London, A/52/10–22, letter from Stuart Barnardo to Thomas Barnardo, 20 August 1902.
61 Lady Broome, *Colonial Memories* (London: Smith, Elder, & Co., 1904), p. 208.
62 Broome, *Colonial Memories*, p. 208.
63 Broome, *Colonial Memories*, p. 208.
64 *Census 1911: Preliminary Returns of Census Taken on 7th May 1911* (Pretoria: The Government Printers and Stationary Office, 1911), p. 2. As numerous scholars have demonstrated, census categories are highly problematic. These categories were constantly changing and being redefined and, in the process, becoming more racialised. For a greater discussion of the employment of racial classifications in the South African census, see Akil Kokayi Khalfani, Tukufu Zuberi, Sulaiman Bah, and Pali J. Lehohla, 'Population Statistics', in Amson Sibanda, Tukufu Zuberi, and Eric O Udjo (eds), *The Demography of*

*South Africa* (Armonk: M. E. Sharpe, 2005), pp. 9–17. See also Stanley H. Palmer, 'The Power of Numbers: Settler and Native in Ireland America, and South Africa, 1600–1900', in Steven G. Reinhardt, Dennis Reinhartz, and William Hardy MacNeil (eds), *Transatlantic History* (Arlington: University of Texas, 2006), p. 130; and Cecille Swaisland, *Servants and Gentlewomen to the Golden Land: The Emigration of Single Women from Britain to Southern Africa, 1820–1839* (Oxford: Berg, 1993), p. 41.

65 Alfred Milner, 'Reply to Deputation from White Labour League', 2 June 1903, in vol. 2, South Africa, 1899–1905, of Cecil Headlam (ed.), *The Milner Papers* (London: Cassell, 1933), p. 459.

66 For more on this point, see Cheryl I. Harris, 'Whiteness as Property', *Harvard Law Review*, 106:8 (June 1993), especially p. 1758.

67 On this point, see letter from Stuart Barnardo to Thomas Barnardo, 20 August 1902. See also Edith Marion Welch, 'G.F.S. Among the Maoris', *The Empire and Beyond*, Occasional Leaflet XIII (Advent 1916), p. 4. For more on the 'poor white problem' in South Africa, see S. E. Duff, *Changing Childhoods in the Cape Colony: Dutch Reformed Church Evangelicalism and Colonial Childhood, 1860–1895*, Palgrave Studies in the History of Childhood (Basingstoke: Palgrave Macmillan, 2015), especially chapter 5. See also S. E. Duff, 'The Jam and Matchsticks Problem: Working-Class Girlhood in Late Nineteenth-Century Cape Town', in Kristine Moruzi and Michelle J. Smith (eds), *Colonial Girlhood in Literature, Culture and History, 1840–1950*, Palgrave Studies in Nineteenth-Century Writing and Culture (Basingstoke: Palgrave Macmillan, 2016), pp. 124–37.

68 Heath-Stubbs, *Friendship's Highway*, p. 72. *The Book of the G.F.S.*, p. 38.

69 Joyce, *Responsibility to the Church with Regard to Emigration*. Robert Francis Irvine, Oscar Thorwald, and Johan Alpers, *The Progress of New Zealand in the Century* (London: W. & R. Chambers, Limited, 1902), p. 421.

70 Chilton, *Agents of Empire*, p. 45.

71 DRO, D3287/94/16/14, letter from Judith Wimbush to Mrs Gell, 22 November 1907. On this point, see also Barnardo's, A2/53/173, letter from Stuart Barnardo to Thomas Barnardo, 17 December 1902.

72 L., 'Immigration', *The Natal Witness*, 29 May 1880, p. 4. Emphasis in the original.

73 See, for instance, Joyce, *Emigration – A Paper Read at the Barnsley Conference on Women Work*, p. 6; and Hon Mrs Joyce, 'Children under the Poor Law', *The Times* (9 January 1897), p. 2.

74 See, for instance, DRO, D3287/93/4/1, letter from Philip Lyttelton Gell to Lord Grey, 24 September 1902.

75 See DRO, D3287/76/2/2/88, Muriel Dayrell Browning, 'Extract from the private letter of a young married woman to Mrs. Lyttelton Gell', n.d. DRO, D3287/68/1/3, Ellen Joyce (ed.), 'Report for 1887', in *Girls' Friendly Society. Reports of the Department for Members Emigrating. 1883 to 1897*, p. 24.

76 NA, CO 386/129/194, letter from S. Walcott to Sir, 30 April 1857.

77 For more on this point, see Swaisland, *Servants and Gentlewomen to the Golden Land*, p. 77.
78 'A Meeting of the Aid and Reference Committee for the Emigration Department Held at the GFS Central Office, 39 Victoria Street London SW on Thursday 6th May 1915 at 11.30 a.m.', p. 6.
79 Broome, *Colonial Memories*, p. 195.
80 On this point, see also Una Monk, *New Horizons: A Hundred Years of Women's Emigration* (London: HMSO, 1963), p. 103.
81 Joyce, *Emigration – A Paper Read at the Barnsley Conference on Women Work*, p. 5. Kathleen M. Townsend, *Some Memories of Mrs. Townsend*, p. 19. Money, *History of the Girls' Friendly Society*, p. 44.
82 Joyce, *Emigration. A Paper. Read at the G.F.S. Winchester Diocesan Conference*, p. 6.
83 WL, 5GFS/06/106, *The Girls' Friendly Society. London Diocesan Report. January 1st, 1901, to December 31st, 1901* (Bristol: Rose and Harris Printers, 1902), p. 43.
84 Money, *History of the Girls' Friendly Society*, p. 99.
85 WL, 5GFS/02/261, letter from Alice F. Wyche to Miss Rogers, 10 February 1932.
86 WL, 5GFS/02/358, Durban GFS Lodge, 1935, photograph by A. Cecil Covne. WL, 5GFS/02/262, *G.F.S. Hostels and Homes of Rest*, n.d., pp. 19–20.
87 WL, 5GFS/04/128, M. J. Beckwith, 'South Africa', *A Jubilee Chronicle for Overseas* (1935), p. 22. WL, D3287/68/1/3, Ellen Joyce, *Department for G.F.S. Members Emigrating* (1898), p. 4; DRO, D3287/93/3/39, letter from E. Lyttelton Gell to the bishop of Mashonaland, 16 March 1902; and *The Book of the G.F.S.*, pp. 22–35.
88 DRO, D3287/76/2/2/181, 'Mrs. Owen', 29 December 1903.
89 'Overseas Reports. Australia', *The Empire and Beyond*, Occasional Leaflet XXII (Summer 1919), p. 6. See also *The Book of the G.F.S.*, pp. 21–5.
90 Lambeth Palace Library, London, Davidson 143, ff. 215, 'Appeal for £20,000 for the Lodges and Homes of Rest of the Girls' Friendly Society', 1907. See also Brian Harrison, 'For Church, Queen, and Family: The Girls' Friendly Society 1874–1920', *Past and Present*, 61 (November 1972), 124.
91 Charles van Onselen, 'The Witches of Suburbia: Domestic Service on the Witwatersrand 1890–1914', in *Studies in the Social and Economic History of the Witwatersrand 1886–1914, Vol. 2: New Nineveh* (New York: Longman, 1982), p. 24.
92 WL, 5GFS/02/262, 'Girls' Friendly Society, Durban, Natal, 1937', p. 3.
93 Joyce, *Emigration. A Paper. Read at the G.F.S. Winchester Diocesan Conference*, p. 6.
94 WL, 5GFS/02/231, 'G.F.S. Bombay Branch. October 1931–Oct. 1932'.
95 DRO, D3287/68/1/3, Ellen Joyce (ed.), 'Preface' and 'Report for 1887', *Girls' Friendly Society. Reports of the Department for Members Emigrating. 1883 to 1897*, pp. 1 and 24.
96 Beckwith, 'South Africa', p. 22.

97 DRO, D3287/94/16/51, Edith Lyttelton Gell, 'Rhodesia, Contribution to Imperial Colonist', January 1903, p. 2.
 98 DRO, D3287/94/16/68 (iii), Edith Lyttelton Gell, 'Report for B.W.E.A. & S.A.X.', March 1903, p. 2.
 99 DRO, D3287/74/7/5/16, 'Notes on Hostels for Women in Rhodesia', c. 1900.
100 For more on hostels, see Deborah Gaitskell, '"Christian Compounds for Girls": Church Hostels for African Women in Johannesburg, 1907–1970', *Journal of Southern African Studies*, 6:1 (1979), 44–69.
101 WL, GB/106/BWE/4/4, letter from Madeline Skeels to Ellen Joyce, 12 December 1899.
102 Letter from Madeline Skeels to Ellen Joyce, 12 December 1899.
103 WL, 5GFS/02/262, letter from Ruth M. Rudd to Miss Angus, 24 October 1938. Emphasis in the original.
104 DRO, D3287/68/1/3, Ellen Joyce (ed.), 'Report from 1890', in *Girls' Friendly Society. Reports of the Department for Members Emigrating. 1883 to 1897*, p. 37.
105 DRO, D3287/68/1/3, Ellen Joyce (ed.), 'Report for 1886', in *Girls' Friendly Society. Reports of the Department for Members Emigrating. 1883 to 1897*, p. 17.
106 Joyce, *Emigration. A Paper. Read at the G.F.S. Winchester Diocesan Conference*, p. 8.
107 On being 'unjustly treated', see letter from Eliza Hobbs to 'Honoured Madam', 20 January 1902. On being called 'low-grade', see DRO, D3287/67/11/80, 'Two Imported Servants Quietly Leave at Night and Are Arrested. Sequel in Court', *The Bulawayo Chronicle*, 8 February 1902.
108 Letter from Eliza Hobbs to 'Honoured Madam', 11 February 1902.
109 Mrs F. E. Cotton, 'Domestic Servants', in *The National Council of the Women of New Zealand Fifth Session, Dunedin, 3–12 May 1900* (Christchurch: Smith, Anthony, Sellars and Company Ltd, 1900), pp. 63–4.
110 See, for instance, Barnardo's, A2/53/167, letter from Stuart Barnardo to Thomas Barnardo, 6 December 1902; and DRO, D3287/93/4/4 (ii), letter to Mrs Gell, 30 April 1902. For more on the relationship between mistresses and their servants, see, for instance, the work of Fae Dussart, including *In the Service of Empire*.
111 Joyce (ed.), 'Report from 1890', p. 37; and DRO, D3287/68/1/3, Ellen Joyce (ed.), 'Report from 1892', in *Girls' Friendly Society. Reports of the Department for Members Emigrating. 1883 to 1897*, p. 52.
112 DRO, D3287/67/11/84, letter from Eliza Hobbs to Madam, 8 January 1902.
113 Letter from Eliza Hobbs to 'Honoured Madam', 11 February 1902.
114 On this point, see also DRO, D3287/MIL/1/597/1, letter from P. L. Gell to 'My dear Alfred', 23 January 1903.
115 DRO, D3287/76/2/2/122–132, South African Expansion Application Form for Sarah Elliot, 8 January 1903.
116 DRO, D3287/76/2/2/131, letter from E. F. Thompson to Madam, 18 May 1903.

117 DRO, D3287/76/2/2/122, letter from Geraldine R. Glasgow to Madam, 23 April [1903].
118 DRO, D3287/76/2/2/130, extract from Mother Annie's letter, 25 April 1903. On this point, see also Johnston, 'Only Send Boys of the Good Type', 386.
119 Letter from Geraldine R. Glasgow to Madam
120 Letter from Geraldine R. Glasgow to Madam.
121 DRO, D3287/67/11/84, letter from Ellen Joyce to Miss Hobbs, 22 February 1902.
122 For more on emotional labour, see, for example, Arlie Russell Hochschild, *The Managed Heart: Commercialization of Human Feeling*, 3rd ed. (Berkeley: University of California Press, 2012); Sara Ahmed, *The Cultural Politics of Emotion*, 2nd ed. (New York: Routledge, 2014); Kristine Alexander, 'Agency and Emotion Work', *Jeunesse: Young People, Texts, Cultures*, 7:2 (2015), 120–8; and Karen Vallgårda, *Imperial Childhoods and Christian Missions: Education and Emotions in South India and Denmark*, Palgrave Studies in the History of Emotions (New York: Palgrave Macmillan, 2015). For more on cultural work, see, for example, Carol Watts, *The Cultural Work of Empire: The Seven Years' War and the Imagining of the Shandean State* (Toronto: University of Toronto Press, 2007).
123 May Hely-Hutchinson, 'Female Emigration to South Africa', *Nineteenth Century and After*, 51 (March 1902), 77.
124 DRO, D3287/68/1/3, Ellen Joyce (ed.), 'Report for 1892', in *Girls' Friendly Society. Reports of the Department for Members Emigrating. 1883 to 1897*, p. 52.
125 On this point, see, for instance, DRO, D3287/67/11/170, letter from Margaret James to Lady Malmesbury, 10 December; Lady Barker, *Life in South Africa* (Philadelphia: J. B. Lippincott & Co., 1877), p. 33; and 'Domestic Servants', *The Poverty Bay Herald* (10 June 1910), p. 5.
126 See, for instance, DRO, D3287/68/1/7/4, Girls' Friendly Society, *Department for Members Emigrating* (n.d.), p. 2.
127 Joyce (ed.), 'Preface', *Girls' Friendly Society. Reports of the Department for Members Emigrating. 1883 to 1897*, p. 1.
128 Barnardo's, A3/1/33, 'Table AA: A Seven Years' Record of Village Home Girls', *33rd Annual Report of the Institutions known as 'Dr. Barnardo's Homes' for Orphan & Waif Children*, 1898, p. 104.
129 DRO, D3207/67/11/84, letter from Sidonia C. Robinson to Miss Lefroy, 23 December 1901.
130 'Two Imported Servants Quietly Leave at Night and Are Arrested'.
131 Veracini, *Settler Colonialism*, pp. 4, 3.

# 4

# Contested ideas of whiteness and race in the Girls' Friendly Society

In 1929, GFS associates of the Mill Hill branch in London received an alarming report that sent shockwaves through the branch. One of their members, Violet Paul, intended to travel to India to marry a man named W. E. Davis. What made the situation particularly worrisome to the GFS associates was that one of Paul's friends believed that Davis was a 'half-caste', adding that 'his mother was the native'.[1] In response to this report, Mabel Sisley, an associate of the Mill Hill branch, wrote to the GFS branch in Rawalpindi, asking them to investigate if Davis was 'desirable'.[2] In making this request, Sisley emphasised the 'need to safeguard her [Paul's] welfare in case the man proves to be a rogue or even an agent of the white slave traffic'.[3] The GFS deployed an effective global information network. Within a month, Mrs Marshall, a GFS associate in Rawalpindi, wrote back to Sisley, describing Davis as 'Undesirable' since he was an 'Indian man with Christian name, not Anglo-Indian'.[4] In a subsequent letter, Marshall elaborated on her verdict, explaining that Davis was '*extremely* black' and reflected on the damaging consequences of such a relationship: 'I cannot believe that any decent English girl would be happy if she married a very black man like this, decent fellow though he is. She would find herself cut off from English people and her only company would be Anglo Indians of the lower sort and Indians – also of the lower sort.'[5] As indicated by the repeated emphasis on Davis as 'very black' and 'extremely black', his Indian background and the colour of his skin made the potential marriage of Paul and Davis intolerable to the GFS associates.

Despite Marshall's concern that Paul's marriage to an Indian man would likely have an adverse effect on her social status, correspondence between London and Rawalpindi suggests that Davis was relatively affluent and could provide a comfortable life for Paul, including a home in which she 'will be waited on by servants'.[6] However, this prospect did not ease the fears of GFS associates, who wrote that 'her early home life and education have not fitted her to play the role of hostess'.[7] This correspondence implies that the relationship between Paul and Davis violated not only racial hierarchies but class ones as well. Despite trying to convince Paul that her decision to travel to India to marry Davis would 'wreck her life', correspondence between GFS associates indicates that Paul remained committed in her choice. The conclusion of the case is not clear from the archival records of the GFS, but the available evidence suggests that Paul did go to India, since the last correspondence regarding Paul's case is from Caroline Mytton, the secretary of the GFS Central Council, who wrote that they have done 'everything possible' and 'if the girl persists in going out, she will only have herself to blame'.[8]

The previous chapters examined how the GFS employed various educational activities to turn English girls into empire builders who would help build up white societies abroad through the creation of white homes and the maintenance of English domesticity. Yet, as the story of Paul and the case of Eliza Hobbs and Eliza Cook described in the previous chapter indicate, girls did not always adhere to these prescribed roles. Girls – and particularly working-class girls – were viewed as questionable and unstable racial and cultural bulwarks. By eloping with an Indian man, Paul subverted the goal of GFS's programmes: to create 'good homes' that were 'white'.[9] The GFS's response to Paul and Davis's impending marriage elucidates how racial, class, and gendered anxieties were intertwined within the GFS and colonial societies more broadly.

The GFS presented itself as an organisation that transcended social and racial divisions. Mary Elizabeth Townsend, the GFS's founder, described how one of the organisation's goals was 'welding together those whom differences of race so often keep apart'.[10] In her official history of the GFS, Agnes Money similarly heralded its role in uniting different races: 'In that great work which England to-day is doing for her Indian Empire, I have proud hopes that our G.F.S. may play its part, helping to break down racial distinctions, binding together Anglo-Indian, Eurasian, and Christian native with its cord of love and sympathy and prayer'.[11] However, GFS policies and attitudes towards girls of different races revealed the hollowness of these pronouncements. As Julia Bush observes in her study of the organisation, the GFS 'stood emphatically for purity, especially racial purity'.[12] This commitment to preserving ideas of whiteness and purity was at odds with the realities of colonial societies, particularly in places like India, where white people composed a minority of the population and the experiences of that minority were very different from those of white people in England.

This chapter analyses the GFS's work in India and specifically its efforts to reform two groups that provoked considerable anxiety among the colonial government and the GFS: poor white and multiracial girls. In India, these two groups formed the domiciled community, and the distinction between them was often blurred. The confusion over Davis's background indicates how racial identities were contested and racial designations in flux during this period. 'Anglo-Indian' was initially used to designate a British person resident in India, while 'Eurasian' described a person of Indian and European descent. The multiracial community increasingly resisted the term 'Eurasian' and its derogatory associations with miscegenation, eventually taking over the designation of 'Anglo-Indian', a change reflected in the 1911 census.[13] GFS records reflect this instability of racial categories, with associates using both 'Eurasian' and 'Anglo-Indian' to refer to those of Indian and European descent and also using the term 'Anglo-Indian' to refer to a British person living permanently in India. For the sake of consistency, I use the term 'Anglo-Indian' to refer to those of Indian and European descent and 'domiciled European' to refer to a British person living permanently in India. As this chapter explores, the existence of domiciled Europeans and Anglo-Indians seemingly threatened ideas of whiteness and purity by complicating binary racial distinctions and raising the spectre of racial degeneration. The previous chapters examined the GFS's efforts to make the empire white through educational initiatives and emigration schemes for English girls to the settler colonies. This chapter considers another facet of these efforts by analysing educational and reform programmes for domiciled girls. As with the GFS's plans for emigration, problems beset these programmes, revealing contradictions and fault lines over race within the GFS and the colonial project more broadly.

### 'The G.F.S. Jewel': establishing the GFS in India

The GFS established its first branches in India within ten years of its foundation. Lahore was the first Indian branch founded in 1885, and in the subsequent years, it extended its work to Calcutta, Lucknow, Bombay (present-day Mumbai), and to other areas in southern Asia, including Rangoon (present-day Yangon) and Colombo.[14] Within the imperial family of the GFS, India occupied a special place as '[t]he G.F.S. Jewel', and the branches in India and Ceylon emphasised their 'closer relationship with the Home G.F.S. than the daughter Societies in the Dominions'.[15] The organisational structure reflected this singular place of India within the GFS. In 1902, the GFS Central Council decided that India needed to be governed directly from London.[16] Mary Elizabeth Townsend argued that this greater control was necessary due 'to the vast distances' in India.[17] Under this centralised structure, it was argued that the 'G.F.S. in India might form an integral part of our own Society ... claiming all possible help from us in the organisation and development of the work'.[18] Townsend contended that such an arrangement allowed the GFS in India to 'become more closely linked with the G.F.S. at home, preserving at the same time its freedom and power of adaptation to local needs and surroundings'.[19] Yet such arrangements did not hold India as an equal partner.[20] Indian dioceses could appoint a representative in England to attend and speak at meetings of the Central Council, but they could not vote. Townsend's view that this arrangement would ensure 'its freedom and the power of adaptation' was not shared by the Indian branches themselves, and, as the next chapter explores, the lack of control over their own affairs would cause increasing resentment in the 1920s and 1930s.

The GFS in India initially focused on providing a community to English girls and young women who had recently arrived in India. These girls and young women travelled to India typically to work as governesses, teachers, and nurses. GFS associates in India detailed the special challenges faced by newly arrived emigrants in the region. For instance, a report by the Indian branches to the GFS Central Council in London described how an emigrant 'is plunged into an utterly different life and the loneliness is perfectly awful'.[21] The GFS aimed to remedy this problem in part by seeking to fill girls' lives with wholesome interests. The activities of the GFS in India broadly mirrored those in England, with branches hosting social events, including dances and festivals, and holding meetings and lectures.[22]

Pervasive fears over the potentially degenerative effects of the Indian environment on people's health gave an impetus to the GFS's work in the region.[23] Correspondence from GFS associates in India emphasised how girls faced greater moral dangers in India. Olive Carden, the president of the GFS's Diocesan Council in Lahore, and Ethel Shepard, the head deaconess of St Hilda's Society in Lahore, wrote about the greater challenges facing girls – and the GFS – in the region: 'Here in India, where, owing to the circumstance of their lives, European girls mature young, and are often faced with temptations and a knowledge of evil beyond their years'.[24] As Elizabeth Buettner relates in her study of British families in India, the tropical climate and children's close proximity to Indian people generated fears that children would lose their British identity and adopt Indian habits, endangering white respectability and prestige.[25] GFS associates shared these fears that India lacked 'civilising' influences and consequently left girls idle and apathetic. For instance, an article in *The Empire and Beyond* observes:

> One hears of girls in India, higher up in the social scale, being frivolous and given up to amusement, but is it their fault? They are in a country where there are no advantages; there is no music of our kind, no literature, no lectures, nothing on which a girl can feed her mind after she has left school. Naturally these girls turn to amusements, and their humbler sisters follow suit.[26]

The GFS feared not only the effects of the environment on English girls' behaviour but also the reverberations of these girls' behaviour throughout Indian society and their influence on other girls, namely domiciled European and Anglo-Indian girls. These concerns about the effect of the Indian environment made hostels an especially vital part of the GFS's imperial work.[27] As discussed in Chapter 3, hostels provided a sense of community for girls, offering accommodations and entertainment.[28] The hostels also importantly ensured that girls were surrounded by the 'right influences' and acted as 'a safe and happy refuge' that protected girls from the 'temptations everywhere' in India.[29] The GFS established hostels and lodges in major cities in the region, including Delhi, Murree, Lahore, Calcutta, Rangoon, and Bombay.[30]

## 'A pressing need': the GFS and the 'Anglo-Indian problem'

The GFS in India – like the organisation in other parts of the empire – faced difficulties in attracting and retaining English members, which led associates to focus more of its efforts on working with Anglo-Indian girls. In contrast to English girls, who moved around India or between India and England, Anglo-Indian girls provided a more stable source of membership, since, as noted by Agnes Money in her *History of the Girls' Friendly Society*, they 'live[d] there always'.[31] In addition to the need for more members, the decision for the GFS to work with Anglo-Indian girls stemmed from the growth of the Anglo-Indian population and the increasing preoccupation with the 'Anglo-Indian problem' or 'Eurasian question' in the late nineteenth and early twentieth centuries.[32] The GFS recognised that there was 'a pressing need for lady workers, especially for the Eurasian girls and women' and used the justification of helping the Anglo-Indian population to extend its foothold in India.[33] Articles in GFS periodicals, especially *The Empire and Beyond*, tout the importance and influence of the GFS's 'civilising' guidance on Anglo-Indian girls and how '[t]he Eurasian girl, properly trained, can rise to higher things'.[34] The GFS saw the effects of such work reverberating to the wider Indian society. An article from *The Empire and Beyond* expresses this belief, describing how the GFS was 'bringing other girls to join our sisterhood, and helping them to a higher standard, thus doing our part in bringing the whole of Christian girlhood in India to reflect Christ more than it does at present'.[35] The GFS thus framed its work with Anglo-Indian girls as contributing to the broader reformation of girlhood and, by extension, Indian society.

The admittance of multiracial girls experienced less resistance in India than it did in areas like southern Africa, which is discussed later in this chapter. This difference is partly due to British racial ideology, which placed Indians higher on the civilisational scale than African peoples.[36] The GFS argued that multiracial children in India were essentially English in temperament. Such a view is reflected in Money's *History*:

> Our Government classes them as Europeans; they are Christians; they dress like ourselves, and their daughters go to the High Schools with our English girls. They have the greatest love for England and for all that belongs to it, and will speak of England as "home", though they have never seen it, and know that they can never expect to do so.[37]

Money's outwardly welcoming and conciliatory views were not shared by all GFS associates. Hazel Palmer, the wife of the bishop of Bombay and the president of the GFS's Diocesan Council in Bombay, wrote about Anglo-Indian girls in *The Empire and Beyond*, describing how their character 'sings to all the weaknesses and drawbacks of the Indian race'.[38] Some associates recognised that the problems facing Anglo-Indian girls were not inherent in their character, as often implied by associates, but the product of broader racism by the British. For instance, in 1927, M. F. Down – the secretary of the GFS's Diocesan Council in Calcutta – wrote to Caroline Mytton that the existence of Anglo-Indian girls posed 'one serious difficulty in this country', but she conceded that 'I'm sorry to say we, as a race, are not always as kind and sympathetic to their difficulties as we might be. We cannot or will not see that their colour is sufficient handicap to them in their life, without adding to it.'[39] Such recognition of the role the British played in the challenges faced by Anglo-Indian girls remained rare. Instead descriptions of Anglo-Indian girls as 'lazy', 'feckless', having 'very little backbone', and being 'very different' from English girls are more common in the reports of GFS associates.[40] These disparaging comments reveal how Anglo-Indian children served as visible and uncomfortable reminders of sexual and racial 'transgressions' and complicated racial boundaries, whose maintenance was viewed as essential to English identity.[41]

The need to broaden its membership base also led the GFS to admit Indian, specifically Indian Christian girls, into the organisation, yet, as with Anglo-Indian girls, it did so with reservations. Its half-hearted efforts meant that the GFS failed to be an effective presence in Indian girls' lives. In 1906, a report by the Committee for the GFS in India and Ceylon admitted that there was still 'a *large* number of Indian girls untouched at all'.[42] Over twenty years later, little had changed. In 1928, Mary Campbell, the GFS's organising worker in India, wrote to Mytton about the struggles to find English members: 'One scarcely realises what stretches there are in India where there are just no European girls at all!'[43] At the same time, she conceded that the GFS had failed to attract Indian girls: 'I don't know whether they will ever see the G.F.S. as be [*sic*] of use to the Indian girls'.⁴⁴ Despite the need for Indian and Anglo-Indian members to sustain the organisation, GFS associates feared that admitting them would leave English girls vastly outnumbered, which in turn would compromise the racial purity of the GFS and its reputation of whiteness. Consequently, even though the GFS admitted Indian and Anglo-Indian girls, it simultaneously worked to limit their interaction with English girls.⁴⁵

## 'A stronger link for the girls': the domiciled community and training programmes in India

The 'Anglo-Indian problem' was not an isolated issue that involved only multiracial groups but was intricately connected to the status of other groups, particularly poor whites in India.⁴⁶ In contrast to 'respectable' Europeans in India whose residence in India was viewed as temporary, poor white Europeans lived in India permanently and, along with Anglo-Indians, formed part of the domiciled community. As Satoshi Mizutani observes in his study of the domiciled community in India, 'the visibility of their degraded condition was feared to undermine fatally the collective self-image of the British as respectable agents of imperial civilization in India'.⁴⁷ Like Anglo-Indians, domiciled Europeans were not viewed as 'authentically white'.⁴⁸ As demonstrated by the eponymous character in Rudyard Kipling's *Kim* (1901), poor white children, like Anglo-Indian children, remained on the margins of the colonial social order, blurring class and racial lines and threatening the cohesion of white society. Their danger to white respectability and prestige led Henry Durant, the bishop of Lahore (1913–32), to describe the domiciled community as 'one of our most pressing problems out here'.⁴⁹ As the GFS worked to establish its presence on the subcontinent, it increasingly turned its attention to the domiciled community, who would eventually compose the majority of its membership in branches in India and Ceylon, including the one in Colombo pictured in Figure 4.1.⁵⁰

Children of the domiciled community were considered especially susceptible to the supposedly degenerative forces of India and thus key targets of reform and intervention by the colonial state.⁵¹ The colonial government established low-cost and free elementary and industrial schools to teach children literacy and practical skills, arguing that such educational work would safeguard them against the disadvantages of their background and dangerous influences posed by the colonial environment.⁵² The GFS supported these efforts by sending workers to orphanages and schools for domiciled children and collecting money to pay for workers' passages to India. It also formed branches connected to schools and orphanages for the domiciled community. For instance, it had a branch at the St Lawrence

**Figure 4.1** Candidates in Colombo (Women's Library, London, 5GFS/04/127, 'Candidates of Colombo, Ceylon', November 1931, photo from Block Book VII, 1926–31)

Military Asylum at Sanawar, which was founded in 1846 and, according to historian Dane Kennedy, 'was the earliest and most influential institution established to redeem orphans and other poor white children by transferring them to the hills'.[53] It also had a branch connected with St Andrew's Colonial Homes, which was founded in 1900 and built along the same lines as Dr Barnardo's Homes in England, seeking to separate domiciled children from Indian society and emigrate them abroad to work as artisans, farmers, and servants in other parts of the empire, including New Zealand.[54] The GFS moreover allied with other organisations – like the Young Women's Christian Association (YWCA), the Society for the Propagation of the Gospel, and Mothers' Union – that organised programmes for domiciled European and Anglo-Indian girls.[55]

In addition to working with other institutions and organisations, the GFS started its own programmes in major cities throughout India – including Bombay, Delhi, and Allahabad (present-day Prayagraj) – during the first decade of the twentieth century. For instance, it established a programme in Bombay with St Christopher's Nursery Training School, primarily for 'orphans from the very poorest class of the community'.[56] It also developed the Punjab Industrial Training Scheme (PITS). As with the programme in Bombay, children who were part of PITS came 'mostly from the poorest of European and Eurasian homes, have invariably lost one or both parents, and are often rescued from most undesirable surroundings'.[57]

A pamphlet about PITS provided more information about the purpose of the programme: 'The Girls' Friendly Society in the Punjab long ago realised its responsibilities to the Anglo-Indian Girls of the Punjab where the honourable employment of girls of this class presents even a more difficult problem than that with which the English G.F.S. is endeavouring to deal'.[58] To solve this 'difficult problem', PITS aimed 'to give any Member of the G.F.S. in India the opportunity for training and perfecting herself in a branch of occupation in which she may require to make herself independent and self-supporting'.[59] Like schools, these programmes prepared girls to enter the labour market and 'earn a living by honourable and useful work'.[60] Their ultimate goal was that girls would lead self-sufficient lives, so that they were no longer contributing to greater poverty in India and a drain on the resources of the colonial state.

The GFS programmes prepared girls for specific fields where there was a dire need for workers. St Christopher's Nursery Training School in Bombay taught girls domestic skills and, as suggested by its name, to be children's nurses. While some girls did become servants and nurses, others pursued positions at hostels and offices and as dressmakers.[61] Similarly, PITS initially trained girls 'either in domestic service or public offices and institutions'.[62] It later prepared girls to become children's nurses, because they 'are a great necessity, and difficult to secure in India; and the Anglo-Indian, with a little training, makes an excellent nurse for a child'.[63] Other training programmes, like the one in Delhi, concentrated on educating girls to become medical and health workers.[64]

As described in previous chapters, girls' education had special importance, due to girls' perceived malleability and destined roles as wives and mothers.[65] The first chapter discussed how middle-class and upper-class associates justified the purpose of the GFS by casting doubt on the ability of working-class parents to raise their children properly and provide them with morally respectable, 'pure' homes, and similar rationales also circulated in colonial societies. GFS associates doubted that parents within the domiciled community could be trusted with the proper upbringing and especially moral training of their children. Sister Veronica, who worked at the Bishop Westcott School for Girls in Ranchi, wrote, for instance, to Caroline Mytton that girls' 'homes are often a hindrance rather than anything else'.[66] Like the GFS in England, the GFS in India effectively tried to take the place of the family and ensure that girls were placed under the 'right' influences as a way to remedy the perceived problems of the domiciled community.

The training programmes developed by the GFS for domiciled girls were broadly modelled on the same lines as its training programmes for working-class girls in England. They included classes on religious instruction, domestic science, sewing, singing, laundry work, and the management and care of babies – skills that they would need as servants or nurses but also as future wives and mothers.[67] The GFS targeted girls at schools, hoping that they would retain their connection with the GFS – and, by extension, the church and religious life – after their formal education ceased. As noted at a meeting of the GFS Diocesan Council in Lahore, the GFS wanted to serve as 'a stronger link for the girls between school and the time when they had left school and went to live in the Plains – something which might keep them in touch with the Church and the standards of life they learnt in school'.[68] The GFS's decision to target girls at school also stemmed from the desire to reach them before they could be 'corrupted' by the environment. Margaret Arbuthnot, the president of the GFS Central Council from 1931 to 1933, wrote about the importance of influencing girls when they are younger: 'It would, therefore, seem to me that it is even more desirable in India to get hold of the girls early, just as we try to do in England', since '[t]he whole purport of the Society is to help girls to maintain a high moral standard'.[69] Domesticity, respectability, and morality were seen as inextricably tied, and the GFS viewed the reform of home life and girlhood as a means to reform the domiciled community and Indian society more broadly.

One key impetus behind the GFS's training programmes was 'the learning of place and race'.[70] In *The Magic Mountains*, Kennedy describes how St Lawrence, like other schools and orphanages, 'offered an education that stressed discipline, obedience, piety, respectability, and acquiescence to a future of limited opportunity'.[71] The GFS programmes had a similar purpose. They did not promote upward social mobility but instead reinforced racial and class hierarchies.[72] The GFS stated that its work in India was 'to train the girls from the very beginning in industrial methods and bring them up to work for their livings in the capacity they are best fitted for'.[73] Its emphasis on the 'capacity they are best fitted for' underscores how the GFS's programmes endeavoured to teach domiciled girls their 'proper' role in society and make them useful to the empire. These programmes, like colonial education more broadly, also served as a way for the GFS to extend its influence and authority over marginal members of colonial societies.[74]

Anxieties about whiteness and white prestige lay at the heart of the GFS's educational programmes in India. In his work on the domiciled community, Mizutani argues that 'the invention of whiteness depended *both* on the securing of a "bourgeois" social milieu for middle-class whites *and* on the vigilant control of the impoverished domiciled'.[75] White hegemony was never secure and always contested, and poor whites and people of mixed-race descent destabilised notions of white prestige, leading to concerted efforts to reform these groups, particularly through schools and other instructional programmes. As Mizutani observes, 'Colonial authorities found education as one of the most effective measures to control white pauperism'.[76] The GFS's programmes were part of these broader mechanisms of control and contributed to efforts by the colonial state to raise the status of the domiciled community. The associates of the GFS, who largely belonged to the class of 'respectable' upper-class and middle-class women, recognised that their privileged position within Indian colonial society was intricately connected to the status of the domiciled community, and their investment in these efforts at reform was thus a way to fortify their own whiteness.

## 'The dream of "home" has been too big': training programmes for domiciled girls in England

In addition to developing training programmes for girls in India, the GFS sponsored programmes for domiciled girls to travel to and receive training in England. The majority of the GFS's migration programmes assisted girls travelling from England to other parts of the empire, but girls' movement in the empire was not unilateral and instead involved more complex, multi-directional networks of mobility.[77] In line with the GFS's original remit to protect girls travelling within England, its programmes for girls from India were intended to 'safeguard Eurasian girls coming to London' for educational and employment purposes, specifically to pursue 'training in Kindergarten, musical, and nursing professions'.[78] As it had done in the colonies for English girls, the GFS initially focused its efforts on facilitating travel by furnishing a correspondent who could provide advice to members coming to London, making introductions for new arrivals, providing a meeting place for girls in England, and developing an 'English Scholarship Fund' to subsidise travel costs of GFS members.[79] It also worked with organisations, like the YWCA, to facilitate the travel of girls and young women from India to England.[80]

Myriad motives underlay these migration programmes for girls to India, some of which overlapped with the rationales behind its migration programmes for English girls discussed in the previous chapter. On a practical level, these programmes fulfilled a critical labour shortage. Bringing Indian girls and women to work as domestic servants was viewed as a potential solution to the servant problem in England. Over time, the demand grew for nurses in England, leading the GFS to shift the focus of its training.[81] These programmes were envisioned as not only fulfilling a critical labour need but also strengthening imperial ties by expanding the GFS's presence on the subcontinent and creating an additional bond between different parts of the empire.[82]

Beyond these practical impetuses, the programmes were rooted in a growing belief by the turn of the century that schools and other institutions in India could not adequately solve the 'Anglo-Indian problem'. Schools sought to shield children from the supposedly negative influences in India, yet concerns persisted that schools, even boarding schools, could not entirely protect children from the surrounding environment.[83] Moreover, the continued presence and visibility of children of the domiciled community threatened to undermine notions of white prestige.[84] This belief in turn led to calls for them to be isolated – or more precisely removed – from India altogether.[85] To remedy the problems posed by the domiciled community, organisations like the GFS thought that sending children from India to England ensured that they received a superior, unquestionably English education. As described in the previous chapter, the belief that children needed to be removed from the dangerous and degenerative environments of poor urban areas provided the impetus for emigration programmes from England to settler colonies, and such rationales also worked in reverse and led to programmes to emigrate children from the colonies to England.

Despite the professed importance and need for these training programmes, instituting them was not without its challenges. For instance, PITS originally intended to send members to England to receive training, but the GFS had to remodel the plan along less ambitious lines. Instead of sending girls to England, the GFS ultimately recruited and paid the salary and passage for a GFS associate 'thoroughly trained in all Industrial Work' to travel to India to serve as the matron of the Cathedral Orphanage in Lahore.[86] The lack of workers and the mobility and fluidity of the English community in India hindered the development these training programmes.[87] Paying for the workers' salaries, workers' and girls' passages to and from India, and the training and lodging of girls required considerable financial investment.[88] The GFS raised money through a variety of means, including subscriptions, grants, voluntary efforts, and contributions from the trainees themselves.[89] Branches in India and other parts of the empire would often host fundraisers, including doll pageants, to support the education of girls in these programmes.[90] PITS in particular received the support of influential figures, including the Countess of Minto and the bishop of Lahore, who described the programme as 'too little known though it is deserving of the fullest support'.[91] Despite this high-profile support, programmes like PITS still struggled with financial difficulties. The First World War exacerbated these financial constraints, interrupting the programme and diverting finances and attention to 'the more immediate and pressing requirements of war work'.[92] These financial difficulties persisted even after the war ended.

While the GFS publicly attributed the difficulties in developing these programmes to finances, deeper structural issues beleaguered PITS and other training schemes.⁹³ A 1922 report on PITS conceded that there were 'no girls to train' and that there was 'no use for it'.⁹⁴ Similarly, a 1913–14 report from Bombay admitted that the St Christopher's Nursery Training School 'does not grow' and failed to attract girls.⁹⁵ Two years later, St Christopher's closed.⁹⁶ The GFS attributed the failure in part to the stigma of work and service. The St Christopher's report acknowledged: 'There are probably many people in India, like the man who told the Lucknow Diocesan Secretary, when she offered to send his daughter to us, "I'd rather see her starve than let her go into Service!"'.⁹⁷ GFS associates blamed the domiciled community's reluctance to work on their European ancestry and 'pride of race'.⁹⁸ In a 1914 report, the Lucknow Diocese noted that it struggled with 'the deep-rooted hereditary instinct that for Anglo-Indians as well as Indians, except of the lowest caste, all manual labour is degrading'.⁹⁹ Just as it tried – and largely failed – to change the connotation of domestic service in England, the GFS worked to change negative associations of labour in India, but the lack of girls indicates that its efforts met with limited success. Domiciled Europeans and Anglo-Indians recognised that – contrary to the rhetoric of GFS associates – domestic service would not improve the lives of girls but instead was a mode of exploitation.

Even when the problems of these programmes were apparent, the GFS was keen to portray them as a success. For instance, the *Girls' Friendly Society Leaflet for India and the Far East* from 1925 recounted the accomplishments of one student, Dorothy Winter, who was born in Rawalpindi and educated at St Denys Girls' Diocesan School in Murree. Winter trained as a nurse and, after winning a scholarship, moved to England. The leaflet encouraged other girls to emulate her: 'we hope this record of a G.F.S. Member will inspire other Members in India to follow her example, and by hard steady work and devotion to duty show that Girls in India and trained there, can hold their own when they come to England without any difficulty arising from that fact'.¹⁰⁰ Yet such success stories were not universal, and associates often wrote about the 'most unsatisfactory and difficult experiences' faced by girls from India travelling to England.¹⁰¹ Like the English migrants who travelled to other parts of the empire, girls from India experienced loneliness and difficulties adapting to a new country and climate, with some returning to India because they felt 'absolutely miserable in England'.¹⁰² Contrary to Winter's experiences, girls reported experiencing discrimination in England due to their Indian background. When the GFS associate Agnes Attree wanted to send two members from her branch in Calcutta to England, Caroline Mytton advised her to dissuade the members from going, writing: 'The Anglo-Indian girl seems mad to come to England, and we on our side are bent on trying to prevent it, if we possibly can'.¹⁰³ Mytton disclosed that girls from India who wanted to stay at GFS lodges faced resistance and '[i]t is very difficult to find posts in England for Anglo-Indians'.[104] Mytton's correspondence reveals how racist and discriminatory attitudes towards girls from India prevented them from finding employment and places to stay in England. In correspondences with Margaret Scott, the secretary of the GFS Diocesan Council in Lahore, Mytton likewise spoke about the inadvisability of having girls from India travel to England, writing: 'it is rather hard on our workers in England who do not understand the Anglo-Indian at all ... I do not think the Anglo-Indian ought to consider England is home, and we want to discourage them coming for their own sake'.[105] In response, Scott asserted: 'we cannot *make* the Anglo-Indian stay in India ... the dream of "home" has been too big to be drowned in cold water'.[106] As described in Chapter 2, the GFS encouraged girls to think of England as home, but Mytton's correspondence reveals a divergence between rhetoric and reality and the true purpose behind the emphasis on England as 'home'. Such discourses were intended to strengthen England's position as the head of the imperial family, not to make girls in the empire – and especially girls of colour – feel that they were equal members of a community. The difficulties with the training programmes laid bare the hollowness of the GFS's pronouncements about being an inclusive society and instead demonstrated its deep commitment to keep England white.[107]

## 'A difficult position': disputes between colonial branches and the Central Council

The training programmes' lack of success reveals the GFS's ineffectiveness at addressing the 'Anglo-Indian problem' and failure of the GFS in London to understand fully the conditions in different parts of the empire. These issues exacerbated tensions between the Central Council and branches in the colonies and dominions. Their deleterious effect on the GFS's imperial work is exemplified by the problems created by the appointment of Mary Thomas to take over the GFS's hostel in Calcutta. When Thomas landed in Calcutta in February 1930, it was clear that the task before her would not be easy. Yet Caroline Mytton and Finetta Bruce, the GFS Central Council secretary and vice-president respectively, placed great faith in Thomas and her abilities. They vetted her and found her a 'capable' worker, commending her 'her appearance and manner' and her knowledge of the GFS – noting she 'has been G.F.S. for a great many years, first as a Member, and then as an Associate'.[108] Even though Thomas was older, fifty-four years of age, Mytton reported that she was in good health. Yet such reassurances did little to assuage sceptical GFS associates in India. They needed workers who knew the climate and language and were 'in touch with the modern girl'.[109] Thomas had none of these attributes, and her GFS background and appearance had little value amid the different, challenging conditions of India. Mytton and Bruce claimed Thomas had the requisite experience because she performed 'Rescue Work' in the Cape Colony.[110] However, Vera Westmacott, the president of the GFS Diocesan Council in Calcutta, made it clear that running a hostel was very different from rescue work and India was not the same as South Africa.[111] When Westmacott expressed her dissatisfaction with Thomas's appointment, Mytton rebuffed her criticism by stating 'it is not easy to get people to volunteer to go out to India'.[112] Westmacott was fatalistic about Thomas's tenure even before her arrival, writing to Mytton: 'We cannot afford to send her home when she breaks down'.[113] In the end, her assessment was prescient.

From the moment she reached Calcutta, Thomas encountered numerous difficulties, including political riots and troubles acclimatising to life in India.[114] Thomas was not alone in her struggles; the different conditions of life in India and other parts of the empire meant that other GFS workers, like emigrant girls, found themselves unprepared for colonial life. Those who went out to the colonies and dominions found that their ideas 'had to be readjusted to suit a new country'.[115] Thomas confided to Mytton about her struggles, writing that 'the language and the money baffle me' and that the hostel 'needs much to make it really comfortable'.[116] Thomas found 'the heat trying' and had difficulties adjusting to the climate.[117] After Thomas's arrival, Westmacott wrote to Mytton, describing how ill-equipped Thomas was to undertake the work at the GFS hostel: 'She assures me she is accustomed to heat and prefers it, but to plunge a woman of her age into a temperature already 102 in the shade with the responsibilities of 23 girls of all ages and professions, knowing nothing of the language, servants, food or conditions is contrary to all reasonable theories with regard to health and endurance in a hot climate'.[118] The repercussions of Thomas's lack of knowledge about India and how to run a hostel became readily apparent, and, just four months after her arrival in India, Westmacott wrote to Mytton that Thomas's appointment was an 'absolute failure'.[119]

One key reason for this assessment was Thomas's lack of training for work in India and her inability to understand the conditions and needs of girls at the hostel. In her letters to Mytton, Thomas described her difficulties with the girls at the hostel and wrote disparagingly of them: 'I am astonished to find how artificial the lives of the girls are – even worse than at home'.[120] While Thomas blamed the girls for their tenuous relationship, Westmacott placed the responsibility on Thomas and specifically her lack of experience with Anglo-Indian girls. In a letter to Mytton, Westmacott described how Thomas 'does not get on with the Anglo Indians and openly dislikes them, and they are frightened of her ... She is full of complaints of the girls [sic] bad manners and undisciplined behaviour'.[121] Her letter continued: 'In her dislike of Anglo Indian girls Miss Thomas is unfair to them, and several of the complaints she has made to me of them appear to be grossly exaggerated and untrue'.[122] Thomas's prejudicial attitudes towards Anglo-Indian girls and lack of understanding of Indian society form a recurring theme in Westmacott's reports about Thomas. She noted that Thomas 'disliked the Anglo Indians very much, and she treated some of the younger girls as prostitutes, threatening to turn one out on the street – Her rule has been a most unfortunate one.'[123] Westmacott's letters also reveal the consequences of Thomas's inability to work with girls in India. Westmacott mentioned that girls in the hostel 'no longer respect her' because 'she gets so angry with them'.[124] She reiterated the problems caused by Thomas's antipathy of Anglo-Indians in a later letter: 'Her relations with the girls were not always happy, possibly because she did not understand them, and altogether she had created a difficult position'.[125] As a result of Thomas's actions, many girls left the hostel.[126]

In addition to her attitudes toward Anglo-Indian girls, Thomas's poor health and her drinking exacerbated the already difficult situation. The girls at the hostel reported that Thomas 'has been lounging about in a dressing-gown smelling so strongly of drink that they don't like going near her'. Westmacott visited the hostel and found that, although 'she was to all appearances sober', she was 'worried at the strong smell of drink'.[127] Westmacott later observed that Thomas 'was intemperate in her temper language and habits' and 'she is looking a wreck and her hands tremble'.[128] Westmacott attributed this drinking problem to the challenges posed by hostel work and Thomas's lack of preparation for life in India. In a letter to Mytton, she explained:

> [F]rom the start she has not got on with the girls, and as the hot weather has progressed she has got more and more exhausted and unable to deal with petty grumbles calmly. Her health has undoubtedly suffered, and it is for this reason I imagine she has found it necessary to resort to stimulants to help her carry on. That being the case, it is obvious she is unfit for work in this country.[129]

She reiterated this view in another letter:

> I was aware she was taking spirits as I frequently smelt it, but never saw it, or any real reason for speaking about it, and it was not till a deputation came to me and complained of unjust treatment, temper, and her accusation of some of them in no mean language did I realise what a hopeless position prevailed.[130]

These factors created an 'unhappy atmosphere in the Hostel', leading Westmacott to ask if Thomas 'would consent to go home'.[131] In justifying her request, Westmacott wrote: 'knowing India as we do, and the type of girl living in the Hostel, we have no hesitation whatever in saying that Miss Thomas was the last person in the world to be placed in charge'.[132] Thomas departed Calcutta and arrived back in London in August 1930.

Thomas arrived during 'a time of problems in India', and her brief – only around five months – but disastrous time at the hostel seemed to put the nail in the coffin of the GFS in Calcutta.[133] Writing three months after Thomas returned to England, Westmacott reported to the GFS in London: 'We are seriously contemplating closing the Hostel, and if we do G.F.S. becomes a mere shadow, but we cannot carry on unless full ... I am afraid during Miss Thomas [sic] short reign the hostel got a bad name, one only hears now in round-a-bout ways the aspersions she seems to have cast upon the character of the inmates, and it is having a bad effect now'.[134] Struggling with poor finances and having alienated its girl residents, the GFS hostel in Calcutta closed the following year in July 1931.[135] Westmacott conceded that Thomas alone was not responsible: 'I think she merely hastened the end – and possibly had she been more sympathetic and tactful we might have saved the situation, but as I say, looking back on the last years work, I find it hard to blame anyone or any thing'.[136] Indeed Westmacott's prediction that the GFS would become a 'mere shadow' in India came true. As the next chapter examines, two years later, in 1933, the GFS would close its branches in India.

Thomas was not alone in her struggles to understand Anglo-Indian girls and adapt to India. Other GFS associates and workers wrote about their difficulties with Anglo-Indian girls.[137] Around the same time as Thomas's ruinous tenure in Calcutta, the GFS found itself in a comparable situation in Bombay, when Mabel Goodrich was forced to resign her position as the superintendent of the White House Lodge in Bombay by the GFS's Diocesan Council in the city. As it had done with Thomas, the GFS in London orchestrated Goodrich's appointment and had high expectations, noting that '[h]er knowledge of G.F.S. procedure is a great advantage'.[138] Yet, as made evident by Thomas, an understanding of the GFS was not enough, and instead Goodrich faced similar problems in acclimatising to India and understanding Indian society and the Anglo-Indian community. Correspondence about and by Goodrich chronicles her arguments with girls at the hostel and with the Anglo-Indian woman in charge of the hostel before her arrival.[139] Lady Winifred Cocke, the president of the GFS's Diocesan Council in Bombay, conceded that Goodrich

> was not a success with the girls. She did not seem to understand them in the least though I am sure she tried to very hard. I think you would realise how much we hoped Miss Goodrich would settle down and get to know the very difficult type of girl – the Eurasian or Anglo-Indian as they are called now-a-days, by keeping her on as long as we did.[140]

Like Thomas, Goodrich felt overwhelmed at the situation in Bombay and wrote to Mytton: 'Personally I feel that I have never tackled such a tough job in my life'.[141] In a later letter, she admitted to making mistakes but reasoned: '*It takes time* for a person who has never been to India before or seen an Anglo Indian'.[142] The situation did not noticeably improve with Goodrich's successor, Theodora Ackland. Like Goodrich, she seemed uninterested and unsympathetic towards the girls she worked with in Bombay, dismissively describing them as 'extremely apathetic' and 'lethargic'.[143] Anglo-Indian girls faced discrimination not only from associates – like Thomas, Goodrich, and Ackland – but also from English girls, who often refused to interact with them and regarded them as a race apart.[144]

For years before the appointment of Thomas and Goodrich, associates from the colonial branches had written to Mytton that they did not want workers from England due to their lack of preparation and prior disastrous experiences, particularly with Anglo-Indian girls.[145] They impressed upon Mytton that working with girls in India was not the same as working with girls in England. For instance, Margaret Scott wrote to Mytton that 'to be a girl here is much more difficult than in England'.[146] Other reports and correspondence from branches in India similarly drew contrasts between life in England and life in other parts of the empire and argued for the necessity of greater adaptability and freedom for colonial branches to operate effectively.[147] A report about the GFS's work in Ceylon from 1935 noted: 'Eastern conditions, naturally, differ very greatly from Western ones, and a large amount of elasticity in organisation is necessary if the Society is to meet the needs of the Ceylonese girls'. It continued: 'Much freedom must be allowed, I am sure, for the proper development of G.F.S. work in the island'.[148] Mrs Joseph from the Murree Lodge wrote about how rules formed in England were not suitable for lodges in India: 'I do see that conditions here are so absolutely different from home that English Rules and Regulations are not helpful'.[149] Yet their appeals for greater understanding and flexibility went unheeded, with members of the Central Council continuing to view themselves as head of the imperial family who did not need to listen or adapt to the needs of its 'Colonial Daughters'.

The situation was not unique to India, with similar frustrations expressed by GFS workers in other parts of the empire.[150] Fanchette G. Parrish – the secretary of the GFS branch in Port Elizabeth (present-day Gqeberha) – described the challenges facing the organisation there and how '[t]he working of a Branch in South Africa is very different from that of working a Branch in England'.[151] Other associates and workers in South Africa wrote about the 'many Sharp difficulties and perplexities' they encountered and reported needing a worker who 'knows us in S. Africa and our peculiar difficulties'.[152] Yet the GFS Central Council in London ignored such concerns and continued to believe that it knew better than associates on the ground in places like India or South Africa. This attitude is reflected in its decision to send one of its workers, Ada Gardner Williams, to Colombo for a year in 1926 to provide advice about how the GFS could operate more effectively in the region. While in Ceylon, Gardner Williams gave speeches that discussed the aims and activities of the GFS in England. These talks had little relevance for members and associates in Ceylon, with one associate in Colombo commenting: 'Being new to the Island she was not able to suggest any methods of work as conditions were different out here'.[153] GFS associates in the colonies and dominions recognised that the structure, ideals, and programmes of the GFS operated on metropolitan models that could not necessarily be applied beyond England.

The response of the GFS in London compounded the challenges faced by colonial branches. For Westmacott, the appointment of Thomas was just one of a long-standing list of grievances and reaffirmed feelings that the GFS had 'completely ignored' her views and 'neglected' the GFS in India.[154] Even before the appointment of Thomas, Westmacott and other associates in India bemoaned the apparent lack of concern of the Central Council to the difficulties facing the GFS in India and how it blamed hard-working associates on the ground in India for the shortcomings of the GFS.[155] Ackland also criticised the lack of understanding from the Central Council, contending: 'I doubt whether anyone at home realises altogether what we are up against'.[156] E. Mabel Smith, a long-time GFS associate in Port Elizabeth, similarly described the distinct challenges the GFS faced in South Africa, writing that the 'G.F.S. is by no means an easy thing to keep alive in a country like this with its cosmopolitan population and variety of religious denominations'.[157] She noted that '[w]e still struggle along' but '[u]nless you were here to see you could not be expected to know what odds we have to face to keep the GFS flag flying'.[158] She admitted that 'many times I have asked myself "is it worth it"'.[159] M. Sleading also wrote from South Africa in 1935 that branches there felt 'depressed and disconsolate, chiefly in connection with treatment by Headquarters'.[160] Yet Mytton and other members of the Central Council remained unmoved by such testimonies. While acknowledging that the situation in places like India and South Africa was 'terribly difficult', Mytton placed the onus on GFS associates and wrote that 'more enthusiasm is required amongst the workers'.[161] Such indifference to the broader problems contributed to widening and ultimately irreconcilable divisions between the Central Council and GFS branches in the colonies and dominions, a topic returned to in the following chapter.

The growing challenges and repeated failures of workers in the colonies and dominions ultimately led Mytton to realise what associates in India and other parts of the empire had been trying to tell her for years: workers from England could not solve the GFS's problems in India and in fact were the cause of many of its difficulties. In 1931, Mytton wrote to Finetta Bruce, who had assisted her in the selection of Thomas and other workers for the colonies, 'that hardly any woman in England is temperamentally fitted to deal with Anglo-Indians' and they 'do not understand the Anglo-Indian at all'.[162] She continued: 'Our experiences with workers, one after another, seem to bear this out, no matter who the person may be'.[163] Mytton also conceded that their criteria for workers was faulty: 'I have not found that previous G.F.S. experience in England seems to have counted much with the work in India'.[164] Yet the realisation came too late. The GFS had already developed a reputation that it did not 'appreciate the Anglo-Indian girls' and was not 'of use to the Indian girls'.[165] Other organisations were instead more effective at reaching these girls.[166] The YWCA in particular was successful in appealing to Indian and Anglo-Indian girls in ways that the GFS was not.[167] The problem of finding effective workers to undertake work in the empire spoke to its continued prioritisation of England above the interests of other branches and a larger problem within the GFS, namely that its model of girlhood – based on ideal notions of white girlhood – could not be readily adapted for different parts of the empire.

### 'They are not on an equal footing': girls of colour in southern Africa and other parts of the empire

The GFS's struggles to accommodate and include girls of colour are similarly evident in its operations in other parts of the empire, particularly southern Africa. The GFS established its first branch in southern Africa in Cape Town in 1889, followed by branches in Grahamstown (present-day Makhanda), Bloemfontein, and Pretoria.[168] Despite early inroads, work in the region was beset by problems, including the diffuse nature of the population, the relative lack of transportation and communication infrastructure, and the mobility of the British population. As described in Chapter 1, these problems were ubiquitous and affected branches throughout the empire, but the GFS in London attributed its difficulties in southern Africa to the admittance of Coloured and Black girls.[169] From the early 1890s, Coloured and Black girls participated in the organisation.[170] Missionaries formed candidates' classes for Black and Coloured girls that helped the organisation extend its reach in the region.[171] However, the GFS did not intend for these girls to be full members of the GFS in the same way that white girls were. It refused financial support for branches and hostels for Coloured girls and insisted on separate branches for white and Black and Coloured girls and even worked to exclude Coloured and Black girls from the GFS altogether.[172]

The lack of equality between GFS branches for white girls and 'Coloured branches' led Coloured girls to leave the GFS. In 1906, a branch for Coloured girls in Cape Town withdrew from the GFS stating that 'they are not on an equal footing with the white members, they gain nothing by belonging to the GFS, the Society gains strength from them'.[173] A report by the GFS's Sectional Committee for South Africa indicates that the withdrawal of Coloured branches was a common occurrence, citing similar incidents in East London and Port Elizabeth and at other branches in Cape Town.[174] Despite the closure of the branch, the GFS's Diocesan Council in Cape Town refused to consider any form of integration or greater support for the Coloured girls but instead advocated for the extension of its segregationist policies, proposing 'in future only white girls be admitted to the G.F.S. in Capetown [sic]'.[175] However, this proposal to admit only white girls experienced resistance from other branches, who remarked on the infeasibility of excluding Coloured members altogether. For instance, the head of the GFS branch in Grahamstown wrote that 'they could not lose their coloured members' and instead advocated for continuing segregationist policies by keeping the branches for white and Coloured girls 'quite distinct' so 'that the Members should not be invited to visit the other Members'.[176] At the time of these debates in 1906, the GFS concluded that the matter of what to do with Coloured branches was 'one of grave and increasingly difficulty'.[177] Two years later, in 1908, Laura Ridding, who was involved in the GFS, toured South Africa and described the GFS as '[u]nsuccessful' in the region. She observed that it would be better suited to helping 'native or coloured girls' but that white women within the GFS eschewed such work.[178] GFS associates in the region wanted to keep the GFS white, but this commitment to whiteness meant that it failed to attract girls of colour who had a need for the organisation. The GFS's operations in the region reveal its prioritisation of whiteness over the welfare of girls.

Over the next decades, the GFS continued to adopt discriminatory policies that relegated Coloured and Black girls.[179] In 1929, the GFS's Imperial and Overseas Committee received repeated entreaties for financial help in establishing a hostel for 'native girls' but unanimously decided that its funds should not be used for this purpose. The GFS instead said it would contribute to the cause by forming GFS classes for the girls.[180] Such classes would enlarge the membership of the organisation but not provide what girls actually needed, a hostel, exposing the self-interested motives of the GFS. In justifying its refusal to provide funds, the GFS used a familiar tactic, stating that its hands were tied since it needed the clergy's approval. Yet correspondence from the clergy indicates that they encouraged the GFS to do more work among Black and Coloured girls, viewing these as the groups most in need of aid.[181] While there was a demand for the GFS's work, the GFS failed to fulfil this need, since it was not among the desired population of white girls and would compromise its ideal of purity.

Instead of leading to its growth and strengthening its position in the region, the GFS's segregationist policies weakened the organisation. In 1948, the GFS's Imperial and Overseas Committee again revisited the question of girls of colour in the organisation. The discussions reflect continuing divisions and misunderstandings over its policies towards Coloured and Black girls.[182] The committee acknowledged that its exclusion of these girls had irrevocably damaged the organisation's reputation in the region and the decision 'had met with much disfavour, and the Society was now considered to be "old fashioned" and it did not appear to meet the girls' needs; therefore it was not well thought-of or wanted in the Union'.[183] Faced with exclusionary policies, African girls instead joined other groups, including the Women's Help Society, the YWCA, and the Girl Guides. Girls perceived these organisations as more tolerant and welcoming, although, as scholars like Jennifer Helgren, Mary Clare Martin, and Kristine Alexander have shown, they also upheld segregationist policies.[184]

The GFS faced similar situations regarding girls of colour in other parts of the empire, including the West Indies. When the GFS began its work in the West Indies in 1905, the development was welcomed by GFS leaders and especially Mary Elizabeth Townsend, who 'was anxious that the West Indian link might be made to complete the Girls' Friendly Society chain encircling the Empire'.[185] Townsend emphasised the importance of the GFS in 'raising the whole spiritual tone among the girlhood of that tropical country'.[186] However, its work faltered in the West Indies too. In 1929, Marion Turner, a deaconess who ran a GFS branch in connection with a school in Kingston, Jamaica, wrote that the GFS 'had practically died out'. In particular, she pinpointed the inability of the organisation 'to face the colour difficulty' as one of the factors contributing to making the organisation 'extinct'.[187] As in India and southern Africa, this problem was further complicated by workers from England who lacked an understanding of West Indian society and 'the difficulties connected with conditions of life there'.[188] In other areas, including China, similar reports emerged, blaming the GFS's failure to make inroads in the region because of its discriminatory policies.[189]

In 1936, Edith Gordon Clark, vice president of the GFS Central Council, wrote to Caroline Mytton asking for clarification on the position of the GFS regarding 'native races'. As with her other writings on the topic, Mytton's response to Gordon Clark reveals how she viewed the presence of girls of colour as a regrettable problem. She confided to Gordon Clark: 'In all cases where coloured girls have joined the Society, it has not been done without full understanding of the difficulties'. Mytton attempted to obviate criticisms of the GFS's treatment of girls of colour by noting that '[t]he G.F.S. has no lack of care and consideration for natives of any country, as is made quite clear by its numerous Missionary activities'.[190] The organisation indeed frequently classified its work with girls of colour as under the purview of missionaries, which shows that the GFS viewed them as targets of conversion and reform rather than equal members of the organisation.[191] The GFS's ambiguous and often contradictory policies towards girls of colour reveal its continued unease with race and its inability to reconcile its commitment to whiteness and racial purity with the needs of girls in different parts of the empire.

## Conclusion

The treatment of girls of colour exposes the disparities and disunities within the 'very large family' of the GFS. The GFS positioned itself as an organisation of racial unity. Its official history, *Friendship's Highway*, stated that 'there are divisions of race ... Links and bridges are needed, and the G.F.S. has a unique opportunity for supplying them'.[192] Despite this harmonious message, the GFS's ultimate goal was the preservation of white supremacy. Its exclusionary policies were rooted in anxieties over whiteness, which was not as stable and enduring as GFS organisers would have liked to believe. Through its training programmes in India, the GFS sought to raise the status of domiciled girls and thereby avert the supposed degeneration of the white race. It also sought to uphold white hegemony through racial exclusion. Instead of building '[l]inks and bridges', it constructed barriers to bar girls of colour. While the GFS professed its commitment to 'the care of the girlhood of the empire' and its dedication 'to embrace all kinds of girls', it served in reality as a means of exclusion and marginalised girls who were not white or did not adhere to the middle-class values of the organisation's leadership.[193] Contrary to its rhetoric, only racially 'pure', white girls could be part of the 'Imperial sisterhood' of the GFS.

When I set out to write this chapter, I intended to forefront the voices and experiences of girls of colour in the organisation, but the nature of the GFS archives complicated this endeavour. The GFS archives replicate the power dynamics of the organisation, centring the perspectives of the adult leaders and containing limited information about girls, especially girls of colour. In her magisterial *Wayward Lives, Beautiful Experiments: Intimate Histories of Riotous Black Girls, Troublesome Women, and Queer Radicals*, Saidiya Hartman reflects on these power relations within the archive, observing: 'Every historian of the multitude, the dispossessed, the subaltern, and the enslaved is forced to grapple with the power and authority of the archive and the limits it sets on what can be known, whose perspective matters, and who is endowed with the gravity and authority of historical actor'.[194] To contend with the challenges of the archive, Hartman 'elaborates, augments, transposes, and breaks open archival documents so they might yield a richer picture'.[195] Following in the footsteps of Hartman, Ann Laura Stoler, and others, I have read both along and against the archival grain to uncover the involvement – and resistance – of girls in the organisation, despite their attempted silencing.[196] Violet Paul's decision to travel to India to marry Davis, girls' decision to leave the Calcutta hostel during the oppressive rule of Mary Thomas, and the withdrawal of Coloured girls from GFS branches in southern Africa demonstrate that the inequities within the organisation did not go uncontested and girls were not passive participants but actively shaped the GFS in accordance with their interests, sometimes disrupting the organisers' plans in the process. The next chapter returns to this theme and further explores the ways that girls challenged the directives of the GFS leadership.

While the GFS saw its commitment to whiteness as a strength and an integral part of its identity, it ultimately proved to be a weakness. In 1923, the GFS's Committee for Extension Work in India and Ceylon declared that the '[r]ace difficulty *can* be overcome'.[197] Yet over twenty-five years later in 1949, the GFS was forced to admit that it continued to struggle with 'difficulties owing to the colour-bar', even though other organisations, like the Mothers' Union and Girl Guides, had 'happily surmounted' them.[198] Although the GFS continued its work in places like India and South Africa, its failure to reach girls of colour signalled the GFS's waning influence. The next chapter returns to this topic and explores in more depth the reasons behind the organisation's decline in the interwar years.

## Notes

1 Women's Library, London (hereafter WL), 5GFS/02/235, letter from Mabel C. Sisley to Caroline Mytton, 26 January 1929, p. 1.
2 WL, 5GFS/02/235, letter from Mabel C. Sisley to Mrs Marshall, 31 January 1929.
3 Letter from Mabel C. Sisley to Caroline Mytton, 26 January 1929, p. 4.
4 WL, 5GFS/02/235, telegram from Marshall re W. E. Davis, 20 February 1929.
5 WL, 5GFS/02/235, letter from Norman E. Marshall to Caroline Mytton, 18 February 1929, pp. 1 and 2. Emphasis in the original.
6 Mabel C. Sisley to Caroline Mytton, 26 January 1929, p. 4.
7 Mabel C. Sisley to Caroline Mytton, 26 January 1929, pp. 2, 4.

8 WL, 5GFS/02/235, letter from Caroline Mytton to Mrs Bruce, 22 March 1929. Searches of newspaper archives for references to Paul and Davis did not yield any further information about Paul, Davis, or their possible marriage.
9 WL, 5GFS/05/017, Question 50 of *The GFS Who Knows: A Game for Candidates*, 2nd series, 1940s.
10 Agnes L. Money, *History of the Girls' Friendly Society*, 2nd ed. (London: Wells, Garner, Darton & Co., Ltd, 1911), p. 70.
11 Money, *History of the Girls' Friendly Society*, pp. 70–1. For a similar sentiment, see WL, 5GFS/01/107, 'Meeting of the Committee of Council for the G.F.S. in India, Ceylon, and the Far East Held at the G.F.S. Central Office, 39 Victoria Street, S.W. on Wednesday, November 6th 1914 at 2.45 p.m.'; and 'Overseas Reports. India', *The Empire and Beyond*, Occasional Leaflet VI (1914), p. 12.
12 Julia Bush, 'Edwardian Ladies and the "Race" Dimensions of British Imperialism', *Women's Studies International Forum*, 21:3 (1998), 285.
13 For more on this shift, see Satoshi Mizutani, *The Meaning of White: Race, Class, and the 'Domiciled Community' in British India, 1858–1930* (Oxford: Oxford University Press, 2011), p. 10 and chapter 3.
14 WL, 5GFS/05/011, Mary E. Campbell, *A Handbook of the Work of the Girls' Friendly Society in India and Ceylon* (February 1928), p. 9.
15 WL, 5GFS/01/107, 'Minutes of a Meeting of the Committee of Council for the G.F.S. in India, Ceylon, and the Far East Held at the GFS Central Office, 39 Victoria Street, S.W., on Friday November 8th, 1918 at 2.30 p.m.', p. 185. WL, 5GFS/05/008, *Girls' Friendly Society Leaflet for India and the Far East*, 1:5 (February 1925), p. 3.
16 Money, *History of the Girls' Friendly Society*, p. 67.
17 WL, 5GFS/01/096, M. E. T. [Mary Elizabeth Townsend], 'G.F.S. in India', c. 1901, p. 46.
18 Money, *History of the Girls' Friendly Society*, p. 67.
19 M. E. T., 'G.F.S. in India', p. 46
20 There are parallels with the Boy Scouts and how their affiliation with the Indian scouting movement was motivated by a desire to control the Indian scouts rather than feelings of brotherhood or equality. For more on this point, see Scott Johnston, '"Only Send Boys of the Good Type": Child Migration and the Boy Scout Movement, 1921–1959', *The Journal of the History of Childhood and Youth*, 7:3 (Fall 2014), 389.
21 WL, 5GFS/02/235, 'The India "At Home"', n.d., p. 1.
22 WL, 5GFS/05/011, *Girls' Friendly Society Leaflet for India and the Far East*, 2:6 (September 1931), p. 2.
23 Elizabeth Buettner, *Empire Families: Britons and Late Imperial India* (New York: Oxford University Press, 2004), especially chapter 1. Mizutani, *The Meaning of White*, pp. 28 and 103. See also Ann Laura Stoler, *Carnal Knowledge and Imperial Power: Race and the Intimate in Colonial Rule* (Berkeley: University of California Press, 2002), especially chapter 5.
24 WL, 5GFS/02/230, letter from Olive Carden and Ethel J. Shepard to Miss Mytton, 14 January 1932.

25 Buettner, *Empire Families*, pp. 28–30.
26 'Industrial Training Scheme for the Punjab', *The Empire and Beyond*, Occasional Leaflet II (1913), p. 5.
27 WL, 5GFS/01/107, 'Minutes of a Meeting of the Committee of Council for the G.F.S. in India, Ceylon, and the Far East held at the G.F.S. Central Office, on Tuesday, March 12th 1918 at 2.30 p.m.', p. 176.
28 For more on hostels and their role and importance, see Lambeth Palace Library, London, Davidson 143, ff. 215, 'Appeal for £20,000 for the Lodges and Homes of Rest of the Girls' Friendly Society', 1907; Derbyshire Record Office, Matlock (hereafter DRO), D3287/68/1/3, Ellen Joyce, *Department for G.F.S. Members Emigrating* (1898), p. 6; DRO, D3287/93/3/39, letter from E. Lyttelton Gell to the bishop of Mashonaland, 16 March 1902; and *The Book of the G.F.S.: What It Is and What It Does* (June 1920), pp. 22–35. For a description of staying at a hostel in India, see 'From A G.F.S. Letter-Bag', *The Empire and Beyond*, Occasional Leaflet XXI (Spring 1919), p. 11.
29 'Overseas Reports. India', *The Empire and Beyond*, Occasional Leaflet VI (1914), p. 12. WL, 5GFS/02/234, letter from Sister Veronica to Miss Mytton, 22 August 1933, p. 1. See also 'Overseas Reports. India', *The Empire and Beyond*, Occasional Leaflet XXII (Summer 1919), p. 5; 'Overseas Reports', *The Empire and Beyond*, Occasional Leaflet XVII (Epiphany 1918), p. 6; and Edith Marion Welch, 'Lahore', *The Empire and Beyond*, Occasional Leaflet XI (Easter 1916), pp. 7–8.
30 WL, 5GFS/01/107, 'Minutes of a Meeting of the Committee of Council for the G.F.S. in India, Ceylon, and the Far East Held at the GFS Central Office, 39 Victoria Street, S.W., on Friday June 7th, 1918 at 2.45 p.m.', p. 182. See also Money, *History of the Girls' Friendly Society*, p. 67. For a photograph of the Murree hostel, see WL, 5GFS/02/358, India, Barbados and Africa album, 1930s.
31 Money, *History of the Girls' Friendly Society*, p. 66. Campbell, *A Handbook of the Work of the Girls' Friendly Society in India and Ceylon*, p. 6.
32 WL, 5GFS/01/108, 'Indian Committee', 5 October 1904.
33 WL, 5GFS/01/107, 'Minutes of Committee of Council for the G.F.S. in India Held on June 16th 1905', p. 24.
34 'Industrial Training Scheme for the Punjab', *The Empire and Beyond*, p. 5.
35 'Overseas Reports. India', *The Empire and Beyond*, Occasional Leaflet XXII (Summer 1919), p. 4.
36 Bush, 'Edwardian Ladies and the "Race" Dimensions of British Imperialism', 287.
37 Money, *History of the Girls' Friendly Society*, p. 66.
38 'Overseas Reports. India', *The Empire and Beyond*, Occasional Leaflet IX (1915), p. 9.
39 WL, 5GFS/02/229, letter from M. F. Down to Miss Mytton, 17 February 1927, p. 3.
40 On lacking 'backbone', see WL, 5GFS/02/230, letter from Miss Mytton to Miss Combe, 31 August 1931. On girls in India being different, see, for

Contested ideas of whiteness and race    157

instance, WL, 5GFS/02/231, letter from Winifred Cocke to Miss Mytton, 31 August 1931. On being 'feckless', see WL, 5GFS/02/235, letter from Deaconess Thomson to Miss Mytton, 3 January 1930.
41 For more on this point, see Durba Ghosh, *Sex and the Family in Colonial India: The Making of Empire* (New York: Cambridge University Press, 2006); Lionel Caplan, *Children of Colonialism: Anglo-Indians in a Postcolonial World* (Oxford: Berg Publishers, 2001); Ann Laura Stoler, 'Sexual Affronts and Racial Frontiers: European Identities and the Cultural Politics of Exclusion in Colonial Southeast Asia', *Comparative Studies in Society and History*, 3:4 (1992), 514–51; and Ann Laura Stoler, *Carnal Knowledge and Imperial Power: Race and the Intimate in Colonial Rule* (Berkeley: University of California Press, 2002).
42 WL, 5GFS/01/107, 'Committee for the G.F.S. in India and Ceylon', 23 May 1906. Emphasis in the original.
43 WL, 5GFS/02/234, letter from Miss Campbell to Miss Mytton, 1 November 1928.
44 Letter from Miss Campbell to Miss Mytton, 1 November 1928.
45 WL, 5GFS/01/102, 'Minutes of a Meeting of the Committee for Extension Work in India and Ceylon, held at Townsend House, Greycoat Place, S.W., on Thursday, June 9th, 1927, at 11 a.m.', p. 95. For more on this point, see Bush, 'Edwardian Ladies and the "Race" Dimensions of British Imperialism', 284.
46 For more on the perceptions of poor white children, see Ann Stoler 'Making the Empire Respectable: The Politics of Race and Sexual Morality in 20th-Century Colonial Cultures', *American Ethnologist*, 16:4 (1989), 634–60. For more on poor children in the specifically British context, see Harald Fischer-Tiné, *Low and Licentious Europeans: Race, Class and 'white Subalternity' in Colonial India*, New Perspectives in South Asian History (Hyderabad: Orient Blackswan Pvt Ltd, 2009); Teresa Hubel, 'In Search of the British Indian in British India: White Orphans, Kipling's *Kim*, and Class in Colonial India', *Modern Asian Studies*, 38:1 (2004), 227–51; David Arnold, 'European Orphans and Vagrants in India in the Nineteenth Century', *The Journal of Imperial and Commonwealth History*, 7:2 (1979), 104–27; and David Arnold, 'White Colonization and Labour in Nineteenth-Century India', *The Journal of Imperial and Commonwealth History*, 11:2 (1983), 133–58.
47 Mizutani, *The Meaning of White*, p. 46. See also Satoshi Mizutani, 'Historicising Whiteness: From the Case of Late Colonial India', *Australia Critical Race and Whiteness Studies Association Journal*, 2:1 (2006), 1–15.
48 Mizutani, *The Meaning of White*, p. 49.
49 WL, 5GFS/01/110, *The Girls' Friendly Society in India* (Lahore: Girls' Friendly Society, 1917), p. 8.
50 Grenside, 'G.F.S. in India', p. 3. 'Overseas Reports. India', *The Empire and Beyond*, Occasional Leaflet IX (1915), p. 9. WL, 5GFS/04/127, 'Candidates of Colombo, Ceylon', November 1931, photo from Block Book VII, 1926–31.
51 See, for instance, 'Industrial Training Scheme for the Punjab', *The Empire and Beyond*, p. 5.

52 'The India "At Home"', p. 3.
53 Dane Kennedy, *The Magic Mountains: Hill Stations and the British Raj* (Berkeley: University of California Press, 1996), pp. 136–7. For more on the connection between St Lawrence and the GFS, see Money, *History of the Girls' Friendly Society*, p. 28; and WL, 5GFS/02/230, letter from Winifred Paine to Miss Mytton, 29 January 1930.
54 WL, 5GFS/05/010, 'Girls' Friendly Society', *The Church Monthly of St. Andrew's and St. Oswald's Churches, Lahore*, 12:135 (April 1926), 6. GFS newsletters featured stories about working with poor and destitute children at St. Andrew's Colonial Homes. See, for instance, 'From A G.F.S. Letter-Bag', *The Empire and Beyond*, Occasional Leaflet XX (All Saints 1918), p. 11. For more on St Andrew's Colonial Homes, see Jane McCabe, *Race, Tea, and Colonial Resettlement: Imperial Families, Interrupted* (London: Bloomsbury Academic, 2017). See also Mizutani, *The Meaning of White*, chapter 5.
55 WL, 5GFS/01/107, 'Minutes of a Meeting of the Committee of Council for the G.F.S. in India, Ceylon, and the Far East Held at the GFS Central Office, 39, Victoria St. S.W. 1 on June 4, 1920 at 2.45 p.m.', p. 210.
56 WL, 5GFS/02/102, 'Report of G.F.S. Lodge and S. Christopher's Nursery Training School, Bombay. For 1914', *Girls' Friendly Society, Bombay. Report Dec. 1913–14* (Bombay: M. J. Joseph at the 'Bombay Guardian' Mission Press, 1915), p. 14.
57 WL, 5GFS/01/110, 'Punjab Industrial Training Scheme', in *The Girls' Friendly Society in India* (Lahore: Girls' Friendly Society, 1917).
58 WL, 5GFS/01/110, 'General Review.', in *The Girls' Friendly Society in India* (Lahore: Girls' Friendly Society, 1917), p. 4.
59 'Home Reports. Province of York', *The Empire and Beyond*, Occasional Leaflet XXI (Spring 1919), p. 10.
60 WL, 5GFS/01/110, 'Letter of Commendation from the Bishop of Lahore', in *The Girls' Friendly Society in India* (Lahore: Girls' Friendly Society, 1917), p. 8.
61 WL, 5GFS/02/102, Susannah Marsh, 'Report of G.F.S. Lodge and S. Christopher's Nursery Training School, Bombay. For 1913', *Girls' Friendly Society, Bombay. Report Dec. 1912–13* (Bombay: M. J. Joseph at the 'Bombay Guardian' Mission Press, 1914), pp. 8–9.
62 WL, 5GFS/02/164, 'Diocesan Conference', in *Lahore Diocesan Leaflet*, 1:7 (April 1911), p. 3.
63 WL, 5GFS/01/110, 'Girls' Friendly Society. Punjab Industrial Training Scheme', in *The Girls' Friendly Society in India* (Lahore: Girls' Friendly Society, 1917), p. 5. See also 'Overseas Reports. India', *The Empire and Beyond*, Occasional Leaflet VII (1914), p. 7; 'Industrial Training Scheme for the Punjab', *The Empire and Beyond*, p. 5; 'Home Reports. Province of York', *The Empire and Beyond*, Occasional Leaflet XXI (Spring 1919), p. 10.
64 WL, 5GFS/01/107, 'Minutes of a Meeting of the Committee of Council for the G.F.S. in India, Ceylon, and the Far East Held at the GFS Central Office, 39 Victoria Street, S.W., on Friday June 7th, 1918 at 2.45 p.m.', p. 181.

C. F. Andrews, 'India', *The Empire and Beyond*, Occasional Leaflet III (1913), pp. 4–5.

65 'Essays', *Girls' Friendly Society Leaflet for India and the Far East*, 1:5 (February 1925), p. 21.
66 Letter from Sister Veronica to Miss Mytton, 22 August 1933, p. 3. See also 'The India "At Home"', pp. 3–4.
67 Marsh, 'Report of G.F.S. Lodge and S. Christopher's Nursery Training School, Bombay. For 1913', pp. 8–9.
68 WL, 5GFS/05/011, 'Lahore Diocese', in *The Girls' Friendly Society Leaflet for India and the Far East*, 2:6 (September 1931), 9. For a similar statement, see 'The India "At Home"', pp. 3–4; WL, 5GFS/01/107, 'Minutes of Committee of Council for the G.F.S. in India and Ceylon Held on May 23rd 1906', p. 33; and Campbell, *A Handbook of the Work of the Girls' Friendly Society in India and Ceylon*, p. 9.
69 WL, 5GFS/02/230, letter from Margaret E. Arbuthnot to Mrs Carden, 11 February 1932.
70 Stoler, *Carnal Knowledge and Imperial Power*, p. 112.
71 Kennedy, *The Magic Mountains*, pp. 136–7.
72 For more on this point, see Mizutani, *The Meaning of White*, p. 137.
73 'Punjab Industrial Training Scheme', in *The Girls' Friendly Society in India*.
74 For more on this point, see Ghosh, *Sex and the Family in Colonial India*, p. 13; and Fischer-Tiné's *Low and Licentious Europeans*.
75 Mizutani, 'Historicising Whiteness', 1. Emphasis in the original.
76 Mizutani, 'Historicising Whiteness', 9.
77 Jane McCabe highlights these different networks in *Race, Tea, and Colonial Resettlement*.
78 WL, 5GFS/01/107, 'Minutes of a Meeting of the Committee of Council for the G.F.S. in India and Ceylon Held at the GFS Central Office, 39 Victoria Street, London, S.W. on Friday 25th February 1910 at 2.30 p.m.', pp. 72–3.
79 'General Review', in *The Girls' Friendly Society in India*, p. 4. WL, 5GFS/01/107, Kathleen M. Townsend, 'Report of the Sub-Committee Appointed by the Committee of Council for the GFS in India and Ceylon to Consider What Steps Can Be Taken to Safe-Guard Eurasian Girls Coming to London', p. 78. 'Industrial Training Scheme for the Punjab', *The Empire and Beyond*, p. 5. 'Overseas Reports. India', *The Empire and Beyond*, Occasional Leaflet VII (1914), p. 7. WL, 5GFS/01/107, 'Committee of Council for the G.F.S. in India, Ceylon, and the Far East Held at the G.F.S. Central Office, 39 Victoria Street, S.W. on Wednesday, March 6th 1914 at 2.45'.
80 'Overseas Reports. India', *The Empire and Beyond*, Occasional Leaflet VI (1914), p. 10. 'Committee of Council for the G.F.S. in India, Ceylon, and the Far East Held at the G.F.S. Central Office, 39 Victoria Street, S.W. on Wednesday, March 6th 1914 at 2.45'. On the efforts of the YWCA to provide accommodations for Indian students in Britain, see Modern Records Centre, University of Warwick, Coventry, MSS 243/4/12/1–12, Emily Kinnaird,

'Indian Women Students in Great Britain', *The Blue Triangle Gazette*, 50:3 (March 1932), p. 14.
81 WL, 5GFS/01/108, 'Sub-Committee appointed by the Committee for the G.F.S. in India and Ceylon Feb. 1910 to consider what steps can be taken to safeguard Eurasian Girls coming to London, held at the G.F.S. Central Office, 39 Victoria Str. London, S.W. on Tuesday 24 May 1910 2.15 p.m.'.
82 BL, IOR/L/PG/6/480, File 993, 'Scheme for the employment of young Indian women as domestic servants in the UK', 13 May 1898. 'India', *The Empire and Beyond*, Occasional Leaflet V (1914), p. 5.
83 Buettner, *Empire Families*, p. 157.
84 Mizutani, 'Historicising Whiteness', 10.
85 Mizutani, *The Meaning of White*, p. 103.
86 'Punjab Industrial Training Scheme', in *The Girls' Friendly Society in India*.
87 'Girls' Friendly Society. Punjab Industrial Training Scheme', in *The Girls' Friendly Society in India*, p. 5.
88 'Girls' Friendly Society. Punjab Industrial Training Scheme', in *The Girls' Friendly Society in India*, p. 5.
89 'Girls' Friendly Society. Punjab Industrial Training Scheme', in *The Girls' Friendly Society in India*, p. 6. See also 'Overseas Reports. India', *The Empire and Beyond*, Occasional Leaflet VII (1914), p. 7.
90 'Home Reports', *The Empire and Beyond*, Occasional Leaflet VI (1914), p. 9. WL, 5GFS/02/164, The Editor, '"Dream Pictures." commonly called "The Doll's Pageant"', in *Lahore Diocesan Leaflet*, 1:7 (April 1911), 3–4.
91 'Letter of Commendation from the Bishop of Lahore', in *The Girls' Friendly Society in India*, p. 8.
92 'Girls' Friendly Society. Punjab Industrial Training Scheme', in *The Girls' Friendly Society in India*, p. 6.
93 'Overseas Reports. India', *The Empire and Beyond*, Occasional Leaflet VI (1914), pp. 9–13. See also Mary Heath-Stubbs, *Friendship's Highway: Being the History of the Girls' Friendly Society, 1875–1935* (London: G.F.S. Central Office, 1935), pp. 150–1.
94 WL, 5GFS/01/109, 'Agenda for the Meeting of the Committee of Council for the G.F.S. in India Ceylon and the Far East, held at the Central Office on Friday March 4th at 2.45 p.m.'. WL, 5GFS/01/111, 'Minutes of a Meeting of the Committee of Council for the G.F.S. in India, Ceylon and the Far East, held at the G.F.S. Central Office in 39 Victoria St. S.W. on Friday June 2nd 1922 at 2.45 p.m.', p. 4. On the end of PITS, see also WL, 5GFS/01/107, 'Minutes of a Meeting of the Committee of Council for the G.F.S. in India, Ceylon and the Far East, held at the G.F.S. Central Office on Friday March 4th 1922 at 2.45 p.m.', p. 240.
95 'Report of G.F.S. Lodge and S. Christopher's Nursery Training School, Bombay. For 1914', *Girls' Friendly Society, Bombay. Report Dec. 1913–14*, p. 14.
96 WL, 5GFS/01/107, 'Minutes of a Meeting of the Committee of Council for the G.F.S. in India, Ceylon and the Far East held at the G.F.S. Central Office, 39

Victoria Street, London, S.W. on Friday, 3rd November 1916 at 2.45 p.m.', p. 161.
97 'Report of G.F.S. Lodge and S. Christopher's Nursery Training School, Bombay. For 1914', *Girls' Friendly Society, Bombay. Report Dec. 1913–14*, p. 14.
98 Mizutani, *The Meaning of White*, p. 95. See also Mizutani, 'Historicising Whiteness', 9.
99 'Overseas Reports. India', *The Empire and Beyond*, Occasional Leaflet VI (1914), p. 12.
100 'Essays', *Girls' Friendly Society Leaflet for India and the Far East*, p. 23.
101 WL, 5GFS/02/235, letter from Secretary to Deaconess Margaret, 15 March 1930.
102 Letter from Secretary to Deaconess Margaret, 15 March 1930.
103 WL, 5GFS/02/229, letter from Secretary to Miss Attree, 13 February 1930. WL, 5GFS/02/229, letter from Agnes Attree to Miss Mytton, March 1930.
104 Letter from Secretary to Deaconess Margaret, 15 March 1930. On the difficulties facing Indian servants in England, see also BL, IOR/L/PJ/6/518, File 1676, 'The case of Nasiban, a female servant and native of India, destitute in England', 2 September 1899.
105 Letter from Secretary to Deaconess Margaret, 15 March 1930.
106 WL, 5GFS/02/235, letter from Margaret Scott to Miss Mytton, 16 March 1930. Emphasis in the original.
107 The phrase 'to keep England white' is used by Heath-Stubbs, *Friendship's Highway*, p. 111, and discussed more in the fifth chapter below.
108 WL, 5GFS/02/229, letter from Secretary to Mrs Westmacott, 30 January 1930. WL, 5GFS/02/229, letter from Caroline M. Mytton to Mrs Westmacott, 10 January 1930. See also WL, 5GFS/02/229, letter from Secretary to Miss Thomas, 17 December 1929; and WL, 5GFS/02/229, 'Calcutta Post'.
109 WL, 5GFS/02/229, letter from Secretary to Mrs Gladstone, 10 October 1929.
110 Letter from Secretary to Mrs Westmacott, 30 January 1930. Letter from Caroline M. Mytton to Mrs Westmacott, 10 January 1930.
111 WL, 5GFS/02/229, letter from V. Westmacott to Miss Mytton, 5 March 1930. See also WL, 5GFS/2/229, letter from Secretary to Mrs Westmacott, 12 March 1930.
112 WL, 5GFS/02/229, letter from Secretary to Mrs Westmacott, 13 February 1930.
113 WL, 5GFS/02/229, letter from V. Westmacott to Miss Mytton, 19 February 1930.
114 WL, 5GFS/02/229, letter from Secretary to Miss Thomas, 7 May 1930.
115 'Overseas Reports', *The Empire and Beyond*, Occasional Leaflet IX (1915), p. 8.
116 WL, 5GFS/02/229, letter from Mary Thomas to Miss Mytton, 11 March 1930.
117 WL, 5GFS/02/229, letter from Mary Thomas to Miss Mytton, 21 April 1930.
118 WL, 5GFS/02/229, letter from V. Westmacott to Miss Mytton, 5 March 1930.
119 WL, 5GFS/02/229, letter from V. Westmacott to Miss Mytton, 14 June 1930.

120 Letter from Mary Thomas to Miss Mytton, 21 April 1930.
121 Letter from V. Westmacott to Miss Mytton, 14 June 1930.
122 Letter from V. Westmacott to Miss Mytton, 14 June 1930.
123 WL, 5GFS/02/229, letter from V. Westmacott to Mrs Bruce, 18 July 1930.
124 WL, 5GFS/02/229, letter from V. Westmacott to Miss Mytton, 19 June 1930.
125 Letter from V. Westmacott to Mrs Bruce, 18 July 1930.
126 Letter from V. Westmacott to Mrs Bruce, 18 July 1930.
127 Letter from V. Westmacott to Miss Mytton, 14 June 1930.
128 Letter from V. Westmacott to Mrs Bruce, 18 July 1930. WL, 5GFS/02/229, letter from V. Westmacott to Miss Mytton, 26 June 1930.
129 Letter from V. Westmacott to Miss Mytton, 19 June 1930.
130 Letter from V. Westmacott to Mrs Bruce, 18 July 1930.
131 Letter from V. Westmacott to Miss Mytton, 19 June 1930.
132 Letter from V. Westmacott to Mrs Bruce, 18 July 1930.
133 Campbell, *A Handbook of the Work of the Girls' Friendly Society in India and Ceylon*.
134 WL, 5GFS/02/229, letter from V. Westmacott to Miss Grenside, 20 November 1930.
135 WL, 5GFS/01/111, 'Minutes of a Meeting of the Committee for Extension Work in India, Burma and Ceylon, held at Townsend House, Greycoat Place, Westminster, on Thursday February 14th, 1933, at 2.30 p.m.', p. 181.
136 WL, 5GFS/02/229, letter from V. Westmacott to Miss Grenside, 16 July 1931.
137 WL, 5GFS/02/230, letter from Margaret Scott to Mrs O'Dell, 4 April 1927.
138 WL, 5GFS/02/235, letter from Secretary to Mrs Bruce, 4 March 1930.
139 WL, 5GFS/01/111, 'Minutes of a Meeting of the Committee for Extension Work in India, Burma and Ceylon, held at Townsend House, Greycoat Place, S.W. 1 on Wednesday, February 5th 1930 at 3 p.m.', p. 130.
140 WL, 5GFS/02/231, letter from Winifred Cocke to Miss Mytton, 31 August 1931.
141 WL, 5GFS/02/231, letter from Mabel R. Goodrich to Miss Mytton, 20 February 1931.
142 WL, 5GFS/02/231, letter from Mabel R. Goodrich to Miss Mytton, 8 May 1931. Emphasis in the original.
143 WL, 5GFS/02/231, letter from Hon. Sec. GFS Lodge Bombay to Caroline Mytton, 8 April 1932.
144 WL, 5GFS/01/112, 'India and Ceylon Extension Work Committee, at Townsend House. Friday, March 4th, 1927, at 2.30 p.m.'.
145 See, for instance, WL, 5GFS/02/231, letter from H. Palmer to Miss Mytton, 18 October 1927; and WL, 5GFS/01/112, 'Meeting of the Committee for Extension Work in India, Burma and Ceylon, held at Townsend house, Greycoat Place, Westminster, on Tuesday, May 5th, 1931, at 2.30 p.m.'.
146 WL, 5GFS/02/235, letter from Margaret Scott to Caroline Mytton, 26 November 1928.

147 'Overseas Reports. Ceylon', *The Empire and Beyond*, Occasional Leaflet IX (1915), p. 9.
148 WL, 5GFS/04/128, 'Ceylon', *A Jubilee Chronicle for Overseas* (1935), p. 23.
149 WL, 5GFS/02/164, 'Extract from Mrs. Joseph's letter', c. 1911–12. For a similar situation in Bombay, see WL, 5GFS/02/237, letter from Winifred Cocke to Mrs Arbuthnot, 9 June 1933.
150 WL, 5GFS/01/098, 'Meeting of the Imperial & Overseas Committee of the Girls' Friendly Society held at the Central Office on Monday March 16th 1925 at 2.30 p.m.', p. 37.
151 WL, 5GFS/02/263, F. G. Parrish, 'Girls' Friendly Society. Grahamstown Diocese. Port Elizabeth. St. Paul's Branch', p. 2.
152 WL, 5GFS/02/261, letter from M. M. Stevens to Miss Mytton, 6 December 1932. 'Overseas Reports', *The Empire and Beyond*, Occasional Leaflet XVII (Epiphany 1918), p. 7.
153 WL, 5GFS/05/008, E. Mendis, 'Colombo', *Girls' Friendly Society Leaflet for India and the Far East*, 1:9 (January 1927), p. 5.
154 WL, 5GFS/02/229, letter from Secretary to Mrs Westmacott, 13 February 1930. WL, 5GFS/02/229, letter from V. Westmacott to Miss Mytton, 5 March 1930.
155 WL, 5GFS/02/229, letter from V. Westmacott to Miss Mytton, 13 December 1927.
156 WL, 5GFS/02/231, Hon. Sec. GFS Lodge Bombay to Caroline Mytton, 8 April 1932. For a similar sentiment, see 'Industrial Training Scheme for the Punjab', *The Empire and Beyond*, p. 5.
157 WL, 5GFS/02/263, letter from E. Mabel Smith to Miss Rogers, 20 February 1937.
158 Letter from E. Mabel Smith to Miss Rogers, 20 February 1937.
159 Letter from E. Mabel Smith to Miss Rogers, 20 February 1937.
160 WL, 5GFS/02/261, letter from M. Sleading to Secretary, 16 October 1935.
161 WL, 5GFS/02/238, letter from Caroline M. Mytton to Miss Paine, 12 May 1932.
162 WL, 5GFS/02/235, letter from Secretary to Mrs Bruce, 22 June 1931.
163 Letter from Secretary to Mrs Bruce, 22 June 1931.
164 Letter from Secretary to Mrs Bruce, 22 June 1931.
165 WL, 5GFS/01/112, 'India, Burma, and Ceylon Committee held at Townsend House, on Tuesday, February 3rd, 1931, at 3 p.m.'. Letter from Miss Campbell to Miss Mytton, 1 November 1928.
166 WL, 5GFS/01/107, 'Minutes of Committee of Council for the G.F.S. in India Held on June 9th 1903', p. 9.
167 WL, 5GFS/02/230, letter from Winifred Paine to Miss Grenside, 28 April 1931. Letter from Miss Campbell to Miss Mytton, 1 November 1928.
168 Money, *History of the Girls' Friendly Society*, p. 100.
169 WL, 5GFS/01/102, 'Sectional Committee for South Africa: Minutes of a Meeting Held on Sept. 19th 1906', p. 8.

170 WL, 5GFS/01/091, 'Sectional Committee for South Africa. Minutes of a Meeting held on Friday Nov. 17th 1905', pp. 141–2.
171 'What Candidates Are Doing', *Our Letter: For G.F.S. Candidates all over the World* (September 1907), p. 3. 'Sectional Committee for South Africa: Minutes of a Meeting Held on Sept. 19th 1906', p. 8.
172 DRO, D3287/68/1/3, Ellen Joyce (ed.), 'Report for 1893', in *Girls Friendly Society. Reports of the Department for Members Emigrating. 1883 to 1897*, p. 54. WL, 5GFS/01/098, 'Minutes of a Meeting of the Imperial & Overseas Committee held on Monday, March 18th, 1929 at Townsend House at 2.30 p.m.', pp. 53–4.
173 WL, 5GFS/01/102, 'Sectional Committee for South Africa: Minutes of a Meeting held on May 22nd, 1906', p. 5.
174 'Sectional Committee for South Africa: Minutes of a Meeting held on May 22nd, 1906', p. 5.
175 'Sectional Committee for South Africa: Minutes of a Meeting held on May 22nd, 1906', p. 5.
176 'Sectional Committee for South Africa: Minutes of a Meeting held on May 22nd, 1906', p. 5.
177 'Sectional Committee for South Africa: Minutes of a Meeting held on May 22nd, 1906', pp. 5–6.
178 Hampshire Archives and Local Studies, Winchester, 9M68/61/1, Diary of Lady Laura Ridding's foreign travels, to South Africa, 1908, pp. 20–1. See also WL, 5GFS/01/098, 'Meeting of the Imperial & Overseas Committee of the Girls' Friendly Society held at G.F.S. Headquarters, Townsend House, Greycoat Place, London, S.W. 1, on Thursday 1st July 1948, at 11.30 a.m.', p. 231. For more on Laura Ridding and her time in South Africa, see Sue Anderson-Faithful, *Mary Sumner: Mission, Education and Motherhood: Thinking a Life with Bourdieu* (Cambridge: Lutterworth Press, 2018), p. 140; and Julia Bush, *Edwardian Ladies and Imperial Power* (London: Continuum, 1999), p. 119.
179 WL, 5GFS/02/261, letter from Overseas Secretary to Mrs Head, 2 December 1933.
180 WL, 5GFS/01/098, 'Minutes of a Meeting of the Imperial and Overseas Committee held on Monday, March 18th, 1929 at Townsend House at 2.30 p.m.', p. 50. WL, 5GFS/01/098, 'Minutes of a Meeting of the Imperial and Overseas Committee held at Townsend House, Greycoat Place, S.W. 1 on Monday, June 24th 1929 at 11 a.m.', p. 58.
181 See, for instance, 'Minutes of a Meeting of the Imperial and Overseas Committee held at Townsend House, Greycoat Place, S.W. 1 on Monday, June 24th 1929 at 11 a.m.', p. 58.
182 WL, 5GFS/01/098, 'Minutes of a Meeting of the Imperial and Overseas Committee of the Girls' Friendly Society, held at G.F.S. Central Office, Townsend House, Greycoat Place, London, S.W. 1, on Tuesday 17th February 1948, at 11.30 a.m.', p. 222.
183 'Minutes of a Meeting of the Imperial and Overseas Committee of the Girls' Friendly Society, held at G.F.S. Central Office, Townsend House,

Greycoat Place, London, S.W. 1, on Tuesday 17th February 1948, at 11.30 a.m.', p. 220.
184 For more on this point, see Kristine Alexander, 'Similarity and Difference at Girl Guide Camps in England Canada, and India', in Nelson R. Block and Tammy M. Proctor (eds), *Scouting Frontiers: Youth and the Scout Movement's First Century* (Newcastle: Cambridge Scholars, 2009), pp. 108, 114–17; Mary Clare Martin, 'Race, Indigeneity and the Baden-Powell Girl Guides: Age, Gender and the British World', in Shirleene Robinson and Simon Sleight (eds), *Children, Childhood and Youth in the British World*, Palgrave Studies in the History of Childhood (Basingstoke: Palgrave Macmillan, 2016), pp. 161–79; Jennifer Helgren, *American Girls and Global Responsibility: A New Relation to the World During the Early Cold War* (New Brunswick: Rutgers University Press, 2017), p. 8; and Bush, *Edwardian Ladies and Imperial Power*, p. 119.
185 WL, 5GFS/02/299, *Girls' Friendly Society. Report of a Conference for the Consideration of the Central Rules, held at the G.F.S. Central Office 29 Victoria Street, S.W. 1, on Friday and Saturday, June 13th and 14th, 1919*, p. 61. Heath-Stubbs, *Friendship's Highway*, p. 162.
186 Kathleen M. Townsend, *Some Memories of Mrs. Townsend: Foundress of the Girls' Friendly Society* (London: G.F.S. Central Office, 1923), pp. 35–49.
187 WL, 5GFS/01/104, 'Minutes of a Meeting of the West Indies Sectional Committee held on Monday, March 18th 1929 at 11.30 a.m. at Townsend House', pp. 39–40. See also WL, 5GFS/01/098, 'Minutes of a Meeting of the Imperial and Overseas Committee held at Townsend House, on Monday, June 16th 1930 at 11.30 a.m.', p. 74.
188 'Minutes of a Meeting of the Imperial and Overseas Committee held on Monday, March 18th, 1929 at Townsend House at 2.30 p.m.', p. 53.
189 'Overseas Reports. China', *The Empire and Beyond*, Occasional Leaflet IX (1915), p. 11. WL, 5GFS/01/098, 'Minutes of a Meeting of the Imperial & Overseas Committee Held at Townsend House on Monday, October 24th 1929 at 2.30 p.m.', p. 37.
190 WL, 5GFS/02/227, letter from Caroline Mytton to Miss Gordon Clark, 20 January 1936.
191 WL, 5GFS/01/098, 'Minutes of a Meeting of the Imperial and Overseas Committee held on Monday October 26th 1936 at Townsend House at 2.30 p.m.', pp. 159–60. Heath-Stubbs, *Friendship's Highway*, p. 147.
192 Heath-Stubbs, *Friendship's Highway*, p. 151.
193 *The Book of the G.F.S.*, p. 12.
194 Saidiya Hartman, *Wayward Lives, Beautiful Experiments: Intimate Histories of Riotous Black Girls, Troublesome Women, and Queer Radicals* (New York: W. W. Norton & Company, 2019), p. xiii.
195 Hartman, *Wayward Lives, Beautiful Experiments*, p. xiv.
196 Hartman, *Wayward Lives, Beautiful Experiments*, pp. 87–8. Ann Laura Stoler, *Along the Archival Grain: Epistemic Anxieties and Colonial Common Sense* (Princeton: Princeton University Press, 2008).

197 WL, 5GFS/01/109, 'Committee for Extension Work in India and Ceylon, 1st Meeting Jan. 29th 1923'.
198 WL, 5GFS/01/098, 'Minutes of a Meeting of the Overseas Council of the Girls' Friendly Society held at G.F.S. Headquarters, Townsend House, Greycoat Place, London, S.W. 1, on Wednesday 22nd June 1949, at 3.0 p.m.', p. 258.

# 5

# Shifting colonial relations and ideas of girlhood and the decline of the Girls' Friendly Society

As the GFS marked its jubilee year in 1925, the organisation celebrated its growth throughout the empire and its transformation from a 'small body' to 'become a vast body stretching through all the English speaking world'.[1] When the governor of Burma (present-day Myanmar), Sir Harcourt Butler, opened the GFS hostel in Rangoon (present-day Yangon) a year earlier in 1924, he similarly touted the GFS's imperial work and how 'the Society has made considerable progress in the Indian Empire'.[2] Yet such outward pronouncements conflicted with a sense of uncertainty within the organisation about its progress in India and other parts of the empire. Such pessimism was not new. When the Committee for the GFS in India and Ceylon (present-day Sri Lanka) met in 1906, it acknowledged that that it had to contend with the widespread perception that the 'G.F.S. was dead', 'defunct', and '*unpopular*'.[3] Around a decade later in 1914, Lady Sydenham, the wife of the governor of Bombay (present-day Mumbai) and a member of the Committee for the GFS in India, Ceylon, and the Far East, provided a sobering assessment of the GFS in the region, describing India as a 'Land of Regrets' and portraying the GFS's work as a lost cause: 'the G.F.S. there has had quite a struggle to live since it was started and had it not been for the dogged determination of a few English ladies, in spite of cold water thrown on their schemes, it would have died a natural death'.[4] Her presentiments about the GFS dying out would come true, and in 1933, the GFS would 'lose India altogether' and close all its branches in the country.[5]

This chapter examines how and why the GFS 'lost' India and its broader decline across the empire. The previous chapter detailed the problems posed by race, and the first chapter described logistical difficulties faced by the organisation in establishing branches in the colonies and dominions, including how distances between branches, the mobility of the population, the climate, and the lack of workers complicated organisational efforts. Other endemic problems beleaguered the organisation and became more pronounced in the interwar period. The First World War transformed the lives of girls and women, but the GFS struggled to adapt to these changes.

Girls increasingly viewed the society as antiquated and instead found other organisations more amenable to their lives. Prolonged debates over the possible amendment of the GFS's central rule on purity highlighted how out of touch the society had become with girls and their needs. The historian Vivienne Richmond has analysed debates over this rule and its connection to the decline of the organisation in her article '"It is Not a Society for Human Beings but for Virgins": The Girls' Friendly Society Membership Eligibility Dispute 1875–1936'.[6] The decline of the organisation has also been studied by Brian Harrison in his article 'For Church, Queen and Family: The Girls' Friendly Society 1874–1920'. Harrison ties the GFS's waning presence to the decrease in domestic service and growing democratisation during the period.[7] These factors all contributed to the organisation's diminishing influence and are discussed in this chapter, but its decline cannot be understood fully without consideration of the imperial context. Disputes within the organisation mirrored growing divisions within the empire, as members and associates in the colonies and dominions increasingly challenged the undemocratic and hierarchical structure of the organisation. As explored throughout this chapter, the decline of the GFS is not simply a chronicle of one organisation's struggle – and failure – to solve the problems it faced; instead, it reveals a larger story about the shifting social and political order in the interwar period marked by dramatic changes in girlhood and imperial relations.

### 'More difficult than I imagined': the impact of the First World War and social and political changes in the interwar period

When the First World War broke out in 1914, GFS associates hoped the conflict would provide an opportunity to reinvigorate the organisation and strengthen its imperial connections. There were grounds for such optimism. The UK government asked for the GFS's assistance in the war effort, specifically in providing accommodations for women war workers and care and goods for the troops. GFS publicity showcased the important role played by candidates, members, and associates in the war effort, including collecting waste paper for Red Cross funds and gardening to increase food supplies.[8] The conflict underscored the close-knit, interdependent nature of the empire, with articles in GFS newsletters praising its 'colonial daughters' for their contributions to the war.[9] *Friendship's Highway* extolled how 'the Colonies responded so willingly to the call of the Society, as they rallied to the help of the Empire itself and did their share in meeting the needs of the girlhood of the nation in that time of trial'.[10] An article in *Our Letter* encouraged girls in England to follow the example of those in the colonies and dominions:

Look at the British Empire. Do we 'fly at Mother's call' in the splendid way that Canada and Australia and New Zealand and South Africa and many other parts of the Empire have done in this last year. Look at them sending ships and men and motors and money and everything they can think of that the mother country needs. They speak of the old country as home.[11]

While the article celebrated the efforts of the colonies and dominions, it simultaneously reasserted imperial hierarchies by singling out the white settler colonies for praise and placing itself at the head of the imperial family as 'the mother country'.

Although the First World War bolstered the purpose of the GFS in certain ways, it also exacerbated underlying problems. As described in the previous chapter, the war diverted finances from GFS projects, like the training programmes in India. Girls' and women's involvement in the war effort as volunteers and workers limited their time and ability to participate in GFS activities.[12] Their greater responsibilities during wartime, along with the new employment opportunities, meant that they had less use for the GFS. With a great demand for women workers in fields like manufacturing, girls and young women increasingly turned away from domestic service.[13] These professions were less solitary, meaning that girls had less need for the community provided by the GFS, which continued to have a reputation as a society primarily for servants. Following the conclusion of the war, the GFS encouraged its members 'to return to their pre-war occupations' and developed new schemes to raise the respectability of domestic work and attract girls to service, since, as Mary Heath-Stubbs observed in her history *Friendship's Highway*, 'The Society found itself confronted by the "Servant Problem" in an accentuated form'.[14] The schemes were largely unsuccessful; girls had little interest in returning to life in service and the prewar status quo.

The war also brought changes in the geopolitical landscape, with ideas of nation, empire, and race increasingly contested – all of which further complicated the GFS's work abroad. While the war did reinforce imperial bonds, it also exposed weaknesses within the empire, which became especially apparent in the postwar years. In the 1920s and 1930s, reports and correspondence by GFS associates described the growth of the independence movement and 'the anti-British spirit in parts of India'.[15] In 1920 and 1921, as India was in the throes of Gandhi's Noncooperation Campaign following the massacre of hundreds of Indians at Amritsar, GFS reports warned potential workers about the 'terrible unrest in India' and the 'unsettled state' in the region.[16] Beyond the growing independence movement, the GFS faced other difficulties in the region. The 'terrible' influenza outbreak in 1919 and later the Bago earthquake near Rangoon in 1930 impeded the GFS's outreach there, and the global depression in the 1930s further hindered its work in India and other parts of the empire.[17]

Such challenges were not confined to South Asia. In southern Africa, the GFS's work was complicated by – in the words of M. Steele, who was the honorary secretary of the Durban branch – 'the different conditions out here' and specifically the problems posed by the 'unhappy divisions in this country'.[18] The GFS struggled with the political and racial situation in the region. In a letter to the GFS Overseas Secretary Sarah Angus, Fanchette G. Parrish, the secretary of the GFS branch in Port Elizabeth (present-day Gqeberha), described how the branch was 'carrying on' but expressed concern about the effects of rising Afrikaner nationalism in the 1930s by figures like D. F. Malan, who implemented the system of apartheid during his term as prime minister of South Africa from 1948 to 1954. Parrish detailed the growing '[r]acial hatred between Dutch and British, fostered by the ignorant element, which is worked upon by Dr. Malan and quite a few more, who if they were out for S. Africa's good, instead of their own Political advancement would and could raise this country at least from the depths of misery caused by ignorance, hunger and disease'.[19] The apartheid regime hindered the operations of the GFS in the region, a point returned to in the conclusion.

Shifts in the relationships among GFS branches mirrored these broader changes of the interwar period. The GFS attested that 'people in the Dominions and Colonies liked to belong to the same Societies as did people in Great Britain', but, as described in the previous chapter, instead of feeling a bond with Britain and the empire, imperial branches felt abandoned by the Central Council, which in turn generated greater feelings of isolation and resentment.[20] Vera Westmacott, the president of the GFS Diocesan Council in Calcutta, wrote to Caroline Mytton, the secretary of the GFS Central Council, that 'the feeling amongst girls too, is that they are subscribing to something miles away, with which they can never be in touch'.[21] The GFS in England continued to see itself as the head of the GFS family, the 'mother' to its 'colonial daughters', but branches in other parts of the empire did not view the organisation in such hierarchical terms and wanted greater control over their own affairs.[22] In making a plea for 'our independence' in 1928, Mary Campbell, the GFS's organising worker in India, pushed back against the notion by the Central Council that the 'India G.F.S. [is] a rather tiresome and greedy child'.[23] Mytton expressed little sympathy to such pleas, derisively referring to Campbell as 'our Gandhi' due to her agitation for reform and greater freedom for the Indian branches. Mytton instead lamented branches' resistance to 'any attempt at control' by the Central Council.[24] The indifferent responses of Mytton and other associates in England to the challenges faced by the GFS in the empire did little to ease the concerns of branches in the colonies and dominions and only reaffirmed the need for them to have control over their own affairs.[25]

While calls for greater independence were especially pronounced in India because it was directly controlled by the Central Council, branches in other parts of the empire also expressed a desire for greater autonomy.[26] This movement towards independence emerged at a time when colonies and dominions were seeking to redefine their relationship with Britain. The 1931 Statute of Westminster of the UK Parliament marked a shift in imperial relations with the formal establishment of the British Commonwealth of Nations. This statute largely removed Britain's right to legislate for South Africa, Australia, Canada, Ireland, and New Zealand. At the same time, GFS branches in these regions sought to move away from the control of the Central Council in England. Winifred Preston, an associate from England, witnessed the growing divergence between the GFS in England and the 'colonial daughters' when she travelled to New Zealand in 1939 to assess the state of activity of the GFS in the country. The goal of her trip was to strengthen the bond between the GFS in England and New Zealand, but upon her arrival, Preston found that her objective was complicated by the peculiar situation in New Zealand.[27] Preston's accounts to the Central Council in London contrast with public reports that portrayed the GFS there as flourishing.[28] She detailed the various challenges she encountered in a letter to the Central Council: 'I must confess it is more difficult than I imagined it would be. Conditions out here are so entirely different to what they are at home, so that what applies there does'nt [sic] apply here at all, and I see that "Home" does'nt [sic] really know a great deal about New Zealand.'[29] Preston was disappointed to find that New Zealanders were 'so very self-satisfied' and 'in fact horribly insular in outlook' and that 'they are not really very interested in English things as far as they touch themselves. You can talk to them about home but they are far more interested in their own local gossip and affairs.'[30] As reflected in Preston's correspondence, the ties among the GFS branches – and England and New Zealand more broadly – had weakened. Contrary to the expectations of English associates, members and associates in the colonies and dominions did not express unquestioned deference and loyalty to the 'mother country' and instead remained more focused on their own matters. Consequently, despite hopes that the war would bolster the GFS, the wartime and postwar experiences intensified divisions within the society.

## 'A strange transition period': the modern girl and generational divisions within the GFS

GFS associates appreciated that the war marked a transformative moment for its members. Such recognition is apparent, for instance, in an article in *Our Letter* by the editor, Constance Thomas, who urged girls to realise that 'when you are grown up you will have splendid chances of helping your country such as no women have ever had since the world began ... Everything outward is changing and women and girls are doing all sorts of work to help their country.'[31] While the GFS encouraged girls to embrace their new responsibilities, the GFS leadership was not prepared for the changes that were to come. The war brought opportunities for girls and young women to step outside the confines of traditional feminine roles and exercise greater freedom and independence. Yet the GFS urged girls to participate in the war effort through their domestic roles. An article in *Our Letter* redoubles on the GFS's long-standing messages of duty and self-sacrifice and particularly emphasises how homes served as national bulwarks: 'We are proud of the "homes of England." It is in our homes that we serve our country. When you help Mother and go errands without grumbling or being selfish, when you make the little ones happy, you are a home-maker; you are doing what God means you to do, and you have a good conscience.'[32] This theme of girls' domestic responsibilities and homes as the basis of a strong nation similarly comes across in another article from *Our Letter* by the GFS's founder, Mary Elizabeth Townsend, who encouraged girls to serve their country through their roles in the home: 'it is in your homes that you must learn to serve your country and to witness for Christ in the great days that are to come, when you are grown and take your place as brave women of the Motherland'.[33] As it had done in the previous decades, the GFS framed the creation and maintenance of good homes as the primary way for girls to contribute to the nation and empire.

The GFS clung to its Victorian foundations, even as that social order was being uprooted during and after the First World War. The organisation remained disengaged from pressing questions of women's social situation during this period, notably the suffrage movement. Leaders, like Ellen Joyce, were anti-feminist and anti-suffrage.[34] The GFS also eschewed other social changes, including 'the pagan tendencies, the developments of birth control, the greater freedom between the sexes', which it regarded as among 'the great perils and temptations in the modern world'.[35] In the face of these upheavals, the GFS reaffirmed its traditional ideals and launched the 'Forward Movement' to fortify the organisation's mission in the postwar world. The goal of the Forward Movement was to 'obtain Crusaders in the Fight for Purity and Friendship', and one cornerstone of the Forward

Movement was the White Crusade, whose 'aim was not only to bear strong witness before the world to the value and reality of the ideals of the Society, but to educate public opinion'.[36] The White Crusade sought to reaffirm the GFS's commitment to purity and ensure that girls and women 'maintain the purity and strength of their ideals' amid the changes and opportunities 'which had been opened to them by the War'.[37] As signalled by its name, the ultimate goal of the White Crusade was 'to keep England white'.[38] Yet its focus was keeping not only England white but also the empire white, with the GFS envisioning the White Crusade spreading throughout the empire.[39] In 1919, the GFS held a conference dedicated to the Forward Movement where it discussed how 'the powers of English girlhood extended all over the world through the Englishmen who left England to civilise the earth. It was of the profoundest meaning to the Empire that the influence of girls on their menfolk should be everywhere a power for purity.'[40] This rhetoric – which tied girlhood to purity and purity to civilisation and framed girls' primary imperial responsibility as the propagation of purity – echoed earlier discourses by associates like Joyce and highlighted how little the GFS had evolved from the 1870s. The official history of the organisation applauded the success of the White Crusade, but other records paint a contradictory picture.[41] Reports from Australia noted that the Crusade had to be abandoned, since there was little enthusiasm for it.[42] Consequently, while the GFS hoped that the Forward Movement and White Crusade would serve as a source of strength, it instead further highlighted how out of touch the organisation was.

The GFS undertook the White Crusade amid growing anxieties about the modern girl. For GFS leaders, the modern girl was a manifestation of the changing world order, and their reaction to the modern girl revealed their lack of adaptability and discomfort with these vicissitudes. Their scepticism regarding the modern girl comes through in GFS periodicals. One article on 'The Psychology of the Flapper' in the *Associates' Journal and Advertiser* describes how the girl 'is puzzling her elders more than ever she did before. The war has brought to us many surprises, and amongst them has been a sudden development of independence and disregard of conventionalities on the part of our younger girls which has made us tremble for the issue'. It proceeds to underscore the broader feeling of unease: 'We scarcely know – we are half afraid – we are dimly conscious that we are on the brink of a revolution which will be more far-reaching in its influence than any previous revolution'.[43] Another article, this one in *The Girls' Quarterly*, is not as alarmist but still critical of the modern girl and what she represented. The author of the article describes how they are living through 'a strange transition period', especially regarding women's position in society. Amid these changes, the author cautions readers that they 'do not forget the older roads in which those other women walked long ago – the ways of past generations, which, if they were narrower than ours in some ways, had beauties all their own, nevertheless'. The article continues: 'I confess the modern girl often makes my heart burn within me. She has the habit of – may I say? – elbowing her way through the world as though it belonged exclusively to her.'[44] The modern girl – with her independence, assertiveness, and penchant for fashion, parties, consumerism, and freedom – represented the antithesis of the GFS's ideal of girlhood, which continued to be rooted in Victorian notions of femininity. While the GFS preached a motto of 'self last', the modern girl seemed to flout the traditional roles of daughter, wife, and mother and, for GFS associates, crystallised fears that girls 'are fast growing to be like boys'.[45] The modern girl disrupted not only gender distinctions but class and racial ones as well, all of which were integral to the GFS and the British colonial project more broadly.[46]

The GFS's discomfort with the modern girl and the modern world and lack of adaptability meant that girls found the society increasingly irrelevant.[47] Associates bemoaned the difficulties faced by the organisation in competing with 'many counter attractions' and the GFS's failure to keep in touch with girls.[48] Mrs Wilkinson, the head of the Mayo School in India, remarked: 'The present day girl has little or no use for G.F.S. … she feels herself capable of looking after herself'.[49] Girls resented the paternalism of the organisation and efforts to control their mobility. They instead 'like[d] to be free agents'.[50] Associates expressed frustration at their inability to reach girls more effectively. For instance, Westmacott described how her work in India 'is terribly up-hill, and I myself am utterly dispondent [sic], and feel that G.F.S. is not meeting the needs of the girls of today. My own experiences leave me with nothing but disappointment and a feeling that all time and trouble are entirely wasted.'[51] Like Westmacott, Edith Sanders, who worked at the GFS hostel in Durban, South Africa, recognised the underlying problems but felt unable to effect a solution. She reported that 'some new stimulus is needed' and that the GFS 'must move with the times and change many of our methods'.[52] She continued: 'we should be doing something in preparation for a "new order" that must come. Here we have wonderful opportunities and I feel ashamed I am only just realising my failure to use them.'[53] Yet many within the GFS failed to heed calls to work with the modern girl and embrace this 'new order'.

The lack of adaptability deprived the GFS of not only members but also younger associates who could have potentially reinvigorated the organisation. The dearth of workers to carry on its work in regions like India, Ceylon, and Burma had been a perpetual concern for the GFS, but as the case of Mary Thomas who is discussed in the previous chapter illustrates, a further complication to this problem was that women who were willing

*Shifting colonial relations and ideas of girlhood* 175

to undertake this work were often older and ill-equipped to run a branch or hostel and work effectively with members and candidates. Branches throughout the empire wrote to the Central Council that they had enthusiastic workers who 'are wonderful in their ideals', but 'they are getting too old, and there is no one to take over the work'.[54] The ageing leadership compounded the image of the GFS as old-fashioned and primarily an 'Old Maids' Club' filled with 'Godforsaken Spinsters'.[55] Winifred Preston came to this realisation during her tour of New Zealand. She recounted her experience of visiting a branch and finding 'there was quite a crowd there, but my heart sank to see so many elderly, grey heads'.[56] She confided that the associates 'are far too old to understand and hold the girls'.[57] Other reports similarly commented on how associates were 'unequipped for dealing with the personal problems of Members' and the many challenges facing girls.[58] The dominance of older associates made younger members feel unwelcome. One associate observed how girls wanted a greater say in the organisation: 'Girls need more scope to express their opinions, run their own show, make decisions'. Another associate similarly remarked that 'girls are too often 'talked at and talked to, but not talked enough *with*'.[59] Such reports indicate that girls often found their opinions and interests ignored and resented the hierarchical nature of the organisation.

## 'Wipe out the G.F.S.': the rising popularity of the YWCA and Girl Guides

The growing sense that the GFS was estranged from and even antagonistic towards girls led them to leave the GFS for other organisations. Although the GFS acted as a precursor to many youth organisations and succeeded in making early inroads in different areas of the empire, other groups – in particular the Young Women's Christian Association (YWCA) and Girl Guides – supplanted the GFS by the interwar years.[60] The GFS professed that these organisations were not rivals.[61] For instance, Mrs. Wilkinson emphasised how 'Girl Guides ideals coincided entirely with those of G.F.S. and their purpose was achieved if they succeeded through that avenue in turning out pure, honest, helpful, human women. G.F.S. had heralded the Guide movement, and could never be dissociated from it.'[62] Yet discussions among associates paint a different picture. They lamented the loss of both leaders and members to other groups and how organisations like the Guides and YWCA seemed 'to appeal to more folk'.[63] Katherine Hughes, the secretary of the GFS Diocesan Council in Lucknow, described how the Guides had supplanted the GFS in a letter to Mytton in 1932: 'Was it [the GFS] meeting the needs of the girls in India? The general opinion seemed to be that it was not, mainly because in itself it was not constructive, and did not inculcate responsibility and initiative as did the Guide Movement.'[64] These sentiments were echoed in other parts of the empire.[65] When Winifred Preston travelled to New Zealand, her reports commented on the loss of members and resources to other organisations, which instead were 'fulfilling the work of the G.F.S.'.[66] Preston related her conversation with Mrs White, a seventy-five-year-old associate in New Zealand, who observed that 'everyone feels that unless fresh younger people are drawn in it will die down' and 'unless the G.F.S. does something *now* about it, the Y.W.C.A. *will*, and at the same time will wipe out the G.F.S.'.[67] Cecil de Carteret, the bishop of Jamaica (1916–31), similarly noted that, in his diocese, 'the G.F.S. Branch was extinct and had been replaced by what he considered were organisations more suitable to the conditions of the country'.[68] In Canada, the GFS also found itself usurped by other organisations, specifically the Women's Auxiliary, which provided 'for the needs of young women and girls entirely, leaving the G.F.S. no power'.[69] Recognising their greater appeal, the GFS sought to utilise the methods of the other organisations to bolster its own membership. It even formed its own Girl Guide companies beginning in 1916 (see Figure 5.1).[70] Yet participation in the GFS Girl Guides remained limited. In 1925, there were around four thousand GFS Girl Guides.[71] By comparison, the Girl Guides had a membership of 430,000 in 1928 and 600,000 by 1933.[72]

The greater popularity of the YWCA and Girl Guides demonstrates that girls found these organisations more relevant to their lives. Girls viewed the Guides in particular as a more amenable avenue to gain friendship and camaraderie and engage in various activities. This point was conceded in an article in *The Empire and Beyond* from an unnamed 'correspondent' in Wakefield:

> Girl Guides are going ahead, and since seeing the work of Girl Guides in other parts of England, I cannot help feeling that it is just the movement required for our younger Members; they are full of life and energy, imbued with all the stir in the air just now, and very impatient of the 'sitting-round-sewing and being-read-to style of meeting' some of us have indulged in. The Girl Guides have so much to interest them; they are led on from one thing to another, and in the background is always a sense of 'the great adventure' which even stirs the blood of some of us older ones in this wonderful time.[73]

As evident in this report, girls – and even GFS associates – found themselves attracted to the more modern and active lifestyle promoted by the Guides, rather than the Victorian activities that still defined the GFS. The contrast between the GFS and Guides underscored the perception that GFS associates were out of touch with the lives and concerns of the girl members.

*Shifting colonial relations and ideas of girlhood* 177

**Figure 5.1** GFS Girl Guides (Women's Library, London, 5GFS/04/113, '6th Poplar G.F.S. Girl Guides at Fryerning', in *The Book of the G.F.S.: What It Is and What It Does*, June 1920)

The Girl Guides were also more effective at reaching the main membership base of the GFS: working-class girls. Despite its attempts to be 'an agency by which *all* classes of working women may be effectively reached', social hierarchies within the GFS remained in place in the interwar years, with the leadership dominated by middle-class and upper-class women.[74] By contrast, the Guides were a more effective multi-class organisation and importantly provided the opportunity for working-class women to rise in the ranks and serve in leadership positions.[75] Although the GFS saw itself as performing a necessary role in girls' lives, the waning popularity of the organisation shows girls themselves had less interest in the GFS.[76]

## 'A real hindrance to our work': divisions over the central rule

The central rule epitomised how estranged the GFS had become from the girls it claimed to help. The GFS's third central rule stipulated that 'No girl who has not borne a virtuous character to be admitted as a Member; such character being lost, the Member to forfeit her card'.[77] The rule had been a perennial topic of debate since the organisation's early years. While critics of the rule contended that it placed purity above friendship and contrasted with the founding principles of the organisation, its proponents asserted that it was one of the cornerstones of the GFS's identity and that admitting girls who 'had sinned' would mean – in the words of Mrs Leigh, the vice president of the Central Council – 'the whole position of the G.F.S. would be fatally weakened'.[78] The GFS's uncompromising ideas of sexual purity, like its adherence to ideas of racial purity, contributed to the organisation's decline and exposed fault lines within the society.

At the end of the First World War, the GFS found itself at a crossroads as it faced declining membership and myriad difficulties. The uncertainties and disquiet over the rule were increasingly viewed as an impediment to the GFS's attempts to re-energise the organisation during and after the First World War.[79] As a result, GFS associates decided to revisit the rule and held two rounds of special meetings – the first from 1917 to 1919 and the second from 1932 to 1936 – to decide whether there should be any modifications of the rule. Following the first round of meetings, the GFS reaffirmed its stipulation of purity and in fact gave the rule greater prominence, making it the first rule instead of the third. The GFS additionally modified it to – what was claimed to be – the more positive wording of 'All those who join the Society must have borne a virtuous character, and must promise to uphold the Object of the Society by the witness of their lives. Those failing to bear witness in life and conduct forfeit their card.'[80] These meetings also reasserted the purpose of the GFS was '[t]o unite for the Glory of God in one Fellowship of Prayer and Service, the girls and women of the Empire, to uphold Purity in Thought, Word, and Deed'.[81] Despite this affirmation in 1919, the issue remained an acute one, and a little over a decade later, in 1932, a special meeting of the GFS Central Council reconsidered the rule again and specifically whether it should remove the strict stipulation of purity for membership by rewording the rule to 'All who join the Society pledge themselves, God helping them, to uphold the Christian standard of purity in heart and life'.[82] As this section explores, debates over the central rule expose differing ideas about girlhood and the role of the GFS in girls' lives. It also contributed to a growing divergence between the GFS Central Council in London and its branches in other parts of the empire.

Discussions about the central rule reveal the organisation's struggle to define its place in a changing world. When the GFS convened a special conference to discuss the possibility of changing the rule in 1919, the deliberations reflected an ongoing tension between holding firm to the past and adapting to the present. For instance, Mrs Philips, president of the St Asaph Branch in Wales and a member of the Imperial and Overseas Committee, framed the organisation's purpose in traditional terms, proclaiming: 'our Society has the glorious opportunity of making a better, nobler, purer and more religious England through its girlhood, the future mothers of our Empire'. Like other associates, she continued to view girls in terms of their prospective maternal roles and the reformation of girls as key to the reformation of society. Yet Philips conceded that times had changed: 'you cannot make 1919 see things the same as 1875 did'. Her speech proceeded to explain why adaptation was necessary to the survival of the GFS:

> Reconstruction is in the air, and is the only word that quite fits to describe all that is taking place whichever way we look. We, as the Pioneer Girls' Society, have got to take our place in it and to set our own house in order if we are going to continue to be the great force for good which we have been in the past. In any department of life this reconstruction element is full of difficulty, but our task seems doubly hard because we have got to combine marching with the times and adhering with unswerving loyalty to those principles which are the very reason of our being as a Society, and we have to realize that the need for new methods becomes compulsory in the face of new dangers.[83]

While Philips was wary of the changes taking places, she also acknowledged that the society could not be useful if it did not adapt with the times. Yet the GFS was unable to resolve this tension, and it emerged again when the GFS revisited the rule change in 1932. At that special meeting, an associate, Mrs Marshall Brooks, testified:

> I am quite sure that the best type of our modern girlhood hates the Rule. I think we shall have a great fight for our home and our girls, and a great many people think it is not the moment to relax one inch. But to my mind we go into the fight shackled by the Rule, and I do beg the Council to think deeply before turning down this movement, which is certainly not lowering our principles but only trying to remove a disability.[84]

Like Marshall Brooks, associates in favour of the rule change recognised how the GFS's inflexibility hindered, rather than helped, the organisation and that disaffection over the rule meant that the GFS increasingly lost its importance for girls.[85]

The perception of the rule as an impediment to the GFS's work was pronounced among the branches in the colonies and dominions. There were some associates in the colonies and dominions who supported the rule, especially in the initial discussions about it between 1917 and 1919, but the greater opinion was that it was 'a mistake' and 'a real hindrance to our work'.[86] Mary Campbell described the rule as 'a great stumbling block' that contributed to 'the very difficult period' experienced by the GFS in India.[87] Campbell eventually resigned her position as the organising worker in India 'on the ground that she was no longer in sympathy with the Central Rule, which she felt needed modifying for work in these countries'.[88] The branches in the colonies and dominions already faced myriad difficulties, and the rule posed further problems to their 'work Overseas and with all Races'.[89] Echoing Campbell's observation, E. Mabel Smith wrote from South Africa that the 'Central rule as now worded has been a distinct bone of contention. I have more than once been attacked on account of it.'[90] Debates over the central rule brought into sharp relief a long-standing issue of contention by associates in the colonies and dominions, namely the lack of understanding by associates in England about the differential conditions they faced.[91]

## The 'handmaid of the church'?: debates between the clergy and GFS

The central rule brought to the fore antagonism between members of the Anglican clergy and the GFS. The GFS trumpeted its close ties with the church.[92] Yet reports by GFS workers from branches throughout the empire bemoaned the 'indifferent attitude of the clergy' towards the organisation and their lack of support.[93] In 1905, associates in southern Africa lamented that the clergy were 'often apathetic' 'if not in opposition to the GFS'.[94] Thirty years later, the relationship had not improved and, if anything, had deteriorated.[95] From the GFS's perspective, the clergy's antipathy stemmed from their lack of understanding of the society and how it was distinct from other organisations.[96] When, as described in Chapter 4, Mabel Goodrich was forced to resign her position as the superintendent of the Bombay Lodge, she placed the blame in part on the clergy. Goodrich contended that the clergy made it impossible for her to do her job in Bombay effectively: 'If the church out here was in any degree keen on GFS I should probably have decided to remain ... but it is not and one is all the time up against an impassable barrier.'[97] Mytton was sympathetic to her criticisms, writing to Goodrich: 'I agree with you that we do find a great deal of indifference amongst the clergy, largely arising from utter ignorance and in some cases peer prejudice'.[98] Mytton elaborated on her problems with the clergy and described how they wanted the GFS to do more work among girls who 'had sinned' and needed help but who fell beyond the GFS's purview because of the central rule: 'those clergy who shun GFS because it will not do rescue work will never find a society which can properly do both things ... the clergy are making an impossible thing that they want one society which can do all classes of work amongst girls and young women'.[99] As evident in the correspondence between Mytton and Goodrich, associates envisioned the GFS as a 'handmaid of the church', but in reality, the relationship between the church and GFS was marked by distrust and resentment.[100] While associates like Goodrich and Mytton faulted the clergy and their misapprehensions for the poor relationship, the problem lay more in the divergent visions and goals of the GFS and clergy. The clergy understood the GFS's purpose but did not feel that the GFS's role as a preventative society was useful to the church's work, especially in different parts of the empire.[101]

As reflected in Goodrich's and Mytton's letters, the central rule was a key reason for the enmity between the church and GFS. The GFS's continued condemnation of girls' lifestyles conflicted with the Anglican Church's approach to sexuality during the interwar period. The Anglican Communion placed less emphasis on condemning sexual 'sin' and instead focused on offering sympathy, understanding, and support.[102] The decision by Anglican bishops to accept artificial methods of birth control in certain circumstances at the 1930 Lambeth Conference reflected this move towards greater acknowledgement of personal choices and freedom.[103] The GFS's central rule stood in contrast to this attitude, and clergy condemned it as 'unchristian' and doing more harm than good to the church's mission.[104] In her report on Australia, an associate, Miss Way, remarked that the clergy saw the GFS's strict adherence to purity as incompatible with what should be a more welcoming spirit of the church: 'some Bishops [are] very antagonistic to [the] rule … They felt they wanted a Society in which everyone could be drawn. They do not need a Society that stands definitely for purity.'[105] According to Way, associates and bishops in New Zealand shared this view and '[f]elt G.F.S. might cease in New Zealand if rule not altered'.[106] Lena Atwell, the secretary of the GFS diocese in Bunbury, echoed Way and wrote about the reticence of parishes in her diocese in West Australia to embrace the GFS 'because of this old Rule which was based on the standards of the world and not on those of Christ'.[107] While the central rule was far from the only issue that plagued the relationship between the clergy and GFS, members of the clergy indicated that they would be more willing to work with the GFS if it changed the rule. This point was acknowledged by the GFS special committee in 1932, which found that 'if the Rule were altered in the way that they recommended, very many of the clergy would welcome G.F.S. in their parishes where now their consciences will not agree to having it'.[108] These reports underscore how the clergy considered the GFS out of step with the work of the church and the needs of girls.[109]

This view comes across unmistakably in the criticisms of Mark Carpenter-Garnier, the bishop of Colombo (1924–38). Like other clergy, he pointed out how the rule contradicted the spirit of the church in a letter to Winifred Cary, the president of the GFS Diocesan Council in Ceylon: 'I acknowledge that I have never felt happy with the rule as it stands. Indeed it has in the past been the reason why I could never feel enthusiastic about the society.' He drew on his previous experience in London to underscore how the GFS turned its back on women and girls who needed help the most: 'This always made me think there was something wrong with the society, for who needed friendship in London more than a girl who's struggling to follow the Lord in the midst of great difficulties?'[110] He also drew attention to the inherent problems of the rule: 'In times past this Rule may have been a strength; but nowadays it is only in certain cases, outside those living in openly bad life, that the world can judge of a girl's moral character. For any company to judge who is disqualified under Rule I is a farce.'[111] As a result, the bishop reported that many people in his 'Diocese are not in favour of going on with the G.F.S.: they do not find it suitable'.[112] He also wrote to Ada Gardner Williams, who had visited in Ceylon in 1926, about how the rule epitomised how out of touch the GFS had become: 'G.F.S. has probably shot its bolt ... it is too Victorian and patronizing for modern youth who resent "kind ladies and tea parties"!'[113] For the bishop, the central rule highlighted the need for branches in the empire to have greater independence from the Central Council, which he conveyed in a letter to Winifred Cary: 'I hope we shall be given the liberty to develop on our own lines ... I feel pretty sure that there will be an increasing desire for an alteration of the Rule and for freedom to adapt the Society to our needs'.[114] Other clergy and associates shared his view that the GFS was no longer useful to the girls and needed to be adapted to suit their needs.[115] As the bishop made clear in his criticisms, the rule had become emblematic of broader, long-standing issues within the organisation.

The long-awaited and long-debated rule change finally came in the spring of 1936. A majority of members and associates voted in favour of the rule change, with 59,350 votes supporting the change and 16,625 opposing it. The Central Council approved the change by a vote of 72 to 15.[116] Following the alteration of the rule, some branches wrote to the Central Council with optimism that the change would provide the opportunity to restart the work of the GFS. For instance, the president of the GFS's Diocesan Council in Brisbane related that the '[g]reater elasticity may mean that more Rectors will feel able to start branches in their parishes'.[117] Yet others, like Katherine Hughes, acknowledged that 'the time had come for the rule to be altered' but conceded that the alteration 'would not revive the work in the Diocese'.[118] The rule change came too late; the damage had been done. The prolonged debates exposed the weaknesses and deepened divisions within the GFS. Moreover, by the time the change was enacted, the GFS had lost its 'Jewel' of India.[119]

## 'A long drawn out demise after a bitter struggle': the end of the GFS in India

The broader challenges facing the GFS – the ageing leadership, its failure to keep in touch with the modern girl, debates over the central rule, and antagonism with the clergy – contributed to the waning popularity of the GFS and led many to question what future, if any, the GFS had in India, but it was actually a brief report in an Anglican newspaper that set the wheels in motion for the closure of its branches in the region. In March 1932, *The Church Times* published an account of a recent meeting held by the General Council of the Church in India. The article relayed several topics discussed at the meeting and included a report about a speech by Norman Tubbs, the bishop of Rangoon (1928–34). Many readers of *The Church Times* probably took little notice of the bishop's speech – it appeared in a single short paragraph towards the end of the article under the section of 'Other Business' – but its damning critique of the GFS ignited a firestorm among the society's leadership that precipitated its withdrawal from India. The article described how '[t]he Bishop of Rangoon expressed grave doubts as to the suitability in India of the Girls' Friendly Society, with its present rules, and strongly urged that a society in the Province for girls of all classes, something along the lines of Toc H [Talbot House, an international Christian movement], be organized'.[120] The bishop questioned whether the 'G.F.S. was the best society for work amongst girls and women in India'.[121] A year after the publication of this article, the bishop reaffirmed these sentiments in a letter to the president of the GFS Central Council, Margaret Arbuthnot:

> The church both at home and abroad needs constructive and not destructive statesmanship, and while G.F.S. as it is at present constituted, is in the unanimous opinion of the committee appointed by our General Council, unsuited to meet the situation in the province of India, it does not mean that it could not be adapted to that purpose. As you know, Central Rule 1 is a great stumbling block. It is regarded with pain and even horror by a large number of our best Churchwomen. Then we also feel the need of a more forward-looking motive. G.F.S. seems to stand for 'safety first' and young people are not attracted. They want adventure, service, symbolism such as Toc H and Guides provide. Cannot G.F.S. see this point of view and think out a way of advance, which will welcome these new elements and yet not lose the gains of the past? The Church in India is not ungrateful for the help and generosity of G.F.S. in the past, but the present position of the Church's work among women and girls is far from satisfactory and we cannot sit still and do nothing.[122]

His critiques of the GFS were not new – others within and outside of the organisation had noted similar problems for years – but his letter elucidates the repercussions of the GFS's intransigence. The society not only ceased to be an effective force in the lives of girls and young women and lost the support of 'our best Churchwomen' but its negative reputation also endangered the position of the church in India.

Associates referred to the bishop of Rangoon as 'the original adversary of the G.F.S.', but he gave voice to the general feeling among high-ranking church officials in the region.[123] Foss Westcott, the bishop of Calcutta

(1919–45), affirmed that the wider General Council was 'of the opinion that it [the GFS] is unsuited to meet the needs of the young people with whom we have to deal'.[124] While acknowledging that the GFS had done valuable work, they agreed that its time had come and gone.[125] The General Council concurred with the bishop of Rangoon that 'the G.F.S. as a Society will probably give place to some younger and more suitable organisation' and was 'of the opinion that modern girls want more democratic control and more symbolism such as the Guide Movement and Toc. H give'.[126] At the conclusion of its meeting in 1932, the General Council made no definite decisions about the future of the GFS in India but instead appointed a committee to investigate how to work most effectively among women and girls in India and then make a final decision on the role of the GFS in India when it met again in 1935.[127]

What surprised the church – and some within the GFS – was the extreme reaction of the GFS's leadership to the report.[128] A year after the publication of the article in *The Church Times*, a special committee of the GFS Central Council convened in March 1933 and decided to cease the GFS's work in India, Burma, and Ceylon at the end of the year.[129] *The Church Times* report left the GFS humiliated and, for Arbuthnot and other members of the Central Council, made clear that 'the Society's organized existence in India was no longer welcomed by the Church there'.[130] Members of the Central Council maintained that they did not wish to cease GFS work in the region but felt that the report had given them 'no option … but to withdraw the Society from Dioceses in India, Burma and Ceylon'.[131] They professed that the public condemnation led the GFS to lose credibility and forced the closure of several of its dioceses in India.[132]

The radical response of the GFS was the culmination of long-standing tension between the church and the organisation. The GFS professed that it was closing down only in accordance with the bishops' wishes, but the General Council of the Church claimed that it did not intend for the GFS to cease its operations immediately and completely.[133] Several clergy, including two of the GFS's most outspoken critics, the bishops of Colombo and Rangoon, indicated that they would support the continuation of the GFS in their dioceses if it implemented changes, particularly regarding the central rule.[134] The bishop of Rangoon tried to mend fences with the GFS and wrote to Margaret Arbuthnot that his statement was not meant to be the final word:

> I too regret that your Council has taken such drastic action, although I think your Council had considerable provocation from the report in the 'Church Times'. That paper however is not the official Church paper and its reports on the Church in India are not always reliable. If I had realized that your Council

would have taken a correspondent's obiter dicta so seriously, I would have written you and I wish you could have written me.[135]

The bishop's letter pointed to one of the systemic problems, namely miscommunication, that led to the deteriorating relationship between the church and GFS.

The disagreements over issues like the central rule and the *Church Times* report were also rooted in broader contestations of power between the GFS and the church. While the bishop of Rangoon and General Council claimed that their disapproval with the GFS lay in its outdated rules, GFS associates had a different view and felt it was instead due to the autonomy exerted by the GFS. In a letter about the GFS's impending closure, C. Hilda Wood, who worked at St Luke's Hospital in Chabua, opined: 'It doesn't seem to us that the Clergy who speak so much against G.F.S. are quite honest about it. Right down at rock-bottom one finds what they mainly object to is that they haven't full control over a thing which calls itself a Church Society.'[136] As debates about the central rule demonstrated, the GFS wanted to run the organisation in its own way and not according to the dictates of the clerical authorities. The GFS's seemingly rash decision to withdraw from India signalled a desire to end the organisation on their own terms, before the church could make the decision for them.

Battles for control were at the root of the conflict not only between the church and the GFS but also between GFS associates in the empire and the Central Council in London. The closure of the Indian branches brought to the fore long-standing tension within the GFS, with associates in India, Burma, and Ceylon expressing their frustration that they had minimal input in the decision of the Central Council to cease its operations in the region. Winifred Cary described the general feeling in India of 'great amazement and indignation at the arbitrary and sudden resolve of the Central Council'.[137] Associates resented having to follow the dictates of the Central Council in London and argued that their work could have continued if they had greater freedom to adapt to local needs and conditions.[138] This grievance came through in other correspondence about the GFS's closure, with one associate writing to Mytton that the Central Council 'lays blame for the failure of G.F.S. at the door of the local workers' and 'evades the main issue altogether, which is Central Rule I'.[139] Workers in India, Burma, and Ceylon believed that the GFS used them as scapegoats instead of addressing more systemic problems and acknowledging the challenges posed by the different conditions in South Asia.

The GFS's Central Council followed a familiar pattern in its response to associates in India, Burma, and Ceylon, refusing to compromise and instead remaining adamant in its decision to exercise strict control over the GFS in the region. When the bishop of Rangoon wrote to Arbuthnot about his desire for the GFS to continue its operations in his diocese if it made changes to the central rule, Arbuthnot refused to contemplate its amendment, stating: 'The Central Rule of the Society about which you speak as a stumbling block is by us regarded in a different light'.[140] Arbuthnot and Edith Gordon Clark – the vice president of the Central Council and chair of the Committee for GFS Extension Work in India, Burma, and Ceylon – also conveyed this opinion in a letter to the diocesan presidents in South Asia and expressed their belief that the GFS in London was more capable of running the affairs of its 'colonial daughters' than the branches themselves: 'without help from the centre, it would have been difficult for the GFS in India to stand by itself'.[141] Other letters from the members of the Central Council revealed the continued prioritisation of England over other areas of the empire. For instance, as the GFS contemplated the closure of the branches in 1932, Winifred Cary wrote to Arbuthnot that 'the Society had been condemned in India' but that it could be an effective presence in the region if the GFS enacted changes and specifically altered the central rule.[142] Arbuthnot remained unmoved by Cary's pleas and instead reminded her that the GFS had been founded for 'English girls at home'.[143] She elaborated on this point further in the letter: 'I can quite understand that it may not be the best Society for work among girls in these Countries, but it seems to me rather unreasonable to suggest that the Home Society should be invited to change its basis on this account'.[144] In her letter, Arbuthnot acknowledged a point that had long been made by associates in the empire: one model of girlhood was not applicable to all. Yet her unwillingness to amend its policies reveals the continued prioritisation of white girls and English interests. For all its familial rhetoric and trumpeting of 'Imperial sisterhood', the GFS in England refused to give credence to the grievances of its 'colonial daughters' or consider granting them greater independence in managing their affairs, fearing that it would diminish its position. Yet, in trying to preserve the power of the GFS in England, Arbuthnot and the Central Council weakened the organisation overall.

While the decision to close its branches in India, Burma, and Ceylon may have appeared 'hasty' and 'drastic' to the clergy and some associates, it came as little surprise to others, especially workers on the ground in the region.[145] They had seen the writing on the wall. Vera Westmacott described the end of the GFS as 'a long drawn out demise after a bitter struggle'.[146] As discussed in the previous chapter, Westmacott had frequently battled with the Central Council and warned that such an end was inevitable unless the Central Council took the concerns of the GFS associates and the situation they faced in India more seriously. Associates in the region had long recognised the inequalities inherent within the GFS and how it hindered their ability to reach girls, especially Anglo-Indian girls. Like other associates in India, Winifred Paine came to India 'with a keen desire to make G.F.S. a real help to the girls' but grew increasingly disillusioned and 'had come to the conclusion that it did not meet the need in India at the present time'. She instead 'felt they were somehow working on the wrong lines' and that the 'G.F.S. was failing in its aim'.[147] In correspondence with Mytton, Paine reiterated her belief that the GFS did not and could not meet the needs of girls in India: 'I shall be very sorry if the necessity arises for me to say "Goodbye" to India and my work among the Anglo Indian girls, but as things are at present I see no alternative. One must be ready for change, especially in India in these days.'[148] Other members of the Diocesan Council in Lahore, including its president, Olive Carden, concurred with Paine. In a meeting to discuss the future of the GFS in the diocese in February 1932, she conceded that the GFS 'had almost entirely failed in keeping in touch with the Anglo-Indian girls in Lahore'.[149] An organisation built for 'English girls at home' in the Victorian period could not survive in twentieth-century India without some adaptation.

Over the course of 1933, the GFS made preparations to close down its branches in India and Burma at the end of the year.[150] By the time it made the decision, some branches, including Calcutta, already 'had given up'.[151] In other areas, the GFS either closed or transferred control of its lodges and hostels to other organisations.[152] For instance, the YWCA took over the GFS lodge in Bombay.[153] Ironically, despite the bishop of Colombo's strong criticism, the GFS continued to operate in Ceylon.[154] In 1937, the GFS in Ceylon finally got its own constitution that it could develop to suit its local needs and conditions.[155] In Rangoon, the diocese decided to reconstitute the work of the GFS under a successor organisation, known as the Girls' Guild of Service (GGS), with a structure and aim – 'to help its members to learn to know Christ, and through fellowship to fit themselves to serve Him' – not dissimilar to those of the GFS.[156] Over a year after the branches closed in India and Burma, Edith Gordon Clark reported that she hoped the GFS 'may yet have a future in India' but, at the same time, expressed doubts about this possibility, since 'many clergy and workers, with very great responsibilities in India, have come to think sadly that the old order does not fully meet the needs, as they know them, of young India'.[157]

The closure of the branches in India and Burma was indicative of systemic problems within the organisation and a harbinger of the GFS's decline throughout the empire. Accounts from other branches – including ones in Australia, Singapore, Shanghai, and Hong Kong – echoed reports from South Asia.[158] For instance, at the same time the organisation's fate was being debated in India, the GFS in Canada noted that it 'was going through a critical time and was in danger of dying out'.[159] Other branches similarly reported that they kept 'the flag flying', but its activities were far from robust.[160] Even the 'youngest members of a long family' – including newer branches in Jerusalem, Cairo, Beirut, Kenya, and the Seychelles – gave a correspondingly bleak picture. Associates started GFS work with great optimism only for 'the inevitable' to happen and for their idealism to descend into disappointment over the GFS's failures.[161] The GFS's commitment to sexual purity – in its adherence to the central rule – and racial purity – in its continued prioritisation of 'English girls at home' – precipitated its demise in South Asia and its waning influence in other areas of the empire.

## Conclusion

The decline of the GFS in the interwar years symbolised an increasing scepticism and disillusionment with the GFS's professed commitment to caring for, preserving, and protecting 'the Girlhood of Our Empire'.[162] Significantly the GFS's primary focus was on *girlhood*, not girls themselves. The GFS's policies reveal that the GFS was less interested in girls' well-being. It instead used its ideal of girlhood – centred on purity and whiteness – to bolster its position and reinforce colonial, racial, social, and gendered structures of power. However, amid the shifting gender and imperial relations of the interwar years, this model of girlhood and the foundational principles of GFS were increasingly challenged and ultimately could not hold.

In debates over the central rule and the future of the organisation, the GFS leadership, particularly the women of the Central Council, largely ignored the voices of members, especially those outside of England, but they did so to their own detriment. This marginalisation of girls was not new or anomalous in the history of the society. Chapter 3 detailed how emigrant girls' concerns and well-being were often regarded as secondary or even immaterial to broader organisational and colonial objectives. Chapters 2 and 4 discussed how the GFS attempted to silence and exclude girls of colour in places like India and South Africa. Yet girls found ways to push back against these efforts to disempower them. As discussed in the previous chapters, archival records of the GFS primarily consist of sources by the adult leaders, presenting a top-down perspective of the society's interwar decline. Although sources by girls are largely missing in the archives, it is clear that girls were not simply bystanders in this process. They did not unquestioningly follow the plans of the organisers, illustrated by the lack of interest by members and associates of the colonial branches in news about England and the failure of the Forward Movement. Myriad issues – including misunderstandings and debates among the GFS leadership – afflicted the organisation and contributed to its waning popularity and influence, but girls' decision to leave the organisation – or not join it at all – was the decisive factor in its decline. Even though the archival record centres the perspectives and actions of the adult leaders, the success or failure of the GFS ultimately rested in girls' hands.

## Notes

1 Women's Library, London (hereafter WL), 5GFS/05/008, *Girls' Friendly Society Leaflet for India and the Far East*, 1:5 (February 1925), p. 2.
2 WL, 5GFS/05/012, 'Girls' Friendly Society in Rangoon: Sir Harcourt Butler Opens a Hostel', *Daily Mail*, (7 December 1924).
3 WL, 5GFS/01/107, 'Committee for the G.F.S. in India and Ceylon. May 23rd, 1906'. Emphasis in the original.
4 'Overseas Reports. India', *The Empire and Beyond*, Occasional Leaflet VI (1914), pp. 11, 9.
5 WL, 5GFS/02/238, letter from C. Hilda Wood to Miss Rogers, 29 January 1933.
6 Vivienne Richmond, '"It Is Not a Society for Human Beings but for Virgins": The Girls' Friendly Society Membership Eligibility Dispute 1875–1936', *Journal of Historical Sociology*, 20:3 (September 2007), 304–27.
7 Brian Harrison, 'For Church, Queen, and Family: The Girls' Friendly Society 1874–1920', *Past and Present*, 61 (November 1972), 135–6.
8 Editor, 'National Service', *Our Letter: For G.F.S. Candidates all over the World* (June 1917), p. 3.
9 See, for example, Editor, 'As Others See Us', *The Empire and Beyond*, Occasional Leaflet VII (1914), pp. 14–15.
10 Mary Heath-Stubbs, *Friendship's Highway: Being the History of the Girls' Friendly Society, 1875–1935* (London: G.F.S. Central Office, 1935), p. 153.
11 'The Objects', *Our Letter: For G.F.S. Candidates all over the World* (September 1915), p. 3.
12 'New Zealand', *The Empire and Beyond*, Occasional Leaflet XIX (Trinity 1918), p. 6.
13 Richmond, 'It Is Not a Society for Human Beings but for Virgins', 306.
14 Heath-Stubbs, *Friendship's Highway*, pp. 39, 40.
15 WL, 5GFS/02/236, letter from E. Winifred Cary to Miss Mytton, 9 March 1932.
16 WL, 5GFS/05/011, Sibyl Wilbraham, 'Report for 1920', in *G.F.S. Missionary Fund for Cawnpore. Report for 1920*, p. 2. WL, 5GFS/02/231, letter from Mabel R. Goodrich to Miss Mytton, 8 April 1932. See also WL, 5GFS/01/107, 'Minutes of a Meeting of the Committee of Council for the G.F.S. in India, Ceylon, and the Far East Held at the GFS Central Office on Friday, June 3rd, 1921 at 2.45 p.m.', p. 224; and WL, 5GFS/05/011, 'Jubilee Year, 1875–1925', in *Girls Friendly Society Leaflet for India and the Far East*, 1:5 (February 1925), p. 3.

17 'From A G.F.S. Letter-Bag', *The Empire and Beyond*, Occasional Leaflet XXI (Spring 1919), p. 11. See, for instance, WL, 5GFS/02/227, letter from W. J. Jordon to Mrs Clark, 19 April 1938; and WL, 5GFS/02/229, letter from Bishop of Calcutta to Miss Grenside, 26 March 1931. On the earthquake, see WL, 5GFS/02/229, letter from Secretary to Miss Powell, 10 May 1930.
18 WL, 5GFS/02/263, letter from M. Steele to Miss Calvert, 8 November 1942.
19 WL, 5GFS/02/262, letter from FGP [F. G. Parrish] to Miss Angus, 21 October 1939.
20 WL, 5GFS/01/098, 'Meeting of the Imperial & Overseas Committee of the Girls' Friendly Society held at G.F.S. Headquarters, Townsend House, Greycoat Place, London, S.W. 1, on Thursday 1st July 1948, at 11.30 a.m.', p. 231.
21 WL, 5GFS/02/229, letter from V. Westmacott to Miss Mytton, 3 March 1932.
22 On references to the GFS in London as the 'mother branch', see letter from M. Steele to Miss Calvert, 8 November 1942.
23 WL, 5GFS/02/235, letter from M. E. Campbell to Miss Mytton, 12 May 1928.
24 WL, 5GFS/02/238, letter from Secretary to Mrs Gordon Clark, 20 October 1933. See also WL, 5GFS/02/235, letter from Katherine Hughes to Miss Mytton, 9 November 1933.
25 See, for example, letter from M. E. Campbell to Miss Mytton, 12 May 1928; and WL, 5GFS/01/112, 'Committee for Extension Work in India, Burma and Ceylon, held at Townsend House on Friday, October 19th, 1928 at 3.30 p.m.'.
26 See the fourth chapter for more on the control of the GFS in India by the Central Council.
27 WL, 5GFS/02/248, Winifred Preston, 'Report on New Zealand Tour for the Girls' Friendly Society, 1940'; WL, 5GFS/02/248, letter from Ethel Hervey to Miss Angus, 13 July 1939.
28 See, for instance, WL, 5GFS/02/246, 'A Successful Year Reported: Work of the Girls' Friendly Society', 1937; and letter from W. J. Jordon to Mrs Clark, 19 April 1938.
29 WL, 5GFS/02/248, letter from Winifred Preston to Miss Angus, 1 May 1939.
30 WL, 5GFS/02/248, letter from Winifred Preston to Miss Angus, 8 July 1939.
31 The Editor [Constance M. Thompson], 'My Dear Candidates', *Our Letter: For G.F.S. Candidates all over the World* (March 1918), p. 2.
32 'The Objects', *Our Letter*, p. 3
33 M. E. Townsend, 'For Home and Country', *Our Letter: For G.F.S. Candidates all over the World* (March 1915), p. 2.
34 Harrison, 'For Church, Queen, and Family', 120–1. Julia Bush, *Edwardian Ladies and Imperial Power* (London: Continuum, 1999), p. 13.
35 WL, 5GFS/02/306, *Report of the G.F.S. Special Committee* (October 1932), p. 2.
36 Heath-Stubbs, *Friendship's Highway*, p. 111. See also p. 114.
37 Heath-Stubbs, *Friendship's Highway*, p. 113.

38 Heath-Stubbs, *Friendship's Highway*, p. 111.
39 WL, 5GFS/01/097, 'Minutes of a Meeting of the Imperial Committee held on Monday, November 15th, 1920, at the G.F.S. Central Office, 39 Victoria Street, S.W. 1, at 2.15 p.m.', p. 322. WL, 5GFS/05/008, 'Sunday School Forward Movement', *Girls Friendly Society Leaflet for India and the Far East*, 1:4 (June 1924), pp. 18–19.
40 M. F., 'On, to the City of God', *The Empire and Beyond*, Occasional Leaflet XXIII (Winter 1919), p. 6.
41 Heath-Stubbs, *Friendship's Highway*, p. 111.
42 WL, 5GFS/01/097, 'Minutes of a Meeting of the Imperial and Overseas Committee held at the G.F.S. Central Office, 39 Victoria Street, S.W. 1, on Monday, March 19th, 1923, at 2.30 p.m.', p. 377.
43 WL, 5GFS/04/024, 'The Psychology of the Flapper', *Associates' Journal and Advertiser* (September 1916).
44 'The Modern Girl', *The Girls' Quarterly: A Paper for Workers in the Girls' Friendly Society*, 22 (April 1900), p. 35.
45 On 'self last', see 'Our Work in the Colonies and India', *The Girls' Quarterly: A Paper for Workers in the Girls' Friendly Society*, 27 (July 1901), p. 156. On girls becoming like boys, see Rev. Harry Jones, 'G.F.S.', *The Girls' Quarterly: A Paper for Workers in the Girls' Friendly Society*, 2 (March 1895), p. 26.
46 For more on 'the modern girl', see, for example, The Modern Girl around the World Research Group (ed.), *The Modern Girl Around the World: Consumption, Modernity, and Globalization* (Durham, NC: Duke University Press, 2008), especially the introduction; and Carol Dyhouse, *Girl Trouble: Panic and Progress in the History of Young Women* (London: Zed Books, 2013), especially chapter 3.
47 See, for instance, 'Overseas Reports. Canada', *The Empire and Beyond*, Occasional Leaflet XX (All Saints 1918), pp. 4–5; and WL, 5GFS/01/103, 'Minutes of a Meeting of the S. America Sectional Committee held at the G.F.S. Central Office, 39 Victoria Street, London, S.W. 1 on Monday, April 16th 1923, at 3 o'clock', p. 35.
48 See, for instance, WL, 5GFS/02/307, letter from Cecilia to Miss Gardner Williams, 28 October 1936. WL, 5GFS/05/011, 'Lahore Diocese', in *Girls Friendly Society Leaflet for India and the Far East*, 2:6 (September 1931), p. 9. Letter from M. Steele to Miss Calvert, 8 November 1942.
49 WL, 5GFS/02/229, letter from Olive Carden to Miss Mytton, 26 November 1932.
50 WL, 5GFS/02/262, letter from E. Mabel Smith to Miss Rogers, 20 February 1937.
51 WL, 5GFS/02/022, letter from V. Westmacott to Miss Grenside, 5 March 1931.
52 WL, 5GFS/02/262, letter from Edith F. Sanders to Miss Thwaites, 20 December 1941.
53 Letter from Edith F. Sanders to Miss Thwaites, 20 December 1941.

54 WL, 5GFS/02/263, 'G.F.S. in South Africa', [c. 1937]. WL, 5GFS/02/263, Sarah Angus, 'Report of Visits to Branches in South Africa, 1937', 27 May 1937, p. 2.
55 On the GFS as a society for 'Old Maids', see WL, 5GFS/02/317, *Girls' Friendly Society Report of the Special Commission* (March 1939), p. 2. On the GFS as 'Godforsaken Spinsters', see Miriam Glucksmann, *Cottons and Casuals: The Gendered Organisation of Labour in Time and Space* (New York: Routledge, 2000), pp. 99–101. On the GFS as 'old-fashioned', see letter from V. Westmacott to Miss Mytton, 3 March 1932.
56 Letter from Winifred Preston to Miss Angus, 8 July 1939.
57 Preston, 'Report on New Zealand Tour for the Girls' Friendly Society, 1940'.
58 *Report of the G.F.S. Special Committee*, p. 3.
59 *Girls' Friendly Society Report of the Special Commission*, p. 3. Emphasis in the original.
60 Letter from Olive Carden to Miss Mytton, 26 November 1932. WL, 5GFS/02/238, letter from Caroline Mytton to Miss Marsh, 4 December 1933.
61 WL, 5GFS/01/107, 'Minutes of a Meeting of the Committee of Council for the G.F.S. in India, Ceylon, and the Far East Held at the GFS Central Office, 39 Victoria Street, S.W., on Friday November 8th, 1918 at 2.30 p.m.', p. 185. WL, 5GFS/05/011, Mabel R. Goodrich, 'Bombay Diocese', in *Girls Friendly Society Leaflet for India and the Far East*, 2:6 (September 1931), p. 4.
62 Letter from Olive Carden to Miss Mytton, 26 November 1932.
63 WL, 5GFS/02/262, letter from E. Mabel Smith to Miss Rogers, 8 February 1936.
64 WL, 5GFS/02/235, letter from Katherine Hughes to Miss Mytton, 8 April 1932. For a similar view, see letter from Olive Carden to Miss Mytton, 26 November 1932.
65 WL, 5GFS/02/270, letter from Overseas Secretary to Mr Bradshaw, 12 September 1935. WL, 5GFS/01/098, 'Minutes of a Meeting of the Imperial and Overseas Committee held at the Townsend House, Greycoat Place, S.W. 1, on Monday June 29th, 1931 at 2.15 p.m.', pp. 89–90. WL, 5GFS/02/238, letter to Miss Anderson, 11 July 1933.
66 Letter from Winifred Preston to Miss Angus, 1 May 1939.
67 WL, 5GFS/02/248, letter from Winifred Preston to Miss Angus, 3 August 1939.
68 WL, 5GFS/01/104, 'Minutes of a Meeting of the West Indies Sectional Committee held on Monday, March 18th 1929 at 11.30 a.m. at Townsend House', pp. 39–40.
69 WL, 5GFS/01/098, 'Minutes of a Meeting of the Imperial and Overseas Committee held at Townsend House, Greycoat Place, S.W. 1 on Monday, March 19th 1928 at 2.30 p.m.', p. 45.
70 WL, 5GFS/04/113, 6th Poplar G.F.S. Girl Guides at Fryerning', in *The Book of the G.F.S.: What It Is and What It Does* (June 1920). WL, 5GFS/02/302, *The Girls' Friendly Society: Constitution of the Society By-Laws of Central*

*Committees, and Minutes of Council Binding on the Whole Society* (London: G.F.S. Central Office, 1927), p. 40.
71 Richmond, 'It Is Not a Society for Human Beings but for Virgins', 320.
72 Kristine Alexander, *Guiding Modern Girls: Girlhood, Empire, and Internationalism in the 1920s and 1930s* (Vancouver: UBC Press, 2017), p. 37. See also Tammy M. Proctor, *On My Honour: Guides and Scouts in Interwar Britain* (Philadelphia: American Philosophical Society, 2002), pp. 69–70; and Tammy M. Proctor, '(Uni)Forming Youth: Girl Guides and Boy Scouts in Britain, 1908–1939', *History Workshop Journal*, 45 (Spring 1998), 106.
73 'Home Reports', *The Empire and Beyond*, Occasional Leaflet XIX (Trinity 1918), p. 11.
74 The quote comes from Lambeth Palace Library, London (hereafter LPL), Tait 268 ff. 234, 'Some Remarks on the Present Crisis in the Girls' Friendly Society, By One of its Earliest Associates and Member of a Diocesan Council', 1880. Emphasis in the original.
75 Proctor, '(Uni)Forming Youth', 109.
76 Letter from Caroline Mytton to Miss Marsh, 4 December 1933. WL, 5GFS/02/230, letter from Winifred Paine to Caroline Mytton, 26 February 1931.
77 The Central Rules are frequently reprinted. See, for instance, *The Girls' Friendly Society* (London: Hatchards, 1877), p. 2.
78 *Report of the G.F.S. Special Committee*, p. 26. WL, 5GFS/02/304, Margaret E. Arbuthnot, *A Statement Drawn up to Show How Any Change in Its Central Rules Would Endanger the Work of the Girls' Friendly Society* (June 1932), p. 3. WL, 5GFS/02/306, *Report of the Special Meeting of the Incorporated Central Council of the Girls' Friendly Society, Held at Townsend House, Greycoat Place, Westminster on Wednesday, April 27th, 1932 at 11 a.m.*, p. 26.
79 WL, 5GFS/02/299, *Girls' Friendly Society. Report of a Conference for the Consideration of the Central Rules, held at the G.F.S. Central Office 29 Victoria Street, S.W. 1, on Friday and Saturday, June 13th and 14th, 1919*, p. 6.
80 Arbuthnot, *A Statement Drawn up to Show How Any Change in Its Central Rules Would Endanger the Work of the Girls' Friendly Society*, pp. 1–2.
81 The Editor [Constance M. Thompson], 'The G.F.S. Objects', *Our Letter: For G.F.S. Candidates all over the World* (September 1918), p. 1.
82 *Report of the G.F.S. Special Committee*, p. 4.
83 *Report of a Conference for the Consideration of the Central Rules*, pp. 4–5.
84 *Report of the Special Meeting of the Incorporated Central Council of the Girls' Friendly Society*, p. 27.
85 *Report of the Special Meeting of the Incorporated Central Council of the Girls' Friendly Society*, p. 16. See also, for instance, Miss Cropper's statement, p. 13.
86 WL, 5GFS/02/306, Rev. Scott's views in 'Notes from Evidence Given on May 26th. and 27th. 1933'. WL, 5GFS/02/307, letter from Mrs Head to Mrs Gordon Clark, 27 September 1936.

87 WL, 5GFS/01/111, 'Minutes of a Meeting of the Committee for Extension Work in India, Burma and Ceylon, held at Townsend House, Greycoat Place, Westminster, on Tuesday, May 5th 1931, at 2.30 p.m.', p. 156.
88 'Minutes of a Meeting of the Committee for Extension Work in India, Burma and Ceylon, held at Townsend House, Greycoat Place, Westminster, on Tuesday, May 5th 1931, at 2.30 p.m.', p. 156.
89 *Report of the Special Meeting of the Incorporated Central Council of the Girls' Friendly Society*, p. 6.
90 Letter from E. Mabel Smith to Miss Rogers, 8 February 1936.
91 For more on this point, see, for instance, *Report of a Conference for the Consideration of the Central Rules*, p. 27; *Report of the Special Meeting of the Incorporated Central Council of the Girls' Friendly Society*, p. 6; and WL, 5GFS/02/270, letter from Rachel Anson to Miss Rogers, 29 January 1934.
92 Heath-Stubbs, *Friendship's Highway*, p. 9.
93 WL, 5GFS/01/102, 'Minutes of a Meeting of the S. African Sectional Committee, held at the G.F.S. Central Office on Friday, June 17th [1917] at 2.15 p.m.', p. 91. See also WL, 5GFS/02/261, letter from [Rev.] W. Eaton to Miss Rogers, 19 September 1933.
94 WL, 5GFS/01/091, 'Sectional Committee for South Africa Minutes of a Meeting Held on Friday Nov. 17th 1905', p. 142.
95 WL, 5GFS/02/238, letter from the President [Margaret Arbuthnot] to Lord Bishop, 28 March 1933.
96 WL, 5GFS/01/098, 'Minutes of a Meeting of the Imperial and Overseas Committee of the Girls' Friendly Society, held at G.F.S. Central Office, Townsend House, Greycoat Place, London, S.W. 1, on Tuesday, 17th February 1948, at 11.30 a.m.', pp. 217 and 221; WL, 5GFS/02/262, letter from E. Mabel Smith to Miss Rogers, 29 February 1936; Letter from Caroline Mytton to Miss Marsh, 4 December 1933.
97 WL, 5GFS/02/231, letter from Mabel R. Goodrich to Miss Mytton, 8 May 1931.
98 Letter from Secretary to Miss Goodrich, 29 January 1931.
99 Letter from Secretary to Miss Goodrich, 29 January 1931.
100 Heath-Stubbs, *Friendship's Highway*, p. 65.
101 WL, 5GFS/04/128, Edith Gordon Clark, 'India', *A Jubilee Chronicle for Overseas* (1935), p. 22.
102 Laura Monica Ramsay, '"The Relation of the Sexes": Towards a Christian View of Sex and Citizenship in Interwar Britain', *Contemporary British History*, 34:4 (2020), 555–79. For more on Liberal Anglicanism in this period, see Matthew Grimley, *Citizenship, Community and the Church of England: Liberal Anglican Theories of the State between the Wars* (Oxford: Clarendon, 2004).
103 Ramsay, 'The Relation of the Sexes', 571. See also Timothy Willem Jones, 'Contraception, Sex, and Pleasure', chapter 5 in *Sexual Politics in the Church of England 1857–1967* (New York: Oxford University Press, 2012), pp. 131–61; and Ross McKibbin, 'Sexuality and Morality', chapter 8 in *Classes and*

*Shifting colonial relations and ideas of girlhood* 195

Cultures: England 1918–1951 (New York: Oxford University Press, 1998), pp. 308–10.
104 Mrs Nicholl's views in 'Notes from Evidence Given on May 26th. and 27th. 1933'. See also WL, 5GFS/02/230, letter from Margaret Scott to Miss Mytton, 27 May 1927; and *Report of the Special Meeting of the Incorporated Central Council of the Girls' Friendly Society*, p. 6.
105 'Notes from Evidence Given on May 26th. and 27th. 1933'.
106 'Notes from Evidence Given on May 26th. and 27th. 1933'.
107 WL, 5GFS/02/307, letter from Lena A. Atwell to Madam, 30 October 1936.
108 *Report of the G.F.S. Special Committee*, p. 4.
109 Letter from Bishop of Calcutta to Miss Grenside, 26 March 1931.
110 WL, 5GFS/02/238, letter from Mark Colombo to Mrs Cary, n.d.
111 WL, 5GFS/02/238, letter from Mark Colombo to Miss Gardner Williams, 16 December 1932.
112 Letter from Mark Colombo to Miss Gardner Williams, 16 December 1932.
113 Letter from Mark Colombo to Miss Gardner Williams, 16 December 1932.
114 Letter from Mark Colombo to Mrs Cary.
115 WL, 5GFS/05/011, letter from C. M. Ricketts, Vicar, in 'G.F.S. St. Michael's Branch', 30 October 1920.
116 WL, 5GFS/02/236, 'Minutes of the G.F.S. Council held at the G.F.S. Hall on July 4th, at 9.30 a.m.', p. 1. WL, 5GFS/02/236, 'Minutes of the G.F.S. Council held on December 7th, at the G.F.S. Hall at 9.30 a.m.', p. 1. Richmond, 'It Is Not a Society for Human Beings but for Virgins', 322.
117 WL, 5GFS/02/306, letter from Katherine S. Stevenson to Miss Gordon Clark, 30 August 1936.
118 Letter from Katherine Hughes to Miss Mytton, 8 April 1932.
119 'Minutes of a Meeting of the Committee of Council for the G.F.S. in India, Ceylon, and the Far East Held at the GFS Central Office, 39 Victoria Street, S.W., on Friday November 8th, 1918 at 2.30 p.m.', p. 185.
120 WL, 5GFS/02/237, 'General Council of the Church of India', *The Church Times*, 4 March 1932.
121 WL, 5GFS/01/111, 'Minutes of a Meeting of the Committee for Extension Work in India, Burma and Ceylon, held at Townsend House, Greycoat Place, Westminster, on Wednesday, March 9th, 1932, at 2.30 p.m.', p. 164. 'General Council of the Church of India'.
122 WL, 5GFS/02/237, letter from Norman Rangoon to Mrs Arbuthnot, 27 July 1933.
123 WL, 5GFS/02/238, letter from Margaret E. Arbuthnot to Mrs Gordon Clark, 11 July 1933.
124 WL, 5GFS/02/235, letter from Foss Calcutta to Mrs Arbuthnot, 5 February 1933.
125 'Minutes of a Meeting of the Committee for Extension Work in India, Burma and Ceylon, held at Townsend House, Greycoat Place, Westminster, on Wednesday, March 9th, 1932, at 2.30 p.m.', p. 164.
126 Letter from Foss Calcutta to Mrs Arbuthnot, 5 February 1933.

127 'General Council of the Church of India'.
128 Letter from Margaret E. Arbuthnot to Mrs Gordon Clark, 11 July 1933.
129 WL, 5GFS/01/111, 'Minutes of a Meeting of the Committee for Extension Work in India, Burma and Ceylon, held at Townsend House, Greycoat Place, Westminster, on Thursday, October 12th, 1933, at 2.30 p.m.', p. 185.
130 WL, 5GFS/02/235, letter from Margaret E. Arbuthnot to Lord Bishop [Calcutta], 18 May 1933.
131 WL, 5GFS/02/235, letter from the President, Incorporate Central Council of the Girls' Friendly Society, and Chairman, Committee for G.F.S. Extension Work in India, Burma and Ceylon, 5 May 1933. WL, letter from Secretary to Mrs Marshall, 11 July 1933.
132 Letter from Margaret E. Arbuthnot to Mrs Gordon Clark, 11 July 1933.
133 'Minutes of a Meeting of the Committee for Extension Work in India, Burma and Ceylon, held at Townsend House, Greycoat Place, Westminster, on Thursday, October 12th, 1933, at 2.30 p.m.', p. 186. WL, 5GFS/02/238, untitled report, c. 1933–34.
134 Untitled report, c. 1933–34. 'Minutes of a Meeting of the Committee for Extension Work in India, Burma and Ceylon, held at Townsend House, Greycoat Place, Westminster, on Thursday, October 12th, 1933, at 2.30 p.m.', p. 186.
135 Letter from Norman Rangoon to Mrs Arbuthnot, 27 July 1933.
136 Letter from C. Hilda Wood to Miss Rogers, 29 January 1933.
137 WL, 5GFS/02/237, letter from E. Winifred Cary to Mrs Arbuthnot, 3 June 1933. On this point, see also WL, 5GFS/02/235, letter from Mark Colombo to Mrs Arbuthnot, 20 June 1933.
138 WL, 5GFS/02/238, letter from Secretary to Mrs Gordon Clark, 7 February 1933. Letter from Mark Colombo to Mrs Arbuthnot, 20 June 1933. WL, 5GFS/02/235, letter from E. Winifred Cary to Mrs Arbuthnot, 20 May 1933.
139 WL, 5GFS/02/238, letter from C. Anderson to Miss Mytton, 12 June [1933].
140 WL, 5GFS/02/238, letter from the President [Margaret Arbuthnot] to Lord Bishop [Rangoon], 19 July 1933. See also WL, 5GFS/02/238, 'Minutes of Diocesan Council held on Saturday, July 15th 1933 at the G.F.S. Hall at 9.30 a.m.'.
141 Letter from the President, Incorporate Central Council of the Girls' Friendly Society, and Chairman, Committee for G.F.S. Extension Work in India, Burma and Ceylon, 5 May 1933.
142 WL, 5GFS/02/237, letter from Winifred Cary to Mrs Arbuthnot, 24 October 1932.
143 WL, 5GFS/02/235, letter from Margaret Arbuthnot to Mrs Cary, 14 November 1932.
144 Letter from Margaret Arbuthnot to Mrs Cary, 14 November 1932.
145 Letter from C. Anderson to Miss Mytton, 12 June [1933]. Letter from Mark Colombo to Mrs Arbuthnot, 20 June 1933.
146 WL, 5GFS/02/238, letter from V. Westmacott to Miss Clark, 25 May 1933.
147 WL, 5GFS/02/238, 'A Meeting of the Lahore Diocesan Council was held on Tuesday, 23rd February, 1932, at St. St. [sic] Hilda's House, Lahore', p. 2.

148 WL, 5GFS/02/238, letter from Winifred Paine to Miss Mytton, 16 April 1932.
149 'A Meeting of the Lahore Diocesan Council was held on Tuesday, 23rd February, 1932, at St. St. [sic] Hilda's House, Lahore', p. 1.
150 WL, 5GFS/02/238, letter from Secretary to Miss Atwool, 22 May 1933.
151 'Minutes of a Meeting of the Committee for Extension Work in India, Burma and Ceylon, held at Townsend House, Greycoat Place, Westminster, on Thursday, October 12th, 1933, at 2.30 p.m.', p. 185. See also WL, 5GFS/02/229, letter from V. Westmacott to Miss Grenside, 28 November 1931; and letter from the President, Incorporate Central Council of the Girls' Friendly Society, and Chairman, Committee for G.F.S. Extension Work in India, Burma and Ceylon, 5 May 1933.
152 WL, 5GFS/02/238, letter from Secretary to Miss Anderson, 23 November 1933. Gordon Clark, 'India', *A Jubilee Chronicle for Overseas*, p. 22.
153 WL, 5GFS/02/238, T. Ackland, 'Girls' Friendly Society. Bombay', April 1934.
154 Letter from Caroline Mytton to Miss Marsh, 4 December 1933.
155 WL, 5GFS/02/236, *Girls' Friendly Society Diocese of Colombo*, January 1937, p. 2.
156 WL, 5GFS/02/238, 'Report on the work of the Committee appointed by the G.F.S. Diocesan Council to re-organize girls' work in the Diocese of Rangoon', [c. 1935–36].
157 Gordon Clark, 'India', in *A Jubilee Chronicle for Overseas*, p. 22.
158 WL, 5GFS/04/128, 'Australia', *A Jubilee Chronicle for Overseas* (1935), pp. 17–19. WL, 5GFS/01/098, 'Minutes of a Meeting of the Imperial and Overseas Committee held at Townsend House on Monday, October 24th 1929 at 2.30 p.m.', p. 38. WL, 5GFS/04/128, 'Non-Treaty Areas', *A Jubilee Chronicle for Overseas* (1935), p. 25.
159 WL, 5GFS/01/098, 'Minutes of a Meeting of the Imperial and Overseas Committee held at Townsend House, Greycoat Place, Westminster, on Monday March 20th 1933 at 2.30 p.m.', p. 107. See also WL, 5GFS/01/098, 'Minutes of a Meeting of the Imperial and Overseas Committee held at the National Society's House on Monday, June 25th 1934 at 2.30 p.m.', p. 128.
160 'Non-Treaty Areas', p. 25.
161 'Non-Treaty Areas', p. 25.
162 LPL, Davidson 143, ff. 215, 'Appeal for £20,000 for the Lodges and Homes of Rest of the Girls' Friendly Society', 1907. Variations of this phrase can be found throughout GFS literature. See, for instance, 'Vision and Mission Slides', *The Empire and Beyond*, Occasional Leaflet XII (Anniversary Week 1916), p. 14. See also Kathleen M. Townsend, *Some Memories of Mrs. Townsend: Foundress of the Girls' Friendly Society* (London: GFS Central Council, 1923), p. 19.

# Conclusion

When the GFS marked its centenary in 1975, it produced a book that celebrated the organisation's past, present, and future and heralded how 'the GFS continues to meet change with change and to fulfil in new times its purpose'.[1] Yet a different picture emerged from other reports. Five years later, the chair of the GFS's Overseas Subcommittee, Miss P. Palmer, travelled to Barbados to celebrate the seventy-fifth anniversary of the GFS on the island. Echoing associates in the 1920s and 1930s, Palmer 'found no G.F.S. work among girls. The majority of members were middle-aged and elderly, one 90.' Despite the efforts of Palmer and others to promote the organisation among girls, they had little success and found girls were instead drawn to the Scouts and Guides. The organisation also failed to reach girls of colour and instead remained a bastion of whiteness, with Palmer reporting: 'Members were nearly all white, despite coloured people forming 85% of the population and a majority of church worshippers'.[2] Palmer's report suggested that, instead of 'meet[ing] change with change', the GFS was still perceived as out of touch and outdated. Despite its efforts, the GFS struggled to resolve systemic problems that had troubled the organisation since its early years.

In the period following the Second World War, the GFS, like Britain, struggled to find its place and redefine its identity. This conclusion provides a brief overview of the organisation's history during and after the Second World War and discusses the ways that it has adapted – and not – to broader social and political changes. In *The Afterlife of Empire*, Jordanna Bailkin argues that decolonisation was not a monolithic or solely political, diplomatic process, but it 'was built into the lives of ordinary Britons, reshaping their experiences and identities at the most intimate level'.[3] The GFS in the postwar years illuminates this more personal dimension of decolonisation. Its history in the decades following the Second World War cannot be disentangled from the broader context of decolonisation, and, as this chapter explores, British colonialism and its legacies continue to shape the GFS down to the present day.

## To 'help a new generation of girls': the GFS during and after the Second World War

As with the First World War, the Second World War brought a renewed sense of purpose to the GFS. Associates seized upon the war as a 'great opportunity' to demonstrate the 'crusading power of the Girls' Friendly Society'.[4] It assisted with efforts on the home front by launching training schemes for girls, raising money to support girl and women workers, and offering Townsend House, its headquarters in London, as a public air raid shelter.[5] The war and postwar years also marked a time when the state increasingly recognised the power and utility of youth organisations.[6] Broader anxieties converged around youth. The postwar 'baby boom', concerns about the 'generation gap', Britain's changing position in the world, and the Cold War all reaffirmed the importance of youth organisations.[7] With the end of the war, the GFS embarked on a period of rebuilding to 'help a new generation of girls'.[8] It launched various reforms to increase its membership, revising its constitution and increasing member involvement in the running of the organisation. It also attempted to raise greater public awareness about the organisation, including hosting a rally and pageant at the Royal Albert Hall in 1946 and 1955 respectively.[9] At the same time, it continued similar initiatives that had existed since its inception, including providing girls with living accommodations and advice about jobs.[10]

The changing landscape for girls and women required a reconfiguration of key cornerstones of the GFS's imperial work. The outbreak of First World War suspended migration programmes, and, while new emigration schemes emerged after the war, they did not receive the same level of enthusiasm as prewar programmes.[11] As a result, the GFS's work among migrant girls declined. M. M. Stevens, who visited the GFS branches in Durban and Cape Town, noted this shift in a letter in 1932: 'The Migration of girls from home wh[ich] filled the Lodges in our Colonies in the old days has almost ceased and they have quite changed'.[12] The GFS continued to sponsor programmes, like scrapbook competitions, to stimulate interest in emigration, but girls expressed little enthusiasm for them.[13] Following the end of the First World War, the GFS took a less direct role in migration and handed the responsibilities of making travel arrangements over to the Society for the Overseas Settlement of British Women (SOSBW), and in 1934, it ceased having a separate migration department.[14] During and after the Second World War, there were discussions about restarting the migration department, but, with the SOSBW taking over its work, the GFS found there was little need to have its own department.[15] Economics was not the sole reason for the decline of emigration. As Ellen Boucher details in *Empire's Children: Child Emigration, Welfare, and the Decline of the British World*,

1869–1967, the eventual turn away from British child emigration was bound up with the decline of a sense of shared culture and racial identity throughout the empire, and this led to the articulation of distinctly national identities as well as new definitions of Britishness.[16] These shifting imperial and national exigencies contributed to the cessation of the GFS's migration programmes, although smaller-scale migration did continue through the GFS's missionary work.

### 'A life based on Christian principles': the development of GFS missionary work

When the GFS closed its branches in India in 1933, there was hope that the closure would be temporary and that, as stated in *A Jubilee Chronicle for Overseas* of 1935, the GFS 'may yet have a future in India'.[17] Yet clergy in the region remained reluctant to support the organisation, with the bishops of major cities, including Bombay (present-day Mumbai) and Lucknow, writing in 1949 that they did not see any prospect of the GFS being restarted in the country.[18] Nevertheless, the GFS did maintain some presence in the region through its missionary programmes, with GFS members undertaking charitable work, often in association with organisations like the Church Missionary Society (CMS).[19] Members worked in churches and hospitals, including the St Barnabas Hospital in Ranchi, St Luke's Hospital in Bihar, and St Stephen's Hospital in Delhi.[20] In the 1970s, the GFS made new efforts to restart work with girls in India, particularly in South India. As it had done in the past, it targeted girls 'morally at risk' after leaving school with the aim of 'enhancing the lifestyle and outlook of village girls'.[21] To this end, it provided girls with professional instruction and offered advice about marriage and motherhood.[22] Yet efforts to re-establish the organisation in India ultimately had little impact, and the GFS does not have a presence in India today.[23] GFS work continued in Ceylon (present-day Sri Lanka) but faced ongoing challenges in the postwar years.[24] As an Anglican organisation, it particularly struggled with the multi-religious nature of the country.[25] A report from 1989 indicated that the Sri Lankan GFS had been 'dying' since the Second World War.[26] Despite these unpromising reports, the GFS does continue to operate in Sri Lanka today and, in line with its original remit, offers professionalisation workshops and religious programmes.[27]

As the GFS's work in India illustrates, the organisation's imperial and overseas efforts continued in the postwar period but under the guise of missionary work. The line between its overseas and missionary programmes was often blurred, causing confusion even among GFS associates as to what

Conclusion 201

qualified as overseas work and what was missionary work.[28] Similar to the GFS's initial purpose, the GFS's missionary programmes prepared girls who were leaving school for employment and 'to prevent them being placed in a position of moral danger'.[29] It also aimed to teach 'the importance of Christian marriage and a life based on Christian principles'.[30] These aims reveal the continuation of the GFS's original efforts to extend notions of white English middle-class morality. As discussed in the first chapter, the GFS's missionary programmes were premised on the idea that white women needed to teach people in other parts of the empire how to create 'pure' 'Christian' homes. This same notion of expertise pervaded postwar missionary programmes. Missionary programmes provided an acceptable way to carry on the GFS's imperial work and also aligned with Britain's foreign-policy objectives. As scholars like Emily Baughan have shown, humanitarian programmes served as a way to forestall anticolonial resistance and bolster Britain's geopolitical power amid the fracturing of the empire.[31] The missionary programmes supported these objectives by fostering connections between Britain and other parts of the world and perpetuating the notion that these regions could benefit from British intervention and 'civilisation'.

As it had when its missionary programmes were first developed in the late 1800s, the GFS in the postwar years supported missionaries in various ways, including fundraising and the provision of goods, and trained girls and young women to work as missionaries.[32] In 1951, the GFS had twenty-five missionaries in regions of Africa, Japan, India, Pakistan, and Iran and helped fund others in China and British Malaya.[33] Over the course of the second half of the twentieth century, the organisation turned its outreach to areas where it traditionally had little or no presence and encouraged missionaries already on the ground to establish GFS branches. Some of the missionaries belonged to the GFS, but even those who were not members viewed the GFS as a means to an end, namely a way to extend Christianity in the region.[34] As a result, the GFS's presence grew in Guyana, the Philippines, Brazil, Japan, Korea, Sudan, Kenya, Ghana, Liberia, and The Gambia.[35]

## 'To keep the GFS mission ... ablaze': the development of the GFS World Council

In addition to the expansion of its missionary work, the development of the World Council in 1955 illustrates how the GFS worked to redefine its structure and purpose amid a shifting international order.[36] When the World Council first met in Switzerland in 1956, it had a membership base of 66,000 across twenty-five countries.[37] The framework of the World Council sought to improve upon some of the problems that had troubled the GFS previously. For instance, it afforded countries greater independence and freedom by keeping the structure more informal and making the directives as elastic as possible.[38] It also made an effort to involve girls, recommending that one of the two representatives from each country at World Council meetings be a 'junior delegate' between the ages of sixteen and twenty-one.[39] With the empire no longer a unifying thread for the GFS's branches throughout the world, the development of the World Council served as a way to connect disparate GFS branches and acted as the GFS's own version of the Commonwealth. Described in the centenary booklet as 'one of the most important developments of the Society in the last 20 years', the Council aimed '[t]o promote fellowship between the members of the society throughout the world by the exchange of information and ideas'.[40] To facilitate communication and cultivate the sense of a global community, the World Council organised 'world assemblies, camps, exchange visits and correspondence between members'.[41] It also started a 'Day of Prayer Around the World' and a world newsletter with updates from different branches.[42]

The World Council mirrored other initiatives in the Commonwealth. For instance, the World Assembly of Youth (WAY) was founded in 1949 as a co-ordinating body of national youth councils and organisations to facilitate international co-operation and interracial friendship among young people, as well as acting as a bulwark against communism.[43] In *The Afterlife of Empire*, Bailkin describes how WAY was one of a variety of programmes devised by the British government to promote personal connections among young people in the Commonwealth. The Commonwealth Youth Trust similarly sought to promote interracial understanding and respect through the development of scholarships, travel opportunities, and camps. In her study of these programmes, Bailkin shows how they aligned with Britain's Cold War and Commonwealth objectives in the postwar era, observing: 'The forging of sentimental ties between young people would strengthen the Commonwealth's economic interconnectedness, and avoid the "ignorance and insularity" that plagued adults'.[44] The GFS's activities – and the creation of the World Council in particular – can be seen as part of these broader efforts to create bonds and a greater sense of awareness and understanding among the youth of different parts of the Commonwealth. As noted in a scrapbook celebrating the centenary of the organisation in 1975, the World Council was 'an opportunity for representatives for young people from diverse cultures to meet, discuss and learn'.[45] While the Cold War and the threat of communism did not loom large on the GFS's agenda, the World Council's work did align with Britain's Cold War objectives in cultivating a stronger 'special relationship' with the United States. In a break from the imperial structure of the past, membership in the World Council was 'open

# Conclusion

to G.F.S. in all countries whose purposes are in fundamental agreement'.[46] Prior to the development of the World Council, there was limited collaboration between the GFS in the United States and the branches in Britain and the empire, but, with the inauguration of the World Council, the US and its affiliated branches – many started as part of its own empire-building projects, including ones in the Philippines and Puerto Rico – were brought under a common aegis.[47]

The most prominent innovation of the World Council was arguably its world mission projects, in which member countries embark on a multi-year service project, typically to benefit newer branches in the Global South. The first project, which ran from 1957 to 1962, created a leadership training programme in Mombasa, Kenya. This project was followed by similar ones in West Africa – specifically Ghana, Liberia, and The Gambia – and Korea and Guyana.[48] The projects provided girls and women with skills needed for leadership roles in their churches and communities.[49] The impetus was not solely altruistic; the projects served as an important means for the GFS to grow in these regions.[50] The World Council believed that developing these branches in newer regions required a 'trained group of dedicated leaders that will keep the GFS mission ... ablaze'.[51] Other projects focused on providing resources to communities. For instance, the project from 1974 to 1976 raised money for a hostel for girls in Sri Lanka.[52] Even though the projects have encountered challenges – including a lack of necessary workers – over the years, the world mission projects remain a key part of the GFS's work today.[53] Recent projects include providing assistance to tsunami survivors in Japan (2014-17), equipping Sri Lankan girls from low-income families with English language skills to enhance their employment prospects (2017–20), and providing training and assistance to poor girls and young women in Cameroon (2021–23).[54] Among the stated objectives of the Cameroon project were '[t]o assist members of the Anglican church of Cameroon to understand the ministry of GFS' and '[t]o promote GFS to the secular community, growing membership and sponsorship'.[55] As these aims reveal, these projects continue to serve as a way to foster the GFS's growth in different countries.[56]

Chapter 3 detailed the myriad ways that the GFS sought to educate girls about the empire, and this educative dimension endured in the post-imperial world. For instance, when a country was chosen as the focus of a world mission project, girls from branches in other parts of the world were encouraged to learn more about that country and its history and culture.[57] Like the study circles of earlier generations, the GFS developed study courses on areas like Ghana, Japan, and Kenya. Girls were encouraged not only to learn as much as they could about these countries but also to explore the missionary connections of these places and specifically to make use of material available from the CMS.[58] The GFS continued its tradition of linked branches and penfriend programmes to generate interest in the work of the GFS and especially its missionaries.[59] It also launched an overseas birthday card scheme, in which girls would receive a card on their birthday along with encouragement to make a donation to an overseas diocese. This programme raised money for the GFS's overseas work and strengthened its global networks.[60]

## 'Is G.F.S. in its present form relevant?': continued difficulties

Despite efforts to revitalise the organisation and extend its outreach, the GFS in the latter half of the twentieth century faced endemic problems that remained unresolved from the interwar era. The GFS struggled to recruit girls and found itself competing with other activities and organisations.[61] It endeavoured to develop branches in areas like Zambia, Lesotho, and Japan but found there was little desire since they already had the Girl Guides, YWCA, and other groups, like the Girls' Brigade, Girls' Auxiliary, the Guild of St Agnes, and the Anglican Girls' Society.[62] Financial and logistical problems also impeded the GFS's ability to start branches.[63] Even with technological advancements, branches struggled with unreliable mail that hindered communication between branches and with having few workers to traverse vast distances.[64] A shortage of workers deterred the growth of the GFS in regions where it had a longer presence, like Ireland, and in newer areas where it hoped to expand its reach, like Japan.[65] The problem, which the GFS had also faced in the interwar years, was not only the lack of workers but also that 'the right people are not forthcoming'.[66] Those who did volunteer were regarded as not 'suitable' and too old to undertake work overseas.[67] Political changes and unrest continued to present obstacles to the GFS's outreach plans. As it had before the Second World War, the growth of independence movements and political agitation affected the operations of the GFS.[68] Postwar emigration to Britain from areas like the West Indies led to the loss of associates and members, placing a heavy strain on the workers who remained there.[69]

Race and the place of girls of colour within the organisation remained a persistent source of difficulty for the organisation. The GFS increasingly recognised that the issue of race was one of the utmost importance. For instance, when the GFS held its first World Council meeting in 1956, one of the central items on the agenda was 'How can we solve our differences – racially – economically?'[70] Debates over race and the inclusion of girls of colour were most acute in southern Africa. As discussed in the fourth chapter, the segregation and unequal treatment of Coloured and Black girls had been an issue of contention since the establishment of the GFS in the region. The GFS revisited the issue of whether branches should include white and Coloured girls in the postwar years, but, with the implementation of apartheid, it was concluded that it would be impossible.[71] The GFS in South Africa ultimately forfeited its membership in the World Council in 1955 after pressure from other members to include girls of colour.[72] Despite this withdrawal from the World Council and the closure of branches in South Africa, the GFS did maintain a presence in the region through branches in Transkei.[73] Led by African women and composed entirely of African women and girls, there were seventy-one branches with around five hundred members in Transkei by 1965.[74] Following the end of apartheid in 1994, the GFS re-established branches throughout South Africa, and, as discussed more below, GFS activity in the region is robust, with members from South Africa composing around 44 per cent of the GFS total worldwide membership in 2017.[75]

Another continuation from the interwar years was that the GFS found itself more often at odds rather than in harmony with the clergy. Even though the GFS is considered 'the oldest of the church's youth organisations', organisers and workers overseas bemoaned that clergy did not support the GFS's efforts to expand its work and even were unaware of the organisation's existence.[76] Over a decade after the organisation updated its contested rule on purity, GFS associates were dismayed to find that members of the clergy thought the rule remained unchanged.[77] The clergy's concern continued to centre on the traditionalist image of the GFS and how this reputation would affect the church's image. Echoing clergy a generation earlier, the bishop of Lincoln, Kenneth Riches, wrote a letter in 1964, stating: 'I'm bound to say that I have for some time felt that the old pattern of the GFS was quite outmoded and unless it was given some new and vigorous form there was little real place for the work of the society in the modern world'.[78] Twenty years later, the GFS continued to have an uneasy relationship with the clergy, which is evident in its attempts to re-establish its presence in the West Indies in 1986. Even though the effort received support from priests in certain regions, like St Lucia and Grenada, it stalled after opposition from the archbishop, who 'did not wish GFS to be revived' and instead thought that other organisations operating there were fulfilling the work of the GFS.[79]

The GFS continued to struggle to find its place in a rapidly changing world and articulate its relevance to girls. A scrapbook produced by the organisation to commemorate its centenary in 1975 indicated its desire for change, stating 'it would like nothing better than to lose its crusty, somewhat Victorian image'.[80] The president reaffirmed this sentiment, writing: 'We can change course, if that is necessary'.[81] Yet other parts of the scrapbook suggest that the GFS still clung to its Victorian foundations. Organisers believed that the solutions devised by Mary Elizabeth Townsend to address social problems in the Victorian era could be applied in the 1970s.[82] The centenary of the organisation took place during the second-wave feminist movement, but, as it had done during the suffrage movement, the GFS encouraged its members not to disregard their traditional feminine roles.[83] The scrapbook featured pictures of recent activities, including pageants, that indicated little had changed in fifty or even a hundred years (Figure 6.1).[84] Over and over again, organisers had to confront the question: 'Is G.F.S. in its present form relevant to girls of today?'[85]

## 'Open new conversations': the GFS today

As the GFS prepares to mark its sesquicentennial in 2025, it is confronted with old and new questions. The GFS's relationship with the Anglican Church and the place of religion within the GFS continues to be debated. The world body of the GFS remains a religious organisation closely connected to the Anglican Communion.[86] However, the GFS in England and Wales has moved away from its Anglican roots and is no longer a religious organisation.[87] As its website notes:

Figure 6.1 Festival service marking the GFS's centenary at Chester Cathedral, 1975, photograph by Clifford Shirley (Women's Library, London, 5GFS/06/178, Girls' Friendly Society Centenary Scrapbook, 1975)

> Over the years, the work of the organisation has evolved to keep pace with the changing needs of girls and young women. We no longer provide groups with religion-based content, however those groups who choose to are free to incorporate elements of faith. These groups are clearly identified on this website, to ensure parents are aware of any elements of faith.[88]

This shift is part of the GFS in England and Wales's efforts to broaden the organisation to meet the changing needs of girls.

Like other youth organisations, including the Guides and Scouts, the GFS is grappling with the extent to which single-gender organisations are relevant and needed.[89] In some countries, the GFS is no longer exclusively a girls' organisation.[90] In the 1990s, the GFS in South Africa adopted the name 'Girls Friendly Society & Boys Friendly Society' (GFS & BFS).[91] According to its website, its decision to include boys was rooted in part in the belief that issues of gender, and especially gender-based violence, cannot be addressed without the inclusion of boys and teaching boys and girls the same values.[92] Girls still vastly outnumber boys in the GFS & BFS. For instance, the Diocese of Mthatha in the Eastern Cape has 3,014 members, of whom 399 are boys.[93] The inclusion of boys and men also raises questions about what role they should have in the organisation: Should they assume leadership roles, or should the GFS remain a women-led organisation?[94] Despite the inclusion of boys in some countries, other countries – including England and Wales – have argued that the organisation should work only with women and girls.[95] A related issue is about the inclusion of transgender children in the organisation, which is a question that the Scouts have also faced. The website of the GFS in England and Wales has stated that it is trans-inclusive and 'proud to say that at GFS, trans women and girls will always be welcome, valued and supported'.[96]

The original purpose of the GFS, which centred on assisting and educating girls, continues to inform the organisation today, but the GFS of the 2020s looks different from the GFS of 1875. No longer is control solely in the hands of upper-class English women, but girls themselves take a greater role in the leadership of the GFS.[97] The World Council provides GFS members with a global community, but, in contrast to the Central Council that dominated the governance of the GFS through the Second World War, it does not dictate rules for branches thousands of miles away. Branches instead have independence and flexibility to adapt their activities and organisation to their local needs. The current composition of the World Council reveals a shift in power within the organisation. Seventeen countries – more than half of the thirty-one countries in the World Council – are in Africa, and African branches account for over 70 per cent of the GFS worldwide membership of 20,355.[98] While England and Wales once had the largest number of members, its membership is only around

702. Instead the country with the greatest number of members is South Africa with 8,909 members, followed by Zambia with 2,871 members.[99] Two South African women have served as chairs of the World Council, Nobantu Makunga from 1996 to 1999 and Thembeka Pama from 2017 to 2023.[100] South Africa also hosted the World Council meeting in 2023, which was originally scheduled for 2020 but delayed due to the COVID-19 pandemic.[101]

In contrast to previous years when it often placed blame on others for their misunderstanding or ignorance of the organisation, the GFS today appears more self-reflective and willing to admit its shortcomings, including when it comes to matters of race. The Black Lives Matter movement led organisations, including the GFS, to confront their history of racism. The website of the GFS in England and Wales expressed its support of the Black Lives Matter movement and explained its efforts to promote diversity: 'Following the murder of George Floyd in 2020, we realised it was past time for us to open new conversations about racism and privilege within GFS and across the charity sector as a whole'.[102] It launched a new Equity, Diversity, and Inclusion strategy with eight key objectives, including ensuring greater representation of different communities and that all girls feel welcome and heard.[103] In the wake of the Black Lives Matter movement and COVID-19 pandemic, the chair of the GFS in England and Wales acknowledged in the annual report that 'we have not remained as forward thinking and relevant as we would like to be'.[104] As examined in this chapter and the previous one, the GFS was often reticent to embrace change, but its ability to evolve – even if belatedly at times – and the continued questioning of its relevance may be one of the reasons for its longevity.

## Future directions

This conclusion only scratches the surface of important issues related to organisation's development in the latter half of the twentieth century. More research is needed to understand the GFS's transition from an imperial to international organisation and from one based in England to one led by South Africa. As noted in the Introduction, *Empire's daughters* did not set out to provide a comprehensive organisational history of the GFS. Given the extensive history of the organisation, it would have been impossible to do so. This book instead used the GFS to understand the role of girls in the empire and how the construction of girlhood, whiteness, and empire were interconnected. This focus means many aspects of the organisation have not been covered in this book, like its work in areas beyond the empire, including in the United States and on the European continent, and

## Conclusion

its welfare initiatives in England, such as providing convalescent care for girls.[105] Other areas that are touched upon only briefly in this book, like its contribution to war efforts and its relationship with the Anglican Church, merit further exploration. Greater work especially needs to be done on how girls of colour engaged with and navigated the organisation.

This book endeavoured to bring the perspectives of girls out from the shadows of empire to the forefront. However, as reflected on throughout the book, the marginalisation of their voices within the archive posed a formidable challenge to this undertaking. Even within the archives of the GFS, individual girls, and especially girls of colour, rarely appear, and instead the perspectives of upper-class women – like Mary Elizabeth Townsend and Ellen Joyce – dominate the archival record. Their memoirs, correspondence, and reports form the core of the GFS archives, and, within these writings, financial matters and debates over the logistics about building hostels and organising events eclipse the stories of girls. Little space is given to girls' voices or concerns, even on issues directly impacting their lives, such as education, employment, and emigration. The GFS's official records contain only trace references to girls of colour, indicating that its primary focus was white girls.

To contend with the challenges of the archive and to give a more holistic picture of girls' experiences, I employed a variety of sources, including literature, correspondence, official reports, and scrapbooks. While the written records of the GFS largely obscure the experiences of girls, they do emerge from the shadows of the archives and became visible through photographs in the scrapbooks discussed in Chapter 3. Photographs are not unproblematic sources and present new challenges and questions, but they can help fill in some of the silences and gaps of textual records and enhance the visibility of girls. The GFS recognised the power of visual media in conveying the significance of its work, as evidenced by its prominence in newsletters and the creation of scrapbooks. Further study of the organisation's rich photographic records can provide insights into questions about the role of photographs and visual media in the GFS and other colonial organisations, girls' use of photography, and the relationship between visual and textual media in studying colonial girlhoods.

### Final reflections

This book has explored how, far from being peripheral figures in the empire, girls had a critical role in constructing colonial identities and societies and ideas of whiteness. Girls' lives and ideas of girlhood were intertwined with conceptualisations of the nation, empire, and race. In line with the imperatives of the colonial state, the GFS sought to affirm ideas of whiteness and class, gender, and racial hierarchies through its concerted education and emigration programmes. Through these myriad programmes, the GFS not only helped to construct ideas of girlhood, race, and empire but also served as a conduit for these ideas to circulate globally. The images of empire and colonial societies that emerge in the GFS's newsletters, pageants, plays, and scrapbooks centred whiteness, and by extension white girls, and simultaneously marginalised girls of colour and obscured the violent realities of colonialism. The GFS's programmes desired to make girls, specifically white girls, good empire builders who would fortify white communities and white hegemony. However, concerns over the poor white problem indicated that girls were an unreliable line of defence. Poor white and multiracial girls provoked considerable anxieties because they called into question ideas about the stability – and by extension superiority – of whiteness.

Girls' participation in the empire was not straightforward and defies easy categorisation, and this complexity of girls' engagement with and experiences of colonialism forms a recurring theme in *Empire's daughters*. While girls did act as empire builders and bolster colonial power, as GFS organisers envisioned, they also remained indifferent to the empire and sometimes undermined imperial goals. Despite the GFS's concerted efforts to instil a sense of patriotism and duty in girls, personal interests, rather than lofty imperial ideals, often motivated girls to emigrate – and abscond their situations if they were unhappy. Even though GFS leaders sought to exert control over girls, girls found ways to resist these efforts. The protests and withdrawal of 'Coloured branches' in South Africa, girls' departure from the hostel in Calcutta when they faced hostility and abuse, and the decision of girls to leave – or not even join – the organisation because their voices were ignored reveal some of the ways that girls pushed back against the imperatives of the GFS. By the interwar years, the irreconcilability of the GFS's commitment to the empire and its model of girlhood – centred on ideas of whiteness and Victorian femininity – with the needs of girls and the realities of their lives became increasingly apparent and led to the society's decline.

The history of the GFS reveals that the construction of girlhood does not occur in isolation. Today, as in the past, girlhood is shaped by cross-cultural exchanges and shifting racial, imperial, national, and social exigencies. The legacies of colonialism continue to inform the global politics of girlhood. Discourses about girlhood and girls' culture, labour, and migration during the late nineteenth and early twentieth centuries reverberate down to the present day, with ideas of girlhood often deployed to advance political and social agendas. Stories about Malala Yousafzai and the kidnapping of the Chibok school girls, for instance, echo earlier discussions about girlhood in their employment of similar paternalist and colonialist language and assumptions, including portraying girls as non-agential figures, using the status of girls as measures of modernity and civilisation, and emphasising the need for white men and women in 'saving brown girls from brown men'.[106] Children remain at the centre of migration politics, starkly demonstrated by US policies towards undocumented migrants. In justifying the separation of migrant parents from their children at the US–Mexico border in 2018, the Trump administration employed similar tactics used by organisations in the nineteenth century, including placing blame on parents and framing such actions in terms of national interest and security. Domestic labour continues to be the defining experience of childhood for over 11.5 million girls worldwide.[107] These continued resonances highlight the importance of integrating historical insights and approaches with contemporary discussions about girls' experiences. They also illustrate an ongoing process of negotiation among different conceptions of girlhood and how girls continue to serve as central sites of contestation in broader political, social, economic, and cultural debates.

## Notes

1 Women's Library, London (hereafter WL), 5GFS/05/021/1, *1875–1975: One Hundred Years of the Girls Friendly Society*, 1975, p. 1.
2 WL, 5GFS/01/106, 'Minutes of the meeting of the Overseas Sub-committee held on Wednesday 1st October, 1980', p. 1.
3 Jordanna Bailkin, *The Afterlife of Empire*, Berkeley Series in British Studies (Berkeley: University of California Press, 2012), p. 253. See also Stuart Ward (ed.), *British Culture and the End of Empire* (Manchester: Manchester University Press, 2001).
4 WL, 5GFS/03/052, *The Girls' Friendly Society Sixty-Sixth Annual Report and Statement of Accounts for the Year ended December 31st, 1940*, p. 22.
5 WL, 5GFS/06/178, Girls' Friendly Society Centenary Scrapbook, 1975, p. 4.
6 *The Girls' Friendly Society Sixty-Sixth Annual Report*, p. 21.
7 Jean Seymour, *A Century of Challenge: A History of the Girls' Friendly in Western Australia from 1888–1988* (Perth: Girls' Friendly Society, 1988), p. 111. WL, 5GFS/02/350, 'World Chairman's Report 1981', in Girls' Friendly Society 10th World Council, 19–26 July 1981, p. 5. For more on youth organisations in this period, see Sian Edwards, *Youth Movements, Citizenship and the English Countryside: Creating Good Citizens, 1930–1960* (London: Palgrave Macmillan, 2018); and Jennifer Helgren, '"Homemaker Can Include the World:" Female Citizenship and Internationalism in the Postwar Camp Fire Girls', in Jennifer Helgren and Colleeen Vasconcellos (eds), *Girlhood: A Global History* (New Brunswick: Rutgers University Press, 2010), pp. 304–22. For a discussion of youth in this period, see David Fowler, *Youth Culture in Modern Britain, c.1920–c.1970* (Basingstoke: Palgrave Macmillan, 2008);

Melanie Tebbutt, *Making Youth: A History of Youth in Modern Britain* (Basingstoke: Palgrave Macmillan, 2016); Bailkin, *The Afterlife of Empire*, particularly chapter 2 on 'Young Britons: International Aid and Development in the Age of the Adolescent'; Jean Spence, 'Feminism and Informal Education in Youth Work with Girls and Young Women, 1975–85', in Sarah Mills and Peter Kraftl (eds), *Informal Education, Childhood and Youth: Geographies, Histories, Practices* (London: Palgrave Macmillan, 2014), pp. 197–215; Carol Dyhouse, *Girl Trouble: Panic and Progress in the History of Young Women* (London: Zed Books, 2013), especially chapter 5; and the work of Catherine Ellis, including 'The Younger Generation: The Labour Party and the 1959 Youth Commission', *Journal of British Studies*, 41:2 (2002), 199–231.
8 Seymour, *A Century of Challenge*, p. 107.
9 See 'Bear Ye One Another's Burdens: The Girls' Friendly Society 1875–2005: A Virtual Exhibition by Vivienne Richmond', 2006, originally published on the Women's Library Website, text available at https://www.academia.edu/1345061/Bear_Ye_One_Anothers_Burdens_The_Girls_Friendly_Society_1875_2005, accessed 7 December 2022. On the pageant, see WL, 5GFS/05/015, A. E. King, 'The Triumph of Harmony', in G.F.S. World Council Newsletter, March 1956.
10 Girls' Friendly Society Centenary Scrapbook, 1975.
11 Edith Marion Welch, 'Home Reports', *The Empire and Beyond*, Occasional Leaflet XI (Easter 1916), p. 13. WL, 5GFS/01/006, 'Minutes of a Meeting of the Employment and Migration Committee Held at Townsend House, Greycoat Place, Westminster, S.W. 1 on Friday, November 7th 1930 at 11:30 a.m.', p. 109. For more information, see, for instance, Katie Pickle, 'Empire Settlement and Single British Women as New Zealand Domestic Servants during the 1920s', *New Zealand Journal of History*, 35:1 (2001), 22–44.
12 WL, 5GFS/02/261, M. M. Stevens to Miss Mytton, 6 December 1932.
13 WL, 5GFS/01/098, 'Minutes of a Meeting of the Imperial and Overseas Committee Held at Townsend House on Monday March 16th 1936 at 2.30 p.m.', p. 152.
14 Mary Heath-Stubbs, *Friendship's Highway: Being the History of the Girls' Friendly Society, 1875–1935* (London: G.F.S. Central Office, 1935), p. 75. WL, 5GFS/02/263, letter from Wolfe to Miss Calvert, 12 January 1940. WL, 5GFS/01/098, 'Minutes of a Meeting of the Imperial and Overseas Committee (now Council) of the Girls' Friendly Society, Townsend House, Greycoat Place, London, S.W. 1 on Monday, 11th October 1948 at 3.0 p.m.', p. 252. Seymour, *A Century of Challenge*, p. 17. WL, 5GFS/01/134, 'Minutes of a Meeting of the Overseas Executive Committee with Mission Committee held on January 23rd, 1950'. WL, 5GFS/01/098, 'Minutes of a Meeting of the Imperial & Overseas Committee Held on Friday, October 26th 1934 at Townsend House, Greycoat Place S.W., on at 3 p.m.', p. 133.
15 'Minutes of a Meeting of the Imperial and Overseas Committee (now Council) of the Girls' Friendly Society, Townsend House, Greycoat Place, London, S.W. 1 on Monday, 11th October 1948 at 3.0 p.m.', p. 252. See also WL,

5GFS/02/227, 'G.F.S. Hostel in Melbourne, Australia, *The Church of England Newspaper*, 11 March 1938.
16 Ellen Boucher, *Empire's Children: Child Emigration, Welfare, and the Decline of the British World* (Cambridge: Cambridge University Press, 2014), p. 19.
17 WL, 5GFS/04/128, Edith Gordon Clark, 'India', *A Jubilee Chronicle for Overseas* (1935), p. 22.
18 WL, 5GFS/01/134, 'Minutes of a Meeting of the Overseas Committee of the Girls' Friendly Society held at G.F.S. Headquarters, Towsend [sic] House, Greycoat Place, London, S.W. 1, on Thursday 19th May, 1949 at 11.40 a.m.'.
19 WL, 5GFS/02/350, 'Report of the Girls' Friendly Society in Ireland 1978–1981', in Girls' Friendly Society 10th World Council, 19–26 July 1981, p. 12.
20 WL, 5GFS/05/015, 'India', in G.F.S. World Newsletter 1957, pp. 16–18.
21 WL, 5GFS/01/106, 'Minutes of a meeting of the Sub-Committee for Overseas Work, held at Townsend House, 126 Queen's Gate, SW7, on Friday 30 April 1976 at 11.30 am.', p. 2. WL, 5GFS/01/106, 'Minutes of a meeting of the Sub-Committee for Overseas Work, held at Townsend House, 126 Queen's Gate, SW7, on Friday 12 May 1978 at 1100', p. 1.
22 WL, 5GFS/01/106, 'Minutes of a meeting of the Sub-Committee for Overseas Work, held at Townsend House, 126 Queen's Gate, SW7, on Monday 20 September 1976 at 10.45 am.', p. 1.
23 'GFS Countries', Girls Friendly Society, www.gfsworld.org/gfs-countries.html, accessed 8 December 2022.
24 WL, 5GFS/05/015, *The Story of the G.F.S.* (London: The G.F.S. Central Office, 1946), p. 7. WL, 5GFS/05/015, 'Ceylon', in G.F.S. World Council Newsletter, March 1956.
25 WL, 5GFS/01/106, 'Minutes of a meeting of the GFS Worldwide sub-Committee held on Thursday 9th March 1989, at Townsend House, 126 Queen's Gate, South Kensington, London, SW7'.
26 WL, 5GFS/02/350, 'Report of the Girls' Friendly Society Sri Lanka', in Girls' Friendly Society 10th World Council, 19–26 July 1981, p. 21.
27 'Sri Lanka', Girls Friendly Society, https://www.gfsworld.org/sri-lanka.html, accessed 8 December 2022.
28 'Minutes of a Meeting of the Overseas Committee of the Girls' Friendly Society held at G.F.S. Headquarters, Towsend [sic] House, Greycoat Place, London, S.W. 1, on Thursday 19th May, 1949 at 11.40 a.m.'. WL, 5GFS/01/098, 'Minutes of a Meeting of the Overseas Council of the Girls' Friendly Society Held at G.F.S. Headquarters, Townsend House, Greycoat Place, London, S.W. 1, on Wednesday, 22nd June 1949 at 3.0 p.m.', p. 262. WL, 5GFS/01/106, 'Minutes of a meeting of the Overseas Sub-Committee, held at Townsend House, Greycoat Place, London S.W.1, on Tuesday, 13th February 1973 at 11 a.m.', p. 2.
29 WL, 5GFS/01/098, 'Minutes of a Meeting of the Overseas Sub-Committee held at Townsend House, Greycoat Place, London, S.W. 1, on Tuesday, 20th February 1968, at 2 p.m.', p. 1.

30 WL, 5GFS/10/189, Family Life Project, Information Sheet No. 18, c. 1977, p. 1.
31 Emily Baughan, *Saving the Children: Humanitarianism, Internationalism, and Empire* (Berkeley: University of California Press, 2021), p. 19. See also Charlotte Riley, '"The winds of change are blowing economically": the Labour Party and British overseas development, 1940s–1960s', in Andrew W. M. Smith and Chris Jeppesen (eds), *Britain, France and the Decolonization of Africa: Future Imperfect?* (London: UCL Press, 2017), pp. 43–61. For more on children and humanitarianism programmes in postwar Europe, see Tara Zahra, *The Lost Children: Reconstructing Europe's Families after World War II* (Cambridge, MA: Harvard University Press, 2015). For children and humanitarianism in the US context during the Cold War, see Sharon Park, 'Constructing Americans' Responsibility to Give: Shifting Debates about Foreign and Humanitarian Aid to Child Refugees, 1945–1989' (PhD dissertation, University of Minnesota, 2016); and Sara Fieldston, 'Little Cold Warriors: Child Sponsorship and International Affairs', *Diplomatic History*, 38:2 (2014), 240–50.
32 Seymour, *A Century of Challenge*, p. 113. WL, 5GFS/01/106, 'Minutes of a meeting of the Overseas Work Sub-Committee held at 126 Queen's Gate, S.W.7, on Monday 4th February 1980 at 11.15.', p. 4.
33 Richmond, 'Bear Ye One Another's Burdens'.
34 See, for example, WL, 5GFS/05/015, 'New Guinea', in *G.F.S. World Council Newsletter to G.F.S. Members around the World 1962*; and 'Australia', in G.F.S. World Newsletter 1957, pp. 22–3.
35 On expansion in southern Africa and the West Indies, see WL, 5GFS/01/098, 'Minutes of a Meeting of the Overseas Committee was held on Tuesday October 13th, 1959 at 12.30 p.m. at Townsend House, Greycoat Place, London, S.W. 1', p. 344; and 'Lesotho', in Girls' Friendly Society Centenary Scrapbook, 1975. On Sudan, see WL, 5GFS/05/015, 'Diocese of the Upper Nile' and 'South Sudan, Juba', in G.F.S. World Newsletter 1957, p. 5. On Ghana, see WL, 5GFS/05/015, 'Ghana', in *G.F.S. World Council Newsletter to G.F.S. Members around the World 1962*. On The Gambia, see WL, 5GFS/01/106, 'Minutes of a meeting of the Sub-Committee for Overseas Work, held at Townsend House, 126 Queen's Gate, SW7, on Tuesday 7 October 1975 at 10.45 am.', p. 2. On expansion in Guyana and the Philippines, see 'World Chairman's Report 1981', in Girls' Friendly Society 10th World Council, p. 5. On the Philippines, see WL, 5GFS/05/015, 'Outposts', in G.F.S. World Council Newsletter, March 1956. On the Philippines, Kenya, Korea, and Guyana, see WL, 5GFS/05/015, *The GFS Today* [c. 1960s–70s], p. 3. On China, see WL, 5GFS/01/134, 'Minutes of a Meeting of the Overseas Executive Committee with Missions Committee held on January 23rd, 1950'; and *The Story of the G.F.S.*, p. 8.
36 WL, 5GFS/02/051, World Council: Note concerning inception, 1965. WL, 5GFS/05/015, 'GFS World Council', in G.F.S. World Council Newsletter, March 1956.
37 *1875–1975: One Hundred Years of the Girls Friendly Society*, p. 10. 'GFS World Council', in G.F.S. World Council Newsletter, March 1956.

38 'GFS World Council', in G.F.S. World Council Newsletter, March 1956. WL, 5GFS/01/098, 'Minutes of a Meeting of the Overseas Committee Held at Townsend House, Greycoat Place, London, S.W. 1 on Tuesday, October 8th, 1957', p. 332.
39 'Directives of the World Council of the Girls' Friendly Society'.
40 *1875–1975: One Hundred Years of the Girls Friendly Society*, p. 9. World Council: Note concerning inception.
41 *1875–1975: One Hundred Years of the Girls Friendly Society*, p. 9. World Council: Note concerning inception.
42 'GFS World Council', in G.F.S. World Council Newsletter, March 1956.
43 'About WAY', World Assembly of Youth, https://way.org.my/about-way, accessed 8 September 2023.
44 Bailkin, *The Afterlife of Empire*, p. 83.
45 Girls' Friendly Society Centenary Scrapbook, 1975.
46 WL, 5GFS/05/015, 'Directives of the World Council of the Girls' Friendly Society', c. 1955.
47 World Council: Note concerning inception. 'GFS World Council', in G.F.S. World Council Newsletter, March 1956.
48 On the Mombasa and West African projects, see 'World Chairman's Report 1981', in Girls' Friendly Society 10th World Council, p. 4; and Seymour, *A Century of Challenge*, pp. 92–3, 103. On British Guiana and Korea, see Seymour, *A Century of Challenge*, p. 92; WL, 5GFS/05/015, 'The 5th World Council Meets in Ireland', in *G.F.S. World Council Newsletter to G.F.S. Members around the World 1962*; and WL, 5GFS/05/015, 'Mombasa World Country Project 1957–62', in *G.F.S. World Council Newsletter to G.F.S. Members around the World 1962*.
49 Seymour, *A Century of Challenge*, p. 106.
50 On this point, see Bailkin, *The Afterlife of Empire*, p. 205.
51 WL, 5GFS/02/350, 'Report of the Diocesan Girls' Friendly Society Diocese of Liberia – July 1981', in Girls' Friendly Society 10th World Council, 19–26 July 1981, p. 16. See also WL, 5GFS/01/106, 'Minutes of a meeting of the Overseas Sub-committee, held Wednesday 1st October, 1980', pp. 1–2.
52 Girls' Friendly Society Centenary Scrapbook, 1975.
53 WL, 5GFS/01/106, 'Minutes of a meeting of the Sub-committee for Overseas Work, held at Townsend House, 126 Queen's Gate SW7, on Friday 20 January 1978 at 1100', p. 1.
54 'World Projects', Girls Friendly Society, www.gfsworld.org/world-projects, accessed 8 December 2022.
55 'World Projects'.
56 'History', Girls Friendly Society, www.gfsworld.org/history.html, accessed 8 December 2022. 'Rules of Management, Girls Friendly Society, www.gfsworld.org/rules-of-management.html, accessed 8 December 2022. 'GFS World', GFS Australia Inc., gfsaustralia.org.au/gfs-australia/gfs-world/, accessed 8 December 2022.

57 Girls' Friendly Society Centenary Scrapbook, 1975. Seymour, *A Century of Challenge*, p. 106.
58 WL, 5GFS/01/098, 'A meeting of the Overseas Committee was held at Townsend House on Thursday, 29th January 1959, at 11.15 a.m.', p. 343. See also Family Life Project, Information Sheet No. 18, p. 9.
59 Seymour, *A Century of Challenge*, p. 115.
60 WL, 5GFS/05/015, 'England and Wales', in G.F.S. World Newsletter 1957, p. 30.
61 See, for instance, the report from Barbados in WL, 5GFS/01/106, 'Minutes of a meeting of the Overseas Sub-committee, held Wednesday 5th February 1986 at Townsend House, 126 Queen's Gate London, SW7', p. 2.
62 Seymour, *A Century of Challenge*, p. 109. On Ireland, see WL, 5GFS/05/015, 'Ireland', in *G.F.S. World Council Newsletter to G.F.S. Members around the World 1962*. On Newfoundland, see WL, 5GFS/05/015, 'Newfoundland', in *G.F.S. World Council Newsletter to G.F.S. Members around the World 1962*. On Japan, see WL, 5GFS/05/015, 'Outposts of U.S.A.', in G.F.S. World Council Newsletter, March 1956. On the Girls' Brigade and lack of interest in Zambia, see WL, 5GFS/01/106, 'Minutes of a meeting of the Worldwide Sub-committee, held on Wednesday September 21, 1987, at Townsend House, 126 Queen's Gate London, SW7', p. 3; and WL, 5GFS/01/106, 'Minutes of a meeting of the GFS Worldwide sub-Committee held on Thursday May 5th at 1988 [*sic*] at Townsend House, 126 Queen's Gate London, SW7', p. 4. On Lesotho and the Guild of St Agnes, see WL, 5GFS/01/106, 'Minutes of the meeting of the Overseas Sub-committee, held on Wednesday 21st May 1986 at Townsend House, 126 Queen's Gate London, SW7 5LQ', p. 2.
63 See, for instance, the report by the Bishop of Mauritius in 'Minutes of a Meeting of the Overseas Committee of the Girls' Friendly Society held at G.F.S. Headquarters, Towsend [*sic*] House, Greycoat Place, London, S.W. 1, on Thursday 19th May, 1949 at 11.40 a.m.'. See also the report on the Upper Nile from 'Minutes of a Meeting of the Overseas Executive Committee with Missions Committee held on January 23rd, 1950'.
64 'Minutes of a meeting of the Overseas Sub-committee, held Wednesday 1st October, 1980', p. 4. WL, 5GFS/05/015, 'Australia', in G.F.S. World Newsletter 1957, pp. 21–4. WL, 5GFS/01/106, 'Minutes of the meeting of the Worldwide Sub-Committee held on Wednesday 3rd June, 1987 at Townsend House, 126 Queen's Gate, London, SW7', p. 5. WL, 5GFS/01/106, 'Minutes of a meeting of the Sub-Committee for Overseas Work, held at Townsend House, Greycoat Place, London S.W.1 on Tuesday 18th September 1973 at 11 a.m.', p. 3.
65 'Report of the Girls' Friendly Society in Ireland 1978–1981', in Girls' Friendly Society 10th World Council, p. 13. WL, 5GFS/05/015, 'Union of South Africa', in G.F.S. World Council Newsletter, March 1956.
66 WL, 5GFS/05/015, 'England and Wales', in G.F.S. World Council Newsletter, March 1956.
67 'Union of South Africa', in G.F.S. World Council Newsletter, March 1956. On workers being too old, see WL, 5GFS/01/106, 'Minutes of a meeting of

the Sub-Committee for overseas work, held at 126 Queen's Gate SW7 on Thursday 11th January 1979', p. 1.
68  See, for instance, the report on British Guiana in WL, 5GFS/05/15, *G.F.S. World Council Newsletter to G.F.S. Members around the World 1962*; and 'Minutes of a Meeting of the Overseas Committee of the Girls' Friendly Society held at G.F.S. Headquarters, Towsend [sic] House, Greycoat Place, London, S.W. 1, on Thursday 19th May, 1949 at 11.40 a.m.'.
69  WL, 5GFS/05/015, 'West Indies – St. Kitts', in *G.F.S. World Council Newsletter to G.F.S. Members around the World 1962*.
70  'To GFS Members Around the World', in G.F.S. World Council Newsletter, March 1956.
71  WL, 5GFS/01/134, 'Minutes of a Meeting of the Overseas Executive Committee of the Girls' Friendly Society held at G.F.S. Headquarters, Townsend House, Greycoat Place, London, S.W. 1, on Monday, 24th January, 1949 at 3 p.m.'.
72  'Girls' Friendly Society World Day of Prayer', Girls Friendly Society, 29 September 2018, www.gfsworld.org/uploads/8/4/5/8/84580960/2018_gfs_world_day_of_prayer_service__1_.pdf, accessed 8 December 2022.
73  'Girls' Friendly Society World Day of Prayer'. See also 'South Africa', Girls Friendly Society, https://www.gfsworld.org/south-africa.html, accessed 22 November 2023.
74  WL, 5GFS/05/024, 'South Africa', in *1965 Newsletter to GFS members around the world*.
75  'South Africa', Girls' Friendly Society. 'Membership Statistics', Girls Friendly Society, 2017, https://irp.cdn-website.com/ba9cb555/files/uploaded/world_reports.pdf, accessed 8 December 2022.
76  WL, 5GFS/02/095, 'Launching of the Development Scheme', 23 September 1964. 'Minutes of a meeting of the Overseas Sub-committee, held Wednesday 1st October, 1980', p. 1.
77  'Minutes of a Meeting of the Imperial and Overseas Committee (now Council) of the Girls' Friendly Society, Townsend House, Greycoat Place, London, S.W. 1 on Monday, 11th October 1948 at 3.0 p.m.', pp. 244–5.
78  WL, 5GFS/02/095, letter from Kenneth Lincoln to Mrs Barry, 9 March 1964.
79  'Minutes of the meeting of the Overseas Sub-committee, held on Wednesday 21st May 1986 at Townsend House, 126 Queen's Gate London, SW7 5LQ', p. 1. WL, 5GFS/01/106, 'Minutes of the meeting of the Overseas Sub-Committee, held at 126 Queen's Gate London SW7 on Thursday, 12th February 1981 at 11.15 a.m.', p. 3.
80  WL, 5GFS/06/178, 'One Hundred Friendly Years', in Girls' Friendly Society Centenary Scrapbook, 1975. See also *The GFS Today,*
81  *1875–1975: One Hundred Years of the Girls Friendly Society*, p. 2.
82  *The GFS Today*, p. 1.
83  Girls' Friendly Society Centenary Scrapbook, 1975.
84  Girls' Friendly Society Centenary Scrapbook, 1975.

85 WL, 5GFS/02/350, 'Membership', in Girls' Friendly Society 10th World Council, 19–26 July 1981, p. 7.
86 'Statement on Purpose of the Girls Friendly Society (GFS)', Girls Friendly Society, www.gfsworld.org/statement-of-purpose.html, accessed 8 December 2022; 'Rules of Management'; and 'History'.
87 'Our History', Girls Friendly Society (England and Wales), https://girlsfriendlysociety.org.uk/about-gfs/our-history/, accessed 8 December 2022.
88 'Frequently asked questions', Girls Friendly Society (England and Wales), https://girlsfriendlysociety.org.uk/about-gfs/faqs/, accessed 8 December 2022.
89 For more on this point, see, for instance, Taylor Hosking, 'Why Do the Boy Scouts Want to Include Girls?', *The Atlantic* (12 October 2017), www.theatlantic.com/politics/archive/2017/10/why-did-the-boy-scouts-decide-to-accept-girls/542769/, accessed 8 December 2022. Camp Fire faced a similar dilemma in the 1970s. See Jennifer Helgren, '"It's a New Day": Camp Fire's Reckoning and Restructuring in the 1970s', chapter 9 in *The Camp Fire Girls: Gender, Race, and American Girlhood, 1910–1980* (Lincoln: University of Nebraska Press, 2022), especially pp. 249–55.
90 'Minutes of the Girls Friendly Society 21st World Council, 25th July–4th August [2014], University of Swansea, Swansea', p. 16, Girls Friendly Society, www.gfsworld.org/uploads/8/4/5/8/84580960/2014_wales.pdf, accessed 8 December 2022.
91 'South Africa', Girls Friendly Society, www.gfsworld.org/south-africa.html, accessed 8 December 2022.
92 'South Africa'.
93 'South Africa'.
94 Minutes of the Girls Friendly Society 21st World Council, 25th July–4th August [2014], University of Swansea, Swansea', pp. 15–17.
95 Minutes of the Girls Friendly Society 21st World Council, 25th July–4th August [2014], University of Swansea, Swansea', p. 15.
96 'Frequently asked questions'.
97 For more on this shift, see Seymour, *A Century of Challenge*, p. 153.
98 'GFS Countries'.
99 'Membership Statistics'.
100 'World Chairman', Girls Friendly Society, www.gfsworld.org/uploads/8/4/5/8/84580960/list_of_world_chairmen_2.pdf, accessed 8 December 2022.
101 'GFS World Council 2023 – South Africa', GFS Australia Inc., gfsaustralia.org.au/2022/05/04/gfs-world-council-2023-south-africa/, accessed 8 December 2022. 'Girls Friendly Society World Council is underway in Johannesburg', Anglican Communion News Service, 8 August 2023, https://www.anglicannews.org/news/2023/08/girls-friendly-society-world-council-is-underway-in-johannesburg.aspx, accessed 13 September 2023.
102 'Equity, Diversity and Inclusion (EDI) at GFS', Girls Friendly Society (England and Wales), https://girlsfriendlysociety.org.uk/about-gfs/equity-diversity-and-inclusion-edi-at-gfs/, accessed 8 December 2022.

103 'Equity, Diversity and Inclusion (EDI) Action Plan – September 2021', Girls Friendly Society (England and Wales), https://girlsfriendlysociety.org.uk/about-gfs/equity-diversity-and-inclusion-edi-at-gfs/gfs-edi-plan-sept-2021/, accessed 8 December 2022.

104 Chair's Welcome in 'Annual impact report summary, 1 October 2020–30 September 2021', Girls Friendly Society (England and Wales), https://girlsfriendlysociety.org.uk/wp-content/uploads/2022/05/Double-spread-full-signed-version.pdf, accessed 8 December 2022.

105 Vivienne Richmond has done some work on this last topic. See 'Crafting Inclusion for "Invalid" Women: The Girls' Friendly Society Central Needlework Depôt, 1899–1947', in Janice Helland, Beverly Lemire, and Alena Buis (eds), *Craft, Community and the Material Culture of Place and Politics, 19th–20th Century* (Burlington: Ashgate, 2014), pp. 161–76.

106 Gayatri Chakravorty Spivak, 'Can the Subaltern Speak?', in Cary Nelson and Lawrence Grossberg (eds), *Marxism and the Interpretation of Culture* (Basingstoke: Macmillan Education, 1988), p. 297. See, for instance, Shenila Khoja-Moolji, 'Why Is Malala such a Polarizing Figure in Pakistan?', *Al Jazeera*, 1 April 2018, www.aljazeera.com/opinions/2018/4/1/why-is-malala-such-a-polarising-figure-in-pakistan/, accessed 8 December 2022; and Chitra Nagarajan, 'Focusing on Schoolgirl Abductions Distorts the View of Life in Nigeria', *The Guardian*, 2 March 2018, www.theguardian.com/commentisfree/2018/mar/02/nigeria-boko-haram-abductions-chitra-nagarajan, accessed 8 December 2022.

107 These numbers come from the International Labor Organization, which estimates that 17.2 million children are in paid or unpaid domestic work in the home of a third party or employer and that 67.1 per cent of all child domestic workers are girls. See 'Child Labour and Domestic Work', *International Labor Organization*, www.ilo.org/ipec/areas/Childdomesticlabour/lang--en/index.htm, accessed 8 December 2022.

# Appendix
# List of key figures in the Girls' Friendly Society

**Margaret Arbuthnot**
The president of the GFS Central Council from 1931 to 1933 and a proponent of the central rule

**Finetta Bruce**
Vice president of the GFS Central Council and chair of the Committee for Extension Work in India, Burma, and Ceylon from 1929 to 1931 who was involved in the selection of workers, including Mary Thomas, for the GFS's colonial branches

**Mary Campbell**
Organising worker for India and Ceylon beginning in 1925 who was referred to as 'our Gandhi' for her advocacy of greater independence for GFS branches in India

**Olive Carden**
President of the GFS Diocesan Council in Lahore beginning in 1930

**Winifred Cary**
President of the GFS Diocesan Council in Ceylon beginning in 1928

**Eleanor Chute**
President of the GFS Central Council from 1901 to 1916

**Lady Winifred Cocke**
President of the GFS Diocesan Council in Bombay beginning in 1931

**Lady Cecilie Cunliffe**
President of the GFS Central Council from 1917 to 1931

## Ada Gardner Williams

GFS associate who travelled to Colombo in 1926–27 to provide advice about how the GFS could operate more effectively and later served as the president of the Liverpool diocese and was elected president of the GFS Central Council in 1933 amid the central rule debate

## Mabel Goodrich

GFS associate who resigned her position as the superintendent of the White House, the GFS lodge in Bombay, in 1931 due to her conflict with the girls

## Edith Gordon Clark

Vice president of the GFS Central Council and chair of the Committee for Extension Work in India, Burma, and Ceylon beginning in 1932

## Mary Heath-Stubbs

GFS associate who wrote a history of the GFS, *Friendship's Highway*

## Katherine Hughes

Deaconess of the All Saints' House in Allahabad and the secretary of the GFS Diocesan Council in Lucknow in the 1920s and 1930s

## Ellen Joyce

A prominent proponent of women's emigration who founded and led the GFS's Department for Members Emigrating

## Agnes Money

A long-time friend of Mary Elizabeth Townsend who was a leading figure in the GFS during its early years and wrote a history of the organisation in 1911

## Caroline Mytton

Secretary of the GFS Central Council beginning in 1920 who frequently corresponded with associates in the colonies and was involved in the selection of workers for the GFS's colonial branches, including Mary Thomas

## Winifred Paine

Secretary of the GFS Diocesan Council in Lahore beginning in 1930

## Fanchette G. Parrish

Secretary of the GFS branch in Port Elizabeth in the 1930s and early 1940s

**Winifred Preston**
GFS associate from England who travelled to New Zealand in 1939 to assess the state of the GFS in the country

**Margaret Scott**
Deaconess of St Hilda's Deaconess House in Lahore and secretary of the GFS Diocesan Council in Lahore from 1925 to 1929

**Ethel J. Shepard**
Head deaconess of St Hilda's Society in Lahore in the 1930s

**E. Mabel Smith**
A member and associate of the GFS in Port Elizabeth, South Africa, from 1901 until her death in 1938

**Lady Sydenham**
Wife of the governor of Bombay and member of the Committee of Council for the GFS in India, Ceylon, and the Far East

**Mary Thomas**
GFS associate who travelled to Calcutta in 1930 to run the GFS hostel but was forced to leave less than six months later due to her conflicts with other GFS workers and girls at the hostel

**Mary Elizabeth Townsend**
Founder of the Girls' Friendly Society who lived from 1841 to 1918

**Vera Westmacott**
President of the GFS Diocesan Council in Calcutta beginning in 1928 who clashed with the Central Council, including over the appointment of Mary Thomas

# Bibliography

## Archival collections

Barnardo's, London, United Kingdom
    Personal and Administrative Correspondence, 1896–1905
    Publications: Annual Reports, 1867–1995

The British Library, London, United Kingdom
    General Reference Collection
    India Office Records and Private Papers

Derbyshire Record Office, Matlock, United Kingdom
    Papers of the Gell Family of Hopton

Hampshire Record Office, Winchester, United Kingdom
    Earl of Selborne and Laura Ridding (née Palmer) Papers

Lambeth Palace Library, London, United Kingdom
    Administration of the Girls' Friendly Society
    Correspondence and Papers on the Girls' Friendly Society

London Metropolitan Archives, London, United Kingdom
    Dr Barnardo's Homes: Correspondences and Papers

Modern Records Centre, University of Warwick, Coventry, United Kingdom
    Records of the Young Women's Christian Association

The National Archives, London, United Kingdom
    Records of the Colonial Office, Commonwealth and Foreign and Commonwealth Offices
    Records of the Home Office

University of Liverpool Department of Special Collections and Archives, Liverpool, United Kingdom
    Papers relating to Maria Rye's Emigration Home for Little Girls

Women's Library, London School of Economics, London, United Kingdom
  Records of the British Women's Emigration Association
  Records of the Girls' Friendly Society
  Records of the South African Colonisation Society

## Online sources

### Articles

'Child Labor and Domestic Work'. *International Labor Organization*. https://www.ilo.org/ipec/areas/Childdomesticlabour/lang--en/index.htm. Accessed 8 December 2022.

Hosking, Taylor. 'Why Do the Boy Scouts Want to Include Girls?'. *The Atlantic*. 12 October 2017. https://www.theatlantic.com/politics/archive/2017/10/why-did-the-boy-scouts-decide-to-accept-girls/542769/. Accessed 8 December 2022.

Khoja-Moolji, Shenila. 'Why Is Malala such a Polarizing Figure in Pakistan?'. *Al Jazeera*. 1 April 2018. https://www.aljazeera.com/indepth/opinion/malala-polarising-figure-pakistan-180401054631496.html. Accessed 8 December 2022.

Nagarajan, Chitra. 'Focusing on Schoolgirl Abductions Distorts the View of Life in Nigeria'. *The Guardian*. 2 March 2018. https://www.theguardian.com/commentisfree/2018/mar/02/nigeria-boko-haram-abductions-chitra-nagarajan. Accessed 8 December 2022.

Richmond, Vivienne. 'Bear Ye One Another's Burdens: The Girls' Friendly Society 1875–2005: A Virtual Exhibition by Vivienne Richmond'. 2006. Originally published on the Women's Library Website. Text available at https://www.academia.edu/1345061/Bear_Ye_One_Anothers_Burdens_The_Girls_Friendly_Society_1875_2005. Accessed 7 December 2022.

Vallgårda, Karen, Kristine Alexander, and Stephanie Olsen. 'Against Agency'. Society for the History of Childhood and Youth Featured Commentaries. 23 October 2018. www.shcy.org/features/commentaries/against-agency/. Accessed 27 November 2022.

### Reports

'Equity, Diversity and Inclusion (EDI) Action Plan – September 2021'. Girls Friendly Society (England and Wales). https://girlsfriendlysociety.org.uk/about-gfs/equity-diversity-and-inclusion-edi-at-gfs/gfs-edi-plan-sept-2021/. Accessed 8 December 2022.

'Girls' Friendly Society World Day of Prayer'. Girls Friendly Society. 29 September 2018. www.gfsworld.org/uploads/8/4/5/8/84580960/2018_gfs_world_day_of_prayer_service__1_.pdf. Accessed 8 December 2022.

'Minutes of the Girls Friendly Society 21st World Council, 25th July–4th August [2014], University of Swansea, Swansea'. Girls Friendly Society. www.gfsworld.org/uploads/8/4/5/8/84580960/2014_wales.pdf. Accessed 8 December 2022.

## Websites

'Annual Impact Report Summary, 1 October 2020–30 September 2021'. Girls Friendly Society (England and Wales). https://girlsfriendlysociety.org.uk/wp-content/uploads/2022/05/Double-spread-full-signed-version.pdf. Accessed 8 December 2022.

Bartie, Angela, Linda Fleming, Mark Freeman, Tom Hulme, Alex Hutton, and Paul Readman. 'The Quest'. The Redress of the Past: Historical Pageants in Britain. https://historicalpageants.ac.uk/pageants/1072/. Accessed 1 December 2022.

'Equity, Diversity and Inclusion (EDI) at GFS'. Girls Friendly Society (England and Wales). https://girlsfriendlysociety.org.uk/what-we-do/equity-diversity-and-inclusion-edi-at-gfs/. Accessed 8 December 2022.

'Frequently Asked Questions'. Girls Friendly Society (England and Wales). https://girlsfriendlysociety.org.uk/about-gfs/faqs/. Accessed 8 December 2022.

'GFS Countries'. Girls Friendly Society. www.gfsworld.org/gfs-countries.html. Accessed 8 December 2022.

'GFS World'. GFS Australia Inc. http://gfsaustralia.org.au/gfs-australia/gfs-world/. Accessed 8 December 2022.

'GFS World Council 2023 – South Africa'. GFS Australia Inc. https://gfsaustralia.org.au/2022/05/04/gfs-world-council-2023-south-africa/. Accessed 8 December 2022.

'Girls Friendly Society World Council is underway in Johannesburg'. Anglican Communion News Service. 8 August 2023. https://www.anglicannews.org/news/2023/08/girls-friendly-society-world-council-is-underway-in-johannesburg.aspx. Accessed 13 September 2023.

'History'. Girls Friendly Society. www.gfsworld.org/history.html. Accessed 8 December 2022.

'Membership Statistics'. Girls Friendly Society. 2017. https://irp.cdn-website.com/ba9cb555/files/uploaded/world_reports.pdf. Accessed 8 December 2022.

'Our History'. Girls Friendly Society (England and Wales). https://girlsfriendlysociety.org.uk/about-gfs/our-history/. Accessed 8 December 2022.

'Rules of Management'. Girls Friendly Society. www.gfsworld.org/rules-of-management.html/. Accessed 8 December 2022.

'South Africa'. Girls Friendly Society. www.gfsworld.org/south-africa.html. Accessed 8 December 2022.

'Sri Lanka'. Girls Friendly Society. www.gfsworld.org/sri-lanka.html. Accessed 8 December 2022.

'Statement on Purpose of the Girls Friendly Society (GFS)'. Girls Friendly Society. www.gfsworld.org/statement-of-purpose.html. Accessed 8 December 2022.

'World Chairman'. Girls Friendly Society. www.gfsworld.org/uploads/8/4/5/8/84580960/list_of_world_chairmen_2.pdf. Accessed 8 December 2022.

'World Projects'. Girls Friendly Society. https://www.gfsworld.org/world-projects. Accessed 8 December 2022.

## Printed sources

### Newspapers

*The Bulawayo Chronicle*
*The Natal Witness*
*Poverty Bay Herald*
*The Times* (London)

### Periodicals

*Associates' Journal and Advertiser*
*Cheltenham Ladies' College Magazine*
*The Empire and Beyond*
*For God and Country*
*Friendly Leaves*
*G.F.S. Magazine*
*The G.F.S. Workers' Journal*
*Girls' Friendly Society Leaflet for India and the Far East*
*The Girls' Friendly Society Reporter*
*The Girls' Quarterly: A Paper for Workers in the Girls' Friendly Society*
*Gloucester Diocesan Report for 1911*
*The Imperial Colonist*
*Journal of the Royal African Society*
*Macmillan's Magazine*
*Night and Day: A Record of Christian Missions and Practical Philanthropy*
*Nineteenth Century and After*
*Our Letter: For G.F.S. Candidates all over the World*
*The Personal Rights Journal*

### Primary sources

Barker, Lady. *Life in South Africa*. Philadelphia: J. B. Lippincott & Co., 1877.

Beale, Dorothea (ed.). *Work and Play in Girls' Schools*. London: Longmans, Greens, & Co., 1901.

*The Book of the G.F.S.: What It Is and What It Does*. No place or publisher. June 1920.

Booth, William. *In Darkest England, and the Way Out*. London: International Headquarters of the Salvation Army, 1890.

Bowerman, Elsie Edith. *Stands There a School: Memories of Dame Frances Dove, D.B.E., Founder of Wycombe Abbey School*. High Wycombe: Wycombe Abbey School, 1966.

Broome, Lady. *Colonial Memories*. London: Smith, Elder, & Co., 1904.

Cartwright, Julia (ed.). *The Journals of Lady Knightley of Fawsley*. New York: E. P. Dutton & Company, 1917.

*Census 1911: Preliminary Returns of Census Taken on 7th May 1911*. Pretoria: The Government Printers and Stationery Office, 1911.

Du Bois, W. E. B. *W. E. B. Du Bois: Writings*. New York: Library of America, 1987.

Fanon, Frantz. *Black Skin, White Masks*. Translated by Charles Lam Markmann. London: Pluto Press, 2008.
Greg, William Rathbone. *Why Are Women Redundant?* London: Trübner, 1869.
Hall, G. Stanley. *Adolescence: Its Psychology and Its Relations to Physiology, Anthropology, Sociology, Sex, Crime, Religion and Education.* 2 vols. New York: D. Appleton and Company, 1904.
Heath-Stubbs, Mary. *Friendship's Highway: Being the History of the Girls' Friendly Society, 1875–1935.* London: G.F.S. Central Office, 1935.
Irvine, Robert Francis, Oscar Thorwald, and Johan Alpers. *The Progress of New Zealand in the Century.* London: W. & R. Chambers, Limited, 1902.
Joyce, Ellen. *30 Years Imperial Work with Girls Friendly Society.* London: The Girls' Friendly Society, 1912.
Milner, Alfred. 'Reply to Deputation from White Labour League, 2 June 1903'. In Cecil Headlam (ed.), *The Milner Papers. Volume 2: South Africa, 1899–1905*, p. 459. London: Cassell, 1933.
Money, Agnes L. *History of The Girls' Friendly Society.* Second edition. London: Wells, Garner, Darton & Co., Ltd, 1911.
Murray, Edith. *The G.F.S. in Picture and Pageant.* London: G.F.S. Central Office, c. 1910.
*The National Council of the Women of New Zealand, Fifth Session, Dunedin, 3–12 May 1900.* Christchurch: Smith, Anthony, Sellars and Company Ltd, 1900.
Townsend, Kathleen M. *Some Memories of Mrs. Townsend: Foundress of the Girls' Friendly Society.* London: GFS Central Council, 1923.
Tregear, Edward. *The Aryan Maori.* Wellington: G. Didsbury, 1885.
Wilson, Lady Sarah. *South African Memories: Social, Warlike & Sporting, from Diaries Written at the Time.* London: Edward Arnold, 1909.

## Secondary sources

Aaron, Haley. 'Spaces of self: Girls' scrapbooks at the Alabama Department of Archives and History'. In Tiffany R. Isselhardt (ed.), *A Girl Can Do: Recognizing and Representing Girlhood*, pp. 109–28. Wilmington: Vernon Press, 2022.
Ahmed, Leila. *Women and Gender in Islam: Historical Roots of a Modern Debate.* New Haven: Yale University Press, 1992.
Ahmed, Sara. *The Cultural Politics of Emotion.* 2nd edition. New York: Routledge, 2014.
Alexander, Kristine. 'Agency and Emotion Work'. *Jeunesse: Young People, Texts, Cultures*, 7:2 (2015), 120–8.
Alexander, Kristine. 'Can the Girl Guide Speak?: The Perils and Pleasures of Looking for Children's Voices in Archival Research'. *Jeunesse: Young People, Texts, Cultures*, 4:1 (2012), 132–45.
Alexander, Kristine. *Guiding Modern Girls: Girlhood, Empire, and Internationalism in the 1920s and 1930s.* Vancouver: UBC Press, 2017.
Alexander, Kristine. 'Similarity and Difference at Girl Guide Camps in England, Canada, and India'. In Nelson R. Block and Tammy M. Proctor (eds), *Scouting Frontiers: Youth and the Scout Movement's First Century*, pp. 106–20. Newcastle: Cambridge Scholars, 2009.
Allender, Tim. *Learning Femininity in Colonial India, 1820–1932.* Studies in Imperialism. Manchester: Manchester University Press, 2016.

Anderson, Benedict. *Imagined Communities: Reflections on the Origin and Spread of Nationalism*. Revised edition. New York: Verso, 2006.

Anderson-Faithful, Sue, and Catherine Holloway. '"We do not wish to be sofa cushions, or even props to men, but we wish to work by their side": Celebrating Women as Popular Educators at the Anglican Church Congresses 1881–1913'. *History of Education*, 48:2 (2019), 180–96.

Anderson-Faithful, Susan. 'A "Mission to Civilize": The Popular Educational Vision of the Anglican Mothers' Union and Girls' Friendly Society (1886–1926)'. *Revista Brasileira de História da Educação*, 12:1 (2012), 15–44.

Anderson-Faithful, Susan. *Mary Sumner: Mission, Education and Motherhood: Thinking a Life with Bourdieu*. Cambridge: Lutterworth Press, 2018.

Ariès, Philippe. *Centuries of Childhood: A Social History of Family Life*. Translated by Robert Baldick. New York: Vintage Books, 1962.

Arnold, David. 'European Orphans and Vagrants in India in the Nineteenth Century'. *The Journal of Imperial and Commonwealth History*, 7:2 (1979), 104–27.

Arnold, David. 'White Colonization and Labour in Nineteenth-Century India'. *The Journal of Imperial and Commonwealth History*, 11:2 (1983), 133–58.

Arondekar, Anjali. *For the Record: On Sexuality and the Colonial Archive in India*. Durham, NC: Duke University Press, 2009.

Bagnell, Kenneth. *The Little Immigrants: The Orphans Who Came to Canada*. Toronto: Dundurn Press, 1980.

Bailkin, Jordanna. *The Afterlife of Empire*. Berkeley Series in British Studies. Berkeley: University of California Press, 2012.

Ballantyne, Tony. *Orientalism and Race: Aryanism and the British Empire*. London: Palgrave, 2001.

Banerjee, Swapna M. *Men, Women and Domestics: Articulating Middle-Class Identity in Colonial Bengal*. New York: Oxford University Press, 2003.

Banivanua Mar, Tracey, and Penelope Edmonds (eds). *Making Settler Colonial Space: Perspectives on Race, Place and Identity*. New York: Palgrave Macmillan, 2010.

Bartie, Angela, Linda Fleming, Mark Freeman, Alexander Hutton, and Paul Readman (eds). *Restaging the Past: Historical Pageants, Culture and Society in Modern Britain*. London: UCL Press, 2020.

Bartie, Angela, Linda Fleming, Mark Freeman, Tom Hulme, Paul Readman, and Charlotte Tupman. 'The Redress of the Past: Historical Pageants in Twentieth-Century England'. *International Journal of Research on History Didactics, History Education, and History Culture*, 37 (2016), 19–35.

Bashford, Alison. *Purity and Pollution: Gender, Embodiment, and Victorian Medicine*. Studies in Gender History. New York: St Martin's Press, 1998.

Bates, Rebecca. 'From Suppression to Sponsorship: Juvenile Emigration and the Preservation of Pre-Industrial Labor'. In Maria Ruiz (ed.), *International Migrations in the Victorian Era*, pp. 507–31. Leiden: Brill, 2018.

Baucom, Ian. *Out of Place: Englishness, Empire, and the Locations of Identity*. Princeton: Princeton University Press, 2001.

Baughan, Emily. *Saving the Children: Humanitarianism, Internationalism, and Empire*. Berkeley: University of California Press, 2021.

Bean, Philip, and Joy Melville. *Lost Children of the Empire*. London: Unwin Hyman, 1989.

Belich, James. *New Zealand Wars and the Victorian Interpretation of Racial Conflict*. Auckland: Penguin, 1986.
Belich, James. *Paradise Reforged. A History of the New Zealanders from the 1880's to the Year 2000*. Honolulu: University of Hawaii Press, 2002.
Bernstein, Robin. *Racial Innocence: Performing American Childhood from Slavery to Civil Rights*. New York: New York University Press, 2011.
Bhabha, Homi. *The Location of Culture*. New York: Routledge, 2004.
Blackburn, Geoff. *The Children's Friend Society: Juvenile Emigrants to Western Australia, South Africa and Canada, 1834-1842*. Northbridge: Access Press, 1993.
Boucher, Ellen. *Empire's Children: Child Emigration, Welfare, and the Decline of the British World, 1869–1967*. Cambridge: Cambridge University Press, 2014.
Bradlow, Edna. 'The Children's Friend Society at the Cape of Good Hope'. *Victorian Studies*, 27:2 (1984), 155–77.
Bristow, Edward. *Vice and Vigilance: Purity Movements in Britain since 1700*. Dublin: Gill and Macmillan, 1977.
Brookes, Barbara. 'Gender, Work and Fears of a "Hybrid Race" in 1920s New Zealand'. *Gender & History*, 19:3 (November 2007), 501–18.
Brookes, Barbara, Annabel Cooper, and Robin Law (eds). *Sites of Gender: Women, Men and Modernity in Southern Dunedin, 1890-1939*. Auckland: Auckland University Press, 2003.
Brooks, Van Wyck. 'On Creating a Usable Past'. *The Dial* (11 April 1918), 337–41.
Brysk, Alison, Craig Parsons, and Wayne Sandholtz. 'After Empire: National Identity and Post-Colonial Families of Nations'. *European Journal of International Relations*, 8:2 (2002), 267–305.
Buettner, Elizabeth. *Empire Families: Britons and Late Imperial India*. New York: Oxford University Press, 2004.
Burton, Antoinette. *Burdens of History: British Feminists, Indian Women, and Imperial Culture, 1865–1915*. Chapel Hill: The University of North Carolina Press, 1994.
Burton, Antoinette. *Dwelling in the Archive: Women, Writing, House, Home and History in Late Colonial India*. New York: Oxford University Press, 2003.
Burton, Antoinette (ed.). *After the Imperial Turn: Thinking with and through the Nation*. Durham, NC: Duke University Press, 2003.
Burton, Antoinette (ed.). *Archive Stories: Facts, Fictions, and the Writing of History*. Durham, NC: Duke University Press, 2006.
Bush, Julia. *Edwardian Ladies and Imperial Power*. London: Continuum, 1999.
Bush, Julia. 'Edwardian Ladies and the "Race" Dimensions of British Imperialism'. *Women's Studies International Forum*, 21:3 (1998), 277–89.
Bush, Julia. '"The Right Sort of Women": Female Emigrators and Emigration to the British Empire, 1890-1910'. *Women's History Review*, 3 (1994), 385–409.
Calabria, Tim. 'Agents of Settler Colonialism?: Childhood, Time and Exclusion in the Fairbridge Scheme, 1913–1924'. *Settler Colonial Studies*, 13:1 (2023), 133–55.
Caplan, Lionel. *Children of Colonialism: Anglo-Indians in a Postcolonial World*. Oxford: Berg Publishers, 2001.
Chatterjee, Partha. *The Nation and Its Fragments: Colonial and Postcolonial Histories*. Princeton: Princeton University Press, 1993.

Chilton, Lisa. *Agents of Empire: British Female Migration to Canada and Australia, 1860s-1930*. Toronto: University of Toronto Press, 2007.

Conor, Liz. *Skin Deep: Settler Impressions of Aboriginal Women*. Crawley: UWA Publishing, 2016.

Conor, Liz, and Jane Lydon. 'Double Take: Reappraising the Colonial Archive'. *Journal of Australian Studies*, 35:2 (June 2011), 137–43.

Constantine, Stephen. *Emigrants and Empire: British Settlement in the Dominions before the War*. Manchester: Manchester University Press, 1990.

Cooper, Frederick, and Ann Laura Stoler (eds). *Tensions of Empire: Colonial Cultures in a Bourgeois World*. Berkeley: University of California Press, 1997.

Corbett, Gail H. *Nation Builders: Barnardo Children in Canada*. Toronto: Dundurn, 2002.

Coulter, Natalie, and Kristine Moruzi. 'Woke Girls: From *The Girl's Realm* to *Teen Vogue*'. *Feminist Media Studies*, 22:4 (2020), 765–79.

Cunningham, Hugh. *Children and Childhood in Western Society since 1500*. New York: Longman, 1995.

Cunningham, Hugh. *The Reputation of Philanthropy since 1750: Britain and Beyond*. Manchester: Manchester University Press, 2000.

Davidoff, Leonore, and Catherine Hall. *Family Fortunes: Men and Women of the English Middle Class, 1750-1850*. Revised edition. New York: Routledge, 2002.

Davin, Anna. 'Imperialism and Motherhood'. *History Workshop Journal*, 5:1 (1978), 9–66.

Davin, Anna. 'What Is a Child?'. In Stephen Hussey and Anthony Fletcher (eds), *Childhood in Question: Children, Parents and the State*, pp. 15–36. Manchester: Manchester University Press, 1999.

Devereux, Cecily. '"The Maiden Tribute" and the Rise of the White Slave in the Nineteenth Century: The Making of an Imperial Construct'. *Victorian Review*, 26:2 (2000), 1–23.

Diamond, Marion. *Emigration and Empire: The Life of Maria S. Rye*. New York: Routledge, 1999.

Dillenburg, Elizabeth. 'Constructing and Contesting "the Girlhood of Our Empire": Girls' Culture, Labor, and Mobility in Britain, South Africa, and New Zealand, c. 1830–1930'. PhD dissertation, University of Minnesota, 2019.

Dona, Giorgia, and Andrea Veale. 'Mobility-in-Migration in an Era of Globalization: Key Themes and Future Directions'. In Giorgia Dona and Andrea Veale (eds), *Child and Youth Migration: Mobility-in-Migration in an Era of Globalization*, pp. 234–44. Basingstoke: Palgrave Macmillan, 2014.

Duff, S. E. '"Capture the Children": Writing Children into the South African War, 1899–1902'. *The Journal of the History of Childhood and Youth*, 7:3 (2014), 355–76.

Duff, S. E. *Changing Childhoods in the Cape Colony: Dutch Reformed Church Evangelicalism and Colonial Childhood, 1860-1895*. Palgrave Studies in the History of Childhood. Basingstoke: Palgrave Macmillan, 2015.

Dussart, Fae. *In the Service of Empire: Domestic Service and Mastery in Metropole and Colony*. New York: Bloomsbury Academic, 2022.

Dyhouse, Carol. *Girl Trouble: Panic and Progress in the History of Young Women*. London: Zed Books, 2013.

Dyhouse, Carol. *Girls Growing Up in Late Victorian and Edwardian England*. Boston: Broadway House, 1981.

Edwards, Sian. *Youth Movements, Citizenship and the English Countryside: Creating Good Citizens, 1930–1960*. Basingstoke: Palgrave Macmillan, 2018.

Ellis, Catherine. 'The Younger Generation: The Labour Party and the 1959 Youth Commission'. *Journal of British Studies*, 41:2 (2002), 199–231.

Fabes, Ray, and Alison Skinner. 'The Girls' Friendly Society and the Development of Rural Youth Work 1850–1900'. In Ruth Gilchrist, Tony Jeffs, and Jean Spence (eds), *Essays in the History of Community and Youth Work*, pp. 64-73. Leicester: Youth Work Press, 2001.

Fairburn, Miles. *The Ideal Society and Its Enemies: The Foundations of Modern New Zealand Society, 1850-1900*. Auckland: Auckland University Press, 1989.

Field, Corinne T., Tammy-Charelle Owens, Marcia Chatelain, Lakisha Simmons, Abosede George, and Rhian Keyse. 'The History of Black Girlhood: Recent Innovations and Future Directions'. *The Journal of the History of Childhood and Youth*, 9:3 (2016), 383–401.

Field, Corinne T., and LaKisha Michelle Simmons (eds). *The Global History of Black Girlhood*. Champaign: University of Illinois Press, 2022.

Field, Corinne T., Nicholas L. Syrett, Pat Thane, Bianca Premo, Ishita Pande, Corrie Decker, Sayaka Chantani, and Ashwini Tambe. AHR Roundtable: 'Chronological Age: A Useful Category of Analysis'. *American Historical Review*, 125:4 (October 2020), 371–459.

Fieldston, Sara. 'Little Cold Warriors: Child Sponsorship and International Affairs'. *Diplomatic History*, 38:2 (2014), 240–50.

Fischer-Tiné, Harald. *Low and Licentious Europeans: Race, Class and 'White Subalternity' in Colonial India*. New Perspectives in South Asian History. Hyderabad: Orient Blackswan Pvt Ltd, 2009.

Fowler, David. *Youth Culture in Modern Britain, c.1920–c.1970*. Basingstoke: Palgrave Macmillan, 2008.

Frankenberg, Ruth. *White Women, Race Matters: The Social Construction of Whiteness*. Minneapolis: University of Minnesota Press, 1993.

Frankenberg, Ruth (ed.). *Displacing Whiteness: Essays in Social and Cultural Criticism*. Durham, NC: Duke University Press, 1997.

Gaitskell, Deborah. '"Christian Compounds for Girls": Church Hostels for African Women in Johannesburg, 1907–1970'. *Journal of Southern African Studies*, 6:1 (1979), 44–69.

Garber, Marjorie. *Vested Interests: Cross-dressing and Cultural Anxiety*. New York: Penguin Books, 1993.

George, Abosede. *Making Modern Girls: A History of Girlhood, Labor, and Social Development in Colonial Lagos*. Athens: Ohio University Press, 2014.

Ghosh, Durba. *Sex and the Family in Colonial India: The Making of Empire*. New York: Cambridge University Press, 2006.

Gill, Alan. *Orphans of the Empire: The Shocking Story of Child Migration to Australia*. New York: Vintage, 1998.

Gleason, Mona. 'Avoiding the Agency Trap: Caveats for Historians of Children, Youth, and Education'. *History of Education*, 45:4 (2016), 446–59.

Glucksmann, Miriam. *Cottons and Casuals: The Gendered Organisation of Labour in Time and Space*. New York: Routledge, 2000.

Goldin, Ian. *Making Race: The Politics and Economics of Coloured Identity in South Africa*. Cape Town: Maskew Miller Longman, 1987.

Gorham, Deborah. 'The "Maiden Tribute of Modern Babylon" Re-Examined: Child Prostitution and Childhood in Late-Victorian England'. *Victorian Studies*, 21:3 (Spring 1978), 353–79.

Grimley, Matthew. *Citizenship, Community and the Church of England: Liberal Anglican Theories of the State between the Wars*. Oxford: Clarendon, 2004.

Gust, Omni. *Unhomely Empire: Whiteness and Belonging, c. 1760-1830*. London: Bloomsbury Academic, 2020.

Hadley, Elaine. 'Natives in a Strange Land: The Philanthropic Discourse of Juvenile Emigration in Mid-Nineteenth-Century England'. *Victorian Studies*, 33:3 (1990), 411–39.

Hall, Catherine. *Civilising Subjects: Colony and Metropole in the English Imagination, 1830–1867*. Chicago: The University of Chicago Press, 2002.

Hammerton, A. James. *Emigrant Gentlewomen: Genteel Poverty and Female Emigration, 1830–1914*. London: Croom Helm, 1979.

Harper, Marjory, and Stephen Constantine. *Empire and Migration*. Oxford History of the British Empire Companion Series. New York: Oxford University Press, 2010.

Harris, Cheryl I. 'Whiteness as Property'. *Harvard Law Review*, 106:8 (June 1993), 1707–91.

Harrison, Brian. 'For Church, Queen, and Family: The Girls' Friendly Society 1874–1920'. *Past and Present*, 61 (November 1972), 107–38.

Harrison, Phyllis. *The Home Children: Their Personal Stories*. Winnipeg: Watson and Dwyer, 1979.

Hartman, Saidiya. *Wayward Lives, Beautiful Experiments: Intimate Histories of Riotous Black Girls, Troublesome Women, and Queer Radicals*. New York: W. W. Norton & Company, 2019.

Haskins, Victoria K., and Claire Lowrie (eds). *Colonization and Domestic Service: Historical and Contemporary Perspectives*. New York: Routledge, 2014.

Heathorn, Stephen. *For Home, Country, and Race: Gender, Class, and Englishness in the Elementary School, 1880–1914*. Toronto: University of Toronto Press, 2000.

Helgren, Jennifer. *American Girls and Global Responsibility: A New Relation to the World during the Early Cold War*. New Brunswick: Rutgers University Press, 2017.

Helgren, Jennifer. *The Camp Fire Girls: Gender, Race, and American Girlhood, 1910-1980*. Lincoln: University of Nebraska Press, 2022.

Helgren, Jennifer (ed.). *Girlhood: A Global History*. Piscataway: Rutgers University Press, 2012.

Heywood, Colin. '*Centuries of Childhood*: An Anniversary – and an Epitaph?'. *The Journal of Childhood and Youth*, 3:3 (Fall 2010), 341–65.

Hochschild, Arlie Russell. *The Managed Heart: Commercialization of Human Feeling*. 3rd edition. Berkeley: University of California Press, 2012.

Honeck, Mischa. *Our Frontier Is the World: The Boy Scouts in the Age of American Ascendency*. Ithaca: Cornell University Press, 2018.

Hubel, Teresa. 'In Search of the British Indian in British India: White Orphans, Kipling's *Kim*, and Class in Colonial India'. *Modern Asian Studies*, 38:1 (2004), 227–51.

Humphreys, Margaret. *Empty Cradles*. London: Corgi, 2011.

Ishiguro, Laura. '"Growing up and Grown up [...] in Our Future City": Children and the Aspirational Politics of Settler Futurity in Colonial British Columbia'. *BC Studies: The British Columbian Quarterly*, 190 (2016), 15–37.
Ittmann, Karl, Dennis D. Cordell, and Gregory H. Maddox (eds). *The Demographics of Empire: The Colonial Order and the Creation of Knowledge*. Athens: Ohio University Press, 2010.
Jacobs, Margaret. *White Mother to a Dark Race: Settler Colonialism, Maternalism, and the Removal of Indigenous Children in the American West and Australia 1880–1940*. Lincoln: University of Nebraska Press, 2009.
Jeffery, Chris, and Geoffrey Sherington. *Fairbridge: Empire and Child Migration*. London: Woburn Press, 1998.
Johnson, Morgan Brie. 'Settler Colonial Structures of Domestication: British Home Children in Canada'. *Genealogy*, 5:3 (2021), 78.
Johnston, Scott. '"Only Send Boys of the Good Type": Child Migration and the Boy Scout Movement, 1921–1959'. *The Journal of the History of Childhood and Youth*, 7:3 (Fall 2014), 377–97.
Jones, Timothy Willem. *Sexual Politics in the Church of England, 1857–1967*. New York: Oxford University Press, 2012.
Jordan, Benjamin René. *Modern Manhood and the Boy Scouts of America: Citizenship, Race, and the Environment*. Chapel Hill: University of North Carolina Press, 2016.
Kennedy, Dane. *The Magic Mountains: Hill Stations and the British Raj*. Berkeley: University of California Press, 1996.
Khalfani, Akil Kokayi, Tukufu Zuberi, Sulaiman Bah, and Pali J. Lehohla. 'Population Statistics'. In Amson Sibanda, Tukufu Zuberi, and Eric O Udjo (eds), *The Demography of South Africa*, pp. 3–39. Armonk: M. E. Sharpe, 2005.
Koven, Seth. 'Borderlands: Women, Voluntary Action, and Child Welfare in Britain, 1840 to 1914'. In Seth Koven and Sonya Michael (eds), *Mothers of a New World: Maternalist Politics and the Origins of Welfare State*, pp. 94–135. New York: Routledge, 1993.
Krandis, Rita S. (ed.). *Imperial Objects: Essays on Victorian Women's Emigration and the Unauthorized Imperial Experience*. New York: Twayne Publishers, 1998.
Lake, Marilyn. 'White Man's Country: The Trans-National History of a National Project'. *Australian Historical Studies*, 34:122 (2003), 346–63.
Lake, Marilyn, and Henry Reynolds. *Drawing the Global Colour Line: White Men's Countries and the International Challenge of Racial Equality*. Critical Perspectives on Empire. Cambridge: Cambridge University Press, 2008.
Lal, Ruby. *Coming of Age in Nineteenth-Century India: The Girl-Child and the Art of Playfulness*. New York: Cambridge University Press, 2013.
Lester, Alan. 'Colonial Settlers and the Metropole: Racial Discourse in the Early 19th-Century Cape Colony, Australia and New Zealand'. *Landscape Research*, 27:1 (2002), 39–49.
Levine, Philippa. *Prostitution, Race, and Politics: Policing Venereal Disease in the British Empire*. New York: Routledge, 2013.
Levine, Philippa (ed.). *Gender and Empire*. Oxford History of the British Empire Companion Series. Oxford: Oxford University Press, 2004.
Levison, Deborah, Mary Jo Maynes, and Frances Vavrus. 'Children and Youth as Subjects, Objects, Agents: An Introduction'. In Deborah Levison, Mary Jo

Maynes, and Frances Vavrus (eds), *Children and Youth as Subjects, Objects, Agents: Innovative Approaches to Research across Space and Time*, pp. 1–9. New York: Palgrave Macmillan, 2021.

Levitan, Kathrin. 'Redundancy, the "Surplus Woman" Problem, and the British Census, 1851–1861'. *Women's History Review*, 17:3 (2008), 359–76.

Liebich, Susann. 'Connected Readers: Reading Practices and Communities across the British Empire, c. 1890–1930'. PhD thesis, Victoria University of Wellington, 2012.

Lipsitz, George. 'The Possessive Investment in Whiteness: Racialized Social Democracy and the "White" Problem in American Studies'. *American Quarterly*, 47:5 (1995), 369–87.

Locher-Scholten, Elsbeth. 'Orientalism and the Rhetoric of the Family: Javanese Servants in European Household Manuals and Children's Fiction'. *Indonesia*, 58 (October 1994), 19–39.

Lynch, Gordon. *Remembering Child Migration: Faith, Nation-Building and the Wounds of Charity*. London: Bloomsbury Academic, 2016.

Macdonald, Charlotte. *A Woman of Good Character: Single Women as Immigrant Settlers in Nineteenth-Century New Zealand*. Wellington: Allen & Unwin, 1990.

MacKenzie, John M. *Popular Imperialism and the Military: 1850–1950*. Manchester: Manchester University Press, 1992.

MacKenzie, John M. *Propaganda and Empire: The Manipulation of British Public Opinion, 1880–1960*. Manchester: Manchester University Press, 1984.

MacKenzie, John M. (ed.). *Imperialism and Popular Culture*. Manchester: Manchester University Press, 1986.

Magubane, Zine. *Bringing the Empire Home: Race, Class and Gender in Britain and Colonial South Africa*. Chicago: University of Chicago Press, 2004.

Mangan, J. A. *The Games Ethic and Imperialism: Aspects of the Diffusion of an Ideal*. New York: Viking, 1986.

Mangan, J. A. (ed.). *Benefits Bestowed: Education and British Imperialism*. Manchester: Manchester University Press, 1987.

Mangan, J. A. (ed.). *The Imperial Curriculum*. London: Routledge, 2012.

Mangan, J. A. (ed.). *Making Imperial Mentalities: Socialisation and British Imperialism*. New York: St Martin's Press, 1990.

Marcus, George E. 'Ethnography in/of the World System: The Emergence of Multi-Sited Ethnography'. *Annual Review of Anthropology*, 24 (1995), 95–117.

Martin, Mary Clare. 'Race, Indigeneity and the Baden-Powell Girl Guides: Age, Gender and the British World'. In Shirleene Robinson and Simon Sleight (eds), *Children, Childhood and Youth in the British World*, pp. 161–79. Palgrave Studies in the History of Childhood. Basingstoke: Palgrave Macmillan, 2016.

May, Helen, Baljit Kaur, and Larry Prochner. *Empire, Education, and Indigenous Childhoods*. London: Routledge, 2016.

Maynes, Mary Jo. 'Age as a Category of Historical Analysis: History, Agency, and Narratives of Childhood'. *The Journal of the History of Childhood and Youth*, 1:1 (2008), 114–24.

Maynes, Mary Jo, Birgitte Søland, and Christina Benninghaus (eds). *Secret Gardens, Satanic Mills: Placing Girls in European History, 1750–1960*. Bloomington: Indiana University Press, 2005.

Maza, Sarah, Steven Mintz, Nina Milanich, Robin P. Chapdelaine, Ishita Pande, and Bengt Sandin. AHR Exchange: 'Rethinking the History of Childhood'. *American Historical Review*, 125:2 (April 2020), 1260–322.

McCabe, Jane. *Race, Tea, and Colonial Resettlement: Imperial Families, Interrupted*. London: Bloomsbury Academic, 2017.

McClintock, Anne. *Imperial Leather: Race, Gender, and Sexuality in the Colonial Contest*. New York: Routledge, 1995.

McKibbin, Ross. *Classes and Cultures: England 1918–1951*. New York: Oxford University Press, 1998.

Midgley, Clare. *Feminism and Empire: Women Activists in Imperial Britain, 1790–1865*. London: Routledge, 2007.

Midgley, Clare (ed.). *Gender and Imperialism*. Manchester: Manchester University Press, 1998.

Miller, Susan. 'Assent as Agency in the Early Years of the Children of the American Revolution'. *The Journal of the History of Childhood and Youth*, 9:1 (2016), 48–65.

Miller, Susan. *Growing Girls: The Natural Origins of Girls' Organizations in America*. Rutgers Series in Childhood Studies. New Brunswick: Rutgers University Press, 2007.

Mills, Sarah, and Peter Kraftl (eds). *Informal Education, Childhood and Youth: Geographies, Histories, Practices*. Basingstoke: Palgrave Macmillan, 2014.

Mintz, Steven. 'Reflections on Age as a Category of Analysis'. *The Journal of the History of Childhood and Youth*, 1:1 (Winter 2008), 91–4.

Mitchell, Sally. *The New Girl: Girls' Culture in England, 1880–1915*. New York: Columbia University Press, 1995.

Mizutani, Satoshi. 'Historicising Whiteness: From the Case of Late Colonial India'. *Australia Critical Race and Whiteness Studies Association Journal*, 2:1 (2006), 1–15.

Mizutani, Satoshi. *The Meaning of White: Race, Class, and the 'Domiciled Community' in British India, 1858–1930*. Oxford: Oxford University Press, 2011.

The Modern Girl around the World Research Group. *The Modern Girl around the World: Consumption, Modernity, and Globalization*. Durham, NC: Duke University Press, 2008.

Monk, Una. *New Horizons: A Hundred Years of Women's Emigration*. London: HMSO, 1963.

Moreton-Robinson, Aileen. *The White Possessive: Property, Power, and Indigenous Sovereignty*. Minneapolis: University of Minnesota Press, 2015.

Morrison, Hugh. *Protestant Children, Missions and Education in the British World*. Brill Research Perspectives in Religion and Education Series. Boston: Brill, 2021.

Morrison, Toni. *Playing in the Dark: Whiteness and the Literary Imagination*. Cambridge, MA: Harvard University Press, 1992.

Mort, Frank. *Dangerous Sexualities: Medico-Moral Politics in England since 1830*. New York: Routledge, 2002.

Moruzi, Kristine. 'Encouraging Charitable Work and Membership in the Girls' Friendly Society through British Girls' Periodicals'. In Alexis Easley, Beth Rodgers, and Clare Gill (eds), *Women, Periodicals and Print Culture in Britain, 1830s–1900s: The Victorian Period*, pp. 140–52. Edinburgh: Edinburgh University Press, 2019.

Moruzi, Kristine. 'Feminine Bravery: *The Girls Realm* (1898–1915) and the Second Boer War'. *Literature Association Quarterly*, 34 (2009), 241–54.

Moruzi, Kristine. '"The Freedom Suits Me": Encouraging Girls to Settle in the Colonies'. In Tamara S. Wagner (ed.), *Victorian Settler Narratives: Emigrants, Cosmopolitans and Returnees in Nineteenth Century Literature*, pp. 177–91. London: Pickering & Chatto, 2011.

Moruzi, Kristine. '"I am content with Canada": Canadian Girls at the Turn of the Twentieth Century'. *Jeunesse: Young People, Texts, Cultures*, 4 (2012), 119–31.

Moruzi, Kristine, and Michelle J. Smith (eds). *Colonial Girlhood in Literature, Culture and History, 1840–1950*. Palgrave Studies in Nineteenth-Century Writing and Culture. London: Palgrave Macmillan, 2014.

Murdoch, Lydia. *Imagined Orphans: Poor Families, Child Welfare, and Contested Citizenship in London*. Rutgers Series in Childhood Studies. New Brunswick: Rutgers University Press, 2006.

Nakata, Sana. *Childhood Citizenship, Governance and Policy: The Politics of Becoming Adult*. New York: Routledge, 2015.

Nandy, Ashis. *Traditions, Tyranny, and Utopias: Essays in the Politics of Awareness*. London: Oxford University Press, 1987.

Niedermier, Silvan. 'Colonial Self-positioning. Approaching the Snapshots of an American Woman in the Philippines (1900–1902)'. In Ulrike Lindner and Dörte Lerp (eds), *New Perspectives on the History of Gender and Empire*, pp. 115–48. New York: Bloomsbury Academic, 2018.

Olsen, Stephanie. *Juvenile Nation: Youth, Emotions and the Making of the Modern British Citizen, 1880–1914*. New York: Bloomsbury, 2014.

Olusoga, David. *Black and British: A Forgotten History*. London: Macmillan, 2016.

Painter, Nell Irvin. *The History of White People*. New York: W. W. Norton & Company, 2010.

Palmer, Stanley H. 'The Power of Numbers: Settler and Native in Ireland, America, and South Africa, 1600–1900'. In Steven G. Reinhardt, Dennis Reinhartz, and William Hardy MacNeil (eds), *Transatlantic History*, pp. 85–194. Arlington: University of Texas, 2006.

Park, Sharon. 'Constructing Americans' Responsibility to Give: Shifting Debates about Foreign and Humanitarian Aid to Child Refugees, 1945–1989'. PhD dissertation, University of Minnesota, 2016.

Parr, Joy. *Labouring Children: British Immigrant Apprentices to Canada, 1869–1924*. Toronto: University of Toronto Press, 1980.

Paterson, Lachey, and Angela Wanhalla. *He Reo Wāhine: Māori Women's Voices from the Nineteenth Century*. Auckland: Auckland University Press, 2017.

Perry, Adele. *On the Edge of Empire: Gender, Race, and the Making of British Columbia, 1849–1871*. Toronto: University of Toronto Press, 2001.

Pettitt, Clare. 'Topos, Taxonomy and Travel in Nineteenth-Century Women's Scrapbooks'. In Mary Henes and Brian H. Murray (eds), *Travel Writing, Visual Culture and Form, 1760–1900*, pp. 21–41. Palgrave Studies in Nineteenth-Century Writing and Culture. Basingstoke: Palgrave Macmillan, 2016.

Philips, Jock, and Terry Hearn. *Settlers: New Zealand Immigrants from England, Ireland and Scotland 1800–1945*. AUP Studies in Cultural and Social History Series. Auckland: Auckland University Press, 2008.

Pickering, Michael. *Blackface Minstrelsy in Britain*. New York: Ashgate, 2008.

Pickles, Katie. 'Empire Settlement and Single British Women as New Zealand Domestic Servants during the 1920s'. *New Zealand Journal of History*, 35:1 (2001), 22–44.
Pomfret, David. *Youth and Empire: Trans-Colonial Childhoods in British and French Asia.* Redwood City: Stanford University Press, 2015.
Price, John. *Everyday Heroism: Victorian Constructions of the Heroic Civilian.* London: Bloomsbury 2014.
Price, John. 'Heroism in Everyday Life: The Watts Memorial for Heroic Self Sacrifice'. *History Workshop Journal*, 63 (2007), 254–78.
Proctor, Tammy M. *On My Honour: Guides and Scouts in Interwar Britain.* Philadelphia: American Philosophical Society, 2002.
Proctor, Tammy M. '(Uni)Forming Youth: Girl Guides and Boy Scouts in Britain, 1908–1939'. *History Workshop Journal*, 45 (Spring 1998), 103–34.
Ramsay, Laura Monica. '"The Relation of the Sexes": Towards a Christian View of Sex and Citizenship in Interwar Britain'. *Contemporary British History*, 34:4 (2020), 555–79.
Rehin, George F. 'Blackface Street Minstrels in Victorian London and Its Resorts: Popular Culture and Its Racial Connotations as Revealed in Polite Opinion'. *Journal of Popular Culture*, 15:1 (Summer 1981), 19–38.
Richards, Thomas. *Imperial Archive: Knowledge and the Fantasy of Empire.* London: Verso, 1996.
Richmond, Vivienne. 'Crafting Inclusion for "Invalid" Women: The Girls' Friendly Society Central Needlework Depôt, 1899–1947'. In Janice Helland, Beverly Lemire, and Alena Buis (eds), *Craft, Community and the Material Culture of Place and Politics, 19th–20th Century*, pp. 161–71. Burlington: Ashgate, 2014.
Richmond, Vivienne. '"It Is Not a Society for Human Beings but for Virgins": The Girls' Friendly Society Membership Eligibility Dispute 1875–1936'. *Journal of Historical Sociology*, 20:3 (September 2007), 304–27.
Riley, Charlotte. '"The winds of change are blowing economically": The Labour Party and British Overseas Development, 1940s–1960s'. In Andrew W. M. Smith and Chris Jeppesen (eds), *Britain, France and the Decolonization of Africa: Future Imperfect?*, pp. 43–61. London: UCL Press, 2017.
Robb, George. *British Culture and the First World War.* Basingstoke: Palgrave Macmillan, 2002.
Rosenberg, Gabriel. *The 4-H Harvest: Sexuality and the State in Rural America.* Philadelphia: University of Pennsylvania Press, 2015.
Rowan, Caroline. 'Child Welfare and the Working-Class Family'. In Mary Langan and Bill Schwarz (eds), *Crises in the British State, 1880–1930*, pp. 226–39. London: Hutchinson, 1985.
Ryan, James. *Picturing Empire: Photography and the Visualization of the British Empire.* Chicago: University of Chicago Press, 1998.
Sacks, Janet, and Roger Kershaw. *New Lives for Old: The Story of Britain's Home Children.* London: The National Archives, 2008.
Said, Edward. *Orientalism.* New York: Vintage Books, 1979.
Sandiford, Keith A. P. *Cricket and the Victorians.* Aldershot: Scholar Press, 1994.
Schwarz, Bill. *The White Man's World (Memories of Empire).* Oxford: Oxford University Press, 2012.
Schwebel, Sara L. 'The Limits of Agency for Children's Literature Scholars'. *Jeunesse: Young People, Texts, Cultures*, 8:1 (2016), 278–90.

Sen, Satadru. *Colonial Childhoods: The Juvenile Periphery of India, 1850–1945*. New York: Anthem, 2005.
Seymour, Jean. *A Century of Challenge: A History of the Girls' Friendly in Western Australia from 1888–1988*. Perth: Girls' Friendly Society, 1988.
Siegel, Elizabeth. *Galleries of Friendship and Fame: A History of Nineteenth-Century American Photograph Albums*. London: Yale University Press, 2010.
Sinha, Mrinalini. *Colonial Masculinity: The Effeminate Bengali and the Manly Englishman*. Manchester: Manchester University Press, 1995.
Smith, Michelle. 'Be(ing) Prepared: Girl Guides, Colonial Life, and National Strength'. *Limina*, 12 (2006), 52–63.
Smith, Michelle. *Empire in British Girls' Literature and Culture: Imperial Girls 1880–1915*. New York: Palgrave Macmillan, 2010.
Smith, Michelle. 'Wild Australian Girls?: The Mythology of Colonial Femininity in British Print Culture, 1885–1916'. In Clare Bradford and Mavis Reimer (eds), *Girls, Texts, Cultures*, pp. 237–60. Studies in Childhood and Family in Canada. Waterloo: Wilfrid Laurier University Press, 2015.
Smith, Michelle, Kristine Moruzi, and Clare Bradford. *From Colonial to Modern: Transnational Girlhood in Canadian, Australian, and New Zealand Children's Literature*. Toronto: University of Toronto Press, 2018.
Sorabji, Richard. *Opening Doors: The Untold Story of Cornelia Sorabji, Reformer, Lawyer and Champion of Women's Rights in India*. Delhi: Penguin Books India, 2010.
Spivak, Gayatri Chakravorty. 'Can the Subaltern Speak?' In Cary Nelson and Lawrence Grossberg (eds), *Marxism and the Interpretation of Culture*, pp. 271–313. Basingstoke: Macmillan Education, 1988.
Spivak, Gayatri Chakravorty. 'The Rani of Sirmur: An Essay in Reading the Archives'. *History and Theory*, 24:3 (1985), 247–72.
Springhall, John O. 'The Boy Scouts, Class and Militarism in Relation to British Youth Movements, 1908–1930'. *International Review of Social History*, 16 (1971), 125–58.
Stearns, Peter. *Childhood in World History*. 2nd ed. New York: Routledge, 2006.
Stoler, Ann Laura. *Along the Archival Grain: Epistemic Anxieties and Colonial Common Sense*. Princeton: Princeton University Press, 2008.
Stoler, Ann Laura. *Carnal Knowledge and Imperial Power: Race and the Intimate in Colonial Rule*. Los Angeles: University of California Press, 2002.
Stoler, Ann Laura. 'Colonial Archives and Arts of Governance'. *Archival Science*, 2 (2002), 87–109.
Stoler, Ann Laura. 'Making Empire Respectable: The Politics of Race and Sexual Morality in 20th-Century Colonial Cultures'. *American Ethnologist*, 16 (November 1989), 634–52.
Stoler, Ann Laura. *Race and Education of Desire: Foucault's History of Sexuality and the Colonial Order of Things*. Durham, NC: Duke University Press, 1995.
Stoler, Ann Laura. 'Rethinking Colonial Categories: European Communities and the Boundaries of Rule'. *Comparative Studies in Society and History*, 31:1 (January 1989), 134–61.
Stoler, Ann Laura. 'Sexual Affronts and Racial Frontiers: European Identities and the Cultural Politics of Exclusion in Colonial Southeast Asia'. *Comparative Studies in Society and History*, 3:4 (1992), 514–51.

Sunderland, Helen. '"Politics for Girls": Representations of Political Girlhood in the *Girls' Own Paper* and the *Girl's Realm*'. *Victorian Periodicals Review*, 52:1 (Spring 2019), 1–26.
Swain, Shurlee, and Margot Hillel. *Child, Nation, Race and Empire: Child Rescue Discourse, England, Canada, and Australia, 1850–1915*. Manchester: Manchester University Press, 2010.
Swaisland, Cecillie. *Servants and Gentlewomen to the Golden Land: The Emigration of Single Women from Britain to Southern Africa, 1820–1839*. Oxford: Berg, 1993.
Swartz, Rebecca. 'Child Apprenticeship in the Cape Colony: The Case of the Children's Friend Society Emigration Scheme, 1833–1841'. *Slavery & Abolition*, 42:3 (2021), 567–88.
Swartz, Rebecca. *Education and Empire: Children, Race and Humanitarianism in the British Settler Colonies, 1833–1880*. Basingstoke: Palgrave Macmillan, 2019.
Taylor, David. '"The Minstrels Parade": Blackface Minstrelsy and the Music Hall'. In *From Mummers to Madness: A Social History of Popular Music in England, c. 1770s to c. 1970s*, pp. 197–214. Huddersfield: University of Huddersfield Press, 2021.
Tebbutt, Melanie. *Making Youth: A History of Youth in Modern Britain*. Basingstoke: Palgrave Macmillan, 2016.
Tennant, Margaret. '"Magdalens and Moral Imbeciles": Women's Homes in Nineteenth-Century New Zealand'. *Women's Studies International Forum*, 9:5 (1986), 491–502.
Thomson, David. 'Marriage and Family on the Colonial Frontier'. In Tony Ballantyne and Brian Moloughney (eds), *Disputed Histories: Imagining New Zealand's Past*, pp. 119–42. Dunedin: Otago University Press, 2006.
Tucker, Susan. 'Reading and Re-Reading: The Scrapbooks of Girls Growing into Women, 1900–1930'. In Anne H. Lundin and Wayne A. Wiegand (eds), *Defining Print Culture for Youth: The Cultural Work of Children's Literature*, pp. 1–26. Westport: Libraries Unlimited, 2003.
Tucker, Susan, Katherine Ott, and Patricia Buckler (eds). *The Scrapbook in American Life*. Philadelphia: Temple University Press, 2006.
Vallgårda, Karen. *Imperial Childhoods and Christian Missions: Education and Emotions in South India and Denmark*. Palgrave Studies in the History of Emotions. New York: Palgrave Macmillan, 2015.
van Onselen, Charles. 'The Witches of Suburbia: Domestic Service on the Witwatersrand, 1890–1914'. In *Studies in the Social and Economic History of the Witwatersrand 1886–1914*, pp. 1–73. New York: Longman, 1982.
Veracini, Lorenzo. *Colonialism: A Global History*. New York: Routledge, 2023.
Veracini, Lorenzo. *Settler Colonialism: A Theoretical Overview*. Basingstoke: Palgrave Macmillan, 2010.
Visram, Rozina. *Ayahs, Lascars and Princes: The Story of Indians in Britain 1700–1947*. London: Taylor and Francis Limited, 2016.
Wagner, Gillian. *Barnardo*. London: Weidenfeld and Nicolson, 1979.
Wagner, Gillian. *Children of the Empire*. London: Weidenfeld and Nicolson, 1982.
Walkowitz, Judith R. *City of Dreadful Delight: Narratives of Sexual Danger in Late-Victorian London*. Chicago: University of Chicago Press, 2013.
Walkowitz, Judith R. *Prostitution and Victorian Society: Women, Class, and the State*. Cambridge: Cambridge University Press, 1980.

Ward, Stuart (ed.). *British Culture and the End of Empire*. Studies in Imperialism. Manchester: Manchester University Press, 2001.

Ware, Vron. *Beyond the Pale: White Women, Racism, and History*. New York: Verso, 1992.

Watts, Carol. *The Cultural Work of Empire: The Seven Years' War and the Imagining of the Shandean State*. Toronto: University of Toronto Press, 2007.

Webster, Wendy. *Englishness and Empire 1939–1965*. New York: Oxford University Press, 2005.

White, Holly N. S., and Julia M. Gossard. 'Considering "Double Age" in the History of American Childhood and Youth: An Introduction'. *The Journal of the History of Childhood and Youth*, 15:3 (Fall 2002), 355–61.

Wilson, Adrian. 'The Infancy of the History of Childhood: An Appraisal of Philippe Ariès'. *History and Theory*, 19:2 (1980), 132–53.

Wilson, Kathleen. *The Island Race: Englishness, Empire, and Gender in the Eighteenth Century*. New York: Routledge, 2003.

Wolfe, Patrick. 'Settler Colonialism and the Elimination of the Native'. *Journal of Genocide Research*, 8:4 (December 2006), 387–409.

Wolfe, Patrick. *Settler Colonialism and the Transformation of Anthropology*. London: Cassell, 1999.

Woollacott, Angela. 'New Angles on Whiteness and the Making of the Modern World'. *Itinerario*, 47 (2023), 138–45.

Worsnop, Judith. 'A Reevaluation of "the Problem of Surplus Women" in 19th-century England: The Case of the 1851 Census'. *Women's Studies International Forum*, 13:1 (1990), 21–31.

Zahra, Tara. *The Lost Children: Reconstructing Europe's Families after World War II*. Cambridge, MA: Harvard University Press, 2015.

# Index

Aboriginal people 62, 80–1, 83
African peoples (southern Africa) 12, 62, 80–3, 87, 117, 150–3, 154, 204–5, 210
  see also Black people (southern Africa); Coloured people (southern Africa)
Afrikaner 12, 83, 110, 170
Anglican Church/Communion 12, 180–8, 203, 205, 206–7, 209
Anglo-Indian 131–3, 135–50, 153–4, 186–7
  see also domiciled community
apartheid 170, 204–5
Arbuthnot, Margaret 140, 183–6, 220
archive 4, 9–11, 83–4, 119–21, 153–4, 188–9, 209
Australia
  branches 35, 38, 84–5, 173, 181, 187
  in education programmes 57, 58
  emigration 60–2, 103, 107, 113
  in newsletters 55, 57, 58, 60–2, 169
  West Australia scrapbook 75, 77–84
Ayers, Alice 34–5

Barbados 113, 198
  see also West Indies
Barnardo's 6, 42, 103–4, 119, 138
blackface/brownface 67, 72–5
Black Lives Matter Movement 14, 208
Black people (southern Africa) 12, 80–3, 110–11, 117, 150–3, 204–5
  see also African peoples (southern Africa)

Bombay (Mumbai) 114, 133, 135, 136, 138, 139, 143, 147–8, 167, 180, 187, 200
  see also India
Boy Scouts 29, 207
British Women's Emigration Association (BWEA) 104–5, 110, 114, 115, 119
Broome, (Lady) Mary Anne 110, 112
Bruce, Finetta 144–5, 150, 220
Bulawayo 3, 101–2
  see also Rhodesia (Zimbabwe); southern/South Africa
Burma (Myanmar) 12, 35, 60, 67, 167, 174, 184–7
  see also Rangoon (Yangon)

Calcutta 57, 84, 133, 135, 136, 143, 144–7, 154, 170, 183–4, 187, 210
  see also India
Cameroon 203
Campbell, Mary 136, 170, 179, 220
Camp Fire Girls 29, 84
Canada
  branches 35, 176, 187
  emigration 10, 103, 104, 107, 109, 113, 116
  missions 39
  in newsletters 55, 60–1, 169
Cape Colony 40, 75, 77–84, 86, 110, 113, 115, 145, 148, 149, 150–1, 170, 199
  see also southern/South Africa
Cape Town 113, 115, 150–1, 199
  see also southern/South Africa

Carden, Olive 134, 187, 220
Carpenter-Garnier, Mark, bishop of Colombo 181–2, 184, 187
Cary, Winifred 181, 182, 185, 186, 220
Central Council (Girls' Friendly Society) 35–7, 39, 42, 84, 109, 132, 133–4, 140, 144–50, 152, 170–1, 175, 178, 182, 183–8, 207
central rule 13, 29–30, 36, 205
  debate 14, 42–3, 168, 177–88
Ceylon (Sri Lanka) 12, 35, 57, 60, 63, 133, 136, 137, 138, 148, 149, 154, 167, 174, 181–2, 184–7, 200
  see also Colombo; Sri Lanka
Chibok school girls 210
Children's Friend Society (CFS) 103–4
China 39, 57, 65–6, 152, 187, 201
Church Missionary Society (CMS) 39, 200, 204
*Church Times, The* 183–5
Chute, Eleanor 42, 200
class
  anxieties 4, 7–8, 10–11, 24, 25–9, 102, 105–6, 109–12, 116–17, 121, 131–2, 138–41
  in the Girls' Friendly Society 25–9, 31–5, 37, 43–4, 56, 153, 177, 201, 207, 209
  hierarchies 2, 31–5, 116–17, 140–1, 210
Cocke, (Lady) Winifred 147, 220
Cold War 199, 202–3
Colombo 57, 133, 137–8, 149
  see also Carpenter-Garnier, Mark, bishop of Colombo; Ceylon (Sri Lanka)
Colonial Committee/Imperial Committee/Imperial and Overseas Committee 36, 59, 76, 84, 151, 152, 178
Coloured people (southern Africa) 12, 80–3, 110–11, 150–3, 154, 204–5, 210
  see also African peoples (southern Africa)

Commonwealth 171, 202
Cook, Eliza 3, 101–2, 116–19, 120–1, 132
Criminal Law Amendment Act (1885) 27
Cunliffe, (Lady) Cecilie 109, 220

Davis, W. E. 131–3, 154
decolonisation 14, 198
Delhi 114, 135, 138, 139, 200
  see also India
Department for Members Emigrating 6, 10, 55, 103–5, 107, 109, 112–13, 199
  see also emigration; Joyce, Ellen
doll/doll pageant 75, 142
domesticity/domestic life 13, 25–6, 33–4, 38, 40–1, 55, 65–6, 78, 87–8, 108–10, 131–2, 139–40, 172
domestic servant/service 3, 32–5, 68, 114–19, 131, 145, 211
  decline 168, 169
  emigration 3, 13, 101–2, 107–12, 138
  in Girls' Friendly Society 32–3, 43–4, 169
  servant problem/crisis 32–4, 107–8, 141, 169
  in southern Africa 3, 87, 101–2, 110–19
  training programmes in India 138–44
domestic skills 25–6, 28, 33–4, 110, 139–40, 172
domiciled community 132–3, 135–50, 153–4, 186–7
  see also Anglo-Indian; domiciled European
domiciled European 132–3, 135, 137–44, 153–4
  see also domiciled community
drill
  see exercise/physical activity
Du Bois, W. E. B. 7
Durban 112, 113, 114, 170, 174, 199
  see also southern/South Africa

education 1–2, 4–5, 8, 11, 13–14, 27, 28, 33, 39–40, 44, 55–88, 131, 137–44, 200–1, 207, 209–10
  see also Punjab Industrial Training Scheme (PITS); St Christopher's Nursery Training School; St Lawrence Military Asylum
Education Act (1870) 4, 5
Elliot, Sarah 117–18, 120–1
emigration 2, 3, 5–7, 8, 10, 11, 13, 14, 36, 38, 101–21, 133, 209–10
  criticisms 104, 109–19
  decline 199–200
  and education programmes 55–6, 58, 60–7, 75–83, 86–7
  programmes for domiciled girls 141–4
  and social reform 105–7
  societies/organisations 102–5
  see also Barnardo's; British Women's Emigration Association (BWEA); Children's Friend Society (CFS); Department for Members Emigrating; Fairbridge Society; hostel; Joyce, Ellen; Rye, Maria; Salvation Army; Society for the Overseas Settlement of British Women (SOSBW); South African Colonisation Society (SACS)
*Empire and Beyond, The* 37, 38, 41, 57, 58, 59, 66, 134–5, 136, 176
Empire Education Committee 56
Eurasian question
  see Anglo-Indian
exercise/physical activity 26, 70–1

Factory Act (1833) 4, 103
Fairbridge Society 103–4
family/familial language within the Girls' Friendly Society 14, 25–6, 36–7, 43, 63–5, 77–8, 86, 88, 144, 148, 153, 169, 170–1, 186, 188
  branches as colonial daughters 14, 36, 39, 133, 168–9, 170, 186
  ideas of sisterhood 14, 25, 58–9, 63–5, 77, 84, 88, 135, 153, 186

mother/maternal metaphor 25, 36–7, 119, 168–9
in newsletters 63–5
in scrapbooks 77–8
Fanon, Frantz 7
femininity 24, 26–7, 34, 69, 71, 78, 172, 174, 206, 210
Forward Movement 172–3, 188
*Friendly Leaves* 26, 59, 60–3

garden party 57
Gardner Williams, Ada 149, 182, 221
Gell, Edith Lyttelton 101, 114–15
Ghana 201, 203
Girl Guides 5, 29, 67, 76, 152, 154, 175–7, 184, 204, 207
girlhood 2, 209–11
  anxieties about 24, 25–8, 178–80
  definitions 4–5
  differences 66–7, 72, 84, 150, 153, 186, 188
  in the Girls' Friendly Society 13, 25–32, 37, 56, 57, 59, 64, 66–80, 87–8, 135, 152, 173–4, 188
  and race 8, 10, 13–15, 28, 56, 72–5
  studying and researching 2–3, 4, 9–12, 83–5, 119–21, 153–4, 188–9, 209
  see also girls of colour; modern girl
Girls Friendly Society & Boys Friendly Society (GFS & BFS) 207
Girls' Guild of Service 187
girls of colour 5, 10, 14, 38, 41, 56, 72, 81, 88, 144, 152–4, 188, 198, 204–5, 209–11
  see also Aboriginal people; African peoples (southern Africa); Anglo-Indian; Black people (southern Africa); Coloured people (southern Africa); Māori
*Girls' Quarterly: A Paper for Workers in the Girls' Friendly Society, The* 24, 33, 40, 41, 65, 66, 173–4
Goodrich, Mabel 147–8, 180–1, 221
Gordon Clark, Edith 152, 186, 187, 221
Greg, William Rathbone 105–6

Hall, G. Stanley 26
Heath-Stubbs, Mary 12, 35–6, 43, 169, 221
Hely-Hutchinson, (Lady) May 110, 118
Hobbs, Eliza 3, 101–2, 114, 116–18, 120–1, 132
Hong Kong 60, 187
hostel 167, 175, 187, 199, 203, 209
   in Calcutta 144–7, 154, 210
   for domiciled girls 139, 143–4
   purpose 113–15, 135
   in southern Africa 111–12, 117, 174
   White House Lodge (Bombay) 114, 147–8, 180, 187
Hughes, Katherine 175–6, 182, 221

Imperial and Overseas Committee
   *see* Colonial Committee/Imperial Committee/Imperial and Overseas Committee
*Imperial Colonist, The* 115
Imperial Committee
   *see* Colonial Committee/Imperial Committee/Imperial and Overseas Committee
Imperial Conference (Girls' Friendly Society) 59, 107, 108
India 12
   branches 14, 35, 38–9, 84, 86, 133–7, 154
   decline of the Girls' Friendly Society 167, 169–71, 174–5, 179, 182–9, 200
   in education programmes 57, 58
   hostels 114, 135, 144–50
   migration 131–3
   missionary work 39, 40, 41, 65, 66, 200, 201
   in newsletters/periodicals 24, 55, 59, 60, 65, 66
   in pageants and plays 70, 72–5
   training programmes 137–44, 153, 169
   *see also* Anglo-Indian; Bombay (Mumbai); Calcutta; Ceylon (Sri Lanka); Delhi; domiciled community; domiciled European; Lahore; Lucknow; Murree; St Christopher's Nursery Training School; St Lawrence Military Asylum

Jamaica 37, 152, 176
   *see also* West Indies
Japan 39, 65, 66, 201, 203, 204
Joan of Arc 1–2, 6, 68, 69
Joyce, Ellen 10, 35, 101, 104–9, 111, 113, 114, 115, 116, 117–18, 119–20, 121, 172, 173, 209, 221

Kipling, Rudyard 37, 137
Knightley, Louisa 43

Lahore 67, 133, 134, 135, 137, 140, 142, 144, 187
   *see also* India
Lambeth Conference (1930) 181
lantern lecture 26, 57
lodge
   *see* hostel
Lucknow 58, 133, 143, 175, 200
   *see also* India

Malta 35, 60, 63
Māori 62
membership structure of the Girls' Friendly Society 28–32
Metropolitan Association for Befriending Young Servants (MABYS) 32–3
Milner, Alfred 110–11
missions/missionaries/missionary societies
   in education programmes 55, 57–9
   Girls' Friendly Society programmes 39–41, 42, 150, 153
   in newsletters 63, 65–6
   in pageants and plays 67, 70, 72–5
   in postwar period 200–1, 203–4
   *see also* Church Missionary Society (CMS); Society for the Propagation of the Gospel
modern girl 27, 172–5, 178–9, 182, 184

Money, Agnes 29, 38, 42, 132, 135, 136, 221
Murree 135, 143, 148
  see also India
Mytton, Caroline 132, 136, 139, 143–50, 152–3, 170–1, 175, 180–1, 185, 187, 221

newsletters/periodicals 2, 26, 34, 36, 40, 59–67, 68, 76, 77–9, 84–5, 87–8, 135, 168, 173, 202, 209
  see also Empire and Beyond, The; Friendly Leaves; Girls' Quarterly: A Paper for Workers in the Girls' Friendly Society, The; Our Letter: For G.F.S. Candidates all over the World
New Zealand
  branches 35, 68, 171, 175, 176, 181
  emigration 107, 112, 113, 116, 118, 138
  missionaries 58
  in newsletters 55, 60–5, 169
nurse, children's and medical 35, 58, 68, 72, 114, 134, 138–40, 141, 143

Our Letter: For G.F.S. Candidates all over the World 1–2, 34, 40, 55, 60, 63–6, 68, 70, 72, 168–9, 172

pageant/play 57, 59, 67–75, 84–5, 87–8, 142, 199, 206
Paine, Winifred 187, 221
Parker, Louis Napoleon 67, 68, 69
Parrish, Fanchette G. 148–9, 170, 221
Paul, Violet 131–2, 154
penfriend programme 85–7, 204
photographs 60, 63–4, 72–83, 85, 209
play
  see pageant/play
Port Elizabeth (Gqeberha)
  branches 86, 148–9, 151, 170
  emigration 115
  hostel 113
  scrapbook 75, 77–84
  see also southern/South Africa

Preston, Winifred 171, 175, 176, 222
prostitution
  see sex work
Punjab Industrial Training Scheme (PITS) 138–43
purity 33
  connection to emigration and imperial and missionary work 38, 40–1, 65, 106, 108, 112, 114
  in the Girls' Friendly Society 13, 24, 26, 28–31, 38, 42–3, 44, 58, 68, 83, 168, 172–3, 177–8, 181, 205
  and whiteness 8, 24, 132, 133, 137, 152, 188
  see also central rule; social purity movement

race
  anxieties 4, 7, 10–11, 27–8, 44, 132, 140–1, 210
  definitions 12
  and emigration 102, 106, 107–11, 117, 121
  in the Girls' Friendly Society 5, 13–15, 55–6, 132, 143–4, 152–4, 198, 204–5, 208
  hierarchies 2, 11, 25, 131–2, 136, 140, 210
  representations of 61–2, 66–7, 72–5, 80–3, 84
  see also blackface/brownface; girls of colour; whiteness
Rangoon (Yangon) 60, 133, 135, 167, 169, 183–6, 187
  see also Burma (Myanmar)
reading unions and circles 26, 58
Rhodesia (Zimbabwe) 3, 12, 101–2, 114, 117–18, 120–1
  see also Bulawayo; Salisbury (Harare); southern/South Africa
Ridding, Laura 151
Robinson, Sidonia 101, 116–17, 118, 120
Rye, Maria 103–4, 109

St Christopher's Nursery Training School 138, 139, 143

St Lawrence Military Asylum 137–8, 140
Salisbury (Harare) 114, 117–18
  see also Rhodesia (Zimbabwe); southern/South Africa
Salvation Army 25, 103, 107
school
  see education
Scotland 12–13, 35
Scott, Margaret 144, 148, 222
scrapbooks 9, 75–85, 87–8, 199, 202, 205–6, 209, 210
  competitions 76, 199
  scrapbook exchanges 76–85
servant
  see domestic servant/service
sex work 27, 30, 32, 106, 112
Shepard, Ethel J. 134, 222
Smith, E. Mabel 149, 179–80, 222
Social Darwinism 4, 28
social purity movement 26–8, 30–1, 41, 105, 106
Society for the Overseas Settlement of British Women (SOSBW) 199
Society for the Propagation of the Gospel 39, 138
Sorabji, Mary 59
South African Colonisation Society (SACS) 5, 43, 104–5, 114, 117–18, 119
South African War 4–5, 11, 28, 105
southern/South Africa 12
  apartheid era 204–5
  branches 35, 39, 85, 86, 87, 135–6, 148–54, 170–1, 174, 179–80
  emigration 3, 11, 101–2, 107, 110–19
  in newsletters 60–2, 169
  post-apartheid era 14, 207–8, 210
  in scrapbooks 75, 77–83
  see also Bulawayo; Cape Colony; Cape Town; Durban; Port Elizabeth (Gqeberha); Rhodesia (Zimbabwe); Salisbury (Harare) South African Colonisation Society (SACS); South African War; Transkei

Sri Lanka 12, 200, 203
  see also Carpenter-Garnier, Mark, bishop of Colombo; Ceylon (Sri Lanka); Colombo
Stead, W. T. 27
stamp club 57
study circles 57, 58–9, 203
Sydenham, (Lady) Elizabeth 167, 222

Thomas, Mary 144–8, 154, 174, 222
Townsend, Kathleen 36, 65
Townsend, Mary Elizabeth 24, 25, 27, 31, 34, 37–8, 42, 43, 44, 104, 132, 133–4, 152, 172, 206, 209, 222
transgender children 207
Transkei 205
Travellers' Aid Society 25
Tubbs, Norman, bishop of Rangoon 183–6

United States 35, 202–3, 208, 211

Victoria, Queen 24, 37

Wales 5, 12–13, 74, 178, 206, 207, 208
Westcott, Foss, bishop of Calcutta 183–4
West Indies 35, 60, 63, 152, 204, 205
  see also Barbados; Jamaica
Westmacott, Vera 84, 145–7, 149, 170, 174, 186, 222
White Crusade 172–3
whiteness
  anxieties about 4–5, 10, 11–12, 13–14, 27–8, 33, 44, 62, 63, 109–11, 114–15, 133, 134, 137–8, 140–1, 142
  connection to purity 24, 28–31, 38, 152, 172–3
  in the Girls' Friendly Society 10, 13–14, 24, 30, 38, 56, 66–70, 72–5, 80–3, 87–8, 132, 137, 144, 151, 153–4, 188, 198, 201, 209–10

relationship with colonialism 2, 11–12, 13–14, 24, 37, 38, 41, 44, 55–6, 62, 66–7, 74, 80–3, 87–8, 102, 106, 108–11, 121
scholarship 7–8
white slave trade 27–8, 33, 112
Women's Help 42, 152
World Assembly of Youth (WAY) 202
World Council 201–4, 207–8
world mission project 203–4
World War I 142, 167–9, 172, 178, 199
World War II 14, 198–200

Young Women's Christian Association (YWCA) 138, 141, 150, 152, 175–6, 187, 204
Yousafzai, Malala 210
youth organisation 5–6, 29, 67, 84, 175, 184, 199, 204, 207
*see also* Boy Scouts; Camp Fire Girls; Girl Guides; World Assembly of Youth (WAY); Young Women's Christian Association (YWCA)

Zimbabwe
*see* Bulawayo; Rhodesia (Zimbabwe); Salisbury (Harare); southern/South Africa

EU authorised representative for GPSR:
Easy Access System Europe, Mustamäe tee 50,
10621 Tallinn, Estonia
gpsr.requests@easproject.com

www.ingramcontent.com/pod-product-compliance
Ingram Content Group UK Ltd.
Pitfield, Milton Keynes, MK11 3LW, UK
UKHW021826140426
5217IPUK00004B/111